INTERNET DAEMONS

ELECTRONIC MEDIATIONS

Series Editors: N. Katherine Hayles, Peter Krapp, Rita Raley, and Samuel Weber
Founding Editor: Mark Poster

(continued on page 321)

INTERNET DAEMONS

Digital Communications Possessed

FENWICK McKELVEY

Electronic Mediations 56

University of Minnesota Press

Minneapolis

London

The University of Minnesota Press gratefully acknowledges the generous assistance provided for the open access version of this book by the Concordia Open Access Author Fund.

Portions of chapter 7 were published in a different form in "Algorithmic Media Need Democratic Methods: Why Publics Matter," *Canadian Journal of Communication* 39, no. 4 (2014): 597–613.

Published by the University of Minnesota Press
111 Third Avenue South, Suite 290
Minneapolis, MN 55401-2520
http://www.upress.umn.edu

Printed in the United States of America on acid-free paper

The University of Minnesota is an equal-opportunity educator and employer.

Library of Congress Cataloging-in-Publication Data
Names: McKelvey, Fenwick, author.
Title: Internet daemons : digital communications possessed / Fenwick McKelvey.
Description: Minneapolis : University of Minnesota Press, [2018]
Series: Electronic mediations ; 56 | Includes bibliographical references and index.
Identifiers: LCCN 2018001934 (print) | ISBN 978-1-5179-0153-0 (hc) |
    ISBN 978-1-5179-0154-7 (pb)
Subjects: LCSH: Internet programming.
Classification: LCC QA76.625 .M3825 2018 (print) | DDC 006.7/6–c23
LC record available at https://lccn.loc.gov/2018001934

UMP BMB

CONTENTS

ABBREVIATIONS AND TECHNICAL TERMS

3GPP	Third Generation Partnership Project
ACE	Application Control Engine
ACK	Shorthand for "acknowledgment," often used in packet switching
ACM	Association for Computing Machinery
ANS	Advanced Network Services
ARPA	Advanced Research Projects Agency
ARPANET	A packet-switching digital communication system by Advanced Research Projects Agency
ASN	Autonomous Systems Numbers
AUTOVON	A secure telephone system designed by AT&T for the American military.
BBN	Bolt, Beranek, and Newman Inc.
BBS	Bulletin Board System
BE	Best Efforts delivery guarantee
BEREC	Body of European Regulators of Electronic Communications
BGP	Border Gateway Protocol
BIRD	An internet protocol–routing project targeting Linux and UNIX-like systems. Its acronym stands for "BIRD Internet Routing Daemon," a nod to GNU standing for "GNU Is Not UNIX."
BSD	Berkeley Software Distribution, an operating system derived from UNIX
CAIDA	Cooperative Association for Internet Data Analysis
CAIP	The Canadian Association of Internet Providers
CBC	Canadian Broadcasting Corporation
CDN	Content Distribution Networks

CGO	Canadian Gamers Organization
CIDR	Classless Inter-Domain Routing, a standard that includes a notation method for IP addresses
CMTS	Cable Modem Termination System
CRTC	Canadian Radio-Television and Telecommunications Commission
CSEC	Communications Security Establishment of Canada
CTSS	Compatible Time-Sharing System, one of the first time-sharing operating systems
CYCLADES	French packet-switching project developed in the 1970s
DAEMON	A computer program running in the background of a computer system as an automated process rather than being under the direct command of a user
DARPA	Defense Advanced Research Projects Agency, what Advanced Research Projects Agency (ARPA) is now called
DASH	Dynamic Adaptive Streaming over HTTP
DDoS	Distributed Denial of Service attack
DHT	Distributed Hash Tables
DNS	Domain Name System
DOCSIS	Data Over Cable Service Interface Specification (enable broadband over coaxial cable)
DPI	Deep Packet Inspection
DRM	Digital Rights Management
DSLAM	Digital Subscriber Line Access Multiplexer
E2E	End-to-End principle
eBGP	External Border Gateway Protocol
EFF	Electronic Frontier Foundation
FCC	Federal Communications Commission
FIDONET	A worldwide communication network between electronic Bulletin Board Systems
FTP	File Transfer Protocol
GATEWAY	Generic term to describe hardware that interconnects different systems. The core internet requires gateways to interconnect autonomous systems.
HCI	Human–Computer Interaction
HOST	A device connected to the internet
HSIS	High-Speed Internet Service
HSPA	High-Speed Packet Access

HTML	HyperText Markup Language
HTTP	HyperText Transfer Protocol
Hub	Obsolete piece of network infrastructure that interconnected computers and forwarded packets. Hubs forwarded packets to all ports, unlike their successor, switches.
I2P	The Invisible Internet Project
IANA	Internet Assigned Numbers Authority
iBGP	Internal Border Gateway Protocol
ICANN	Internet Corporation for Assigned Names and Numbers
IEEE	Institute of Electrical and Electronics Engineers
IETF	Internet Engineering Task Force
IMP	Interface Message Processor
IoT	Internet of Things
IP	Internet Protocol address
IPRED	Intellectual Property Rights Enforcement Directive
IPSec	Internet Protocol Security
IPTO	Information Processing Techniques Office, part of the Advanced Research Projects Agency
IRC	Internet Relay Chat
IRE	Institute of Radio Engineers, predecessor to the Institute of Electrical and Electronics Engineers (IEEE)
ISP	Internet Service Provider
ITMP	Internet Traffic Management Practices, a term used by the Canadian Radio-Television and Telecommunications Commission
ITU	International Telecommunications Union
LTE	Long-Term Evolution
MIT	Massachusetts Institute of Technology
M-Lab	Measurement Lab, an open platform for internet measurement
Modem	Modulator-Demodulator, device used to send digital signals over analog lines
MP3	MPEG-2 Audio Layer III, a coding format for digital audio
MPAA	Motion Picture Association of America
MPLS	Multi-Protocol Label Switching
NAC	Network Analysis Corporation
NCC	Network Control Center at BBN
NCP	Network Control Program at University of California, Los Angeles

NMC	Network Measurement Center
NNTP	Network News Transfer Protocol
NPL	National Physical Laboratory
NSA	U.S. National Security Agency
NSFNET	National Science Foundation Network
OLIVER	On-Line Interactive Vicarious Expediter and Responder
OSPF	Open Shortest Path First routing protocol
P2P	Peer-to-Peer
PBE	Priority Best Efforts delivery guarantee
PCC	Policy and Charging Control architecture
PPPoE	Point-to-Point Protocol over Ethernet
PPTP	Point-to-Point Tunneling Protocol
PTS	Policy Traffic Switch
QoS	Quality of Service
RAND	The Research ANd Development corporation
RFC	Request for Comments
RFNM	Request for Next Message
RFQ	Request for Quotations
Router	Generic term to refer to hardware capable of maintaining routing tables and forwarding packets between networks
RSVP	Resource reSerVation Protocol
SABRE	Semi-Automated Business Research Environment
SAGE	Semi-Automatic Ground Environment
SCE	Service Control Engine
SDN	Software-Defined Networking
SNMP	Simple Network Management Protocol
SRT	System Response Time
Switch	Generic term to refer to hardware that forwards packets between devices in a local area network. Switches are intelligent enough to send packets only to the appropriate port for the packet to reach its destination, unlike its predecessor hubs.
TCP	Transmission Control Protocol
TCP/IP	The Internet Protocol Suite (Transmission Control Protocol and Internet Protocol)
TOR	The Onion Router
TPB	The Pirate Bay
UDP	User Datagram Protocol

VoIP	Voice over Internet Protocol
VPN	Virtual Private Network
WAAS	Wide Area Application Services
WELL	Whole Earth 'Lectronic Link
WoW	World of Warcraft

INTRODUCTION

USERS HAVING TROUBLE WITH EMULE, a Peer-to-Peer (P2P) file-sharing application popular in the 2000s, often sought help on its online message board. Frustrations with slow downloads, confusion about internet connections, and worries about uploading echo throughout the hundreds of posts. On July 23, 2006, one user named thelug wondered why "uploaders in the queue keep disappearing"—a problem, since eMule used a credit system to reward users for uploading files.[1] Other users responded to the thread, reporting the same mysterious problem with uploading. Later, thelug posted again with an account of a call to his or her internet service provider (ISP), Comcast, who assured thelug that it did not block eMule connections and was unsure of the cause of the problem.

Something strange was happening for Comcast customers. Two other users also noted they had issues with Comcast as the thread expanded. Over a week later, on August 11, moderator PacoBell entered the thread with a clue: Comcast did not block eMule, but rather throttled eMule traffic. Throttling allowed users to use P2P applications, but they were given lower priority. When thelug uploaded to eMule, the throttled connection was slow, so his or her downloading peers dropped thelug's connection in favor of a faster one.

Details about throttling were sparse in 2006. Comcast had not formally announced any changes to their networks, so users like thelug were left to discover them on their own. Comcast turned out to be not the only ISP behaving strangely. P2P users had created wikis to track their problems with ISPs globally. These lists of known issues represented a user-generated investigation into mysterious happenings on the internet, such as eMule developers starting a list of bandwidth-throttling ISPs in 2006. PacoBell added Comcast to eMule's wiki after posting in thelug's thread.[2] The wiki included columns for both observed problems (throttling and slow uploads/downloads) and workarounds, but questions remained. Problem descriptions were vague, with observations usually consisting only of "slow uploads/downloads." Comcast's entry included the ostensibly more specific error message "Error 10053, dropped upload connections," but only question marks appeared in the workaround column. It was not the only P2P network experiencing problems. Earlier, the popular BitTorrent client Vuze (then Azureus) started a wiki entitled "Bad ISPs" in 2005. By August 2006, the Vuze list included fifty-two ISPs from Canada, the United States, China, Europe, and Australia.[3]

Solutions were scarce because the reasons for the performance issues remained uncertain until May 2007. Robb Topolski, also known as "FunChords," posted a detailed study of his problems with Comcast on the popular internet news site *DSLReports*. Frustrated that he could not share his Tin Pan Alley and ragtime music, he took it upon himself to figure out the problem.[4] By comparing his connection with Comcast to another internet connection in Brazil, he deduced that Comcast had begun installing Sandvine traffic-management appliances in order to dynamically identify new P2P applications and throttle their bandwidth use. He wrote that the Sandvine appliances monitored traffic and interrupted P2P communications when users passed a certain threshold of bandwidth usage.[5] Public interest in Topolski's claims prompted the Associated Press and the Electronic Frontier Foundation to investigate Comcast. Both found that Comcast had deliberately injected packets into communications between peers in BitTorrent networks to disrupt uploaders' ability to establish connections.[6] The connection issues experienced by thelug and other Comcast customers were not accidental, but a direct result of Comcast's attempts to manage P2P networking.

Comcast's unannounced network-policy changes played a part in over ten years of legal activity related to internet regulation in the United States. The case became the leading national example of a new kind of discrimination by an ISP and a violation of the popular network neutrality principle that called for ISPs to take a hands-off approach to internet content.[7] Six lawsuits were filed against Comcast, including one initiated by Topolski, by June 2008. The lawsuits, eventually consolidated into one class-action suit, alleged that defendants did not receive the high-speed, unrestricted internet access promised by Comcast.[8] After receiving formal complaints submitted by the public-interest groups Free Press and Public Knowledge, the Federal Communications Commission (FCC) investigated Comcast. In response, Comcast challenged the FCC's jurisdiction to regulate the internet at all. The FCC won the right to regulate the internet—a major victory that led to the adoption of its Open Internet rules on February 26, 2015, which banned throttling and other net-neutrality violations, until a new administration repealed the order with its Restoring Internet Freedom Order on December 14, 2017. The regulatory uncertainty continues as new lawsuits have begun to contest the repeal and individual states have begun to pass their own network neutrality rules.[9]

As the right to control the internet is worked out (at least in the United States), the internet is moving on. Comcast's treatment of eMule and BitTorrent became the industry standard. While the company did cease throttling P2P traffic, it did not stop trying to manage internet bandwidth in other ways, such as introducing a user-centric traffic management program.[10] From 2005 to 2018, the Vuze list of ISPs managing P2P grew from two ISPs to over one hundred in fifty-six countries. Something had changed, but the shifts were obscured by technical layers and buried deep within the infrastructure of these ISPs. This book is about those changes.

AN INTERNET POSSESSED

The internet is possessed. Something inhuman seizes its cables, copper, and fiber, but it is not supernatural. It has more in common with Norbert Wiener and FreeBSD than with Beelzebub or Zuul. Engineers and hackers have long imagined the functions (and dysfunctions) of computers as "demonic" in a nod to physicist James Maxwell's celebrated thought experiment. To question the second law of thermodynamics, Maxwell conceived of a demon tirelessly transmitting gas particles between two chambers.[11] Famed originator of cybernetics Norbert Wiener employed Maxwell's demon to explain how information processing created meaning in the world. For Wiener, "demons" could be found everywhere working to prevent entropy through their active control of a system.[12] Maxwell's demon also influenced early computer researchers at MIT, especially those working on the Compatible Time-Sharing System, one of the first time-sharing computer networks. For these early hackers, a "daemon" (note their spelling change) was a "program that is not invoked explicitly, but lies dormant waiting for some condition(s) to occur," with the idea being that "the perpetrator of the condition need not be aware that a daemon is lurking."[13] Robb Topolski and other eMule users found their own daemons when diagnosing their connection issues, initially unaware of the daemons' influence until they looked.

Step into a server room and hear the dull roar of daemons today. Watch the flickering lights on servers representing the frenzy of their packet switching. Behind the banks of servers, pulses of electricity, bursts of light, and streams of packets course through the wires, fibers, and processors of the internet. Daemons animate the routers, switches, and gateways of the internet's infrastructure, as well as our personal computers and other interfaces. These computers need daemons to connect to the global internet, and they are met online by a growing pandaemonium of intermediaries that specialize in better ways to handle packets.

While the internet is alive with daemons of all kinds, this book focuses on a specific type: the internet daemons responsible for data flows. These daemons make the internet a medium of communication. Their constant, inhuman activity ensures every bit of a message, every packet, reaches its destination.

Where internet researchers would ask who controls these daemons,[14] my book questions how these daemons control the internet. Programmers in the late 1960s introduced what I call daemons during the development of a kind of digital communication known as "packet switching," which breaks a message down into smaller chunks (or packets) and transmits them separately. Packet switching has numerous origins, and this book focuses on the work of the U.S. government's Advanced Research Projects Agency. At ARPA, researchers tasked daemons with managing flows of packets, an influence that I call "flow control." Daemons read packets, identify their contents and type of network, and then vary the conditions of transmission based on the network's needs, their programming, and the goals of those who program them.

Daemons flourished as ARPA's experimental packet-switching digital communication system, ARPANET, expanded to be part of today's internet. Their inhuman intelligence spread through the global infrastructure. Internet daemons and their flow control allow the internet to be a network of networks, a multimedia medium. Streaming, real-time, on-demand, P2P, broadcasting, telephony—all of these networks coexist online. Such diversity is possible thanks to internet daemons' ability to vary rates of transmission and create different networks as distinct assemblages of time and space. The internet can be a broadcast network, a telecommunication network, and an information service all at the same time because of daemons.

Internet daemons have grown more intelligent since the internet's inception, and the free-for-all of internet usage increasingly falls under their purposive "daemonic optimization," as I call it. Whereas early daemons used their flow control to prove the viability of packet switching, now they produce and assign different rates of transmission, subtly altering the rhythms of networks. Daemons can promote and delay different packets simultaneously, speeding up some networks while slowing down others. But it's not just about being fast or slow; it's how networks perform in relation to one another. A network might seem delayed rather than reliable due to flow control allocating bandwidth unevenly. Thinking about optimization requires taking seriously science fiction writer William Gibson's claim that "the future has arrived—it's just not evenly distributed yet."[15] Daemon optimization occurs across the multiple networks of the internet. It allows for uneven communication by creating a system that places some nodes in the future while relegating others to the past and now marshals the once-improvisational network of networks under a common conductor. Through their flow control, internet daemons influence the success and failure of networks and change habits of online communication.

As the internet grows more complex and crowded, as its infrastructure becomes overworked or oversubscribed, daemonic optimization has become a technological fix for network owners and ISPs. Since daemons decide how to assign and use finite network resources, their choices influence which networks succeed and which fail, subtly allocating resources while appearing to maintain the internet's openness and diversity. Networks depend on instant and reliable rates of transmission to function. Modern computing increasingly relies on the "cloud," where people store their data in distant servers instead of on their home computers.[16] Cloud computing, streaming, downloading, and P2P applications tenuously coexist on limited internet infrastructure. Congestion, delays, lag, and service outages disrupt networking. No one watches a movie that is always buffering. Gamers lose due to lag. Websites succeed only if they load instantly.

Daemonic optimizations matter because they affect how we communicate and participate in contemporary culture, and their impact is not limited to only more marginal media players like eMule. The Canadian

Broadcasting Corporation (CBC) felt the consequences of being deprioritized, for instance, during its experiments with the P2P BitTorrent protocol. After distributing its show *Canada's Next Great Prime Minister* using the protocol, they discovered their audience largely gave up in frustration after the supposedly short download took hours due to Canadian ISPs throttling P2P traffic.[17] CBC eventually stopped experimenting with BitTorrent. Across the world, delayed downloads are an unfortunate but now common effect of internet daemons' influence. In the United States, Comcast not only throttled BitTorrent but also entered into partnership with Microsoft to privilege its Xbox Live Gold service.[18] In Europe, 49 percent of ISPs employed some sort of traffic management on their networks.[19] All over the world, daemons are changing how the internet communicates.

This book analyzes these daemons, their flow control, and their optimizations within this global system of communication. Over its seven chapters, I analyze daemons' flow control from its beginnings in ARPANET to our contemporary moment, when pirates and policy makers struggle over its influence. In what immediately follows, I will introduce the core aspects of my daemonic media studies, specifically the origin of the daemon and my approach to studying their operations, and then move to an overview of the book.

AN INTRODUCTION TO DAEMONIC MEDIA STUDIES

What is a daemon? Linux users—present company included—might assert that the term applies only to background programs in an operating system. While there is truth to that claim, I argue that the term is too productive, too evocative, and too much a part of computer history to live only behind the command prompt. (Perhaps the same could be said for operating systems too.) I am not the first to think of the internet as possessed by daemons. Architecture theorist Branden Hookway uses the metaphor of Pandaemonium, John Milton's capital city of hell in *Paradise Lost*, to imagine the hidden controls in modern design.[20] Sandra Braman, information policy expert, applies Hookway's ideas directly to the internet.[21] Daemons have inspired work outside of academia too. Best-selling science-fiction author Daniel Suarez titled his first book *Daemon*, after the computer program that haunts his cyberthriller.[22] All these works in their own way use the concept of the daemon to understand the software built into today's information infrastructures.

Internet daemons, in my definition, are the software programs that control the data flows in the internet's infrastructures. If scholars in communication studies and science and technology studies share a common interest in how media and information technologies form "the backbone of social, economic and cultural life in many societies,"[23] then daemons are vital to understanding the internet's backbone. Daemons function as the background for the material, symbolic, cultural, or communicative processes happening online.

A daemonic media studies builds on Wendy Chun's seminal work by looking at those programs between the hardware and the user interface. Chun consciously plays with the daemon's spectral and digital connotations in order to question notions of open code and transparent interfaces in software studies. Source code, the written program of software, is a fetish, a magical source of causality too often seen as blueprints for computers. Code creates another source, the user. Chun writes: "Real-time processes, in other words, make the user the 'source' of the action, but only by orphaning those processes without which there could be no user. By making the interface 'transparent' or 'rational,' one creates daemons."[24] Daemons are those processes that have been banished, like the residents of Milton's Pandaemonium, from a user-centered model of computing. The daemon haunts the interface and the source code but is captured by neither. This book responds to Chun's call to understand daemons "through [their] own logics of 'calculation' or 'command.'"[25]

Daemons run on home computers and routers, servers and core infrastructure, and particularly the "middleboxes" between them that are usually installed in the infrastructure of internet service providers. They are everywhere. So much so that Braman has called the internet "pandemonic"[26] because:

> It is ubiquitously filled with information that makes things happen in ways that are often invisible, incomprehensible, and/or beyond human control—the "demonic" in the classic sense of nonhuman agency, and the "pan" because this agency is everywhere.[27]

The internet might also be called Pandaemonium: daemons occupy a seat of power online, just as Satan sat upon the capital's throne. Just as Satan ruled his lesser demons, some internet daemons rule, while others follow.

Such a lively sense of the internet aligns with the vibrant materialism described by Jane Bennett's thinking, drawing on Gilles Deleuze and

Félix Guattari, about infrastructures as assemblages and emphasis on the interconnectedness of technical systems. This books shares her interest in thinking through infrastructure by means of materialism and assemblage theory. Bennett described the 2003 North American electrical blackout in her own study of infrastructure. For reasons still not entirely known, the grid shut down. To understand this event, Bennett thinks of the power grid as:

> a volatile mix of coal, sweat, electromagnetic fields, computer programs, electron streams, profit motives, heat, lifestyles, nuclear fuel, plastic, fantasies of mastery, static, legislation, water, economic theory, wire, and wood—to name just some of the actants.[28]

To Bennett, this volatile mixture has a "distributive agency" that is "not governed by any central head." The task for me is to understand the "agency of the assemblage," not of just one part.[29] Daemons offer a way to embrace the internet as a volatile, living mixture and to think about infrastructure without overstating the "fixed stability of materiality."[30] Daemons belong to the distributed agency that enables internet communication, the millions of different programs running from client to server that enable a packet to be transmitted.

Another vision of Pandaemonium aids our analysis of this volatile mixture and introduces my approach more fully. Oliver Selfridge imagined a digital world filled with what he referred to as "demons." He was an early researcher in artificial intelligence and part of the cybernetics community at MIT. Like others there, he had an interest in daemons.[31] Perhaps his infatuation with daemons started when he worked as a research assistant for Wiener at MIT.[32] Perhaps James Maxwell had an influence. Whatever the cause, Selfridge described an early machine-learning program for pattern recognition as a "demoniac assembly" in a paper presented at the influential 1958 symposium "Mechanisation of Thought Processes" held at the National Physical Laboratory.[33] During an event now viewed as foundational to artificial intelligence and neurocomputing, Selfridge explained how a program could recognize Morse code or letters. Selfridge's work matters to the history of artificial intelligence in its own right, but I borrow his approach here primarily to outline the daemonic media studies used throughout this book. Just as his speculative design inspired future research in artificial intelligence, Selfridge's program titled "Pandemonium" captures the "artificial intelligence" of today's internet daemons.

Selfridge's Pandemonium, illustrated in Figure 1, described how a computer program could recognize letters.[34] He broke each task down by function and referred to them as demons. These demons cooperated by shrieking at each other, forming a "screaming chorus,"[35] a noise that inspired his name for the program.

To observers, Selfridge's Pandemonium is a black box: letters are inputted and digital characters are outputted. Inside, a frenzied demoniac assembly turns the signal into data. The process of recognizing the letter "W" begins with "data demons," who, according to Selfridge, "serve merely to store and pass on the data."[36] These demons convert light signals into binary data and pass it onward. Next, "computational" demons "perform certain more or less complicated computations on the data and pass the results of these up to the next level."[37] A computational demon looks at the data to identify patterns and then passes those patterns to "cognitive" demons. Selfridge imagined numerous cognitive demons for each letter of the alphabet. How a cognitive demon identifies its letter varies, and the process evolves through machine learning. Selfridge noted: "It is possible also to phrase it so that the [letter demon] is computing the distance in some phase of the image from some ideal [letter]; it seems to me unnecessarily platonic to postulate the existence of 'ideal' representatives of patterns, and, indeed, there are often good reasons for not doing so."[38] Without being too platonic, then, a cognitive demon shrieks when it finds a pattern that matches its letter. The better the match, the louder the shriek, and "from all the shrieks the highest level demon of all, the Decision Demon, merely selects the loudest."[39] The decision demon then outputs the correct letter, "W," to end the process.

How Selfridge describes his Pandemonium offers a template for daemonic media studies. The approach begins with an attention to daemons and their specific functions. Together, internet daemons enact a flow control. Daemonic media studies require attending both to the work of each daemon and to their overall effect. For all the talk of a demoniac assembly, Selfridge provided a very well-ordered diagram in his proposal. As I will discuss in chapter 3, daemonic media studies question the arrangement of daemons, the locations both conceptual and physical that they occupy in an infrastructure. Selfridge's demons have a specific goal in mind: being the most efficient letter-recognizing machine imagined. Each of his demons works in their small way to achieve this optimal outcome. Internet daemons also labor to optimize internet communications.

Figure 1. Oliver Selfridge's Pandemonium recognizing the letter "W." Courtesy of John Martz.

Daemonic media studies, finally, question the distributive agency of daemons to enact optimizations.

Daemoniac Assemblies

Selfridge instructs my daemonic media studies first by calling attention to the programs themselves. He describes the specific composition or anatomy of his demons, looking at how their individual designs related to their specific functions. Bennett makes a comparable observation about the electrical grid: "different materialities . . . will express different powers."[40] Each category of Selfridge's demons is programmed and designed differently and, therefore, boasts distinct capabilities. An "image" demon's wide eyes aid in translating a letter into information used by other demons; it encodes the letter but does not interpret it. Cognitive demons interpret signals as letters. Selfridge also believed that demons could evolve and develop better ways of completing their tasks over time. Cognitive demons, through competition, would evolve to outperform each other.

Selfridge's Pandemonium was a lively place with demons quickly spawning to solve the problems they encountered in letter recognition. Selfridge could be said to demonize the work of alphabetic reading by breaking the job into discrete tasks and assigning each task to a specific demon. For problems with multiple possible answers, like feature recognition, Selfridge usually proposed creating more demons. As historian of artificial intelligence Margaret Boden explains, "a relatively useless demon might be removed" and "a new demon might be produced by conjugating two [other demons]," or "a single demon might be randomly 'mutated,' and the best survivor retained."[41]

Selfridge, then, orientates my perspective on the way the internet has been daemonized. How have tasks been broken down into discrete daemons? How have daemons been proposed as a solution to technical issues? How does one daemon beget another when its initial task exceeds its capabilities? The internet, as I will discuss in chapters 1 and 2, started with daemons, and these daemons have proliferated, as we will see in chapters 3 and 4.

Daemonizing relates to critical media studies' concept of "reification," which refers to "a process whereby social phenomena take on the appearance of things."[42] This Marxist term was originally used to describe how, through the process of commodification, the complexity of labor relations becomes obfuscated by the commodity. Beyond appearing like things, reification online creates things, an internet of them. Reification is also at work in my choice to focus on internet daemons rather than those who program them. Approaches from the study of computing bifurcate into studies looking at human coders, on the one hand, and studies focusing on the materiality of code, software, and algorithms, on the other. (The latter could also be seen as part of the "nonhuman turn.")[43]

Daemons can be described through their materiality, or more specifically through the code and its algorithms. An algorithm is "any well-defined computational procedure that takes some value, or set of values, as input and produces some value, or set of values, as output."[44] Algorithms usually solve well-known problems like how to order a queue, which route a traveling salesman should take, or how to sort different sound lengths. For example, Selfridge thought that cognitive demons calculating certainty faced a hill-climbing problem. Like "a blind man trying to climb a hill," how does a demon know when it has reached the highest point, the most certain answer?[45] An algorithm could solve this problem.

Internet daemons implement algorithms, many of which address known problems in computer science. For example, what is the best route to move bits across the internet? This is an old problem and goes by various names. Computer scientists have described it as a problem of flow in networks, while it is considered a transportation logistics problem in operations research.[46] Lester Randolph Ford Jr. and Delbert Ray Fulkerson, both working at the RAND Corporation at the time, defined the problem of routing as follows:

> Consider a rail network connecting two cities by way of a number of intermediate cities, where each link of the network has a number assigned to it representing its capacity. Assuming a steady state condition, find a maximal flow from one given city to the other.[47]

They proposed the Ford–Fulkerson algorithm as one solution to this problem. Using graph theory to model the railway network's makeup, the algorithm calculates the shortest paths between cities. Early internet daemons implemented the Ford–Fulkerson algorithm, as will be discussed, in what became known as "distance vector routing." Other daemons implement algorithms to manage queues or find the best way to classify traffic. Programmers code their own implementation that runs as part of the software program or daemon.

In contrast to the tremendous work already done in the sociology of algorithms, daemonic media studies focus on the materiality of daemons. Daemons possess the internet, inhabit its messy pipes, and make the best communication system they can imagine. Humans are there every step of the way—intervening most often to fix or break the system—but daemons have to be given their due too.

Diagrams: The Ley Lines of the Internet

Daemonic media studies analyze the complex configurations that organize and influence the distributed work of daemons. Selfridge's demons cooperated in a certain layout. Indeed, he describes his Pandemonium as an "architecture": it fixes and outlines both the interactions between demons and their functions in the overall program. The decision demon relies on the cognitive demon, who, in turn, relies on the computational demon. Multiple demons work on the same problem. Cognitive demons can work on different words or the same words at the same time. Selfridge's approach foreshadows parallel processing in computer science, but it also illustrates the complex designs used to implement distributive agency.

I address this configuration of daemons through the concept of the "diagram." The diagram, a concept popularized by Michel Foucault, Gilles Deleuze, and Alexander Galloway, describes "a map of power—diagrammatics is the cartography of strategies of power."[48] Selfridge's Pandemonium has a diagram, cartoonishly approximated in Figure 1, and similar diagrams exist for the internet. For Deleuze, the diagram constructs the real,[49] and these internet diagrams likewise help compose the built infrastructure, guiding the design of cables and switches and edges and cores.

Diagrams arrange daemons and an infrastructure's flows of information, influencing flow control in two ways. First, diagrams arrange how daemons manipulate the flows of packets, stipulating where they can intervene. Second, diagrams influence how daemons share information among themselves. The overall composition is uneven, which is another point shared by Bennett, who suggests that "power is not distributed equally across [an assemblage's] surface."[50] Instead, diagrams create a hierarchy between daemons. If Pandaemonium served as the capital of hell, then some daemon sits on the throne while others sit at its feet. In Selfridge's Pandemonium, the decision demon has the final word. The same applies to internet daemons, with some being more influential than others, occupying the space of flows, so to speak. Diagrams not only arrange daemons but also create abstract locations in which to conjure new ones. In a daemonic media studies, the diagram conceptually prefigures daemonizing by creating spaces and possibilities for daemons to occupy. The evolving diagram of the internet, described in chapter 3, enables new daemons to occupy the infrastructure. ARPANET, for example, proposed using computers in the infrastructure. Its diagrams created the possibility for computers, known as Interface Message Processors (IMPs), to be built and run in its infrastructure. Other diagrams led to more and more possibilities for daemons. Importantly, however, the diagram does not determine subsequent daemons in such a way that daemons become unimportant. As will be discussed, daemons interpret their own functions, locations, and algorithms.

Daemonic Optimization

Finally, Selfridge's Pandemonium illustrates distributive agency under control. As communication scholar Ian Roderick writes, Selfridge's Pandemonium distributive agency worked through "the delegation of tasks amongst disparate actors working individually in a piecemeal fashion to produce more complex patterns of behavior."[51] Such distributed agency, which Galloway called "protocological," now seems commonplace, but at a time of large monoliths and batch computers, Selfridge was only the early inspiration for ideas about computing in the form of distributed, multiagent systems. Even beyond Selfridge's own personal importance in the history of artificial intelligence, his Pandemonium is significant for encapsulating the design decisions of early packet switching. The communication system functioned by allocating work to individual programs whose collective action kept the system running.

Internet daemons collaborate to enact what I have been calling "flow control." The virtual work of daemons is integral to the actual conditions of online communication, which their distributive agency enables. By identifying packets and contextualizing these bits into networks, daemons can vary the conditions of transmission with greater granularity. Some daemons specialize in packet inspection; others manage the selection of routes or allocate bandwidth. A few daemons attempt to manage the overall state of the system. Together, packet by packet, daemons create the conditions of possibility for communication.

My use of "control" deliberately situates this book in ongoing discussions about communication and control. My theorization of control begins with Deleuze, though I draw also on a broader literature that ranges from James Beniger to Wiener. Deleuze notices subtle mechanisms of power overtaking Foucauldian disciplinary societies, what Deleuze calls "societies of control,"[52] and he describes emerging mechanisms[53] that modulate or change dynamically to adapt to varied inputs or tactics. He gives the example of a city pass card that varies entry depending on the time of day: "What counts is not the barrier but the computer that tracks each person's position—licit or illicit—and effects a universal modulation."[54] The concept of control, then, orients critical inquiry toward the more immanent properties of a system that defines the limits of freedom and questions the modulations of control that establish these limits. Subsequently, Galloway focuses on the internet protocol suite as the key mechanism of control in decentralized networks (as well as an example of a "protocological" society).[55] More recently, Scott Lash reaches similar conclusions when he advocates a shift in cultural studies from focusing on hegemony and its tendency toward epistemology to a posthegemonic age emphasizing ontology. The study of ontology in a "society of pervasive media and ubiquitous coding" should focus on "algorithmic or generative rules" that are "virtuals that generate a whole variety of actuals."[56] The modulations of control might be seen as the generative rules that allow for communication.

Flow control serves a higher power: it works to realize an *optimal* state or optimality for the network of networks. Daemons, in other words, optimize a communication infrastructure shared by many networks with their own demands. In engineering, optimization refers to "the process of making [something] as functional, effective, or useful as possible," as well as to "the mechanisms utilized towards these objectives of improved performance."[57] Optimization "problems" refer to the challenge of formulating the problem and composing an algorithm to solve that problem in the most effective manner possible.[58] Etymologically, "optimization" derives from the same root as "optimism." To optimize is to be optimistic, to believe in an ideal solution. These problems and hopes exist throughout engineering, ranging from finding the optimum layout of transistors on a computer chip to solving complex organizational issues, such as deciding the best way to route telephone calls to maximize a limited number of lines.[59] Frederick Taylor's studies into scientific management sought, for example, the optimal shovel load to maximize the labor exerted from the worker.[60] Donna Haraway, in her "Cyborg Manifesto," describes a move in communication sciences toward "the translation of the world into a problem of coding, a search for a common language in which all resistance to instrumental control disappears and all heterogeneity can be submitted to disassembly, reassembly, investment and exchange."[61] Haraway's historical note signals the broader intellectual currents that led to internet daemons. The evolution of the internet involves the coding of information and the formulation of problems related to information flows. Internet daemons reflect and enact an optimism that there might be an optimal way to organize an increasingly ubiquitous medium like the internet.

In this book, I intentionally blur the lines between optimization and the sociopolitical. The daemons encountered in this book were developed and designed to solve the challenge of optimizing communication in a network of networks. As ARPANET developed, it gave rise to optimization problems for the packet-switching model of communication. These problems developed out of utopian ideas from the likes of J. C. R. Licklider, who imagined a new era of "man–computer symbiosis." Licklider's optimism manifested as optimization problems. Kleinrock described packet switching as an optimal solution to the problem of poorly utilized network resources. If "a privately owned automobile is usually a waste of money" because "perhaps [90] percent of the time it is idly parked and not in use," then a private network is also inefficient.[62] Packet switching was an optimal solution because it creates a common data carrier, which maximizes resource utilization. This study of internet daemons is one investigation into an optimization problem, unpacking the ways that computer programs have tried to solve deeply social and political questions about how to share a communication infrastructure between various networks competing for limited resources.

As I explain over the book, advances in optimization do not necessarily include improved ways of deciding the optimal. Better control does not lead to better governance. Rather, optimization asserts those complex, often political, problems of managing the internet as technical ones.[63] Take for example how Leonard Kleinrock, a central figure in the development of ARPANET, described the flow control problem: "the problem of allocating network resources to the demands placed upon those resources by the user population." In Kleinrock's view, this was a strictly technical problem, distinct "from the 'softer' social, political, legal and ecological problems."[64] This early appearance of the desire to separate the technical from the political and social recurs in contemporary network neutrality debates. Even the now-defunct FCC report on "Protecting and Promoting the Open Internet" noted, "in order to optimize the end-user experience, broadband providers must be permitted to engage in reasonable network management practices."[65]

Daemonic media studies overall contribute to the study of media infrastructures, which calls for "interdisciplinary engagements" that explore "issues of scale, difference and unevenness, relationality, labor, maintenance and repair, literacy, and affect."[66] More specifically, examining the internet as infrastructure aligns with what information and communications scholar Christian Sandvig calls "new materialism," an approach that revels in the forgotten importance of "roads, power systems, and communication networks; wires, signals, and dirt."[67] The daemon provides one way to navigate the software side of infrastructure of this new materialism.

THE STRUCTURE OF THE BOOK:
A STUDY OF INTERNET DAEMONS AND FLOW CONTROL

Over its seven chapters, this book elaborates these different components of daemonic media studies. A natural starting place would be: how did demons become associated with computers in the first place? The first chapter explores the intellectual impact of a physicist's thought experiment known as "Maxwell's demon" on early computers and digital communication. The legacy of Maxwell's demon is complex and multifaceted, and interested readers can find a good introduction to it in the work of Philip Mirowski and Katherine Hayles.[68] Within the sciences, James Maxwell's idea inspired great debate that threatened the foundation of thermodynamic theory. Rather than exorcising the demon, these debates culminated in a new theory of information, within which the demon symbolized the idea of a general information processor. Maxwell's demon became part of a larger trend known as the cyborg sciences, which refract many disciplines through computers and computational modeling.[69] Game theory, operations research, information theory, and cybernetics all might be seen as cyborg sciences. These approaches transformed economics, gender, urban planning, possibly political science, and communications. A complete history of the cyborg sciences can be found elsewhere.[70] A connecting thread among these works is the idea that Maxwell's demon contributed to the conceptual shifts that animated the development of systems of control, digital networks, and computers. The first chapter of the present book tracks this shift from demons to daemons by exploring how Maxwell's demon inspired digital communication and control: early computer networks relied on innovative digital computer infrastructures to enable these new forms of communication, and in these infrastructures, the demon made a leap from being an imaginary figure to being a real program running in an operating system. Maxwell's demon, finally, offers a way to understand the constant work that programs do to keep infrastructures online. Researchers at MIT were, in fact, the first to make this connection, calling their programs daemons as a nod to Maxwell.

The second chapter traces the materialization of daemons at the Information Processing Techniques Office (IPTO), a part of the U.S. government's ARPA. While research into packet-switching communication was global, ARPANET was a key point of convergence. Early researchers associated with IPTO sought new digital-first communication channels to better share limited computer resources. This research led to the development of packet switching, the model for internet communication, and to the belief that embedding computers in the infrastructure was the best way to build a packet-switched communication system. These computers would eventually host specific programs managing digital communication—the first internet daemons. The chapter pays special attention to Donald Davies, one of the inventors of packet switching. He described packet switching as nonsynchronous communication, which means that the underlying infrastructure allows for many networks simultaneously. This capacity would allow the internet to function as a multimedia medium, a network of networks. To achieve nonsynchronous communication, researchers involved with IPTO built ARPANET's communication infrastructure out of computers. These Interface Message Processors, the IMPs, were the first internet daemons. IMPs had the difficult task of creating the optimal conditions of transmission in this early network of networks.

The third chapter follows this proliferation by tracing the evolution of packet switching and computer networking. I use the concept of a diagram to conceptualize the nascent internet's shifting abstract arrangements of space and power. Changing diagrams gave daemons new roles to fill, gradually including components for daemons to act at the edges, middle, and core of the emerging internet. The growing complexity of packet-switched communication enabled the internet to act as an infra-structure that supports more than one type of computer network. The internet is significant for being able to provision multiple networks, including home-brewed electronic bulletin boards, early computer dis-cussion groups, and a pirate underground. All these networks converged on the internet's infrastructure, making the life of daemons difficult as they had to decide how best to manage all these networks.

If the internet is full of daemons, what do they do? The fourth chap-ter journeys deeper into their world. I use the metaphor of the congress of demons, Pandaemonium, drawn from computer science, to describe an infrastructure filled with daemons. This chapter journeys through the internet as Pandaemonium, and I have divided it into two parts. The first unpacks the technical operation of today's internet daemons. Daemons inspect, route, and queue packets, as well as coordinate with each other. The second part returns to the problem of daemonic opti-mization to more closely examine two specific kinds of optimization at work in the contemporary internet: nonsynchronous and polychro-nous. These optimizations resonate with concerns around the internet's political economy and governance (often related to the idea of network neutrality), but daemons have an autonomy from regulations and even their owners. This second part explores this world of daemons through a more thorough discussion of the case of Comcast. This tour of the inter-net's Pandaemonium introduces us to the daemons running P2P net-works, sharing cable lines, and optimizing the internet to avoid conges-tion. It reveals the current operations of polychronous optimization and explores some of its future possibilities.

All this attention to internet daemons might make us miss the feel-ings they inspire in users. What is the experience of being delayed? What does it mean to suffer from buffering? In the fifth chapter, I theorize the affective influence of daemons and how ISPs use advertising to articulate these affects into structures of feeling. Flow control exerts an affective influence by disrupting the rhythm of a network, which frustrates users and their attention. Polychronous optimizations create broad structures of feeling with uneven distributions of anxiety and exuberance. The result-ing modulations—prioritized and demoted, instant and delayed, and so on—have a diverse and often deliberate affective influence that mani-fests as valuable feelings sold by ISPs. Taken together, the five commer-cials analyzed in this chapter map out the emotional relations between users and the internet from the initial feelings caused by flow control to their more deliberate use and to a reconsideration of the desires that keep people under the spell of internet daemons.

What can be done about this daemonic influence? The sixth chapter explores the tactics associated with The Pirate Bay (TPB) and the Swedish propiracy movement. Their commitment to an internet without a center prompted them to find ways to elude flow control. In this chapter I analyze two of their tactics: first, an approach of *acceleration* focused on decentralization and popularization and, second, an *escalation* of tactics through the use of virtual private networks (VPNs). Their activities represent another side in the net-neutrality debate, one put forward not by policy makers but by "hacktivists" and pirates who seek to protect and foster their own competing vision of the internet.

How can daemons be made more evident? Given their influence, how can their work be rendered public and perhaps governed? This seventh chapter explores how publics form and learn about daemons. Much of the controversy surrounding traffic management results from publics. As seen above, Comcast's interference with BitTorrent traffic came to light only after hackers analyzed their packets and discovered the invisible work of daemons. In this chapter, I draw on a case from Canada to explore one of the first examples of network neutrality enforcement. This chapter tells the story of Canadian gamers affected by flow control and their two-year journey toward resolution. In the process, they demonstrated the viability of John Dewey's theory of "publics" as a basis for further research investigating both daemons and other digital media.

I conclude with a look toward the future of daemons. What could it mean to embrace the daemon as an analytical tool to study digital media? My conclusion offers a summary of some of the key points found in this book. I also end on a more speculative note as I consider the role of daemons in larger operating systems. How does their flow control cooperate with other kinds of control? How does this ecology of control enable complex systems online today? Daemons, I argue, offer a first step toward understanding these networked operating systems.

The book as a whole offers a different perspective on net neutrality. In the wider public, the issue of flow control has largely been addressed as a matter of network neutrality, a normative stance preventing carriers from discriminating on the basis of content.[71] Although net neutrality has emerged as the popular focus of the debate, it is only one answer to the problem posed by flow control. This book analyzes the root of the problem: the influence of internet daemons. That influence must be made more transparent so as to be better regulated, and in the pages that follow, I will explain how daemons, while they may never be neutral, can be accountable.

My investigation into daemons further relates to ongoing concerns about algorithms as a distributed and dynamic form of social control. Algorithms, as a technical catchall, have become a focal point for accountability and discrimination in a digital society.[72] The study of daemons then connects with a growing literature discussing the implications of algorithms to culture,[73] the public sphere,[74] journalism,[75] labor,[76] and theories of media power.[77] For example, Tarleton Gillespie, continuing his interest in digital control, investigates what he calls "public relevance" algorithms, which are involved in "selecting what information is considered most relevant to us, a crucial feature of our participation in public life."[78] Algorithms also control public attention. Taina Bucher and Astrid Mager consider this designation of relevance in depth in their respective discussions of Facebook and Google.[79] Algorithms make certain people or posts visible or invisible to the user, which means that algorithmic media like Facebook influence matters of representation or inclusion. Martin Feuz, Matthew Fuller, and Felix Stalder investigated how Google's algorithms tailor results depending on who is doing the searching.[80] Gillespie also stressed that algorithms calculate publics and opinions through defining trends or suggesting friends. Social activity—what is popular and who to know—involves the subtle influence of algorithms and addresses the link between material and symbolic processes that interests scholars of media and information technologies.

Internet daemons represent a specific instance of algorithmic power amid this general concern, and their power raises enduring questions about media, time, and communication that are complementary to worries about algorithmic and data discrimination. If media create shared spaces and times, then the internet daemon provides a new concept to describe multimedia communication and the power found in controlling the flows of information within digital infrastructure.

My hope in writing this book is that its study of the internet becomes a model for daemonic media studies, one that attends to the software side of media infrastructures.[81] My approach borrows the concept of the daemon from computer science. There, the daemon is a novel figure to understand the agency of software. Daemons keep the system running until they break down. They are a core technique of control at work in media infrastructure. At times mischievous, daemons also represent being out of control. Both their capacities and their limits help them analyze contemporary digital control. They are also a way to understand the organization of an infrastructure. Daemons are arranged not only in an infrastructure's abstract diagram but also in its server rooms, control centers, and other points in physical space. These arrangements organize a control plane composed of autonomous daemons working in cooperation, following and frustrating each other. My approach attends to both these daemons and their organization as a kind of operating system that optimizes infrastructural activity. Daemons desire some state of the optimal that they are always working to achieve. At a time when achieving the optimal justifies everything from what shows up in Facebook's news feed to which variety of kale to add to your smoothie, my book explores a particular kind of optimization through internet daemons. My framework hopefully has a utility beyond this book and helps to explore these other optimizations at work today.

1 THE DEVIL WE KNOW

Maxwell's Demon, Cyborg Sciences, and Flow Control

"MAXWELL'S DEMON," the celebrated thought experiment by physicist James Maxwell, occupies a strange space, at once both abstract and real. Perhaps the demon is abstract enough to explore the realities of control and communication. What started out as a pure thought experiment inspired decades of speculation about its possible existence and then attempts to build an artificial demon. Maxwell's demon inspired the crucial breakdowns that Donna Haraway identifies as part of postwar computer research, or what has been called the "cyborg sciences." Two breakdowns in particular relate to my interest in networks, infrastructures, and control: between humans and machines and between the physical and nonphysical.[1] This chapter picks up from these breakdowns to track the development of digital communication and control that led to internet daemons.

In contemplating an imaginary demon, the originator of cybernetics, Norbert Wiener, imagined a thinking machine. As Katherine Hayles notes in her influential work on posthumanism and cybernetics, "to pose the question of 'what can think' inevitably also changes, in a reverse feedback loop, the terms of 'who can think.'"[2] If computers thought, were they like humans? How could humans and computers better interact given their similarities? The reconsideration of how humans interact with computers led to digital communication or what I call "networks." J. C. R. Licklider, a defining figure in postwar U.S. computer research,[3] framed the issue as a problem of "man–computer symbiosis" and suggested that the way to achieve harmony between humans and computers was through communication. As Licklider imagined a better world with computers, actual users began to communicate with computers. From chats in time-sharing systems to more elaborate real-time interactions in computer defense systems, these early computer infrastructures foreshadowed the many networks operating online today and continue to inform today's internet.

In addition to provoking reflections on the nature of communication, computers were also used to automate the work of running a communication system. Researchers delegated core communication functions to them, which led to computers becoming communication infrastructure. Maxwell's demon foreshadowed the kind of *control* found in these infrastructures. Maxwell employed his demon to describe an imaginary mechanism able to bring order to the gas molecules' random distribution. The demon's ability to independently keep a system in order resembles contemporary engineering concepts such as feedback, governors, and self-regulating machines. While these principles helped devise more efficient steam engines,[4] Maxwell's demon came to symbolize a force of control in machines and technical infrastructure that inspired subsequent research into a general information processor capable of creating order in the world. This capacity for control, the dream of making order out of chaos, inspired Wiener as he developed the concept of cybernetics. Could real demons be found in nature? Or could humans program demons to combat entropy and create order? Computer infrastructure would become possessed not by Maxwell's demon exactly, but by *daemons*, a term that computer scientists at Massachusetts Institute of Technology (MIT) used to designate the programs running in the background of their computers and keeping a system in working order.

This chapter explores these two turns during the development of digital computing that led to internet daemons. It begins by elaborating on Maxwell's demon's contribution to information theory and computing. From there, the chapter traces the problem of human–computer interaction that materialized in early–Cold War computer infrastructures. At MIT, two early computer systems developed real-time and time-shared approaches to digital communication. Maxwell's demon also made a leap into the real world at these institutions. The latter part of this chapter will address how Maxwell's demon both represents the theory of digital control and became an inspiration to programmers who wrote their own daemons to manage their new computer infrastructures.

"IF WE CONCEIVE A BEING": MATERIALIZING MAXWELL'S DEMON

In the nineteenth century, Maxwell, a seminal figure in physics, engineering, and control theory, conjured a demon into the sciences. In his book on thermodynamics, *Theory of Heat,* published in 1871, he paused to consider a potential refutation of its second law, which states that, generally speaking, entropy increases over time.[5] Maybe the law could be broken, Maxwell speculated, "if we conceive a being whose faculties are so sharpened that he can follow every molecule in its course, such a being, whose attributes are still as essentially finite as our own, would be able to do what is at present impossible to us."[6] In Maxwell's thought experiment, this being acted as a gatekeeper between two chambers containing molecules of gas, opening and closing a door to selectively control the transmission of molecules between chambers. By doing so, the demon isolated hot molecules in one chamber and cold molecules in the other,[7] raising the temperature in the first chamber and lowering it in the second. This redistribution of energy toward an extreme ordered state violated the second law of thermodynamics, which predicted that the two chambers would revert back to a random distribution of molecules (or what was later called "heat death").

The creature in Maxwell's thought experiment became known as a demon, and its being deeply influenced the natural sciences. As Hayles writes:

> Charting the responses to Maxwell's Demon is like mapping the progress of Christopher Columbus across the ocean. From the compass readings we can infer what the prevailing winds and currents were even though we cannot measure them directly. It is like Columbus's route in another respect as well; only in retrospect does the journey appear as progress toward a certain end.[8]

For her part, Hayles traces the influence of entropy and thermodynamics on information and the posthuman. Key figures in the information age such as Wiener and Claude Shannon relied on the debates inspired by Maxwell's demon to formulate their definitions of information. Historian of economics Philip Mirowski, another key figure in the cyborg sciences, traces the long history of refutations of Maxwell's demon that led to Wiener's cybernetics, John von Neumann's computer, and information theory, all of which informed modern economics. For those interested in the longer history of Maxwell's demon, one could find no better guides.[9]

For this book, Maxwell's demon makes two important contributions to conjuring internet daemons. First, it inspired the design of computers and a reconsideration of the nature of communication. Second, it inspired interest in new kinds of digital control. These developments evolved out of the interpretation of Maxwell's demon in information theory.

The theory of information, by most accounts, depended on Maxwell's demon. His thought experiment eased the transference of thermodynamic concepts, specifically probability and entropy, into a mathematical approach to information. The study of thermodynamics treats its laws as "statistical generalizations" with only a probabilistic ability to predict—say, the location of molecules.[10] Entropy refers to the probable distribution of molecules in a space. Maxwell's demon played with both: its gatekeeping moved molecules, altering their probable distribution and overturning the entropic assumption that energy stabilizes at an equilibrium. Efforts to exorcise the demon and confirm the second law turned to its work. How could the demon function? Were there hidden costs that made its work improbable? In answering these questions, theorists began to conceive of the demon's work as information processing. In addition to remembering the location of the molecules, the demon also had to track their movement.

Information became a theoretical concept out of the refutation of the daemon. As Wiener explained, for Maxwell's demon "to act, it must receive *information* from approaching particles concerning their velocity and point of impact on the wall" (italics added).[11] Information about the molecules allowed the demon to control their transmission in a closed system, creating a self-regulating system. In Maxwell's thought experiment, the demon appears to be able to acquire information about the molecules' movement without any cost. How could a demon gain this information? Wiener argued that "information must be carried by some physical process, say some form of radiation."[12] The demon could not operate because "there is an inevitable hidden entropy cost in the acquisition of information needed to run the device."[13] The energy required to transfer information between molecule and demon would eventually, according to Wiener, cause the demon to malfunction.

Maxwell's demon encapsulates information theory research accelerated by World War II. This research redefined probability and entropy around the emerging concept of information developed by the likes of von Neumann, Shannon, Wiener, and Alan Turing.[14] The approach reinterpreted the world in a cultural perception that Hayles describes as understanding that "material objects are interpenetrated by information patterns."[15] Wiener and Shannon both had key roles in developing information theory. Indeed, talks with Wiener and his classified reports on the subject inspired Shannon to publish his theory of information.[16] Shannon, according to Hayles, "defined information as a function of the probability distribution of the message elements."[17] He introduced this definition in his article "A Mathematical Theory of Communication," published in the *Bell Labs Technical Journal*,[18] and it became a foundation for the modern concept of information and digital transmission theory. Decontextualization of information facilitated digital communication. Computer scientists and electrical engineers could focus on transmitting discrete units of information and ignore the complexities of human context and even the physical medium of communication.

Information theory did not distinguish between human and machine, and this is part of the breakdown observed by Haraway. This breakdown prompted a reconsideration of the subjects of communication. Where some scholars had turned to the heavens in the search for intelligent life,[19] early computer scientists found a kindred spirit in Maxwell's demon. Before long, scientists imagined playing games with their newfound companions.[20] Turing, who established the principles of a digital computer, speculated that he could play naughts and crosses (or tic-tac-toe) with a machine.[21] Shannon, a mathematical and electrical engineer whose work was integral to the development of the concept of digital information, thought a computer could play chess.[22] Wiener also saw computing as a way to predict the moves of an unknowable enemy fighter pilot.[23] Turing, in his foundational paper "Computing Machinery and Intelligence," published in *Mind: A Quarterly Review of Psychology and Philosophy* in 1950, popularized the idea of talking to a computer. His "imitation game" (a play on the gendered party game of the same name) asked a human to converse with another unidentified subject.[24] After some time, the human had to decide if they were talking to another human or a machine. The test requires, as a precondition, the breakdown of boundaries between humans and machines. As Friedrich Kittler notes, the Turing test is possible only when the defining traits of humanity can be expressed on a computer printout.[25]

Maxwell introduced the demon as a purely theoretical possibility, but it became a reality when adopted by early computing researchers above, who began to consider the ways that demons could function in the real world. Wiener wrote, "there is no reason to suppose that Maxwell demons do not in fact exist."[26] If demons might be found naturally, could they also be built artificially? In other words, being open to the existence of Maxwell's demon allowed for the possibility of building a real machine designed for generalized control and information processing. Shannon, while he imagined computers playing chess, also suggested that a thinking machine could "handle routing of telephone calls based on the individual circumstances rather than by fixed patterns."[27] Thus, Maxwell's demon made the transition from inspiring the idea of information to providing conceptual fuel for imagining the infrastructures of early computing.

Interpretations of Maxwell's demon finally led to a consideration of computer systems as a force of control in a disordered world. Much of this thinking has roots in lofty interpretations of entropy. Entropy and heat death, in nineteenth-century interpretations, closely tracked the fortunes of the British Empire.[28] Using heat death to ponder the human condition continued in information theory. In brief, Wiener had a negative view of entropy, whereas Shannon had a more optimistic interpretation. Shannon (and his interpreter Warren Weaver) thought entropy could add information. Chaos, noise, and disorder could be seen as "the source of all that is new in the world" (similar to the writings of second-generation cyberneticist Gregory Bateson).[29] Wiener, by contrast, treated entropy as a negative. In his seminal book on cybernetics, he asserted that "the amount of information is the negative of the quantity usually defined as entropy in similar situations."[30] Order and meaning were the opposite of entropy. Wiener's negative view of entropy led him to interpret Maxwell's demon as a noble creature. The demon's "sharpened faculties" allowed it to control the movement of molecules in ways impossible for humans. Wiener found inspiration in this vision of demonic control. Control, according to his own definition, creates order out of chaos; it keeps a signal amid the noise. His science of cybernetics sought to design information systems with feedback mechanisms that would create homeostasis, resulting in a self-regulating system that avoided social entropy.[31] Like a feedback mechanism, Maxwell's demon acts as an agent of homeostasis, exerting control within a system to maintain order and reduce entropy.[32]

Wiener hoped the demon could replace entropy with what he called "metastability." Maxwell's demon also maintained regularity. Wiener argued that "we may speak of the active phase of the demon as *metastable*" (italics added).[33] The "active phase" refers to the time when the demon was working before it lost control. Wiener borrowed the term "metastable" from the sciences to describe the overall effect of Maxwell's demon. It was originally coined by chemists to describe a volatile liquid, and then physicists adopted it to describe the state of the atom.[34] Metastability denotes becoming ordered; it is the phase before a stable state. As such, metastability represents a moment of potential and interaction much like Maxwell's demon trying to organize active molecules. Indeed, this world of molecules might look very disorganized to the demon, but outside observers can perceive its metastability. Later, Wiener speculated that certain biological processes might be similar to Maxwell's demon in their metastability. His reflection on enzymes helps further clarify metastability (in addition to leading to a generalization of the demon, discussed in the next section). He wrote: "The enzyme and the living organism are alike metastable; the stable state of an enzyme is to be deconditioned, and the stable state of a living organism is to be dead."[35] By extension, the stable state of a communication system is to be silent, whereas a metastable communication system is one that is in use.

Internet daemons spawned from these legacies of Maxwell's demon, but not directly. Digital computers came first. As these computers developed, they prompted a reconsideration of communication in addition to actualizing Wiener's dreams of control. In the next section, I elaborate how computers led to new kinds of digital communication. At issue was how to synchronize humans and machines. Answers to the synchronization question, or what was called man–machine "symbiosis," led to the first computer infrastructures and networks. Later in this chapter, I discuss the second contribution of Maxwell's demon: its tireless work moving molecules playfully inspired programmers as they built control mechanisms for their new digital operating systems.

"WHOSE FACULTIES ARE SO SHARPENED": NETWORKS OF HUMANS AND DAEMONS

If people could play games with computers, could they also talk to them? Networks sprang from this communicative impulse, as I elaborate in this next section. The problem became known as man–computer symbiosis, a name that also serves as a reminder of the marginalization of women in the history of computing.[36] The term comes from Licklider, who was an emerging leader in computer science and a figure central to the development of modern computing.[37] After earning a PhD in psychology and psychoacoustics, he took a position as assistant professor of electrical engineering at MIT. There he consulted at one of the early centers of digital computing, the Lincoln Lab, before he left to work as vice president for the high-technology firm Bolt, Beranek, and Newman Inc. (BBN), where he worked on early time-sharing computer services.[38] The Lincoln Lab and BBN were both important centers of work on early computing, and both labs were among the first tasked with solving the problem of finding better applications for computers.

Licklider's influential 1960 paper "Man-Computer Symbiosis" summarized almost a decade of computer research when published in the Institute of Radio Engineers' journal, *IRE Transactions on Human Factors in Electronics*.[39] The novelty, and perhaps the success, of man–computer symbiosis was its ability to define a field of research dedicated to human and computer communication. Licklider drew on his work in early computing, when he had developed some experimental ways to allow for communication between humans and machines. In his paper, he distinguished between "mechanically-extended man" and "man-computer symbiosis." He criticized early computing for being too one-sided. In these systems, "there was only one kind of organism—man—and the rest was there only to help him."[40] The demon got the snub. True symbiosis meant establishing a "partnership" between the two organisms based on "conversation" and "cooperation." Humans would be able to learn from machines, and machines would be able to understand human speech (although simple language recognition remained at least five years off in his estimation). Licklider called for computer science to improve the communication between man and machines, or what today would be called "human–computer interaction" (HCI).

Licklider's vision for man–computer symbiosis implicitly criticized the way communication worked in batch computing, the most common form of computing at the time. Analog computers, and even their earliest digital successors, functioned as batch processors, a paradigm of computing in which programmers inputted commands in batches and then waited for a response. Beginning with the first tabulating machines developed by Herman Hollerith for the U.S. Census, batch computers automated the work of industrial computation that had previously filled rooms with, usually female, "computers."[41] While effective, batch computers provided little chance for interaction. These conditions led to what Herbert Simon later called a man–computer "imbalance," since batch processing meant "the programmer had to wait for the response of the computer."[42]

Licklider recognized that solving the problem of communication between humans and computers was chiefly a matter of time. Even though humans could relate to their computers, they differed in their tempos. Licklider's observation resonated with an earlier assertion by Wiener that the philosophical concept of duration could apply to machines. Henri Bergson used the term "duration" to describe each individual's unique experience of time. Wiener suggested that "there is no reason in Bergson's considerations why the essential mode of functioning of the living organism should not be the same as that of the automaton."[43] Wiener recognized that humans and automatons each had their own durations, and Licklider discovered these durations had what he called a speed "mismatch." He explained that human thinking "move[s] too fast to permit using computers in conventional ways":

> Imagine trying, for example, to direct a battle with the aid of a computer on such a schedule as this. You formulate your problem today. Tomorrow you spend with a programmer. Next week the computer devotes 5 minutes to assembling your program and 47 seconds to calculating the answer to your problem. You get a sheet of paper 20 feet long, full of numbers that, instead of providing a final solution, only suggest a tactic that should be explored by simulation. Obviously the battle would be over before the second step in its planning began.[44]

In addition to reflecting the influence of the Cold War on computing, Licklider's example of a speed mismatch parodied batch computing. It was too one-sided, as "the human operator supplied the initiative, the direction, the integration and the criterion."[45] Genuine symbiosis required the computer and the human to be in a shared time (or what Licklider called "real-time"). Symbiosis would not necessarily mean equality (Licklider expected computers to surpass humans in intelligence), but the two organisms would be together in partnership.

For Licklider, symbiosis provided better access to the past, improved "real-time interactions," and fostered the ability to project into the future. In an ideal state of man–computer symbiosis, human and computer memory would be united to allow for better real-time information retrieval. Humans would "set the goals and supply the motivations," while computers would "convert hypotheses into testable models" and "simulate the mechanisms and models, carry out the procedures, and display the results to the operator."[46] For Licklider, it seemed "reasonable to envision, for a time ten or fifteen years hence, a 'thinking center' that will incorporate the functions of present-day libraries together with anticipated advances in information storage and retrieval and the symbiotic functions."[47] Tremendous optimism, significant for a researcher reflecting on his experiences working in nuclear air defense, abounds in Licklider's writings on man–computer symbiosis. The coming era of man–computer symbiosis "should be intellectually the most exciting and creative in the history of mankind" (at least until "electronic or chemical 'machines' outdo the human brain," bringing an end to the era and to Licklider's optimism about the future).[48]

Licklider's commentary obliquely referenced the state of American computer research. From the time the Soviet Union began testing nuclear weapons in 1949, the U.S. military, especially the Air Force, had invested heavily in computing.[49] Much of the money went to fund research at MIT, continuing its legacy of military science into the postwar era. MIT hosted two major computing projects: the Semi-Automatic Ground Environment (SAGE) and the Compatible Time-Sharing System (CTSS). These two early computer infrastructures directly inspired both a research agenda into digital communication and subsequent infrastructures like the Advanced Research Projects Agency's (ARPA) packet-switching digital communication system, ARPANET. They became prototypes of the early computer networking (real-time and time-sharing) that synchronized humans and machines in distinct ways. Understanding these synchronizations helps explain the networks online today.

Real-Time Computing

Real-time infrastructures delivered, or at least promised, instant or *on-line* responses to user inputs. Early real-time systems required massive budgets. SAGE looms over the early history of digital computing as one of the first attempts to create a *real-time* computer infrastructure. SAGE developed out of Project Lincoln (later the Lincoln Laboratory)—a collaboration among MIT, the RAND Corporation, and IBM begun in 1951—and prior work on the Whirlwind computer at MIT.[50] To mitigate the threat of a Soviet attack, SAGE attempted to create a real-time network using then-experimental digital computers like the Whirlwind.[51] The discourse of real-time control, or what Paul Edwards calls a "closed world discourse," helped justify SAGE's tremendous cost. "A SAGE center," Edwards argues, "was an archetypal closed-world space: enclosed and insulated, containing a world represented abstractly on screen, rendered manageable, coherent and rational through digital calculation and control."[52]

The work done on SAGE advanced computer hardware and communication simultaneously. Over the course of the project's life span, from 1954 to 1984, the U.S. Air Force built an international communication infrastructure. The bulk of the SAGE system consisted of twenty-three bunkers scattered across North America. Known as "detention centers," these gray concrete structures created a real-time simulation of American air space. The centers communicated through AT&T telephone lines to receive radar reports and dispatch orders to pilots in the air. Each center included two IBM AN/FSQ-7 computer systems that cost $30 million each.[53] As SAGE used only one computer at a time, the other was a backup, evidence of the extent to which the needs of real-time, always-on communication overrode cost concerns. These computers calculated the movement of projectiles and rendered their projections on a *display scope,* a predecessor of today's computer monitors. Importantly, the display scope augmented human vision by displaying the full trajectory of a projectile. The computer remembered and displayed both the past known locations of a target and its projected future.

Real-time networking soon found application outside of the military. American Airlines launched one of the first massive initiatives to integrate computer networks into a business model. IBM worked with the airline to translate insights gained from the SAGE project into a distributed airline reservation system, just as telegraphy once coordinated railroads. The project's name, Semi-Automated Business Research Environment (SABRE), directly referenced SAGE. The SABRE system was a massive project: it took five years to build, employed two hundred technical professionals, and cost $300 million. SABRE, which went live in 1965, provided real-time data to airline employees to help them book seats and minimize overbooking. The results revolutionized air travel by synchronizing American Airlines' seat stock with its reservation process. The real-time SABRE system proved immensely valuable, with a return-on-investment rate of 25 percent.[54]

Time-sharing Computer Systems

Time-sharing developed as a more cost-effective way to achieve the online interaction of real-time computing. Time-sharing computers offered a cheaper solution by creating systems that shared one big and expensive machine among multiple users. This approach maximized the use of mainframe computers by allowing many programmers to use the same computer at once. The expense of leaving computers to idle led to time-sharing systems where a queue of programmers shared a high-speed computer that simulated an online or real-time system while continuing to operate under the batch-computing paradigm. Users still submitted batches and waited for a response, but the computers became powerful enough to multitask these requests to simulate a real-time environment.[55] Sharing computer resources allowed universities to justify buying expensive machines.[56]

Although debate surrounds the origins of the phrase "time-sharing,"[57] MIT has a strong claim to being the nucleus of early time-sharing experiments. By 1959, MIT had purchased an IBM 7090 computer[58] to support experiments in time-sharing in its computation center and later at Project MAC, a vague acronym usually stated to stand for "Man And Computer."[59] John McCarthy, one of the developers and a founder of Project MAC, remembered that part of the motivation to write their own time-sharing system came from the high cost of IBM's promised "real-time package" for the computer.[60] Instead, programmers at the center developed the CTSS operating system on their own.

CTSS worked to create a communication network out of this shared infrastructure. The technical work of CTSS attempted to overcome the communication bottleneck imposed by the system's central processor. The CTSS Supervisor software program managed this bottleneck[61] by allocating processor time and priority among users and managing reading and writing information from the system's drum memory.[62] The program's algorithms made decisions based on the status and access level of each user.

The collective activity of CTSS created a common time among the users, the consoles, and the IBM hardware. The storage program allowed users to have a past by saving programs to the system's memory that endured into the future. The scheduling program sorted simultaneous user commands and synchronized users in a queue for the limited common processor. Users never shared the same moment on the processor, but their commands existed in a temporal relation of processed, processing, and to process. This trick, so to speak, meant that the overall CTSS system created an experience with a strong resemblance to concurrent use. It allowed for an early version of computer chat, as terminals could send messages between each other.

Like the rest of the cyborg sciences, time-sharing proliferated both inside and outside the lab.[63] A subsequent time-sharing computer system came from BBN, which was located near MIT. Many computer pioneers from MIT worked at BBN, including Marvin Minsky and Ed Fredkin, who were time-sharing experts like McCarthy, as well as Licklider. By 1960, Licklider was prototyping a Digital Equipment Corporation PDP-1 at BBN and looking for contracts to sell time-shared access to it. BBN sold a time-sharing system to the Massachusetts General Hospital in 1963 and started a subsidiary, TELCOMP, that offered users in Boston and New York City remote access to a digital computer.[64] The idea proved popular, and by 1967, twenty other companies had begun offering commercial clients time-sharing services.[65]

Today, CTSS and SAGE might be seen as a particular kind of infrastructure, namely media infrastructure. Lisa Parks and Nicole Starosielski, in their edited volume on the subject, define media infrastructure as "situated sociotechnical systems that are designed and configured to support the *distribution* of audiovisual signal traffic" (italics added).[66] Their emphasis on distribution resonates with the insights of computer networking historian Paul Edwards, who emphasizes flow as a key function of infrastructure.[67] Manuel Castells, whom Edwards cites, defines "flows" in his study of the network society as "the purposeful, repetitive, programmable sequences of exchange and interaction between physically disjointed positions held by social actors in the economic, political and symbolic structures of society."[68] Flows can be seen as the underlying material conditions that enable communication networks to develop from media infrastructure. SAGE and CTSS exemplify this relationship between infrastructure and network. The budgets of SAGE and SABRE allowed for a much more ambitious but less experimental deployment of real-time computing, whereas CTSS developed a more complicated system to mimic online computing. All three created hardware or infrastructure that could provision a certain kind of flow for networks.

Computers, Networks, and Synchronization

With this history in mind, I would like to elaborate my definition of a network, which is important to understanding the specific influence of a daemon's flow control. Where studies of networks often focus on their topologies or spatial properties,[69] I emphasize their chronologies or properties related to time. Whether running on telegraph wires or the internet, communication networks are unique complexes of time or temporalities.[70] The word synchronization combines the Greek *syn*, meaning "united or connected together," with *khronos*, meaning "time." Crucially, synchronizations are complexes of time (a term borrowed from Gilles Deleuze's philosophy of time) that include pasts, presents, and futures.[71] The internet, as will be discussed, includes many networks that bring humans and machines together in shared pasts, presents, and futures. These networks range from Peer-to-Peer (P2P) networking to live streaming to the on-demand archives of the world wide web.

Networks are productive synchronizations that afford different forms of communication and collaboration (as Licklider suggested). Studies of communication have long considered its influence on time and behavior. Monasteries ringing bells in medieval Europe, according to Lewis Mumford, "helped to give human enterprise the collective beat and rhythm of the machine; for the clock is not merely a means of keeping track of the hours, but of synchronizing the actions of men."[72] The transmission of a tone by a ringing bell imparted a collective rhythm that coordinated and controlled those within hearing range. Without the sound of a bell, serfs and nobles would fall out of synchronization.

James Carey's analysis of the telegraph helps elaborate the idea of synchronization. National telegraph networks facilitated the establishment of a communication system effectively distinct from a transportation system.[73] Telegraphy decreased the time delay in sending messages at a distance and facilitated greater regional coordination, cooperation, and control. In effect, economies could be in contact over larger regions. Commodity traders felt the impact of news transmitted by wire when they began receiving the prices of goods in any city before they shipped. As a result, price disparities between cities lessened. The telegraph, in other words, synchronized disjointed local markets into a coherent national one. Synchronization in the case of the telegraph entailed a united past, future, and present. As Carey argues, "it was not, then, mere historic accident that the Chicago Commodity Exchange, to this day the principal American futures market, opened in 1848, the same year the telegraph reached that city."[74] Commodity traders went from profiting by knowing *where* to buy and sell to *when* to buy and sell.

Networks have uneven temporal relations in which some users might exist in the past relative to other users. Certain users in CTSS could have prioritized access to processing time. The SAGE system, tightly controlled, orientated its time around the decision making of the North American Aerospace Defense Command. In the contemporary internet, social media users have very different levels of access. Social media firms sell access to the real-time system (usually called the firehose) and limit users' ability to participate in the present (through rate limiting or spam filtering). This business model is quite old. The New York Stock Exchange initially delayed telegraph messages by thirty seconds to give trading in the city a competitive advantage; it paid to operate in New York City to receive information live on the floor rather than delayed via the telegraph. The contemporary regime of high-frequency algorithmic trading, as Michael Lewis eloquently describes in his book *Flash Boys,* involves the production of networks to ensure that certain traders operate in what is essentially the future of other traders.[75]

Sarah Sharma, in a larger review of theoretical approaches to time, argues that temporalities are uneven systems of temporal relations. She explains that "temporal" denotes "lived time" and continues:

> The temporal is not a general sense of time in particular to an epoch but a specific experience of time that is structured in particular political and economic contexts. Focusing on the issue of fast or slow pace without a nuanced and complex conception of the temporal does an injustice to the multitude of time-based experiences specific to different populations that live, labor, and sleep under the auspices of global capital.[76]

Certainly, the networks encountered in this book invite discussion about their relation to global capital, but also at work in Sharma's thinking is a sense of a temporality as a system of relations common to humans and, I suggest, machines. Networks require technical labor to function, as will be discussed in the next sections, as well as shared meanings about time. Without getting too ahead in my argument, temporality on the internet works in a more complex fashion than the temporalities of just one network: it supports many temporalities *at once.* As the next section explains, daemonic control allows these infrastructures to share resources among many networks.

"TO DO WHAT IS AT PRESENT IMPOSSIBLE TO US": CONTROL FROM DEMONS TO DAEMONS

How did CTSS manage the demands of its multiple users? (A similar problem vexed the early designers of packet switching.) As mentioned above, CTSS relied on the Supervisor program, which managed the overall data flows in the operating system. It remained active at all times, though users rarely interacted with it directly. Instead, the Supervisor managed users' input and output and scheduled executed jobs. Every job submitted by the user had to go through the Supervisor. Its scheduling algorithm ranked jobs based on their size and time to completion, in effect deciding which jobs finished first and which jobs had to wait. The Supervisor, in short, played a vital role in the time-sharing system: it shared the time. Without its efforts managing the flows of information, the system could crash and the hardware lock up.[77]

The Supervisor greatly resembles Maxwell's demon, and it exemplifies the kind of program through which the metaphor is actualized in computing. Where one manages the flows of molecules, the other handles jobs. One works in a closed system, the other in an operating system. Moreover, these similarities are not accidental. Researchers at the project began to refer to programs as demons or daemons in a direct allusion to Maxwell. As Fernando J. Corbató, a prominent computer scientist at Project MAC, explained later on:

Our use of the word daemon was inspired by the Maxwell's demon of physics and thermodynamics. (My background is Physics.) Maxwell's demon was an imaginary agent which helped sort molecules of different speeds and worked tirelessly in the background. We fancifully began to use the word daemon to describe background processes which worked tirelessly to perform system chores.[78]

The change in spelling from "demon" to "daemon" was intended to avoid some of its older, religious connotations. No matter the spelling, Maxwell's demon provided an evocative imaginary of control and order to explain the computationally routine.

Through Project MAC and CTSS, Maxwell's demon materialized as digital daemons running in computer hardware. The joke became real when the first daemon entered the infrastructure to control tape backup, and the process was known as the Disk And Execution MONitor, or DAEMON. DAEMON shared the infrastructure with other daemons responsible for scheduling time and cleaning up messes made by users. Later on, MIT would invest in the biggest time-sharing project ever, MULTICS, the Multiplexed Information and Computing Service. Although MULTICS struggled to stabilize, it inspired the influential operating system UNIX, which retained the term daemon to refer to the programs running in its background.

From running a printer to managing a tape backup, digital systems require the daemons to maintain control. Of all these daemons, I am interested in the daemons that manage flows in these digital systems (building on my earlier discussion of infrastructure and flow). In doing so, I follow Wiener (as well as many others) by investigating the link between communication and control. His cybernetics (of communication and control) is just one of many definitions of control at work in this book. In this last section, I elaborate on my specific usage of control and its relation to communication. This overview breaks with the historical discussion so far to capture the broad features of digital control in order to contextualize internet daemons.

Control does not so much create constraints as it does influence the conditions of possibility for communication, movement, or action. In infrastructure studies, control works against "the variability inherent in the natural environment."[79] Before the term's use in infrastructure studies, control had been defined by Michel Foucault as a productive power: "It produces pleasure, forms knowledge, produces discourse; it is a productive network which runs through the whole social body, and is far more than a negative instance whose function is to punish."[80] To put it another way, control conceptualizes how *constituent* power *(pouvoir)*—the chaos, noise, and potential—becomes *constituted* power *(puissance)*, a discernible infrastructure or assemblage.[81] Control can be considered an immanent power because it is part of the very system that it holds together, necessary for both its constitution and its continued operation.

Communication is a key mechanism of control, and so much so that it is difficult to distinguish the two at times. To borrow a term from Raymond Williams, communication "imparts" a shared or common existence for those in contact with each other.[82] Imparting can be seen as a form of control, putting people and machines in contact with one another in a common system of communication. Systems of communication encode means of exchange and coordination and cultivate shared meanings and values. Media studies scholars have highlighted this link between the constitution of a system through communication and the control exerted therein. Indeed, theories of "hypodermic needle models," "propaganda," and "culture industries" (terms drawn from early work in communication studies) were developed in response to anxieties about the power of communication media to control society.[83] Yet, these "direct effects" models overlook the complex operation of communication as a form of control in multiagent systems.

Theories of control in communication, however, can be more specific about mechanisms than the theory of hypodermic needles. Organizational studies,[84] infrastructure studies,[85] and media studies[86] complement one another in their attempts to link specific mechanisms of communication within media, organizations, and social forms. Scholars of organizational communication have detailed many of the mechanisms of communication at work in late-nineteenth-century corporate America. For example, James Beniger details a wide array of mechanisms for advanced information processing (such as card-sorting computers developed by IBM) and reciprocal communication (such as the monthly reports train conductors gave to chief engineers). These mechanisms of control allowed corporations to better monitor and regulate their activity: to know the activity of their agents, the deviations from their purpose, and how these deviations might be corrected. However, Jo Ann Yates argues that Beniger's definition of control is too broad. In her study of the same period, she focuses on the rise of *managerial control,* an influence "over employees (both workers and other managers), processes and flows of materials" due to mechanisms "through which the operations of an organization are coordinated to achieve desired results."[87] Yates refines both the agents (employees of a company) and the mechanism of influence (memos, reports, and newsletters).[88] Taken together, Beniger's and Yates's accounts reveal the mechanisms of control that allowed disorganized family companies to evolve into modern corporations, another trajectory of control in communication studies.

Mechanisms of control are more suggestive than deterministic and "range from absolute control to the weakest and most probabilistic form, that is, any purposeful influence on behavior, however slight."[89] They operate through influencing probabilities and likely outcomes, and Maxwell's demon remains helpful, along with the real history of control, in elaborating this probabilistic influence. Importantly, the demon does not directly move the molecules, but rather increases the probability of them ending up in one chamber or another. Probability constitutes open, creative systems that allow their parts to operate with a certain degree of freedom. Deleuze compared control to a highway system: "People can drive indefinitely and 'freely' without being at all confined yet while still being perfectly controlled."[90] According to Raiford Guins, freedom is like the open road, "a practice produced by control."[91] In other words, control creates conditions of possibility, rather than constrictions. Modern personal computers, for example, are designed with no single purpose in mind, so users can repurpose them by installing software such as deep web tools like TOR or P2P applications like BitTorrent. Jonathan Zittrain described this openness as generative, since it allows for innovations to be created by users and other sources.[92] Control often succeeds precisely by capturing these innovations—the unpredictable creativity of users—as feedback to help regulate the overall system.

Maxwell's demon helps pinpoint the particular kind of control to be discussed throughout the rest of this book. The demon works constantly and responds dynamically to molecules' movements. This kind of control resonates with what Deleuze theorizes as "societies of control, which are in the process of replacing the disciplinary societies," and are characterized by "*modulation,* like a self-deforming cast that will continuously change from one moment to the other, or like a sieve whose mesh will transmute from point to point."[93] Whereas discipline sought to compel subjects to internalize mechanisms of control and become docile bodies, modulation is continually adaptive, embracing difference and change while nonetheless maintaining regularity. Yet, where Maxwell imagined only one daemon, I see countless daemons operating in the internet. Flow control, then, may be restated as distributive agency manifest by daemons to modulate the conditions of transmission online.

Control, however, has its limits. Mechanisms of control inherently have many limitations precisely because they operate with great degrees of freedom. William S. Burroughs, who inspired Deleuze to write about control, stresses that "control also needs opposition or acquiescence; otherwise, it ceases to be control."[94] Constituent power exceeds its constituted form. In fact, this excess can drive the development of control technologies by exposing limitations and revealing new possibilities to be harnessed and regularized. Crises in control necessitate new mechanisms. For example, the rapid expansion of railroads and the ensuing rise in the number of train accidents required new mechanisms, such as high-speed telegraphy, standardized time, scheduling, and routine inspections, to bring the system back in order.[95] The limits of control can derive from constituted power as much as from an excess of constituent power. Constituted power has gaps in the system, or what Alexander Galloway and Eugene Thacker call "exploits," that may allow momentary, unintended uses.[96] Hackers, for example, look for exploits in computer systems. Insecurities in the Microsoft Windows operating system have facilitated the spread of worms, viruses, and botnets. More recently, SnapChat, a social media photo-sharing application for mobile devices whose original appeal centered on user privacy, grew from three thousand users to 3.4 million in one year only for a security flaw to leak most of its users' phone numbers.[97]

The outcome of control, I argue, is an optimal state or optimality. In this book, the optimal is not a fixed state, but a metastability (as Wiener suggested). But Wiener was not the only theorist of control to use metastability; Deleuze did too. For the latter, control societies are metastable: "In the societies of control one is never finished with anything—the corporation, the educational system, the armed services being *metastable states* coexisting in one and the same modulation, like a universal system of deformation" (italics added).[98] "Metastability in a control society" refers to the active organization of change established through the relationships between institutions. The emphasis here is on control as dynamic or modulating, and its overall effect is metastable, maintaining a living system. Elsewhere, Deleuze defines metastability as "a fundamental difference, like a state of dis-symmetry," but he goes on to say that "it is nonetheless a system insofar as the difference therein is like potential energy, like a difference of potential distributed within certain limits."[99] Deleuze's definition of metastability also captures the work of Maxwell's demon. Gas molecules of different temperatures and speeds surround the demon. The two chambers (the overall system) are in a state of dis-symmetry. The demon controls this dis-symmetry, modulating the system by channeling the molecules' own energy to create a certain order, a "potential distributed within certain limits."

Internet daemons include all these aspects of control. Their distributive agency has the difficult task of managing an infrastructure filled with many networks, ranging from real-time to more asynchronous communication, like email. Daemons modulate the conditions of transmission to support these different networks. Their *flow control* refers to a control over the flow or conditions of transmission in an infrastructure. This productive power enables networking. In doing so, daemons change networks' temporalities and the relations between networks to create an overall metastability (following Sharma). This metastability is what I call an optimality, a working program of how the network of networks should interact. An optimality influences both the conditions for networks and the overall conditions of communication. Daemons' constant and tireless work of flow control actualizes these optimalities amid and among the networks of the internet.

CONCLUSION

Maxwell's demon has had an unquestionable influence on the history of digital computing, but it has also had a major influence on my own project of daemonic media studies. Maxwell's demon inspired two important developments that enabled the internet daemon. First, information theory and control materialized in actual computer infrastructures. Researchers began to frame these questions of man–machine symbiosis as communication questions. Digital communication crystallized through this research as new computing infrastructures brought together humans and machines in unique synchronizations, particularly around time-sharing and real-time computing. These synchronizations became a sort of prototype for future networks running on the internet. In tandem with the development of digital communication, demons, or rather *daemons*, came to actualize Norbert Wiener's idea of cybernetic control. Where Wiener hoped to find Maxwell's demon in nature, programmers coded their own versions to manage the routine tasks of their new operating systems. Internet daemons followed from these two developments and became a means to control the complex work of running a digital communication infrastructure.

The problem of digital communication exceeded the research agenda of Project MAC and SAGE. Indeed, the growth and popularity of computers altered the problem of man–computer symbiosis. Rather than simply looking for ways to connect humans and machines, the question turned to interconnecting different computer systems to each other. The local computer systems at MIT became models for research into national, international and intergalactic computer communication systems. ARPANET, the internet's progenitor, was an early attempt to interconnect computers' infrastructures. The success of computer networking required ARPANET to abstract one step further and create an infrastructure that could accommodate multiple networks. Just as Shannon proposed that computers could control telephone systems, researchers at ARPANET proposed computers that could manage digital communications. These computers would host a new generation of internet daemons that would be able to control the flow of information in this new infrastructure, enabling what we now call a network of networks.[100]

2   POSSESSING INFRASTRUCTURE

Nonsynchronous Communication, IMPs, and Optimization

DAEMONS HELPED INSPIRE what we now call packet switching. Donald Davies, a researcher at the prestigious National Physical Laboratory (NPL) in the United Kingdom and one of the inventors of packet switching, discovered daemons, the same ones mentioned in the previous chapter, when he visited Project MAC (Man And Computer) at Massachusetts Institute of Technology (MIT). On a research trip in May 1965, he observed the Compatible Time-Sharing System (CTSS) and noted that a "central part of the system" was a "scheduling algorithm" that allowed users to share time on an IBM 7094 computer. While Davies did not mention it in his report, this algorithm was likely part of the Supervisor software program's daemon that allocated computer resources. Davies saw great promise in the daemon, though he also commented that "there does not seem to have been much development of the scheduling algorithm."[1] It is unclear whether this daemon inspired Davies to think of extending the principles of time-sharing into communication infrastructure or, rather, it served only as a model for describing his new design for a digital communication infrastructure. Either way, in 1966, Davies wrote a "Proposal for a Digital Communication Network" that become a foundation of packet switching. Davies envisioned a new, intelligent infrastructure for computer communication. Like a scheduling algorithm accommodating multiple users, Davies proposed building an infrastructure that used programs to accommodate multiple networks on the new digital communication system.

How did daemons make their way from Davies's proposal to the internet? Davies, for his part, faced difficulties winning the British government's support. He did, however, influence a team of researchers working in the heart of the American military-industrial-academic complex. In 1967, at a symposium organized by the Association for Computing Machinery (ACM) in Gatlinburg, Tennessee, Davies's work found a receptive audience in researchers from the Information Processing Techniques Office (IPTO), which was part of the Advanced Research Projects Agency (ARPA). The IPTO researchers were presenting their own work on a new communication system called ARPANET. Soon after the meeting, the researchers aggregated ideas from Davies and numerous others working in computer communication to build this actual experimental communication system.

Central to the history of the internet, IPTO was a key site in the development of packet switching, though the ideas generated there are an example of the product more of a general intellect than of a lone inventor. The names of all the collaborators are too numerous to mention here, and even if an attempt at listing them were made, omissions are inevitable. ARPANET's history has been well covered,[2] but its specific relationship to control, networking, and infrastructure requires greater attention to fully account for the influence of daemons.

Through ARPANET, daemons possessed the internet's core infrastructure. The computers embedded in the network's infrastructure were called Interface Message Processors (IMPs). Daemons resided on IMPs and handled the logistics of sending and receiving information, and Davies helped researchers at the IPTO formalize these functions. As mentioned above, he proposed a digital infrastructure designed for nonsynchronous communication. Where early computer networks (whether batch, real-time, or time-sharing) synchronized humans and machines, his nonsynchronous communication system could modulate transmission to facilitate many kinds of networking. This shift (foundational to the design of packet switching) tasked daemons with managing these different networks. For many reasons, not the least of which was the massive funding dedicated to the task by the U.S. Department of Defense, it was ARPANET's version of packet switching that established the dominant approach to internetworking.

Where the previous chapter introduced the concepts of networks and control, this chapter uncovers the origins of daemons and their flow control. Without daemons, the internet could not be a network of networks, because their flow control allows many networks to coexist simultaneously. Their origins also foreshadow their enduring influence. Daemons historically have been responsible for managing and optimizing the network of networks. As such, they have grown more clever and influential since their beginnings on IMPs and more capable of managing and optimizing traffic. Their influence over the conditions of transmission continues to enable and control the networks of the internet.

FROM LOCAL NETS TO ARPANET:
THE ORIGINS OF PACKET SWITCHING

By the early 1960s, the ambitions for time-sharing computing had grown beyond sharing limited computer resources. It had begun to be seen as a new kind of communication to be shared as widely as possible. Speaking at an early conference imagining the computers of the future, John McCarthy, a key figure involved in time-sharing at MIT, thought that time-sharing computing "may someday be organized as a public utility."[3] Already at MIT, computing had developed its own culture. Tung-Hui Hu vividly describes the feelings of intimacy and privacy that time-sharing engendered.[4] Programmers on different terminals could chat with one another, share private moments, or steal time on the shared device. Sometimes remote users dialed in to access the mainframe computer from home using a then-cutting-edge device known as a modem. If individual users could connect remotely to their local time-sharing systems, could time-sharing systems be interconnected remotely? More broadly, could time-sharing be a model for a new kind of communication?

J. C. R. Licklider figures significantly in the development of ARPANET (and, by extension, of packet switching) because he directed tremendous resources from the U.S. government. His problem of man–computer symbiosis had attracted the attention of ARPA, at that point a new organization (which would be later named the Defense Advanced Research Projects Agency, or DARPA). Two years prior to the publication of Licklider's paper on man–computer symbiosis, the Department of Defense founded ARPA to coordinate research and development prompted by fears over the Soviet Union's launch of the Sputnik 1 satellite in 1957.[5] ARPA sought out Licklider to direct its Command and Control Research project,[6] and he joined as the project's director in 1962. Licklider redefined ARPA's interests in command and control as seeking "improved man-computer interaction, in time-sharing and in computer networks."[7] This change in vision was reflected in a change in nomenclature, and Licklider renamed the project as "the Information Processing Techniques Office," IPTO.

Many of ARPANET's original engineers and developers cite Licklider as a visionary who set a path toward a global computer network during his first tenure as director, from 1962 to 1964.[8] Licklider's optimism about computers stood in stark contrast to the times. Colleagues like Norbert Wiener became more pessimistic about computing over time,[9] while students burned computer punch cards in protest of the Vietnam War.[10] However, Licklider's optimism attracted some of the best minds in computing. IPTO's researchers came from the Stanford Research Institute, the University of California, Berkeley, the University of California, Los Angeles, the Carnegie Institute of Technology, Information International Inc., Thompson-Ramo-Wooldridge, and MIT.[11] The people at these centers had "diverse backgrounds, philosophies, and technical approaches from the fields of computer science, communication theory, operations research and others."[12] These researchers explored numerous applications of man–computer symbiosis, including time-sharing, computer graphics, new interfaces, and computer networking.

At IPTO, packet switching (before it was called that) was codified in four key documents: a memo from 1963, a report from 1966, a paper from 1967, and a final Request for Quotations (RFQ) in 1968. To chart the evolution of packet switching at IPTO, the following section reviews these documents and discusses the important work done by Davies. Taken together, his efforts and IPTO documents reveal the importance of internet daemons to the predecessor of the internet, ARPANET.

INTERGALACTIC, PLANETARY: FROM SYMBIOSIS TO NETWORKING

The link between symbiosis and a research project about computer networking was explicitly established in a memo by Licklider. Given the humorous title "Memorandum for Members and Affiliates of the Intergalactic Computer Network," the memo circulated to members of IPTO in April 1963.[13] In the memo, Licklider seems to be thinking out loud about the benefits of interconnected computer systems. (Literally out loud; in its style, the memo seems to be hurriedly dictated before a plane trip.) The memo signals Licklider's shift in institutional research away from command and control toward researchers interested in "some way connected with advancement of the art or technology of information processing,"[14] hence the subsequent name change to the IPTO. The memo implicitly draws on his "Man–Computer Symbiosis" paper. As discussed earlier, symbiosis was a communication problem. In the 1963 memo, Licklider extends this communication problem from a symbiosis between a human and a computer to a group activity. Indeed, the "Intergalactic Computer Network" in the memo can be read as researchers interested in computer networking, as well as the technical design of a system to connect programs and data stored on remote computer systems or what he might later call "thinking centers."

While Licklider had a vision for intergalactic networks of humans and machines engaged in what he might later call "on-line interactive debugging," the memo focused principally on the design challenge to enable work through interconnected computer systems. How could data shared between computers be kept up to date? How could data encoded in one system be read by another? Licklider sought a balance between local autonomy and collective intelligence, using computers to accommodate for regional differences. As he explains,

> Is it not desirable, or even necessary for all the centers to agree upon some language or, at least, upon some conventions for asking such questions as "What language do you speak?" At this extreme, the problem is essentially the one discussed by science fiction writers: "how do you get communications started among totally uncorrelated 'sapient' beings'?"[15]

In retrospect, Licklider was discussing the question of internetworking protocols, in addition to reiterating the similarities among humans, machines, and other alien intelligences. This process of choosing a language eventually evolved into a formal research program for networking standards and protocols to allow communication between different software systems. Many of these network communication problems emerged out of time-sharing, and Licklider wondered, "is the network control language the same thing as the time-sharing control language?" This question framed the development of ARPANET as an outgrowth of time-sharing.

Computer communication occupied subsequent directors of ARPANET who took research of packet switching from a speculative memo to a request for computer equipment. Licklider was a "visionary . . . not a networking technologist, so the challenge was to finally implement such ideas," according to Leonard Kleinrock, another key figure in the development of the internet.[16] Their motivations were much less otherworldly compared to Licklider's, though no less ambitious. And in 1965, IPTO commissioned a report on interconnecting time-sharing computer systems.

1966: LAWRENCE ROBERTS AND EARLY COMPUTER COMMUNICATION

The report was written by Thomas Marill from the Computer Corporation of America and Lawrence Roberts of the Lincoln Laboratory. Submitted in 1966, the report was entitled "A Cooperative Network of Time-Sharing Computers." It began by stressing the need for the computer networking research community to address fragmentation issues brought about by an increasing number of computer systems and programming languages. The report's authors then turned to the software and hardware issues involved in connecting computer systems. The report "envision[ed] the possibility of the various time-shared computers communicating directly with one another, as well as with their users, so as to cooperate on the solution of problems."[17] Its findings drew on experimental research linking a TX-2 computer at Lincoln Laboratory in Lexington, Massachusetts, with a Q-32 computer at the System Development Corporation in Santa Monica, California.

The hardware issue was simple: there wasn't any. Or, to put it another way, computer communication infrastructure had not yet been formalized. In their paper, Marill and Roberts actively debated infrastructural matters, especially the lines to connect computers. The experimental link between the TX-2 computer and the Q-32 computer sent messages on leased telephone lines. Messages and commands shared the same line. Future infrastructure did not have to be that way. Marill and Roberts wondered whether it would be more efficient to send commands and data on different lines. They also debated adding computers to the infrastructure itself—a move that foreshadowed the design of ARPANET. They wrote: "It may develop that small time-shared computers will be found to be efficiently utilized when employed only as communication equipment for relaying the users' requests to some larger remote machine on which the substantive work is done."[18]

As much as the report questioned the materials of a computer network, it ignored or abstracted the telephone system. The report set a precedent of abstraction—later known as layering—in which certain infrastructural functions can be taken for granted (not unlike the women involved in the research at the time). Telephone switching received no mention, even though it had begun to involve computers as well. Bell had installed the Electronic Switching System No. 1, a computer for telecommunications switching, in 1965.[19] In part, these switches ran a secure telephone system for the U.S. military designed by AT&T and known as AUTOVON.[20] The military referred to AUTOVON as a polygrid: a network of densely linked sites that operationalized a Cold War strategy of distribution to ensure survivability.[21] AUTOVON distributed traffic among these hardened sites to ensure the survival of communication after a nuclear attack.

(Paul Baran, the other inventor of packet switching, developed his own model of *distributed communication* in reference to AUTOVON.)

The report showed more of an interest in software than in hardware. Much of the report discussed the operation of the message protocol that allowed the Q-32 and the TX-2 to communicate directly. The report defined their message protocol as "a uniform agreed-upon manner of exchanging messages between two computers in the network."[22] The protocol established a connection between computers in order for messages to be exchanged. The protocol did not specify the contents of messages, but instead described the command data that preceded and followed every message, which was included to help each computer transmit data and interpret the message. The report referred to this initial data as the "header," a term that was maintained in the transition to packet switching. Headers were sent before the message to indicate whether the forthcoming message contained data for the user or the monitor (the TX-2 had an experimental graphic interface). An ETX command indicated the end of a message to which the receiver could send an ACK to acknowledge receipt and request the next message.

1967: PROPOSING AN ARPANET

The next iteration of ARPANET appeared in a paper in 1967 that introduced daemons into the computer infrastructure. The paper was the product of much collaboration coordinated by Roberts, who joined IPTO at the end of 1966 to direct the office's research into networking. Roberts started what became the Networking Working Group in 1967. The group included researchers from the RAND Corporation (short for Research ANd Development), from the University of California institutions in Los Angeles and Santa Barbara and from the University of Utah. Group discussions led to a paper entitled "Multiple Computer Networks and Intercomputer Communication," presented at the ACM Operating Systems Symposium in Gatlinburg in October 1967. Presented at the Mountain View Hotel nestled in the Smoky Mountains, the document presented ideas developed at a meeting of IPTO's principal investigators earlier that year and in subsequent breakout groups of researchers interested in networking.[23]

In spite of the elevation of the conference location, the paper was markedly grounded. It provided a rough outline of a network design oriented to the computer research community (in contrast to the intergalactic ideals of Licklider), and it proposed a system that allowed "many computers to communicate with each other."[24] The system's benefits included facilitating remote access to specialized hardware and software, sharing programs and data, and limited interactive messaging. The paper anticipated interconnecting thirty-five computers across sixteen locations, creating an infrastructure from the social network of IPTO. These computers connected on leased telephone lines—the lone discussion of common carriage in the paper.

The paper made a decisive recommendation to use computers as the building blocks of the communication infrastructure. In doing so, IPTO ushered daemons into the network. The paper's authors called it an Interface Message Processor (IMP), a delightfully supernatural sounding name[25] suggested by Wesley Clark at the ARPA primary investigator meeting in May 1967.[26] IMPs were responsible for "dial up, error checking, retransmission, routing and verification."[27] IMPs embedded computers in infrastructure. Kleinrock, IPTO researcher and expert in queuing theory, later wrote that the benefit of IMPs is that "[t]he ability to introduce new programs, new functions, new topologies, new nodes, etc., are all enhanced by the programmable features of a clever communications processor/multiplexor at the software node."[28] Cleverness, in short, meant that IMP computers were *programmable,* capable of obeying set instructions.[29]

The report categorized the hypothetical ARPANET as a "store-and-forward" network, a term that situated ARPA in the history of telecommunications alongside the telegraph. Store-and-forward systems use a series of interconnected nodes to send and receive discrete messages. Each node stores the message and forwards it to a node closer to the final destination, similar to other computer data networks at the time. The ARPANET was proposed as a series of interconnected IMPs that could send, receive, and route data. This meant the network was not necessarily real-time, as the hops between IMPs introduced some delay in a message getting passed to its destination. Real-time applications might have required the IMPs to maintain the line, but the report does not elaborate on this application. IMPs forwarded what the report called message blocks. A message's block header included its origin and the destination so daemons could effectively route the message. IMPs communicated intermittently (not unlike batch computing). The report did "not specify the internal form" of a message block.[30] Instead, the message block could contain any sort of data.

While the paper established the need for computers in the infrastructure, their job needed more clarification. IMPs' function came into focus during a 1967 ACM symposium in Teddington, England, when Roberts met NPL's Roger Scantlebury, who was attending to present research on computer networks at NPL led by Davies.[31]

DONALD DAVIES AND NONSYNCHRONOUS COMMUNICATION

The fourth key document, the 1968 RFQ that represented the first step toward actually building the ARPANET, cannot be understood without defining the influence of Davies and his work on what is now called "packet switching." His interest in computers began at NPL, where he worked with Alan Turing. NPL promoted him to technical manager of the Advanced Computer Techniques Project in 1965.[32] That same year, he visited the United States, in part to investigate time-sharing projects at Project MAC and other computer centers at Dartmouth College, the RAND Corporation, and General Electric.[33] He was sufficiently enthused by time-sharing to begin thinking seriously about undertaking it at NPL.[34] The following year, he gave a talk on March 18 based on a report to NPL entitled "Proposal for a Digital Communication Network," mentioned in this chapter's introduction. This report outlined the ideas that later became the paper presented in Gatlinburg in 1967.

The "Proposal for a Digital Communication Network" began with the ambitious goal of creating a "new kind of national communication network which would complement the existing telephone and telegraph networks."[35] The core of the proposal was a call for "a major organizational change."[36] Davies proposed a digital communication *infrastructure* that supported multiple kinds of computer *networks* through innovation in its *flow control*. Davies recognized that a great number of applications of computers already existed and that the number would only increase in the future. While telephone networks could be provisioned with modems to allow digital communication, these analog systems created impediments to the reliability of digital communication. He proposed creating a communication infrastructure that could support these diverse networks. As he and his colleagues later wrote, "the difficulty in such an approach is to develop a system design general enough to deal with the wide range of users' requirements, including those that may arise in the future."[37]

Davies's proposed system supported diverse and multiple applications through an approach that he called "nonsynchronous communication."

The theory's key innovation was to avoid a general synchronization of the infrastructure. While Licklider and others had also faced the problem of connecting multiple durations, they focused on specific synchronization as a solution (e.g., time-sharing or batch computing). Davies avoided synchronization altogether. His hypothetical digital infrastructure differed from the telephone and telegraph networks designed for "synchronous transmission" and "design[ed] for human use and speed."[38] A computer network, Davies observed, did not have only human users; it had "two very different kinds of terminals attached to this network; human users' consoles or enquiry stations working at very slow speed and real time computers working at high speeds."[39] Unlike Semi-Automatic Ground Environment (SAGE) or Project MAC, the proposed system facilitated "non-synchronous transmission, which is a consequence of connecting terminals that work at different data rates."[40] Davies recognized that the infrastructure itself should not decide how to synchronize its users, but rather it should create the capacity for multiple kinds of synchronization at once.

Davies drew on the example of time-sharing systems, particularly Project MAC, to delineate the core functions of nonsynchronous communication. He described in detail the time allocation on a multiaccess computer. The project's CTSS operating system divvied up limited processor time through what Project MAC likely called a "scheduling daemon." The daemon divided jobs into segments and allocated processor time to these smaller segments.[41] Like CTSS, Davies proposed breaking messages into smaller units labeled packets. Where time-sharing systems like Project MAC broke its users' jobs into segments, Davies proposed segmenting messages into what he called packets. Packets made hosting multiple networks on the same infrastructure easier. The infrastructure dealt with smaller requests within its capacity and responded quickly enough to mimic other networks from real-time, multiaccess, online, or batch-processing networks.

Davies also described packet communication as a store-and-forward system. Similar to ARPANET's design, his nonsynchronous communication system was a series of interconnected node computers. Davies encouraged setting up the system to be over-connected so that packets could travel on different routes in case one node became oversaturated. These nodes exchanged packets in a manner similar to that in which Roberts envisioned message blocks in ARPANET, but with a key difference: their smaller size greatly altered the system's operation. These short

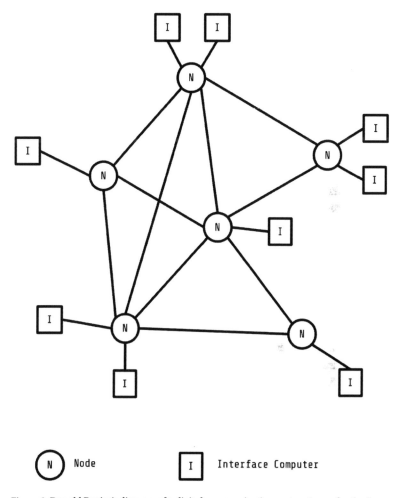

N ⃝ Node   I ⃞ Interface Computer

Figure 2. Donald Davies's diagram of a digital communication system (reproduction).

units required much more activity and greater control in the network, as the node computers had to constantly deal with packets.

At the Gatlinburg ACM conference in 1967, Scantlebury presented an updated version of packet communication entitled "A Digital Communication Network for Computers Giving Rapid Response at Remote Terminals." The report characterized the new digital communication system as a "common carrier" for public, commercial, and scientific computing applications. In keeping with the general purpose of a common carrier network, the report also described three types of networking: "man-computer, computer-computer and computer-machine."[42] Humans communicated among each other or with computers.[43] Computers also communicated with one another. Nonsynchronous communication modulated the conditions of transmission to accommodate these different human and machine applications. The proposal by Davies and his colleagues thus expanded the concept of "common carriage" to mean a communication system capable of accommodating humans and machines alike.

The paper further refined the role of computers in the infrastructure. The report's authors described two types of computers in a diagram of the proposed system, as seen in Figure 2. One computer called an "interface" acted as the single conduit for a local area network to access the system. Interfaces connected to other computers called "nodes" that coordinated the transmission of packets to their destinations. Nodes used an "adaptive routing technique" to transmit packets between each other. The report cited this technique as a form of hot-potato routing developed by Paul Baran (the other inventor of packet switching). Adaptive routing involved daemons maintaining a map (or table) of the network and passing off a packet to the closest node as quickly as possible (much like the children's game "hot potato"). Eventually, by passing the packet from node to node, the daemons routed it to the right location.

Davies left the work of optimization to the node computers, where "each node takes cognizance of its immediate locality." This "simple routing and control policy" enabled the "high data handling rate" in their proposal.[44] Davies was neither the first nor the last to envision network optimization through decentralized nodes. At the same conference, Roberts introduced IMPs as a similar computer embedded in the infrastructure. Both papers avoided central control (no doubt cause for conversation after the panel). Instead, the proper functioning of the infrastructure was left up to the IMPs (or nodes) to determine using their localized knowledge, creating a distributed pattern. Independent IMPs acting collectively led to an efficient network. Davies knew this to be true only through simulation: he modeled and ran a computer experiment to calculate the optimal design of his node computers and their processing power.

Davies's distributed approach stood as a novel optimization at the time. Other calculations of the optimal state might have been the product of linear programming or game theory.[45] Recall Licklider's frustration with batch computing discussed in chapter 1. Waiting for an optimal decision from a batch computer meant that "the battle would be over before the second step in its planning was begun."[46] Researchers at the RAND Corporation turned to computer simulation as a means to calculate the behavior of complex systems as they began to notice the limits of calculating optimal states in game theory.[47] Where these examples used computers to simulate reality, IMPs became a computer simulation made real, knowable only in its distributed operation. A turn to distributed intelligence was also novel at the time. Even popular culture had its versions of a central computer knowing the right answer. In 1966, Robert Heinlein's *The Moon Is a Harsh Mistress* featured a central computer known as HOLMES IV that plots a lunar uprising along with the hero of the book. *Billion Dollar Brain,* a film from 1967, featured a brilliant computer helping to outthink a communist plot. Even the computer villain HAL 9000 from Stanley Kubrick's 1968 movie *2001* was a central processor, capable of being pulled apart.

Packet communication, by contrast, distributed intelligence among daemons who constantly ferried packets between the infrastructure's nodes. These node computers gave new meaning to the nascent idea of an IMP. At least by all accounts, the work of Davies informed ARPANET's design through various late night conversations. Scantlebury introduced Roberts to complementary research for ARPANET, such as Baran's work at RAND, and to NPL's approach to networking. All these ideas informed the final document that led to the construction of the first IMP.

1968: DAEMONIZING THE INFRASTRUCTURE

Roberts submitted the specifications for ARPANET's guidelines in June 1968, and they were sent out as an RFQ the next month.[48] The RFQ solicited major technology firms for bids. Proposals came from familiar companies like Bolt, Beranek, and Newman Inc. (BBN), including a joint bid between Digital Equipment Corporation and the Computer Corporation of America (the same firm that helped author the 1966 report) and a bid from Raytheon.[49] Notably, the RFQ focused on the design and operation of the IMP. Bidders had to propose a design for the IMP and then program and install it at four nodes in less than a year. In the following section, I will trace the connections between the RFQ and its lingering optimality problems.

The IMP, as mentioned in the 1967 report, acted as the interme-diary between a host computer (or a local network) and the wider ARPANET. The IMP functioned as a distributed networking infrastruc-ture needed to send and receive messages between the ARPANET sites. The RFQ described the IMP's tasks as follows: "(1) Breaking messages into packets, (2) Management of message buffers, (3) Routing of mes-sages, (4) Generation, analysis, and alteration of formatted messages, (5) Coordination of activities with other IMPs, (6) Coordination of activi-ties with its HOST, (7) Measurement of network parameters and func-tions, and (8) Detection and disposition of faults."[50] Two of its functions deserve a closer look: buffering and routing. Together, they define the important modulations of flow control.

"Buffering" referred to how IMPs stored and forwarded packets. IMPs had to store packets in their local memory for brief periods of time before sending them to the next IMP, a process called buffering. Limited resources, especially local memory, meant that inefficient buffering could lead to congestion and error. IMPs overloaded or encountered delays that required them to pause packet transmission. Buffering allowed the IMP to control data flows, holding a packet in the buffer to be sent later due to congestion. IMPs stored a copy of a packet in case it needed to be resent due to error. IMPs also signaled each other if, for example, they needed another IMP to stop transmitting because it was congesting the network (also known as "quenching"). The report did not specify the optimal way for an IMP to manage its queue, but it did situate the problem in queu-ing theory.

Theories to manage queues developed out of telephone engineer-ing, mathematics, and operations research as an attempt to find optimal strategies to manage waiting lines in communication systems (though they had numerous applications outside the field). At the time of the RFQ, scholars had just begun to develop the theory beyond the single channel of Claude Shannon's information theory and toward modeling queues in multiple-node, multichannel networks.[51] Kleinrock wrote his dissertation on a mathematical theory for effective queuing to prevent congestion and ensure efficient resource allocation.[52] In it, he suggested that store-and-forward networks had stochastic flows or messages sent at random intervals. Stochastic flows had to be modeled through proba-bility. Based on this model, he contended that an optimal network assigned priority to the shorter messages in queues.[53] His ideas anticipate the kinds of queuing algorithms later developed and implemented on ARPANET in the 1970s and in the contemporary internet.

Queuing also related to resource-allocation issues in time-sharing systems. In his report on Project MAC, Davies noted that the system had four categories of users. Each group had a certain number of lines connected to the machine that regulated system access. Davies explained:

> Two lines are reserved for the top management, six for the systems programmers, two for the people using the special display and [twenty] for the rest. When one group of users' lines is full they can get a stand-by line in another group, if one is free, but may be automatically logged out if that line is wanted by a user in its group.[54]

In other words, Project MAC had begun to design some rudimentary queuing logics into the infrastructure. The scheduling daemon cycled between users connected to the machine, which led to questions about an optimal scheduling system. Should it cycle through in round-robin fashion, as noted by Davies, or use a more complex system?

While these debates continued long after the contract was awarded, the queue illustrates one modulation of flow control in that it specifies which packets have priority over other packets. The RFQ's specifications delegated flow control to the IMPs to solve these queuing issues. Kleinrock later described flow control as a process whereby programs could "throttle the flow of traffic entering (and leaving) the net in a way which protects the network and the data sources from each other while at the same time maintaining a smooth flow of data in an efficient fashion."[55] These flow control programs needed to assign priority to packets arriving simultaneously. Which would be transmitted first? And which packet had to wait in the buffer?

In addition to questions of priority, IMPs had to choose the best route to send a packet to reach its destination. Routing dilemmas and strategies partially emerged out of the literature of telephone engineering, often found in the pages of the *Bell Labs Technical Journal,* as part of the move to automated long-distance telephone switching. Operations researchers also had an interest in figuring out the optimal route to travel when faced with multiple paths (often called the traveling salesman problem).[56] Telephone engineers sought to design both the optimal topology of a network and the best algorithms for routing long-distance calls. A central problem they faced concerned avoiding blocked trunks (or, in IPTO language, congested nodes), and they derived solutions from early applications of probability theory and graph theory. This literature partially framed the challenge faced by the IMP developers. One of the key architects of the IMP, Robert Kahn of BBN, and later IPTO, worked at Bell Labs under the supervision of Roger I. Wilkinson, who wrote an influential article relating to routing.[57] Wilkinson proposed, for example, that automatic switching should be able to calculate multiple possible routes for a call to minimize delay and reduce congestion in the telephone system.

ARPANET routing provided additional challenges to IMPs. Davies and others had suggested that the network's topology should be over-connected, and the RFQ stated: "Each IMP shall be connected to several other IMPs by full duplex [fifty] kbps common carrier communication links creating a strongly interconnected net."[58] This meant that IMPs had options and had to keep track of them to pick the best route. IMPs crashed, became congested, and locked up (for many reasons not originally anticipated by IPTO).[59] As a result, IMPs had to communicate with other IMPs (responsibility 6 from the RFQ), constantly measure performance (responsibility 7), and detect failures (responsibility 8) to maintain an operational model of the network topology. IMPs kept all this information in what became known as a routing table. Routing daemons read these tables to make decisions about where to send a packet. A routing daemon, for example, might follow Baran's hot-potato routing strategy by referring to the routing table, finding the IMP closest to the destination, and passing the packet off to the selected IMP as quickly as possible.

Routing acts as another modulation of flow control, wherein daemons prioritize connections and influence the path of a packet. Daemons then directly overlap with the spatial configurations of the internet's physical infrastructure. While wires and pipes provide possible connections—a plane of immanence—for networks, daemons enact these connections with significant consequences for the temporal conditions of transmission. Does a daemon pick a route that causes greater delay? How does a daemon know the best path? Through routing, daemons wielded another important influence over the conditions of transmission.

Routing and queuing became two important capacities of ARPANET's daemons. A packet communication network allows daemons to be extremely particular about their influence, as will be seen in chapter 4. While they could simultaneously accommodate distinct temporalities, their flow control could also manipulate the response time of certain networks, adding delay or giving priority. New ways to understand and interpret packets augmented daemons' ability to vary transmission conditions. How daemons should use their newfound powers constituted an ongoing debate about the internet's design.

The RFQ gave three ranked criteria for network performance: message delay, reliability, and capacity. Any proposal would be judged on whether it could ensure that "the average message delay should be less than [half a second] for a fully loaded network," that it had a low probability of losing or misrouting a message, and least importantly, that the network had a defined maximum bandwidth per IMP.[60] Delay, the RFQ suggested, could be caused by how the IMP processed and queued packets as well as by the medium of communication. The emphasis on delay, a factor known at the time to cause user frustration (as will be discussed in chapter 5), can be seen as a guideline that the network should prioritize interaction and communication. Perhaps in contrast to the need for reliability in a telephone network, ARPANET's daemons should be more concerned with lessening delay and, by extension, with the communication between host computers. The RFQ did not discuss matters of prioritization or how to manage multiple network at once—questions that lingered.

While the RFQ exhibited an overall preference for technical language, the lack of a vision for the network in the description of the network model is striking compared to the roots of ARPANET. Gone are the ideals of man–computer symbiosis or an intergalactic network. The RFQ did not even mention the concept of multimedia networking suggested by Davies. The lack of details posed a lingering question for daemons to solve: what should a network of networks be?

THE OPTIMALITY PROBLEM

The RFQ provided little direction for the definition of an optimal communication system. The report exemplifies a common issue found in this history: engineers built new systems of control and management without designing ways for these systems to be managed or governed. Robert Frank, Kahn, and Kleinrock, who were all researchers deeply involved in the design of the ARPANET and the IMP, later reflected that "there is no generally accepted definition of an 'optimal' network or even of a 'good' network," a statement that could be viewed as an admission of a constitutive issue in the ARPANET.[61] The word "optimal" is telling. As mentioned in the introduction, optimization originates in mathematics and operations research. An optimal solution is the best one among available options. Nonsynchronous communication created the conditions for the internet to be many kinds of networks without necessarily stipulating what an optimal network is. As a result, daemons are always trying to optimize but do not always agree on how. Even without a clear sense of the optimal, ARPANET included two distinct processes of optimization. On one side, BBN left the management of flow control to the IMPs themselves. BBN's response to the RFQ eschewed centralized control in favor of letting autonomous IMPs handle the work. As they explained:

Our experience convinced us that it was wrong to platform for an *initial* network that permitted a sizable degree of external and remote control of IMPs. Consequently, as one important feature of our design, we have planned a network composed of highly autonomous IMPs. Once the network is demonstrated to be successful, then remote control can be added, slowly and carefully.[62]

In practical terms, optimization occurred through actively autonomous IMPs collectively enabling flow control. There was no central control, only the work of daemons coordinating with each other. This process of optimization continues to this day, with the internet running through the distributed work of millions of pieces of hardware.

As the infrastructure grew, ARPANET augmented IMPs' optimization with a second computer simulation. The Network Measurement Center (NMC) at UCLA and the Network Control Center (NCC) at BBN both monitored the performance of IMPs, analyzing the system for congestion and lock-up and then diagnosing the cause. Both centers' observations led to iterative changes in the design of the IMPs and the overall operation of the system. Simultaneously, programs run at BBN and another contractor, the Network Analysis Corporation (NAC), ran simulations of ARPANET to understand and improve its performance and forecast its growth.[63] Between the simulations and the work of ARPANET, the specific nature of network optimization became apparent. Semiannual reports from NAC provide a concise statement of the logic of optimization used in computer simulation. IPTO first contracted NAC's services in 1969 to help plan its expansion beyond the first four nodes, and NAC submitted six semiannual reports to IPTO from 1970 to 1972.[64]

Like so many of the contractors at IPTO, NAC's President Howard

Frank was a familiar member of the computer science research community, training and using many techniques of the cyborg sciences. He earned his PhD from Northwestern University, where his doctoral work applied network theory to computer communication systems. His research resembled Kleinrock's so greatly that a colleague mistook the library's copy of Kleinrock's published book for Frank's unfinished dissertation. (Upon hearing the news, Frank rushed to the library to find the book, feeling relief that their approaches differed enough that his dissertation still made a contribution.) After graduation, Frank worked with Kleinrock at the White House in an experimental group known as the Systems Analysis Center. Their use of network theory to analyze offshore natural gas pipeline systems saved an estimated $100 million.[65] After Richard Nixon's election, Frank focused on using the same network analysis for other applications like modeling ARPANET.

Unlike the IMPs, NAC had a better sense of the optimal. Building on research in pipeline design, graph theory, and the subfield of network theory,[66] the first of the six reports described a methodology and a recommendation for an optimal topology for ARPANET. This was primarily an infrastructure question: calculating the optimal number and location of nodes, the capacity of the telephone lines that linked them together, and the overall capacity of the system. The report concisely described this problem at the start:

> Each network to be designed must satisfy a number of constraints. It must be reliable, it must be able to accommodate variations in traffic flow without significant degradation in performance, and it must be capable of efficient expansion when new nodes and links are added at a later date. Each design must have an average response time for short messages no greater than 0.2 seconds. The goal of the optimization is to satisfy all of the constraints with the least possible cost per bit of transmitted information.[67]

Topological optimization iteratively calculated the most economic and feasible network design. This process kept static much of the work of IMPs and users, such as fixing the routing calculation, averaging traffic for regular and high-volume nodes,[68] and using the established buffer size of IMPs. Keeping these constant, the optimization program drew a network between nodes, calculated the cost, and then redrew the network. It then compared the two designs, kept the cheaper, feasible network as an input to start the process over again. The program produced a number of different topologies for the ARPANET that Frank analyzed at the end of the report. These designs informed the growth of ARPANET into a twelve-, sixteen-, or eighteen-node infrastructure at a time when it had just four nodes.

The report also recognized the limits of its approach to optimization. Computer power at the time could not calculate an optimal topology beyond twenty nodes using the method of integer programming. As report explained:

Even if a proposed network can be accurately analyzed, the most economical networks which satisfy all of the constraints are not easily found. This is because of the enormous number of combinations of links that can be used to connect a relatively small number of nodes. It is not possible to examine even a small fraction of the possible network topologies that might lead to economical designs. In fact, the direct enumeration of all such configurations for a twenty node network is beyond the capabilities of the most powerful present day computer.[69]

Though advances in computing improved capacity for the calculation, computational capacity set hard limits on the foresight of ARPANET.

Although NAC's report discussed IMPs' flow control and network optimization, it did not solve them through computation modeling. Finding the optimal was left to daemons to figure out by themselves. Daemons provided a very different kind of optimization from the services provided by NAC, expressing optimization through their active flow control. It is a small but crucial step from the algorithmic calculations of topological optimization to the active and dynamic calculations of IMPs. ARPANET turned the simulation into an actual experiment. This latter daemonic optimization became a key feature of the ARPANET and later the internet.

Daemonic optimization did not have a clear solution, unlike the economics of NAC. Davies, for his part, continued to advance distributed solutions to network optimization and even suggested much more radical solutions than what became accepted wisdom. In the early 1970s, he proposed that a packet-switching system should always operate with a fixed number of packets. He called this solution an "isarithmic" network.[70] A colleague of Davies at NPL, Wyn L. Price, later explained that the obscure term "isarithmic" was a combination of the Greek terms for for "equal" and "number."[71] An isarithmic network kept an equal number of packets at all times by limiting the number of total packets at one time. Daemons continuously transmitted the same number of packets, with or without data, to create a constant flow. To send data, daemons switched empty packets for ones containing data. This radical proposal allowed for congestion control "without employing a control center." Central control, he wrote, "could be effective but has bad features: the monitoring and control data increases the traffic load and the controller is a vulnerable part of the system."[72] Running a packet-switching system at full throttle, in retrospect, seems wild compared to much of the literature discussing the economics of bandwidth at the time.[73] Rather than save bandwidth, Davies proposed using it all.

The logic of isarithmic computing is twofold: first, it simplifies calculating the optimal using computer simulation and, second, it solves an information problem for distributed node computers. The latter aspect warrants further discussion, given its relationship to daemonic optimization. Davies suggested that empty packets could share information between node computers. Similar to the ways IMPs later shared their tables for adaptive routing, Davies imagined that empty packets enabled IMPs to better coordinate their flow control. Implicitly, his isarithmic proposal acknowledged the challenges of distributed intelligence. Node computers had to be intelligent for their flow control to be effective. This requirement would become a distinct challenge, as we will see when I discuss packet inspection in chapter 4. A considerable amount has been invested into making daemons more aware.

Davies first made his proposal at the second and seemingly last Symposium on Problems in the Optimization of Data Communications Systems, held in 1971. He later turned the paper into an article published in the 1972 special issue of *IEEE Transactions on Communications*. These venues proved to be an active forum for debate and discussion, but these debates eventually led to Davies's isarithmic proposal being discarded. The idea, according to Vinton Cerf, "didn't work out."[74]

An isarithmic network was just one of many solutions to congestion and the general matter of daemonic intelligence. What was optimal daemonic behavior? How intelligent should daemons be compared to their users? Many of these debates are well known, having been covered as central debates in the history of the internet, and also as ongoing policy issues. Debates, as discussed in chapter 4, centered on how much intelligence to install in the core of the infrastructure, versus leaving it at the ends. Should daemons guarantee delivery or not? Should daemons think of networks more holistically as a circuit or focus just on routing packets? (This is technically a debate known as "virtual circuits" versus "datagrams"). Many of these arguments culminated in a matter of international standards when the Transmission Control Protocol and Internet Protocol (TCP/IP) became the de facto standard instead of the International Telecommunication Union's X.25.[75]

Researchers on ARPANET collaborated on its design through Requests for Comments (RFCs). Archives of the RFCs contain numerous technical and policy discussions about the design of ARPANET.[76] Topics include visions of network citizenship, whether AT&T would run the system, and if so, whether it would run it as a common carrier, and what communication policy expert Sandra Braman summarizes as debates over "the distinction between the human and the 'daemon,' or machinic, user of the network."[77] How would the network balance the demands of the two? Drawing on an extensive review of the RFCs from 1969 to 1979, Braman explains:

> Computer scientists and electrical engineers involved in the design discussion were well aware that the infrastructure they were building was social as well as technical in nature. Although some of that awareness was begrudging inclusion of human needs in design decisions that would otherwise favor the "daemon," or nonhuman, network users (such as software), at other times there was genuine sensitivity to social concerns such as access, privacy, and fairness in the transmission of messages from network users both large and small.[78]

Braman, in this case, meant daemons in a broad sense beyond the specific internet daemons of this book. Daemons and humans had different needs, and their networks had different tempos. How then could ARPANET strike a balance between the various types of networks running on its infrastructure?

Optimization only became more complex as these debates went on. The flexible ARPA protocols allowed users to utilize the networks for a variety of types of transmissions. By 1971, a version of email had been developed and installed on hosts around ARPANET, allowing humans to communicate with one another. The File Transfer Protocol (FTP), on the other hand, focused on allowing users and daemons to exchange computer files.[79] ARPANET even experimented with voice communications, contracting NAC to conduct a study of its economics in 1970.[80] Each application adapted the ARPA protocols to send different kinds of information, and at different rates. How should daemons accommodate these different demands? Could they? These questions, especially those of fairness in the transmission of messages, only compounded as networks proliferated.

The historical nuances of many of these debates are beyond the scope of this project. My story now accelerates a bit in order to get to today's internet daemons. The proliferation of internet daemons began after BBN won the bid to create the IMP and delivered the first modified Honeywell DDP-516 minicomputers to Kleinrock at UCLA in September 1969.[81] IMPs gradually divided into a host of different network devices, including modems, hubs, switches, routers, and gateways. The concept of packet switching crystallized over the 1970s. During Robert Taylor's time as director of the IPTO from 1969 to 1973, both his work and input from researchers like Cerf, Kahn, Kleinrock, and Louis Pouzin elaborated the version of packet switching that defines the modern internet. The next chapter explores this transformation from ARPANET to the internet by focusing on the changing diagrams that informed the design and operation of internet daemons.

CONCLUSION

The internet is now an infrastructure possessed. Embedded in every router, switch, and hub—almost every part of the internet—is a daemon listening, observing, and communicating. The IMP opened the network for the daemons waiting at its logic gates. Network administrators realized they could program software daemons to carry out menial and repetitive tasks that were often dull but essential to network operation. Daemons soon infested computer networks and enthralled engineers and administrators who made use of their uncanny services. Among the many tasks carried out by daemons, one stands out: flow control.

Flow control is the purposive modulation of transmission that influences the temporalities of networks simultaneously sharing a common infrastructure. Daemons' flow control modulates transmissioned conditions for certain packets and certain networks. It modulates the resonance between nodes in a network and the overall performance of any network. Greater bandwidth increases synchronization and reduced bandwidth decreases it. A daemon might prioritize internet telephony and demote file sharing simultaneously. Networks might run in concert or fall out of rhythm. A daemonic influence changes the relative performance of a network, making some forms of communication seem obsolete or residual compared to emerging or advanced networks. Daemons' ability to modulate the conditions of transmission helped the internet remediate prior and contemporaneous networks.

The overall effect of internet daemons creates a metastable system in the network of networks. Networks coexist and daemons manage how they share a common infrastructure. This situation invites comparison to what Sarah Sharma calls a "power-chronography." In contrast to theories of time-space compression, she writes:

> The social fabric is composed of a chronography of power, where individuals' and social groups' senses of time and possibility are shaped by a differential economy, limited or expanded by the ways and means that they find themselves in and out of time.[82]

Where Sharma focuses on the temporal relations of global capital, the work of daemons establishes temporal relations between networks. This is another way to restate the issue of network neutrality: it involves the optimal way for networks to share infrastructural resources. The uneven distribution of flow causes networks to be in and out sync. As discussed in chapter 4, these relations are enacted through optimizations, through how daemons modulate their flow control to create metastability between networks.

These optimizations create power imbalances and inequalities. Different networks' viability relate to each other: a successful network is defined by an unsuccessful one. "There can be no sensation of speed without a difference in speed, without something moving at a different speed," according to Adrian Mackenzie.[83] Paul Edwards comes closest to explaining the comparative value of temporalities when he discusses the SAGE network built by the U.S. Air Force. SAGE linked radar towers together with control bunkers seeking to operationalize the command and control model of military thought. SAGE was a way to control U.S. air space, but its significance lay in being more responsive than the Soviet system.[84] A better model allowed the United States to react more quickly and more precisely than the Soviets' command and control regime. That is why, as Charles Acland notes on the influence of Harold Innis: "It is essential to remember that spatial and temporal biases of media technologies were relational. They were not inherent a-historical attributes, but were drawn out as technologies move into dominance, always in reciprocity with other existing and circulating technologies and tendencies."[85] Flow control, then, has an influence over the relations of networks, over how well they comparatively perform. At the time of ARPANET, optimal flow control was a bounded problem contained in the experimental system. As packet-switching developed elsewhere and these systems stared interconnecting, solutions to flow control expanded, and often different senses of the optimal came into contact.

3 IMPs, OLIVERs, AND GATEWAYS

Internetworking before the Internet

BEFORE THE FIRST INTERFACE MESSAGE PROCESSOR (IMP) had been delivered, former directors of the Information Processing Techniques Office (IPTO) J. C. R. Licklider and Robert Taylor were imagining a world filled with daemons and digital communications (to everyone's benefit, of course). Their optimism abounded in a lighthearted article entitled "The Computer as a Communication Device" for the business magazine *Science & Technology for the Technical Men in Management*. Published in 1968, the article filled in a vision for the Advanced Research Projects Agency's ARPANET that was absent from the IMP Request for Quotations (RFQ) discussed in the previous chapter. The pair imagined a future in which accessible, computer-aided communications would lead to online *communities* of people across the globe sharing research, collaborating, and accessing new services. People would connect through common interest, not common location. Online, people would access new programs to help them perform everyday tasks. Computers would do more than manage flows. Optimism replaced the optimal.

Licklider and Taylor's article provides a bridge from the design of the ARPANET discussed in the previous chapter to the contemporary internet and its problems of optimization addressed in the next. This transition involves changing technical diagrams for packet switching and new desires around computer networking. Licklider and Taylor foreshadow these trends and their article helps me frame these changes conceptually. First, they wanted new computer programs to improve computer-aided communication. Their imaginative paper helps to explain the very real and technical processes that modified what I refer to as the internet's "diagram," as discussed in the Introduction. The changing internet diagram created new components and places for daemons to possess the internet. Second, Licklider and Taylor took inspiration from the prospect of new applications of computer-aided communication. The ARPANET quickly became one of many computer infrastructures. More than merely leading to technical innovations, these infrastructures created new kinds of networks that brought together humans and computers in shared times and spaces. These developments in the internet's diagram eventually led to the bringing together of different networks to be mediated through one global infrastructure called "the internet."

After defining the concept of the diagram in more detail, this chapter traces the changes to the diagram of packet switching as a way to briefly cover the move from ARPANET to the internet. My goal is not to offer a history of computer communication or packet switching; a full history has been told in more depth elsewhere.[1] Rather, my aim is to describe the changing locations and tasks of internet daemons to be discussed further in the next chapter. In doing so, I focus on four iterative diagrams of packet switching. Each involves a change in the diagram and a new kind of daemon. The story begins with the IMP and a largely homogeneous infrastructure before moving to the introduction of the Network Control Program (NCP) at the University of California, Los Angeles. Developed on the hosts to manage their connection to the ARPANET, NCP can be seen as one of the many programs envisioned by Licklider and Taylor. NCP became an essential part of the internet's diagram by defining its edges. The third diagram moves from a lone packet-switching network to a series of interconnected infrastructures. This move preceded the gradual incorporation of ARPANET as part of a global internet comprised of interconnected infrastructures. This new diagram depended on gateways to connect one infrastructure to another. Figure 3 summarizes these first three diagrams.

The growing number of daemons coincides with many innovative designs for computer networking. The second part of the chapter offers an exemplary discussion of some of the key networks that predate today's internet. These networks, often running on custom hardware, enabled new synchronizations between humans and machines. Outside the military-industrial complex, hobbyist, pirate, and academic networks popularized digital computing, creating what can be seen as new visions of human–computer interaction. Many of these networks converged into the internet. Their unique transmission requirements and demands on daemons' flow control have created what I describe, following Fred Turner, as a heterarchy of network demands that daemonic optimizations must resolve.

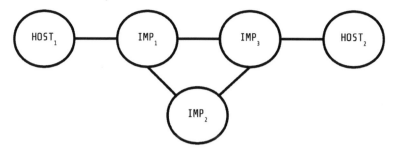

Diagram for Interface Message Processors

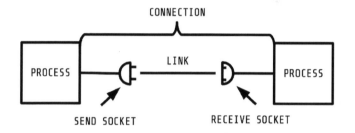

Diagram for Network Control Program

Diagram for Inter-networking

Figure 3. Three diagrams of packet switching communication.

IMPs AND OLIVERs: THE CHANGING DIAGRAMS OF THE INTERNET

Licklider and Taylor thought that people would need some help being online. Their imagined assistants might be seen as an elaboration of

Licklider's earlier work on man–computer symbiosis (a name that reminds us of the marginalization of women in computing). Just as the present book does, they found inspiration in the work of Oliver Selfridge:

> A very important part of each man's interaction with his on-line community will be mediated by his OLIVER. . . . An OLIVER is, or will be when there is one, an "on-line interactive vicarious expediter and responder," a complex of computer programs and data that resides within the network and acts on behalf of its principal, taking care of many minor matters that do not require his personal attention and buffering him from the demanding world. "You are describing a secretary," you will say. But no! Secretaries will have OLIVERs.[2]

The name honored Selfridge, whom they called the "originator of the concept."[3] Imagining a future digital communication system using Selfridge's OLIVERs, their ensuing discussion might be seen as a speculative kind of daemonic media studies and a first glimpse of the internet to be built.

At first pass, OLIVERs seem to resemble the IMPs discussed in the previous chapter. A "complex of computer programs and data that resides within the network" sounds remarkably like the computers that became part of the ARPANET infrastructure. Yet, Licklider and Taylor distinguished OLIVERs as interactive programs distinct from computers implementing what they called the "switching function" in store-and-forward communication. Though they do not mention IMPs by name, they include a discussion of message processors in communications as a way to describe the feasibility of computer-aided communication and to introduce their OLIVERs. These other computers gestured toward programs that resided nearer to end users, on their desktop computers or connected to them through a digital communication system. IMPs were the less interesting intermediaries connecting humans and OLIVERs.

Conceptually, IMPs and OLIVERs specify changes in the infrastructural diagram of the internet. By using the term "diagram," I draw on the work of Michel Foucault, Gilles Deleuze, and Félix Guattari, who use the word in varying ways to describe an abstract arrangement of space and power. One example of a diagram is Foucault's panopticon, which functions as an optical technology used to build prisons and other infrastructures of surveillance. Where Foucault emphasizes the optical nature of the diagram, Deleuze and Guattari prefer the term "abstract machine" to refer to the logics of control that axiomatically construct infrastructures and other systems.[4] As they write, "the diagrammatic or abstract machine does not function to represent, even something real, but rather constructs a real that is yet to come, a new type of reality."[5]

Alexander Galloway makes an explicit link between the diagram and his concept of protocol. Using Paul Baran's diagram comparing centralized, decentralized, and distributed network designs, Galloway argues that the distributed network design is "part of a larger shift in social life," one that involves "a movement away from central bureaucracies and vertical hierarchies toward a broad network of autonomous social actors."[6] This shift, theorized by Galloway as protocol, functions by distributing in all nodes "certain pre-agreed 'scientific' rules of the system."[7] Galloway gives the example of the Internet Protocol Suite, which I discuss in detail later, as one protocol. The early work of IMPs might be understood protocologically. Each IMP ran the same code, so their individual performances enacted a shared optimality.

Such homogeneity was short-lived on ARPANET. By 1975, ARPANET had different kinds of IMPs. At the same time, ARPANET became one of a few packet-switching systems. Internet daemons then became embedded in more complex infrastructures. As diagrams, like Galloway's concept of protocol, function as "a proscription for structure,"[8] attention to the changing diagrams of packet switching tracks the abstractions that created locations and functions for daemons to occupy in the ensuing physical infrastructures.

Diagrams figure significantly in the internet's history. Early design documents, some included in this chapter, sketch out the abstract design for the infrastructure to come. Donald Davies's diagram of this digital communication system, included in chapter 2, is one example of a diagram that helped construct the ARPANET. Lawrence Roberts included his own diagram to describe the unbuilt ARPANET at the fateful Association for Computing Machines conference in Gatlinburg, Tennessee, in 1967. It depicted ARPANET as time-shared computers connected by IMPs to a common carrier. In this chapter, IMPs and OLIVERs refer to the changing components of these diagrams. Licklider and Taylor could be said to be adding to the ARPANET's diagram with the OLIVER. They not only imagined new programs for computer communication; they imagined a new diagram, one that included OLIVERs, host computers, and people connected by IMPs.

Diagrams interact with the work of daemons. Variations in the internet's diagram created spaces and possibilities for daemons to flourish.

This spatial diagram, however, does not entirely determine the kinds of daemons that occupy its nodes and edges. The next chapter will focus on the daemons that appeared within the internet's diagram running on interfaces, switches, and gateways.

The Common IMP

The first diagram comes from the reply by Bolt, Beranek, and Newman Inc. (BBN) to the ARPANET RFQ. BBN's *Report No. 1763*, submitted on January 1969, includes a few diagrams of the proposed ARPANET. The diagram depicted at the top of Figure 3 is reproduced from a section discussing transmission conditions. This diagram best captures the key components of the early ARPANET and its operational sense of abstraction. ARPANET transmits data between hosts through a series of interconnected IMPs. Hosts and IMPs are roughly the same size on the diagram. Researchers at IPTO initially had as much interest in the technical work of packet switching as in its applications, if not more, as illustrated by the diagram. What is missing from the diagram is as interesting as what is represented. The diagram abstracts the common carrier lines and the telephone systems that provisioned the interconnections between IMPs. The whole underlying common-carrier infrastructure is missing. These components simply become lines of abstraction, assumed to be present but irrelevant to understanding ARPANET.

The emphasis on hosts and IMPs represented ARPANET's conceptual design at the time. It abstracted activity into two "subnets": a user subnet filled with hosts and a communication subnet filled with IMPs. These subnets operated separately from one another: the user subnet ignored the work of the IMPs and focused on connecting sockets, while the communication subnet ignored the business of the host computers. Each subnet also contained its own programs. The communication subnet contained daemons running on IMPs. At the user subnet, programs running on hosts handled interfacing with IMPs. Finally, the two subnets used different data formats as well. The user subnet formatted data as *messages*, while the communication subnet formatted *packets*. Nonetheless, the subnets depended on each other. Hosts relied on the IMPs to communicate with each other, and the IMPs depended on hosts for something to do.

Initially a specific piece of hardware, IMPs gradually became an abstract component that served an intermediary function in a packet-switched infrastructure. After delivering the first IMP to Leonard Kleinrock in 1969, the BBN team developed at least four different types of IMP, in part because:

> [It had] aspirations for expanding upon and exploiting the Arpanet technology beyond the Arpanet, both elsewhere in the government and commercially. Relatively early on, a slightly modified version of the 516 IMP technology was deployed in the US intelligence community.[9]

BBN developed the IMP 316, the IMP 516, the Terminal IMP, and the Pluribus IMP. Without enumerating the differences, it is important to recognize that the abstract IMP component of the diagram allowed multiple iterations. In other words, the IMP soon stood for many functions, all having to do with in-between-ness.

The IMP then became an intermediary node in the internet's design, specifying an element between hosts or the "ends" of the communication system. Today, a few different kinds of hardware occupy that intermediary position. Hubs and switches are devices that aggregate and forward packets between parts of the infrastructure. They might be seen as a kind of telephone switching board with multiple inputs and outputs. Hubs and switches differ in their methods of packet forwarding. A hub forwards packets to all its connected lines, whereas switches forward the message only to the specific line. Switches function similarly to another kind of hardware device known as a "router." Routers are designed to learn the topology of a part of the internet and to use that knowledge to send packets toward their destination. Hubs, switches, and routers are a few of the necessary pieces of equipment for packet switching. In addition, a number of other devices known as "middleboxes" exist in this intermediary space. "Middlebox" is a catchall term meant to describe all the intermediary devices that have a purpose other than packet forwarding. As the next chapter discusses, these middleboxes inspect packets and coordinate resources.[10]

A firewall is a good example of a middlebox. It is now an essential part of the internet, but one not necessarily included on the original ARPANET diagram. Firewalls developed as a response to the security risks posed by computer networking. Bill Cheswick and Steven Bellovin, early experts on internet security at Bell Labs, described the problem as "transitive trust." As they explained, "your computers may be secure, but you may have users who connect from other machines that are less secure."[11] Security experts needed a way to secure information transmitted from outside threats. The problem became clear after the Morris worm incident on November 2, 1988. Robert Tappan Morris, a computer science student at Cornell University, wrote a program to measure the internet. The worm's buggy code flooded the internet, overwhelming its infrastructure. Even though Morris was convicted of a crime under the Computer Fraud and Abuse Act, the worm helped to promote technical solutions to transitive trust. Specifically, the worm popularized the usage of firewalls, computers that act as intermediaries between different infrastructures. In a car, a firewall stops engine fires from entering the passenger cabin while still allowing the driver to steer. On networks, firewalls block threats while permitting legitimate traffic to continue. The first firewalls relied on destination and port numbers in the lower layers to identify threats.[12] Digital Equipment Corporation sold the first commercial firewall on June 13, 1991.[13] Firewalls subsequently became a mainstay of any networking infrastructure.

As much as the top diagram in Figure 3 illustrates a packet-switching infrastructure, it misses the activity happening on the host computers. IPTO initially proposed the ARPANET as a way to connect specialized computer infrastructures. Yet, the diagram does not reflect the diversity of the computer systems on the ARPANET, which included computers manufactured by Digital Equipment Corporation and IBM, in addition to different operating systems. This is not to say that ARPANET developers ignored the host computers, but as Janet Abbate argues, users had been ARPANET's "most neglected element."[14] Instead, a second diagram adds a new site of activity on the ARPANET.

Network Control Programs and Transmission Control Programs

Although IPTO encouraged other institutions to use its ARPANET, sites had to develop their own local programs to interface with the IMP. This led to a lot of hurried work developing local programs to interface with IMPs.[15] The second diagram in Figure 3 is one output of that work. It is adapted from a paper by C. Stephen Carr, Stephen Crocker, and Vinton Cerf entitled "HOST-HOST Communication Protocol in the ARPA Network" published in 1970.[16] The paper proposed a new kind of protocol for ARPANET to enable hosts to better communicate with each other in the user subnet. Instead of communicating with different computers, the Host-to-Protocol specified how a host could implement a program that would act as a local interpreter. Carr, Crocker, and Cerf called this new component the "Network Control Program" (NCP).[17]

The NCP represents the first step in the process of separating networks from host computers. It divided the user subnet between host computers and processes running on them. Since many hosts ran time-sharing systems, the NCP needed to target messages for different users and programs running simultaneously. The NCP differentiated messages by including a "socket number" (later called a "port number") in its header. This number was made up of a host number, a user number, and "another eight-bit number" used to identify separate user processes.[18] NCPs read the socket number to know where to send the message locally. NCPs embedded this socket number and other control data in its message header. When a local IMP reassembled the message from its packets and sent it to the host, the NCP read this header to route the message to the right local socket. Through sockets, a user could establish "his own virtual net consisting of processes he had created":

> This virtual net may span an arbitrary number of HOSTs. It will thus be easy for a user to connect his processes in arbitrary ways, while still permitting him to connect his processes with those in other virtual nets.[19]

This quote foreshadows the proliferation of networks on the internet. Through sockets, daemons distinguished different networks on the shared infrastructure.

The second diagram reflects the growing importance of the end computers in the packet-switching systems. Much like Licklider's and Taylor's disinterest in switching computers, the diagram generalizes both the infrastructural connection and the host computer. Neither appears on the diagram. Instead, the diagram depicts processes representing the applications and networks running on the ARPANET. Two lines connect processes in the diagram. The top line refers to the communication subnet. Simultaneously, the link line below illustrates NCPs' work at the user subnet to connect processes to each other. Neither line depicts the computers, IMPs, and telephone lines that enable this communication. These parts of the ARPANET had faded into infrastructure. The omission of the IMP from the diagram had lasting implications for packet switching. The IMP was subsumed into the infrastructure as an assumed intermediary, while the NCP took on more prominence.

This emphasis on the ends endured in the first internet protocols.

By the early 1970s, researchers at IPTO turned from interconnecting time-sharing computers to interconnecting packet-switching infrastructures.[20] The NCP and its new role in creating virtual nets directly informed the development of the internet protocols. In 1974, Cerf and Robert Kahn published an article entitled "A Protocol for Packet Network Intercommunication." The protocol sought to develop standards and software to ease communication across separate packet-switching infrastructures.

The Transport Control Program was a key part of their protocol: it replaced the NCP and had greater responsibility over transmission conditions. It had to. Cerf and Kahn argued that this program was in the best position to understand and make decisions about transmission. Almost ten years later, the Transport Control Program evolved into the Transmission Control Protocol (TCP), part of the Internet Protocol Suite (TCP/IP). On January 1, 1983, also known as "Flag Day," it replaced the NCP as the ARPANET standard.

In many ways, TCP was a revolution, flipping the network design on its head. TCP did not just conceptually replace NCP; it displaced the IMP as the head of ARPANET. Interconnected infrastructures could know their own domain, but not necessarily the whole of the internet. Optimal communication required IMPs and other middleboxes to leave the important decisions to the ends. This arrangement was one of a few ways Cerf and Kahn avoided centralization. They rejected, for example, a suggestion by one of the IMP developers at BBN to build a centralized registry of port numbers. Instead, Cerf and Kahn argued, their solution preserved the premise that "interprocess communication should not require centralized control."[21] These principles were further formalized into what has become known as the End-to-End principle (E2E), discussed in the next chapter.[22] The internet became the outcome of interconnecting packet-switching infrastructures. This metainfrastructure, a network of packet-switching networks, involved another iteration of the internet's diagram and one last component.

Gateways and an Inter-network

In the same paper that introduced the Transmission Control Program, Cerf and Kahn introduced gateways. Figure 3 includes a third diagram adapted from their 1974 paper. This diagram again depicts the act of transmission, but here a message travels across multiple packet-switching infrastructures. As in the previous diagram, processes, referring to the specific applications running on a computer, are the least abstracted element. They also continue to occupy the important ends of the network. Processes connect to each other across two packet-switching infrastructures depicted as hexagons. As in prior diagrams, the infrastructure has been abstracted and processes assume their messages will be transmitted.

The diagram generalizes packet-switching infrastructure as another component just when ARPANET was becoming just one of many infrastructures of its kind. Many of these infrastructures came online after ARPANET. Donald Davies started working on one at the National Physical Laboratory in 1967. Known as the NPL Data Communication Network, it came online in 1970.[23] Other notable packet-switching infrastructures include the CYCLADES project, built in France starting in 1972 and led by a major figure in packet switching, Louis Pouzin.[24] The CYCLADES project, named after a group of islands in the Aegean Sea, aimed to connect the "isolated islands" of computer networks.[25] Bell Canada, one of the country's largest telecommunications companies, launched the first Canadian packet-switching service in 1976.[26] Bolt, Beranek and Newman launched a subsidiary in 1972 to build a commercial packet-switching service known as TELENET (whose relationship to ARPANET was not unlike that of SABRE's to SAGE). By 1973, Roberts had joined as president, and construction began on the commercial infrastructure in 1974.[27] Any of these projects could be represented by the same hexagon.

A new device known as a "gateway" acted as a border between these packet-switching infrastructures, routing packets between them. To enable them to do so, Cerf and Kahn refined an internet address system to allow gateways to locate specific TCP programs across packet-switching infrastructures. Whereas ARPANET needed only to locate a process on a host, this internet had to locate processes on hosts in separate infrastructures. Cerf and Kahn proposed addresses consisting of eight bits to identify the packet-switching infrastructure, followed by sixteen bits to identify a distinct TCP in that infrastructure. Gateways read this address to decide how to forward the message:

As each packet passes through a GATEWAY, the GATEWAY observes the destination network ID to determine how to route the packet. If the destination network is connected to the GATEWAY, the lower 16 bits of the TCP address are used to produce a local TCP address in the destination network. If the destination network is not connected to the GATEWAY, the upper 8 bits are used to select a subsequent GATEWAY.[28]

According to this description, gateways operated on two planes: internally forwarding messages to local TCPs and externally acting as a border between other infrastructures.

The "Fuzzball" was one of the first instances of a gateway and an example of how daemons in the internet developed to occupy these new positions in the diagram. David Mills, the first chair of the Internet Architecture Task Force, developed what became known as the "Fuzzball" to manage communications on the Distributed Communication Network based at the University of Maryland. Mills explained in a reflection on the Fuzzball's development that it had been in a "state of continuous, reckless evolution" to keep up with changing computer architectures, protocols, and innovations in computer science.[29] The Fuzzball was much like an IMP. It was a set of programs that ran on specialized computer hardware designed to facilitate packet-switching communication. The Fuzzball also implemented multiple versions of packet-switching protocols, including TCP/IP and other digital communication protocols. Since they implemented multiple protocols, Fuzzballs could function as gateways, translating between two versions of packet switching.[30]

The gateway, then, completes a brief description of the components of the internet's diagram. Starting at the edges of the infrastructure, the diagram includes processes or local programs. These processes connect through intermediary infrastructures filled with switches, hubs, routers, and other middleboxes. In turn, these intermediary infrastructures connect through gateways, a process that is now called "peering." Together, these three general categories function as an abstract machine creating new internet daemons. Yet, the diagram of the internet has undergone a few noteworthy modifications since the 1974 proposal by Cerf and Kahn.

THE INTERNET

Today's internet incorporates all these prior diagrams: it includes processes, intermediaries, and gateways. They can be seen to directly inspire the layered diagram commonly used to describe the internet, depicted in Figure 4. Layering is a computer engineering strategy to manage complex-

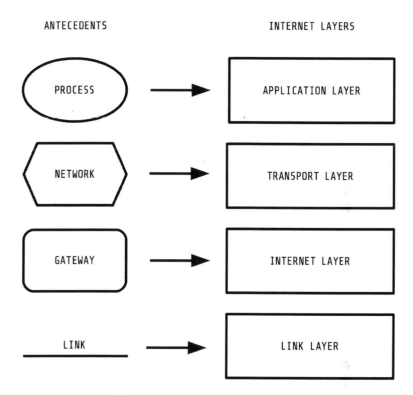

Figure 4. The origins of the Internet Protocol layer.

ity by separating activities into hierarchical layers. Each layer offers "services to higher layers, shielding those layers from the details of how the offered services are actually implemented."[31] ARPANET's communication and user subnets were nascent articulations of this layering approach, more as a way to aggregate functions than as a strict implication of layers. The internet's layers started as the ARPANET's subnets. NCP and TCP bifurcated the user subnet so the host acted as an intermediary for specific users or applications to connect on the ARPANET. Gateways subsequently positioned ARPANET as part of a global system of interconnected packet-switching infrastructures, gesturing toward an internet layer.

The internet's diagram has four layers according to version 4 of TCP/IP. From highest to lowest, they are: the application layer, the transport layer, the internet layer, and the link layer. The application layer contains processes or, in today's terms, applications running on home computers engaged in computer networking. It includes programs for email, the File Transfer Protocol (FTP), and many other "virtual nets" imagined by Cerf and Kahn. The next layer, transport, refers to the location of what became of the Transport Control Program. The transport layer now includes programs using TCP (now the Transmission Control Protocol) and the User Datagram Protocol (UDP). Transport-layer daemons assemble packets and reassemble messages, and they also handle addressing packets using the descendants of sockets or ports. TCP establishes connections between internet nodes, whereas UDP is used more for onetime, unique messages. The internet layer is the domain of intermediaries such as routers, switches, hubs, and gateways. It includes both daemons that forward packets within an infrastructure and daemons that interconnect infrastructures. Finally, the link layer consists of a mix of ARPANET's transmission media: its modems and leased telephone lines. Daemons on this layer handle the transmission of packets accordingly for each particular medium. Where IMPs dealt with modems and telephone lines, contemporary daemons work with Ethernet, copper, coaxial, and fiber lines, which all require custom-encoded protocols to route information.[32]

Another way to interpret the internet's diagram is the Internet Protocol (IP) addressing system, which is used to specify any location on the internet. Until IPv6 arrives, every location on the internet has a 32-bit address, usually divided into four groups of three-digit numbers using the Classless Inter-Domain Routing (CIDR) notation, such as 255.255.255.255.[33] IP addresses are the latest iteration of Cerf and Kahn's network number and TCP identifier discussed in the prior section. The first bits refer to the network number, and the latter bits refer to the local computer. Internet addressing relies on the Internet Assigned Numbers Authority (IANA), which maintains and assigns blocks of IP addresses. IANA allocates these blocks to specific regions, as well as directly to the separately managed parts of the internet known as autonomous systems. As of spring 2018, there were over 60,000 autonomous systems on the internet.[34] IANA distinguishes these different infrastructures through Autonomous Systems Numbers (ASN). Daemons rely on ASNs and IP addresses to ensure that data reaches its destination. A packet might first be sent to the ASN associated with its address, then to the part assigned to its network number, and then finally to its local computer.

Layers and the IP address both express a diagram constructing the internet. This abstraction also informs the development of daemons as components of the diagram. Each layer of the internet fills with daemons, a task now largely carried out by the internet infrastructure industry. The origin of one of the biggest firms, Cisco Systems, is easy to follow from this history. The aforementioned Fuzzball functioned as a gateway because it implemented multiple protocols; it was one outcome of research into multiprotocol routers. Researchers at Stanford University, home of the Stanford Research Institute and a node in the ARPANET, developed their own multiprotocol router to connect various departments to each other. This router became known as the "Stanford Blue Box." By 1982, it could interconnect ARPANET with Xerox Alto computers using Xerox Network Services, as well as other protocols like CHAOSnet.[35] While accounts differ on how exactly the Blue Box escaped the labs of Stanford, it became the first product sold by Cisco Systems, founded in 1984.[36] Today, Cisco Systems is the largest player in the $41-billion networking-infrastructure industry.[37]

The internet, by its very design, supports different kinds of networks. Interconnecting brought together different ideas of computer-mediated communication and their supporting infrastructures. To understand the newfound importance of the internet, it is worth addressing the diversity of networks that developed contemporaneously with the internet beyond time-sharing and real-time. These networks help illuminate the cultural dimension of computer networks prior to the internet, since they acted as infrastructures that synchronized humans and machines around common times, as well as around common visions of a computer network. The internet later remediated these network assemblages and their network cultures.[38]

A BRIEF HISTORY OF NETWORKS

As Licklider and Taylor distinguished OLIVERs from IMPs, they made an interesting comment about communication models. The human mind, according to them, is one communication model, but not the only one. In fact, the mind has some shortcomings. Licklider and Taylor listed a few, including that it has "access only to the information stored in one man's head" and that it could "be observed and manipulated only by one person."[39] Human communication imperfectly shared models between people. A computer, they suggested, might be a better way to share models, in part because it was "a dynamic medium in which premises will flow into consequences."[40] Their article then discusses how a computer might change the nature of work. For example, "at a project meeting held through a computer, you can thumb through the speaker's primary data without interrupting him to substantiate or explain."[41] They go on to speculate that computer communication might enable new forms of interaction beyond the boardroom within "on-line interactive communities" formed on a basis "not of common location, but of common interest."[42] They imagined online communities focused on "investment guidance, tax counseling, selective dissemination of information in your field of specialization, announcement of cultural, sport, and entertainment events that fit your interests, etc."[43] Certainly, this is a telling list of the concerns of two members of the academic elite, but it's also an early attempt to imagine a computer network.

Licklider and Taylor's discussion of online interactive communities and models offers a chance to revisit the idea of computer networks. As discussed in chapter 1, networks are assemblages of humans and machines sharing a common temporality. This temporality includes pasts, presents, and futures. Licklider and Taylor gesture to all three. Online communities would include historical records like computers, afford interactive chats, and allow for computer modeling to predict behavior. These specific applications, however, miss the more evocative aspects of the discussion of models by Licklider and Taylor. Their notion of the shared understandings of communication resembles the discussion of social imaginaries in the information society by the influential political economist of new media Robin Mansell. Where Mansell uses social imaginaries to describe broader visions of the internet as an information commons or as an engine of economic growth, networks might also be seen to include imaginaries shared by their participants. These imaginaries inform networks, especially their senses of time and space.[44]

The next section discusses a few notable examples of this technocultural side of networking. When developed, many of these networks were both new forms of synchronization and novel developments in computer hardware. As the internet became the ubiquitous infrastructure for digital communication, these networks came to run on the common infrastructure. A brief overview of some of these networks elaborates daemons' challenge today. The internet's infrastructure technically converged these networks without dramatically rearticulating their technocultural imaginaries. Daemons then face the difficult tasks of accommodating these different networks while finding an optimal way to manage their infrastructures.

Digest Networks

Some of the first networks would be online discussions oriented around interest, just as suggested by Licklider and Taylor. Two important forums arose in the computer science departments of major research universities: USENET in 1979 and BITNET in 1981. USENET grew out of a collaboration between Duke University and the University of North Carolina and worked by mirroring data between computers. It enabled their users to interact in threaded discussions organized by common topics. By keeping these computers in sync, USENET simulated a shared public, even though computers technically connected only in short updates. Hosts existed in the United States, Canada, and Australia. Early USENET systems also connected with other networks through gateways administered in St. Louis, Missouri.[45] Gradually, USENET offered mail services as well as rich discussion of common interests in newsgroups. Another major network, BITNET ("Because It's Time NETwork"), was developed by researchers at City University of New York and Yale University in 1981. Like USENET, BITNET offered a discussion forum for programmers in the computation departments. In 1984, the BITNET system had 1,306 hosts across the globe, including nodes in Mexico and Canada (where it was called NetNorth).[46] Eventually, when both networks merged with the internet, BITNET became the first email discussion groups and USENET became newsgroups. Both are still common computer networks today.[47] The World Wide Web owes much to this threaded discussion and digest format. Debates about free speech and online participation that animated USENET reverberate in concerns about platform governance today.[48]

Bulletin Board Systems and Amateur Computer Networking

Bulletin Board Systems (BBS) hacked together personal computers and telephone lines to form what computer historian Kevin Driscoll calls the ancestor of social media. The "great snow of Chicago" on January 16, 1978, gave Ward Christensen and Randy Seuss enough time to create the first computer Bulletin Board System. One at a time, users dialed into a modem hacked to boot into a custom program that functioned like a home screen. There, users could select articles to read or post a message for other users.[49] With the arrival of cheap personal modems in 1981,[50] BBSs became an accessible form of computer networking. These ad hoc networks were a way for citizens to start their own local discussion boards and exchanges. By the 1990s, some 60,000 BBSs operated in the United States, and thousands more likely existed internationally.[51]

Culturally, BBSs helped popularize computer communication as a form of virtual community. The Whole Earth 'Lectronic Link (WELL) was perhaps the most famous BBS, and it exemplified a particular strain of optimism that animated computer networks. WELL functioned as a simple online-chat BBS in the San Francisco Bay Area beginning in 1985. Monies from the defunct *Whole Earth Catalog* started WELL. More than just a BBS, WELL served as the vehicle for the movement of the countercultural ethos of Stewart Brand's *Whole Earth Catalog* into the digital age. The network charged a modest fee in comparison to commercial services like CompuServe. Although the site had only a few thousand users, WELL eased the transition from counterculture to cyberculture, according to historian Fred Turner. Countercultural groups like the "new communalists" embraced computers as a means of self-actualization and independence. These ideas, inspired by experiences on WELL, found their way into the trend-setting magazine of early internet culture, *Wired*.[52]

Many of the key expressions of the social value of computer networks came from WELL. WELL and computer networks in general came to be seen by members of the board as a transformational social force. Indeed, the founders of the leading internet rights organization, the Electronic Frontier Foundation (EFF), met on WELL. Mitch Kapor, one of those founders, states: "When what you're moving is information, instead of physical substances, then you can play by a different set of rules. We're evolving those rules now! Hopefully you can have a much more decentralized system, and one in which there's more competition in the marketplace."[53] Parts of WELL exemplified a new mixture of free-market rhetoric and decentralized computing, an approach known as the "Californian ideology."[54] WELL also inspired Howard Rheingold to coin the term "virtual community," which he defines as "social aggregations that emerge from the Net when enough people carry on those public discussions long enough, with sufficient human feeling, to form webs of personal relationships in cyberspace."[55] The term helped frame the internet to the public as a friendly place for people to connect.[56]

BBS culture also inspired antecedents of Peer-to-Peer (P2P) file-sharing and computer pirate cultures.[57] The counterculture of Stewart Brand, the Merry Pranksters, and the Yippies inspired generations of phone and computer hackers who viewed exploiting the phone system as a form of political dissent.[58] These groups were important pioneers in the development of early computing and computer networks. Many of the early phone hackers, or "phreakers," started BBSs to share their exploits and techniques. These groups often freely traded stolen data, and thus attracted the name "pirates": a term that the music industry once applied to people who made tape duplications of music.[59] "What does an underground board look like?" asked Bruce Sterling in a profile of early pirate boards. He explained:

> It isn't necessarily the conversation—hackers often talk about common board topics, such as hardware, software, sex, science fiction, current events, politics, movies, personal gossip. Underground boards can best be distinguished by their files, or "philes," pre-composed texts which teach the techniques and ethos of the underground.[60]

Hackers and pirates traded "warez" on these BBSs or bragged about their exploits in text files or digital copies of the hacker publication *Phrack*. Motivating these activities was a belief that digital systems could copy information indefinitely. Despite their sense of freedom, these BBSs were marked by secrecy and elitism, as only the best pirates could operate in the top networks. Prestige and status had more currency than the value of peers sharing information freely, although iterations of the piracy movement did become more accessible.[61] Today, these pirate networks endure as P2P file-sharing, a popularization of this computer underground.

International and Activist Networks

FIDONET was a worldwide network of BBSs. In 1983, an unemployed computer programmer named Tom Jennings began designing a cheap communication system using computers and telephone lines. Eventually, Jennings's system evolved into the FIDO BBS, named after the mongrel of a machine hosting the server. Unlike home BBSs, FIDO hosts were designed to share data, and Jennings released its code as free software. Anyone could use the code to create a FIDO BBS, provided it was not for commercial use. The decision to release the code mirrored Jennings's anarchist politics. By 1990, FIDONET connected ten thousand local nodes in thirty countries. The cheap network attracted activists and development workers in Latin America, Africa, and Russia. Though community networks like FIDONET eventually assimilated with the internet, the spirit of their organizations and cultures endured in creating community-based internet service providers (ISPs) or new online solidarity networks.[62]

These different networks (in both the technical and cultural sense) have distinct temporalities that continue on the internet today. The rhythms of USENET mailing lists continue in internet newsgroups, as well as in the millions of forums for public discussion online, such as Reddit. Hackers still communicate using Internet Relay Chat (IRC) in the many chat rooms across the internet. They also reside on darknets like "The Onion Router" (TOR), putting up with slow loading web pages for the sake of anonymity.[63] They trade files on P2P networks. These large file-sharing networks are a popular form of the old pirate boards. The virtual communities of WELL endure today in social media. Users log on through the web or mobile apps to chat, share, and like others' posts.

While this short history cannot account for all the computers networks that found their way online, it does outline the problem for daemons slotted into different parts of the internet. They no longer faced the binary challenge of accommodating real-time and time-sharing networks, because now daemons had to accommodate many networks. Conflict loomed. That fact became quickly apparent with the privatization and commercialization of the ARPANET's successor, the National Science Foundation Network (NSFNET), starting in 1991.

CONVERGENCE

While the internet had developed many infrastructures, they eventually collapsed into one using the TCP/IP, the Internet Protocol Suite.[64] The reasons that TCP/IP succeeded over other internetworking protocols are still debated. The factors are neither casual nor simple, but it is helpful to consider the political and economic situation. ARPANET benefited from the tremendous funding of military research during the Cold War.[65] John Day explained the most important factor in a curt but effective summary: "The Internet was a [Department of Defense] project and TCP was paid for by the DoD. This reflects nothing more than the usual realities of inter-agency rivalries in large bureaucracies and that the majority of reviewers were DARPA [or ARPA] contractors."[66] The political context also helps situate the conditions of interconnection.

In 1991, the U.S. Congress's High Performance Computing Act, often called the "Gore Bill" (after its author, then-Senator Al Gore Jr.), mandated that different institutions and networks be combined into one infrastructure. Where his father imagined a national highway system, Al Gore Jr. proposed an information superhighway. The ARPANET, or what was then known as the NSFNET, was a leading contender to be the backbone for this unified infrastructure, but its Acceptable Usage Policy presented a problem. The policy banned any commercial applications, even though the National Science Foundation was already outsourcing its network management to commercial providers.[67] After the Gore Bill passed, the NSF began getting pressure from new customers to offer a unified digital communication infrastructure and to liberalize its Acceptable Usage Policy to allow commercial traffic. The NSF gradually privatized its infrastructure. By 1997, five private infrastructure providers were responsible for running the internet's infrastructure in the United States.[68] The cost of realizing the dream of the Gore Bill was the consolidation of network diversity into a single network largely under the ownership of only a few parties.

CONCLUSION

The internet formed out of the merger of these past networks and infrastructures, but the lack of a definition of an optimal network in its technical design exacerbated tensions between the different remediated networks. These competing networks have an effect like the many users of WELL, leading to Turner's "heterarchy": "multiple, and at times competing value systems, principles of organization, and mechanisms for performance appraisal."[69] Heterarchy complicates optimization, creating even competing different value systems to optimize for. (Benjamin Peters, in a very different cultural and political context, found that the heterarchy of the Soviet state prevented the formation of its own national computer infrastructure.)[70] This heterarchy endures on the contemporary internet, though it is complicated by the proliferation of networks. Their competing values and priorities are latent in "net neutrality" debates. Networks have competing values for how the internet should be managed. Two of these approaches are discussed in the next chapter.

The lack of a clear way to define the optimal—or even an acknowledgment of the problem—haunts internet daemons. In every clock cycle and switch, daemons have to find a metastability between all these networks. Piracy, security, over-the-top broadcasting, and P2P telephony all have become flashpoints where tensions between the various networks converge on the internet. The internet infrastructure struggles to support all these temporalities. Media conglomerates in both broadcasting and telecommunications have been particularly at odds internally over how to manage these issues. Should their approach to the internet fall within a temporal economy of broadcasting or telecommunications? Should networks police their traffic? The situation has only worsened as ISPs have faced a bandwidth crunch for on-demand movies, streaming video, multiplayer games, and music stores, not to mention the explosion in illegal file sharing. The crunch, in short, requires better management of a scarce resource.

The inception of the internet has led to many conflicts over its optimization, but none perhaps as fierce and as decisive as the one over the emergence of P2P file sharing, a new form of piracy. The successful introduction of file sharing offered a mode of transmission that disrupted the conventional broadcasting temporal economy. At first, the associated media industries tried to sue P2P out of existence, but when that failed, they moved increasingly to flow control to contain threats. Technology, instead of law, could solve the problem of file sharing, an example of a *technological fix* in which people attempt to solve social problems through technology.[71] These fixes and their daemons will feature in the debates explored in the following chapters.

4 PANDAEMONIUM

The Internet as Daemons

THE CISCO SERVICE CONTROL ENGINE (SCE) 8000 debuted in 2008. Designed as carrier-grade equipment, the forty-two kilogram metal box requires only five rack units within the tall metal cages of an internet service provider's (ISP) infrastructure. When running, it can manage a million concurrent internet users. The processing power of the SCE 8000 enables "stateful awareness" of packet flows, which means it is able to look into the contents of a sequence of packets and contextualize this data within the overall state of the infrastructure. The SCE's built-in packet inspection detects six hundred known protocols and has adaptive recognition for new Peer-to-Peer (P2P) networks. With stateful awareness, the SCE 8000 is better able to manage bandwidth allocation and assign more or less bandwidth to different networks. But by the time you read this, the SCE 8000 will have reached the end of life,[1] replaced by an even more powerful piece of equipment.

Internet daemons have come a long way. Loosed from the military-industrial complex, daemons are now the products of hackers, free software developers, telecommunication companies, and the $41 billion networking infrastructure industry. This chapter focuses on the daemons produced by this industry. Two of the biggest players in the market are Cisco Systems, with 56 percent market share, and its nearest competitor, Juniper Networks, with 6 to 8 percent market share.[2] Many daemons discussed below come from the subsidiary Deep Packet Inspection (DPI) industry, which has an estimated value of $741.7 million. Two of that industry's biggest vendors appear in this chapter: Procera Networks and Sandvine.[3] Other daemons come from an emerging change in infrastructure design known as software-defined networking, which is estimated to be a $326.5 million market that will grow to $4.9 billion by 2020.[4]

Where this book began with a discussion of Oliver Selfridge's Pandemonium, this chapter describes the internet as its own kind of *Pandaemonium*. In doing so, I build on the prior analysis of the internet's diagram to focus on the daemons that have occupied its infrastructure. Pandaemonium encapsulates how daemons enact flow control, working in collaboration across the infrastructure to create, ideally, smooth conditions for networking. To understand this work of daemons, I have divided the chapter into two parts. The chapter begins with a daemonology of the internet moving from packet inspection to queuing, to routing, to policy management. I begin with a discussion of the daemons on the Interface Message Processor (IMP) as a way to introduce these different functions. The second part examines the internet's architecture to show the collaboration and conflict between demons.

This second half of the chapter proceeds by way of a discussion of some present internet technology that practices the second of two competing kinds of optimizations. The first is type "nonsychronous," a term I borrow from Donald Davies. A nonsynchronous optimization leaves networks unorganized; it draws on the well-known End-to-End principle (E2E) that stipulates daemons at the edges of the infrastructure be responsible for the key decisions during transmission. In a bit of a slight, the principle holds that the core daemons should be dumb. The diagram for a nonsynchronous optimization ignores the center, emphasizing the edge daemons who best know the conditions of networking.

It is hard to blame core daemons for conspiring against this principle, but the consequences led to the "net neutrality" debate. As mentioned in the introduction for instance, unruly P2P daemons such as those in the eMule program prompted internet service providers (ISPs) such as Comcast to install new networking computers known as "middleboxes" into their infrastructure. In doing so, Comcast exemplifies a new trend in networking away from nonsynchronous optimization and toward the second kind of optimization, what I call a "polychronous" internet. This optimization stratifies networks into classes and tiers, allocating bandwidth accordingly. In this new regime, internet daemons in the middle of the infrastructure grow more powerful and influential. Through technical filings submitted by Comcast to the Federal Communications Commission (FCC), I analyze the operations of flow control during the ISP's eMule throttling discussed in the introduction.

Through these two tours of Pandaemonium—the catalogue of daemonic functions and the history of conflicts between users in favor of nonsynchronous optimization and ISPs in favor of polychronous—the chapter analyzes the distributive agency of daemons.

A DAEMONOLOGY OF THE INTERNET

IMPs are a good place to begin the study of internet daemons because the IMPs' core program might be seen as the first of their kind. After Bolt, Beranek and Newman Inc. (BBN) submitted the first IMP, their research team published a paper in 1970 in the *Proceedings of the American Federation of Information Processing Societies* describing its design and operation.[5] They explained:

> The principal function of the operational program is the processing of packets. This processing includes segmentation of Host messages into packets for routing and transmission, building of headers, receiving, routing and transmitting of store and forward packets, retransmitting of unacknowledged packets, reassembling received packets into messages for transmission to the Host, and generating of [Request for Next Message] and acknowledgements. The program also monitors network status, gathers statistics, and performs on-line testing.[6]

From this rather technical description, an IMP:

1. inspected and interpreted packets;
2. stored packets in buffers and managed queues;
3. learned and selected routes; and
4. collected statistics and coordinated with each other to keep the system running.

New daemons handled tasks similar to those of the IMP. Unto the IMP, other internet daemons were born. Their packet inspection begat firewalls and DPI daemons. Their routing algorithms begat internal and external routing daemons. Their buffers begat queuing daemons. And statistics routines begat policy management daemons. Packet inspection, queuing, routing, and policy daemons all modulate flow control. Each one influences the overall conditions of transmission, and thus flow control. Daemons distinguish networks through packet inspection. Conditions of transmission vary depending on routing and queuing. Meanwhile, the interactions between all of these daemons increasingly depend on policy daemons. The internet functions through the delicate orchestration of these daemons.

Packet Inspection

Packet inspection is a daemon's gaze. Daemons read packets to make decisions about transmission. A packet is constructed according to the layering diagram described in chapter 3. A packet is a bit stream that begins with the lower link layer. After the link layer, the packet contains internet layer metadata like source and destination address. Next, the packet encodes the transport layer that includes port numbers and sometimes actual messages. Finally, deep in the packet stream is the application layer that contains both the message and some metadata to help the local application interpret it.

Daemons look at the part of the packet corresponding to their function from the transport layer to the link layer. Consider the daemonic gazes at work when browsing the web. Clicking a link starts a daemonic frenzy. Upper-layer daemons who are part of web browsers send requests in the HyperText Transfer Protocol (HTTP) using the application layer. The server's daemons interpret these requests and send back HTTP responses. Simultaneously, lower-layer daemons on the home computer and the web server encapsulate HTTP data using the transport and internet layers. Finally, daemons at the link layer handle sending the packets, depending on whether the home computer connects to the internet through an Ethernet cable or wirelessly.

Protocols help specify the format of data at each layer of the packet. To be exact, protocols determine the meaning of each bit. A packet is just a binary stream: ones and zeros. These bits do not have any meaning in and of themselves. Rather, daemons are programmed to implement protocols so that they know the meaning of each bit. Protocols, to recall Thomas Marill's and Lawrence Robert's discussion from chapter 2, have to be agreed upon by all parties. Achieving consensus has meant that protocols, especially critical ones like the internet protocol, are slow to change. All daemons must be reprogrammed to interpret the new protocol. Application-layer protocols notably change more quickly, as daemons at the ends are able to understand new data formats.

Protocols, then, have an important influence on the conduct of daemons, and their distributed nature means that they have widespread implications. Protocols are "political," as noted by internet governance expert Laura DeNardis:

> They control the global flow of information and make decisions that influence access to knowledge, civil liberties online, innovation policy, national

economic competitiveness, national security and which technology companies will succeed.[7]

These social topics do not appear much in the early ARPANET technical manuals (though subsequent Requests for Comments [RFCs] actively discussed them),[8] but early design decisions had long-standing consequences. For example, even though BBN developed encryption for the IMP as part of its work with the U.S. intelligence community, the ARPANET protocols did not include it. DeNardis argues that exposure is now a key characteristic of internet protocols. The Edward Snowden leaks revealed the ramifications of unencrypted packets, which eased the global intelligence community's surveillance of the internet. Another unintended consequence of the early design is the exhaustion of internet addresses (preventing new devices from joining the infrastructure) that resulted from version 4 of the Internet Protocol Suite (TCP/IP) assigning only thirty-two bits for signal location, thereby creating a theoretical maximum of 4,294,967,296 locations.[9] The internet is currently in transition to a new version of the protocol (version 6) that will simplify the header content and provision longer, 128-bit addresses. These protocol debates cannot be completely summarized here (and, indeed, they offer a different pathway into internet studies than this book), but they have important ramifications for a daemon's gaze.

Returning to packet inspection, the general trend is that intermediary daemons inspect more of the packet. New forms of inspection allow these daemons to make more insightful decisions. The development of these new daemonic gazes has been driven by demand for better network security, as well as bandwidth management, government surveillance, content regulation, and copyright enforcement.[10] These new gazes include:

1. inspecting packet headers for security threats;
2. tracking the overall state of networks to remember past activity and anticipate routine behaviors;
3. inspecting deep into the packet to read the application layer;
4. and situating the packet in a flow of network activity.

Modern packet inspection uses all these gazes at once, but it is useful to address them in order.

Firewalls directly contributed to the development of the first two gazes. These middleboxes required daemons capable of accessing a packet's probable threat. The first firewall daemons were called "stateful" because they interpreted packets depending on the state of their infrastructure. As one of the first papers about these dynamic packet filters explained, a firewall could inspect "all outgoing TCP [Transmission Control Protocol] and UDP [User Datagram Protocol] packets and only all[ow] incoming packets to the same port."[11] A firewall's daemon remembers whether an internal computer sent a message (an outgoing TCP or UDP packet) and permits only incoming traffic that has been requested locally. Conversely, a daemon could detect the arrival of an unsolicited packet, since it would know that no local host had initiated contact.

A whole industry now tracks global threats against the internet. Arbor Networks, a network security and monitoring firm, runs the Active Threat Level Analysis System (ATLAS) initiative. ATLAS provides real-time threat monitoring by aggregating data generated from more than 330 installations of its equipment by ISPs. The ATLAS website, when accessible, included a small map of the world. Across the globe, dots flickered to indicate detected threats. Below the map, the site listed top attacks, their targets, and sources. ATLAS still functions as a tool to profile risky networks, ports, and domains, though it has become a subscriber service.

ATLAS and programs like it represent a broader imbrication of technology and security oriented around preemption.[12] ATLAS's insights help daemons decide how to treat packets. Daemons download new profiles that update their gazes. At the same time, ATLAS deterritorializes local daemons' gazes. Strange activity on one infrastructure becomes part of a global data set. This cloud of known risk reterritorializes in a loop as the daemons constantly update their profiles to nullify threats before their wider actualization. ATLAS also exemplifies a push to extend the daemon's gaze into the past, in this case with a global log of internet activity.

Most daemons keep detailed activity logs that are used to diagnose threats and to conduct security audits and forensics after attacks. Demand for better data about the past has led to the development of even more sophisticated memory systems. Before going bankrupt in 2015, ISC8 Inc. sold the Cyber NetFalcon appliance, which recorded all the packets that passed through it.[13] The Cyber NetFalcon not only recorded all communications, but its daemons interpreted the entire packet across all layers. Security analysts used the NetFalcon to go back in time by reading these records. Daemons helped too. The appliance's daemons interpreted packets to correlate activity and store records in structured data for easier analysis in the future.

ISC8 was part of an industry developing technologies for DPI,[14] which refers to when daemons, particularly those on middleboxes, read and analyze all layers of the packet, including the application layer.[15] Some of its biggest vendors include Allot Communications, Blue Coat Systems, and Sandvine.[16] In effect, DPI daemons turn packets into a source of big data, or what Jose van Dijck calls "datafication."[17] Using all the data from the packet, DPI daemons make probabilistic guesses about the nature of the packet and look for patterns to detect P2P applications or web traffic. The gaze is probabilistic, since it usually includes some margin of error, according to a survey of the industry, and "both false positives and false negatives are unavoidable."[18] Some appliances inspect the commands embedded in application data to classify the packet's intent or threat level. For example, the Cisco 4700 Series Application Control Engine (ACE) reads HTTP packets to detect key words in web pages and File Transfer Protocol (FTP) packets to identify commands. The ACE could block, for example, packets requesting *.MP3 files to discourage piracy.[19]

DPI vendors describe their products as a solution to the shifting landscape of internet security, specifically the declining value of port numbers as an accurate way to classify traffic. As Sandvine, a leading manufacturer of DPI equipment, wrote:

> DPI is necessary for the identification of traffic today because the historically-used "honour-based" port system of application classification no longer works. Essentially, some application developers have either intentionally or unintentionally designed their applications to obfuscate the identity of the application. Today, DPI technology represents the only effective way to accurately identify different types of applications.[20]

DPI responds to intentional obfuscation or port-spoofing, in which a network self-identifies on unconventional or incorrect ports. Some P2P file sharing networks, in an effort to avoid detection, send packets on HTTP ports rather than their standard ports (or through virtual private networks [VPNs]), as will be discussed in chapter 6. Even when a network mislabels its port, DPI allows a daemon to evaluate the contents of the packet and match it to the correct profile.

Daemons have unintentionally obfuscated networks by using HTTP as a kind of universal transport port.[21] Netflix, Google, and Facebook build their applications to use HTTP ports. For example, Netflix, along with Apple and Microsoft, participate in the Moving Picture Experts Group Committee for Dynamic Adaptive Streaming over HTTP (DASH).[22] DASH delivers video streams over HTTP, which simplifies over-the-top services but confuses older daemons looking to identify networks by port number. Since DPI daemons can read into the application layer, they can distinguish streams in HTTP traffic. Procera Networks, now merged with Sandvine, attracted Netflix's ire when it inspected data from its ISP clients to detect if Netflix subscribers had started to watch the new season of the show *House of Cards*. Using DPI, Procera Networks created a list of the most popular episodes on the streaming service.[23] In reaction, Netflix changed its packets to make it harder for DPI to detect viewing habits.[24]

How DPI works is a dark art usually enshrouded in proprietary code. However, one DPI firm, iPoque, shed some light on the practice by releasing an open-source version of its packet inspection code.[25] OpenDPI version 1.3 classifies 118 different applications, depending on many functions in the source code specific to each application. The code contains 100 separate files dedicated to different applications, including bittorrent.c to classify BitTorrent networks and eDonkey.c to classify eDonkey or eMule networks. The bittorent.c file includes numerous functions that search for particular patterns in the packet that indicate that it is part of a BitTorrent network. A simple function (copied below) compares data in the application layer (the packet→payload variable in the code) to the string "BitTorrent protocol."

```
if (packet->payload_packet_len > 20) {
    /* test for match 0x13+"BitTorrent protocol" */
    if (packet->payload[0] == 0x13) {
        if (memcmp(&packet->payload[1], "BitTorrent protocol", 19) == 0) {
            IPQ_LOG_BITTORRENT(
            IPOQUE_PROTOCOL_BITTORRENT,
            ipoque_struct,
            IPQ_LOG_TRACE,
            "BT: plain BitTorrent protocol detected");
            ipoque_add_connection_as_bittorrent(
            ipoque_struct,
            IPOQUE_PROTOCOL_SAFE_DETECTION,
```

```
IPOQUE_PROTOCOL_PLAIN_DETECTION,
IPOQUE_REAL_PROTOCOL);
    return 1;
}
  }
}
```

If OpenDPI matches a packet, it triggers an event that logs "BT: plain BitTorrent protocol detected." Another function detects packets' uploading data to a BitTorrent network (also called "seeding") by matching the packet payload to a known identifier, in this case, "GET /webseed?info _hash=." OpenDPI also detects specific BitTorrent clients like Azureus and BitComet. The source code includes a simple demonstration that accepts a series of packets (technically a packet dump) as an input and outputs a table listing detected networks.

The use of encrypted services like the VPNs discussed in chapter 6 prompted daemons to find other ways to profile packets. Daemons cannot read the contents of a packet when it is encrypted, so daemons have learned to inspect the sequences of packets, called "flows," instead. These techniques, also called "deep flow inspection," entail tracking the tempo of packets, looking for bursts and other signatures of communication that might indicate a probable network.[26] For example, a Skype conversation sends packets at a rate different from that at which a web browser does, and thus can be easily detected.[27]

Deep flow inspection, however, remains a rule-based system of classification that requires humans to analyze and develop profiles. In coming years, profiling will be automated through machine learning and deep learning. Cybersecurity vendors have already begun to deploy machine learning and artificial intelligence in threat detection. One study found that, through machine learning, daemons could detect BitTorrent networks with 95.3 percent accuracy after observing traffic for about one minute (or two hundred packets).[28]

Companies such as Vectra Networks advertise that they detect threats "using a patent-pending combination of data science, machine learning and behavioral analysis" in real time.[29] Behavioral analysis synthesizes the different forms of packet inspection used by contemporary daemons. The sum of our online communications, encoded as packets, becomes training data for the classifiers with black-boxed algorithms. Daemons once used rules to classify networks by application; now machine learning enables daemons to detect kinds of behaviors that present threats to cybersecurity and to adapt to changing code deployed by new applications. The daemonic gaze will only widen as the computational capacity of the infrastructure increases. Where IMPs tracked fifty-kilobit telephone lines,[30] Saisei Networks today advertises its FlowCommand technology as capable of "monitoring [five] million concurrent flows on a [ten gigabit] link [twenty] times per second, and evaluating and/or taking action on those flows across policies based on more than [thirty] metrics."[31] Future daemons will likely use multiple classifiers at once, being able to detect not just the network type but also its behavior and vector.

What can a daemon do with its improved gaze? It can modulate the conditions of transmission. These modulations happen in what Florian Sprenger calls the "micro-decisions" of the internet. "Micro-decisions" refers to the microseconds of computational cycles allocated for a daemon to modulate transmission conditions.[32] Packet inspection allows flow control to be more targeted, a process Christian Sandvig calls "redlining" in his groundbreaking discussion of the link between packet inspection and net neutrality.[33] Daemons influence the conditions of transmission by modulating "jitter" (variation in packet arrival times), reliability (the level of error in transmission), delay or latency (the time it takes to receive a response to a request), and bandwidth (the rate the ones and zeros or bits of an application pass over a network, usually measured per second, as in ten megabits per second).[34] Daemons intentionally and unintentionally influence these conditions through queuing and routing.[35]

Before moving to a discussion of routing then queuing, the privacy implications of packet inspection must be noted. The ability of ISPs to learn about their subscribers from packet inspection has prompted investigations by regulators into actual and potential privacy harms.[36] These investigations came about in response to companies and ISPs that used DPI to link packets with advertising profiles, as well as to inject data into packets to ease tracking and corporate communications. Phorm, a defunct advertising company, sought to develop DPI equipment designed to connect internet activity to profiles. This prompted privacy investigations by the United Kingdom and the European Union.[37] Packet inspection, more problematically, can lead to packet *injection* where a third party modifies packets on the fly. Canadian ISP Rogers Internet relied on technology from PerfTech to inject messages as a notice to its users. Before Rogers Internet discontinued the program, packet injection would modify web pages to warn users they were reaching their bandwidth cap.[38] Verizon Internet injected an additional identifier often called a "super-cookie" into HTTP packet headers transmitted on their mobile infrastructures. Web advertisers could pay Verizon for access to demographic and geographic information using this identifier to better target advertisements.[39] These issues remain an area of ongoing concern with DPI and other improvements of packet inspection that potentially violate long-standing norms of common carriage.

Routing

"Routing" refers to how daemons decide where to send packets. To make such decisions, daemons require the ability to map available routes and algorithms to select the best route. Where IMPs simply had to know the statuses of their peers before forwarding a packet, now daemons have to understand their location in the larger internet infrastructure and then decide the best route to send their packets. Daemons, however, do not have to map the internet; they just have to learn their domain. "A routing domain," according to an RFC on gateways, "is a collection of routers which coordinate their routing knowledge."[40] Domains gather daemons, in other words, to coordinate how and where to send packets, as well as to share information. Most often, a domain is a single infrastructure or part of an infrastructure, and it has a few daemons that act as routers for it. These daemons constantly collaborate to map possible routes both within their own domain and across domains. Since daemons often know multiple routes, algorithms help them pick one for each packet, though how they make that decision varies by algorithm.

How daemons coordinate routing depends largely on different protocols. These protocols have important implications for how daemons transmit packets. The first IMPs used what became known as a "distance-vector" routing protocol. An IMP chose where to send a packet depending on a routing table kept in its memory. The table included an estimate of the minimum delay to every destination on the ARPANET. Then daemons factored in "queue lengths and the recent performance of the connecting communication circuit" when calculating the delay.[41] When a packet or message arrived, the daemon consulted its routing table to find a route to the packet's destination. It used the Bellman–Ford or Ford–Fulkerson algorithms (developed between 1957 and 1962) to calculate the shortest path before the IMP-to-modem routine sent the packet down the best line.[42] Every half second, IMPs exchanged updated delay estimates to adjacent IMPs. "Each IMP then construct[ed] its own routing table by combining its neighbors' estimates with its own estimates of the delay to that neighbor."[43] Every calculation had a recursiveness—interpreting adjacent routing tables then informing adjacent calculations a half second later. The whole system was distributed, because every routing table was the product of interrelated calculations made on IMPs across the ARPANET.

Even functional routing protocols introduce delay and congestion, depending on how they coordinate daemons. Distance-vector routing, as a distributed system, cascaded any failure. As John McQuillan, an engineer at BBN responsible for the developing of routing, recounted:

> In 1971, the IMP at Harvard had a memory error that caused its routing updates to be all zeros. That led all other nodes in the net to conclude that the Harvard IMP was the best route to everywhere, and to send their traffic there. Naturally, the network collapsed.[44]

This malfunction demonstrates one reason that ARPANET sought to replace distance-vector routing: it "reacted quickly to good news but slowly to bad news."[45] The Harvard IMP's good news happened to be wrong, causing faulty distributed calculations. Conversely, distance-vector routing could cause network delay and malfunctions because, "if delay increased, the nodes did not use the new information while they still [had] adjacent nodes with old, lower values."[46] In other words, IMPs were programmed to be optimistic, to hold on to good news even after the arrival of news of delay and trouble. As a result, IMPs introduced congestion by sending packets to the wrong nodes.

Distance-vector routing did not scale well either when routing across complex, heterogeneous infrastructures. The protocol's replacement, "link-state" routing, arrived in 1978. Link-state routing exemplified a shift from using a universal, homogeneous algorithm (like distance-vector) to more hierarchical, localized algorithms as ARPANET and its successors began to interconnect separate infrastructures. Link-state routing involved minor though significant changes to measurements of delay, signaling, and route calculation, as well as a broader paradigm shift in how daemons conceptualized their network map. In link-state routing,

IMPs and other parts of the communication subnet estimated delay over ten-second periods, rather than instantaneously. The longer time period allowed estimates to smooth out noise and increase stability. A node sent updates to every line—a process now called "flooding"—only when it processed an update. As a result, nodes shared this information less frequently. McQuillan reflected: "We had better, more data for the routing algorithm, delivered less often, only when a meaningful change occurred."[47] Finally, link-state routing changed the route calculation algorithm to a shortest-path-first algorithm designed by Edsger Dijkstra and first published in 1959. The algorithm composed routes in hierarchical trees. Updates changed only the affected branches, not the whole tree. These computational efficiencies made possible a bigger change in routing: "Every node in the network had the entire network 'map,' instead of routing tables from adjacent nodes."[48] Routing calculations became localized instead of distributed. Building on changes to estimates, signaling, and calculation, local nodes calculated their own local map of the infrastructure and network possibilities. Link-state routing went live on ARPANET in late 1978 and early 1979.[49]

Distance-vector and link-state routing inform today's routing protocols, specifically the Border Gateway Protocol (BGP) and the Open Shortest Path First protocol (OSPF). BGP, a descendant of Vinton Cerf's and Robert Kahn's early gateways, is responsible for communication in the core of the internet between autonomous systems, domains under common administration. BGP daemons use a derivative of the distance-vector algorithm to map and decide routes. BGP includes a few protocols, such as the External Border Gateway Protocol (eBGP), which guides how gateways advertise their routes and coordinate with each other. Cooperation varies, and sometimes an autonomous system will configure a daemon to avoid acting as an intermediary between two other systems.[50] BGP also coordinates within domains through the Internal Border Gateway Protocol (iBGP), blurring the boundaries of domains somewhat. OSPF, a descendant of link-state routing, is now the recommended protocol for internal routing. Daemons share link-status updates with their adjacent nodes. The protocol also allows for domains to designate a central router that coordinates its routing.[51]

Since multiple routing protocols coexist, routing daemons have to decide which protocol to use and when. For example, a gateway might be interconnected through the eBGP for networking external to its domain and the OSPF protocol for internal networking. Most daemons then include logics to select the best route and protocol. For example, Cisco ranks protocols through a variable it calls "administrative distance," and so a Cisco daemon will factor in this value when faced with multiple routes using different protocols. Cisco's daemons prefer lower values. By default, Cisco gives an internal BGP route a value of 200 and an OSPF route a value of 110. As a result, a daemon will select the lower OSPF route instead of the iBGP.[52]

The BIRD internet-routing daemon also implements both internal and external routing protocols.[53] At any one time, BIRD might be running a few routines implementing BGP and OSPF, as well as maintaining routing tables. BIRD includes a simple scripting language to help configure how it selects routes. An OSPF configuration, for example, can rank a wired connection higher than a wireless connection so that, when the daemon selects a route from the table, it always selects the wired connection. The same applies for BGP. A BGP configuration might also specify how it will advertise routes and how to pass information to its OSPF routine.

The diversity of routes and routing decisions are an important reminder of routing's relation to flow control. Effective routing avoids delays by routing across the shortest, most reliable lines or, conversely, introduces delay by selecting a slower route. Routing also alters the composition of a network, changing the links between nodes. As Andrew Tanenbaum explains in one of the leading textbooks about computer networks, "typical policies involve political, security, or economic considerations." He suggests, for example, that one should "not use the United States to get from British Columbia to Ontario" and that "traffic starting or ending at IBM should not transit Microsoft."[54] These routing decisions, along with queuing, are the two most important ways daemons modulate transmission conditions.

Queuing

Daemons use queues to decide transmission priority and allocate bandwidth. In computing, "queue" refers to a list stored in a prioritized sequence. Items appearing earlier in a queue are processed sooner than later items. Operations researchers and early computer scientists debated the best algorithms or disciplines to manage queue priorities, as discussed in chapter 2.[55] Davies discussed the round-robin technique of managing queues in time-sharing systems. This technique assigned computing time in equal units, cycling between different processes for the same amount of time so that every process received the same priority.[56] These abstract debates about queue discipline directly influenced the design of the IMP.

Every action on an IMP had a priority. IMPs prioritized routines, interrupts, messages, and packets. Hosts could prioritize messages with a flag in the header, sending these messages to the top of the queue. IMPs also ranked sent packets. Each modem had its own queue that first sent acknowledgments (ACKs), then prioritized messages, and then Requests for Next Messages (RFNMs) and regular packets.[57] These priorities likely did not cause much delay, but they show the roots of queuing in packet transmission.

While the IMP had a lot of moving parts, it did have a few overall priorities, as seen in ACKs and RFNMs being at the front of the transmission queue. IMPs prioritized ACKs and other control messages because early ARPANET researchers preferred an active communication subnet that guaranteed delivery. As ARPANET converted into the internet, this approach gave way to a less active communication subnet developed at the packet-switching infrastructure, CYCLADES. Its design reduced involvement of the communication subnet level and increased responsibility for the host subnet. CYCLADES, as a result, did not ensure the delivery of packets. The approach taken, known as "best efforts," amounted to a daemon doing "its best to deliver [packets]" but "not provid[ing] any guarantees regarding delays, bandwidth or losses."[58] Since networks can be overwhelmed, this approach stipulated that packets should be dropped, forcing a node to resend the packets at a more opportune time.[59] "Best efforts," over time, became a key part of the TCP/IP.

Queue disciplines proliferated even though "best efforts" recommended less involvement of the communication subnet. These disciplines solved queuing problems (which had colorful names like the "diaper-transport problem"[60]) with algorithms that decided how best to send packets down a shared line. Two key queuing algorithms used the metaphor of buckets to describe their logics. The "leaky bucket" algorithm imagines a packet flow as water filling a bucket and leaking out of it through a hole. The bucket acts as a metaphor for a finite packet queue, while the hole represents the average bandwidth. Leaky buckets regulate the intermittent flow of packets by varying queue size (how big a bucket) and average bandwidth (the size of the hole). A queue fills with packets arriving irregularly and holds them until they might be sent at a regular rate. When a bucket overfills, water spills out. When the queue fills, daemons drop packets, signaling congestion.

"Leaky bucket" inspired the "token bucket." Where the leaky bucket kept packet flow constant (the leak has a fixed size), the token bucket accommodates bursts of packets. A token bucket is filled with tokens at a regular rate until it is full. A packet needs a token to be transmitted. Every packet sent removes a token. The maximum transmission rate, then, corresponds to the size of bucket. Thus, the algorithms differ in that "the Token Bucket algorithm throws away tokens (i.e., transmission capacity) when the bucket fills up but never discards packets. In contrast, the Leaky Bucket algorithm discards packets when the bucket fills up."[61] A large burst of packets might be easily accommodated if the token bucket is full, but a leaky bucket, would simply start discarding packets.

Daemons often use these buckets to manage traffic through what is called traffic "shaping" or traffic "policing." Traffic shaping usually works like a leaky bucket, keeping the rate of packet transmission constant. Traffic policing resembles a token bucket, since it attempts to keep an average rate (corresponding to the rate of token refreshing in the bucket) but can accommodate bursts. Both major network equipment manufacturers, Cisco and Juniper, have built-in commands to shape and police traffic as part of their respective operating systems, Cisco's IOS and Juniper's JUNOS. These operating systems run on their routers, switches, and other equipment.[62] The shape command in Cisco's IOS, for example, uses the token-bucket algorithm to limit outbound packets, managing traffic by setting the peak and average bandwidth. By entering "shape average 384000" into the Cisco IOS's command line, a human administrator programs the internal token bucket in a daemon to have a capacity and refresh rate that averages 384,000 bits per second.

The shape command also integrates with packet inspection to treat networks differently. Class-based traffic shaping in Cisco IOS assigns a greater or lesser number of tokens to different networks. Network engineers manually code networks into classes. Classes might include port numbers or other identifiers from DPI and associate through policy maps. Cisco gives the example of a policy map that aggregates classes into gold, silver, and bronze tiers. These tiers receive more or less bandwidth according to a discipline known as "class-based weighted fair" queuing. Different classes receive a set percentage of the token bucket, or bandwidth. The gold tier receives 50 percent, with 20 percent for silver and 15 percent for bronze. (The example does not explain the allocation of the remaining 15 percent.) This is just one example, and Cisco's configuration guide includes numerous queue disciplines and traffic shaping configurations.[63] These queuing configurations demonstrate how flow control easily stratifies networks, ensuring that some receive more bandwidth than others.

Investment in DPI and other forms of advanced traffic management has also led to the development of techniques to accelerate specific networks. Acceleration programs create transmission conditions known to improve certain networks' performances. Another Cisco product, its Wide Area Application Services (WAAS), includes code to accelerate seven networks related to specific applications like HTTP, as well as Windows Media video packets. Acceleration varies, but tweaks such as caching some HTTP traffic lead to better web performance. In addition to these specific accelerations, WAAS includes "200 predefined optimization policy rules" to "classify and optimize some of the most common traffic," according to Cisco Systems.[64] These rules use a combination of different transmission variables like buffer size, "removing redundant information," and compressing data streams to reduce the length of the message.[65] WAAS applies all three techniques to accelerate the Real Time Streaming Protocol used by Skype and Spotify, whereas, by default, it passes on BitTorrent packets without any acceleration.

Other equipment vendors have also begun selling acceleration equipment aimed at improving the performance of other applications and their networks. Allot Communications sells the VideoClass product to improve online video streaming.[66] OpenWave Mobility partnered with a major European mobile network operator to accelerate video game live-streaming sites like Twitch and YouTube.[67] Where shaping and policing deliberately degrade traffic, acceleration technologies lead to uneven communication by improving transmission conditions for select networks.

The ability of a lone daemon to assign queue priority or accelerate packets means little if other daemons cannot identify and indicate high-priority traffic. Numerous protocols have been developed to communicate priority between daemons. Version 4 of TCP/IP includes eight bits in the packet header to signal priority and other transmission conditions to daemons (known as "type of service"). Of the eight bits, the third bit signals if a packet requires low delay, the fourth bit signals a need for high throughput or bandwidth, and the fifth bit signals whether a packet needs high reliability. Each bit signals the daemon to modulate its flow control. Most routers could read the type-of-service bits, but few daemons enforced these instructions.[68]

With the convergence of the internet, great efforts were taken to better signal priority for multimedia and other delay-sensitive packets. The Internet Engineering Task Force (IETF), one of the key standards organizations for the internet, invested heavily in providing multimedia services. The research produced a number of RFCs (the means to publicize and to implement new features on the internet). RFC 2205, released in 1997, outlined the Resource reSerVation Protocol (RSVP) as a means for a host to communicate with networks to reserve a path and resources among them. RSVP provided the foundation for the next protocol, Differentiated Services (DiffServ), outlined in RFCs 2474 and 2475.[69] DiffServ "represented an important modification of the traditional internet paradigm" because "the responsibility to maintain flow information is distributed to all nodes along the network."[70] Using DiffServ, daemons assigned packets to classes according to the type of service specified in their header. Unlike in the Cisco example above, packets included their own priority value.[71] DiffServ classes became a way for network daemons to widen their queue priorities.

Cisco and Juniper developed their own protocol for signaling priority known as Multi-Protocol Label Switching (MPLS).[72] RFC 3031, released in 2001, specified MPLS as a way to label packets entering a part of the internet. The label appears before the IP and TCP data in the bitstream of a packet and includes the class of service among other data for daemons. The label travels with the packet through the infrastructure so that subsequent daemons need only read the MPLS label to decide how to allocate bandwidth.[73]

MPLS works only insofar as daemons agree to abide by its rules, and these pacts work only for a set domain. Where daemons modulate transmission conditions through routing and queuing, they also coordinate themselves through a fourth kind of daemon tasked with policy management.

Policy Management

Policy daemons configure packet inspection, queuing, and routing rules between daemons.[74] They do not necessarily influence transmission conditions directly, but rather coordinate other daemons to set policies that decide how a daemon responds after it inspects a packet. Cisco IOS, for example, includes the POLICY-MAP command to share policies between daemons. Cisco also sells specific products to coordinate policies across domains, usually for enterprise or smaller businesses. Cisco's WAAS, mentioned earlier in relation to acceleration, includes the AppNav feature to coordinate traffic management across multiple pieces of equipment. Typically, the AppNav Controller (ANC) policy daemon monitors incoming traffic and routes it to subservient nodes. An ANC, in other words, administers a cluster of servers. Depending on its configuration, an ANC tries to balance packet flow to avoid overloading the nodes.

The ANC relies on packet inspection to make decisions, matching packets to certain set classes using the class maps discussed above. Cisco's policy-based routing, for example, assigns certain routes to certain classes. This might lead to networks receiving more or less bandwidth if a daemon down the line has been assigned to shape or throttle the packet. A policy daemon might simply pass traffic off to a node or try to balance the load on each node. Finally, policies might accelerate traffic by sending it to a specialized daemon. These are just a few examples of policy management meant to demonstrate how some daemons influence their peers.

A new trend known as Software-Defined Networking (SDN) attempts to further consolidate policy management and control. It is estimated to be a $326.5-million market that will grow to $4.9 billion in 2020.[75] A few ISPs and key players like Google have begun to implement this major new paradigm in network design and management. SDN builds on years of research into internet infrastructure design with the aim of increasing programmability, improving system-wide state awareness, and consolidating control. SDN improves programmability by decoupling daemons from their hardware. Many daemons are hard-coded into purpose-built appliances. Instead, as the name suggests, SDN prefers to use generic hardware and reprogrammable software to carry out functions, exemplifying a trend called "network functions virtualization." This abstraction runs through the whole infrastructure design. Decisions are consolidated in one overall program referenced by the rest of the software infrastructure. SDN advocates sometimes call its implementation a network operating system because it turns all the pieces of an infrastructure into one centrally administered machine. OpenFlow, for example, is the best-known open source implementation of SDN.[76] Juniper advertises its NorthStar Controller as a way to simplify "operations by enabling SDN programmability control points across disparate network elements."[77] Through its web interface, the controller offers a window into infrastructural activity and ways to modify flow control across multiple devices.

The consolidation of policy management through SDN and other distributed management techniques creates an attractive place for daemons. SDN currently requires a human to configure the infrastructure, but in the future, an autonomous daemon empowered with sophisticated artificial intelligence might constantly monitor and manage networks, their different rhythms and tempos orchestrated by an omnipotent descendant of Selfridge's "decision demon." Indeed, a key promise of SDN is to be able to automate traffic management. The NorthStar Controller includes a path optimization feature that inspects the performance of all its nodes. Administrators can click the "Optimize Now" button to automatically reconfigure its daemons to run better.[78]

THE INTERNET AS PANDAEMONIUM: DAEMONS AND OPTIMIZATION

Together, these autonomous daemons orchestrate flow control. Packet inspection daemons profile and contextualize a packet, drawing on its stateful awareness, programmed characteristics of protocol and perhaps behavioral analysis. In concert, policy daemons set the goals for daemons to work toward, such as, for example, a system free of P2P traffic or congestion. Information from packet-inspection and policy-management daemons informs queuing and routing daemons. With a sense of a packet's past and its future, daemons modulate bandwidth and priority at the moment of transmission.

This distributive agency seeks to actualize a programmed optimal state. Internet daemons create a metastability in the network of networks—at least until a network administrator or an autonomous policy daemon changes the rules. Every network differs in what it considers minimum transmission conditions, and it is up to daemons to judge this heterarchy. Netflix requires five-megabytes-per-second bandwidth for high-definition video, while Xbox gaming requires the same bandwidth and less than 150 milliseconds ping time. An optimization decides how a part of the internet accommodates these minimums. A daemon might recognize a few bits in a packet as Voice over Internet Protocol (VoIP) and realize that it needs to be prioritized with low delay to avoid degrading an online conversation. Another daemon might ignore the transmission conditions required by a network, as is often the case with P2P networking. This metastability influences both the life and tempo of networks. How does the internet, as discussed by net neutrality expert Barbara van Schewick, accommodate innovation?[79] Should a new network be treated as a new use or an unknown threat? Should an infrastructure accommodate networks, prioritize some networks over others, or block some networks from operating? It is a matter of the very conditions of communication, the imparting of a shared temporality.

There is no one optimization for the internet. There are multiple definitions of the optimal brought about by the heterarchy of networks and the different versions of packet switching. Two kinds of optimality stand out online: *nonsynchronous* optimization and *polychronous* optimizatton. As mentioned in the introduction of this chapter, these optimizations differ in the daemons they include in the infrastructure, the ways they arrange these daemons, and their shared definition of the optimal. The former largely keeps the networks simple, pushes control to the edges, and prefers to leave the optimal unsettled, while the latter brings in more daemons and uses their flow control toward the center in order to better manage these many networks.

Nonsynchronous Optimization

Nonsynchronous optimization resonates with the ideas that first led to the ARPANET. Donald Davies proposed nonsychronous communication as a way for a common carrier to accommodate diverse networks, but he left the role of the infrastructure somewhat ambiguous. Should it make decisions about accommodating different networks? The next iteration of nonsynchronous optimization made it much clearer that important decisions about the infrastructure should be left to the ends.

This optimization does not call for internet daemons much beyond the original IMP. The optimization expects daemons simply to make their best efforts to control flows.[80] This sense of best efforts can be found again in the E2E principle. Jerome Saltzer, David Reed, and David Clark formalized the principle in a 1984 article entitled "End-to-End Arguments in System Design." Core daemons did little more than route packets, certainly nothing as advanced as discussed above. The principle invites comparison to common carriage, since the core infrastructure has limited control (which, in telecommunications, usually grants the carrier limited liability).

Nonsynchronous optimization privileges the ends over the core, just as the E2E principle prioritized the sender and the receiver. The principle holds that correct message delivery "can completely and correctly be implemented only with the knowledge and the help of the application standing at the end points of the communication system."[81] Only the sender and the receiver can guarantee the accuracy of a message because they alone know its contents. Therefore, control should reside in the endpoints. In this way, the diagram resembled the proposal by Cerf and Kahn mentioned in the previous chapter of this book.

The E2E principle also did not expect an optimal network to be entirely free of error. Consider its approach to voice calls. In the original article, Saltzer, Reed, and Clark thought E2E could easily accommodate delay-sensitive communication, even such as voice, with "an unusually strong version of the end-to-end argument." They reasoned, "if low levels of the communication system try to accomplish bit-perfect communication, they will probably introduce uncontrolled delays in packet delivery." In short, internet daemons should do less to ensure the proper delivery of packets and let the ends of networks (or users) sort out lapses in communication. Etiquette, not optimization, would solve disruptions. They suggested that, if transmission conditions degraded an online conversation, "the high-level error correction procedure" was for the receiver to ask the sender to repeat themselves.[82] Their advice may seem out of touch to anyone who has suffered through an unreliable VoIP conversation, but it demonstrates the sacrifices expected for this optimization.

Nonsynchronous optimization leaves the metastability of the internet unorganized by any central point. Instead, the internet's metastability hinges on the interactions between ends, with each deciding how best to manage its own participation in multiple networks. This arrangement leaves a great deal of uncertainty about how networks share infrastructures. The tempo of the network of networks, in other words, is unknown. E2E requires intermediaries that do little else than carry bits between the ends.[83] Authoritative daemons at the ends command internet daemons to ferry the packet mindlessly to its destination.

Much has been written that defends nonsynchronous optimization. Most significantly, internet legal scholars have argued that E2E fosters innovation and user-led development.[84] Since the ends command the bulk of the authority over transmitting messages, they can easily choose to communicate over new kinds of networks. Jonathan Zittrain calls this the "generative web." He explains: "The end-to-end argument stands for modularity in network design: it allows the network nerds, both protocol designers and ISP implementers, to do their work without giving a thought to network hardware or PC software." He asserts that aspects of E2E invite "others to overcome the network's shortcomings, and to continue adding to its uses."[85] His optimism exemplifies the guiding principle of nonsynchronous optimization: that the infrastructure should accommodate all kinds of networks without being obligated to handle them well.

Polychronous Optimization

In 2002, critical media scholar Dwayne Winseck warned of the "netscapes of power" drawing "intelligence, resources and capabilities back in the network and under the control of those who own them."[86] A multitude of daemons have made good on Winseck's warning. They enact polychronous optimizations. I use "poly" in contrast to "non" to denote this optimization's temporality. The prefix "poly" indicates many. Polychronous optimization works from a belief that a solution exists to manage the knowable, multitudinous networks of the internet. Networks exist within the tempos set by the optimization. The unpredictable "best efforts" approach is replaced by a reasonable management. The unsettled metastability of the internet is replaced by a regulated system of service guarantees and data limits. The diagram shifts from the edges to the core, with infrastructures progressively taking on greater management capacities. To handle this greater responsibility, the poloychronous optimization installs new daemons discussed above.

Polychronous optimization is less a matter of network discrimination than it is one of a broader economics of bandwidth, a push to an optimal metastability of the internet. Perhaps the value of polychronous optimization, more than anything else, is that it captures the productive aspect of traffic management. It rejects the unsettled relations of nonsynchronous optimization and its optimism that networks can coexist without oversight. Instead, this metastability is premised on a knowable diversity of networks whose relations can be ordered into an optimal distribution of infrastructural resources. Bandwidth-hungry applications must be managed to preserve the functionality of "well-behaved" applications. Assigning the labels "bandwidth-hungry" and "well-behaved" involves a network capable of being able to make decisions about the value of a packet. A polychronous optimization does not remove or block problematic networks. This optimization does not stop the innovation of new networks, at least not deterministically, but it incorporates them into an economy of bandwidth in which they have lower value and priority. Discrimination might not even be intentional, but rather an externality of accelerating and prioritizing other users and applications.

The Comcast case discussed next provides a case study of polychronous optimization. As mentioned in the introduction, Comcast's management of eMule in 2007 led to a detailed disclosure of its infrastructural architecture.[87] The FCC compelled Comcast to disclose its practices of traffic management of P2P networks.[88] These filings offer a compelling guide to understanding a polychronous optimization (its daemons, its diagram and its definition of the optimal). The filings demonstrate a conflict between two optimizations of the internet. Home users at the ends proliferated P2P networks, while the descendants of IMPs in Comcast's infrastructure worked to manage and suppress these networks. The introduction of a DPI and traffic management middlebox into Comcast's infrastructure set off the "net neutrality" debate in the United States and provided a glimpse into a future internet under polychronous optimization.

A JOURNEY THROUGH PANDAEMONIUM

This journey begins with activity on home computers. In 2006, the home computer was in the midst of major changes. After Napster, computer piracy grew from an underground phenomenon to a popular activity, an era of mass piracy.[89] Piracy (as well as many legitimate uses) relied on a new kind of networking known as "peer-to-peer," P2P. "Peers," in this case, refers to home users. File transmission before P2P relied on a server–client model in which home users connected to a central file-sharing server. P2P connected home users to each other so they could share files, as well as chat or talk. For example, the popular VoIP service Skype uses P2P. As the music industry learned after the launch of Napster, P2P networks often lacked traditional gatekeepers, so users could move clandestine activities like home taping and underground file-sharing onto the internet. (In many ways, P2P remediated these networks as discussed in the previous chapter.)

P2P developed as advocates of free speech on the internet broadly expanded the implications of the E2E principle.[90] Where the TCP/IP regarded both clients and servers as ends, since they function as the sender and receiver in any session, P2P tried to cut out the server and focus directly on the client, prioritizing home computers above all. As John Perry Barlow, cofounder of the digital rights group the Electronic Frontier Foundation (EFF), once quipped, "the Internet treats censorship as a malfunction and routes around it," a comment that Tarleton Gillespie argues shows that "there is a neat discursive fit between the populist political arrangements [Barlow] seeks and the technical design of the network that he believes hands users power."[91] The ends of the network, proponents like Barlow argued, must be free from the impositions of centralized control. P2P seemed to actualize these desires for an uncensored network of peers, and enthusiasts not only evangelized the concept but also coded P2P networks.[92] For true believers, the closure of Napster and its successors signified the need for a technical project to build a more resilient form of P2P.[93]

P2P users connected to the wider internet through Comcast's infrastructure. At the time, that infrastructure, seen in Figure 5, included seven major points: the end user, the cable modem, the optical node, the Cable Modem Termination System (CMTS), a local market router, a regional network router, and, finally, the internet network backbone.

These points connected through a mixture of repurposed coaxial cables (once used to deliver television) and fiber optic lines. Home users connected to Comcast's infrastructure through a shared network of coaxial cable. These local loops connected to an optical node that transferred signals to fiber optical cables connected to the CMTS. The CMTS aggregated multiple optical nodes, sending traffic to higher-level regional routers and eventually to the core internet. Comcast averaged at the time 275 cable modems per downstream port of a CMTS and 100 cable modems for its upstream port. In total, 14.4 million customers connected to the internet using approximately 3,300 shared CMTS points across Comcast's entire network.

Comcast had also begun to monitor P2P networks in its infrastructure. Several years before 2007, they had begun to investigate changes in internet use that might be causing congestion on their lines, another sign that keeping pace with innovation on the internet challenged the infrastructure itself. The company's research found five problematic P2P file-sharing networks: Ares Galaxy, BitTorrent, eDonkey/eMule, FastTrack, and Gnutella. Each embodied a different version of P2P with its own challenges for Comcast. Gnutella, one of the first P2P networks developed

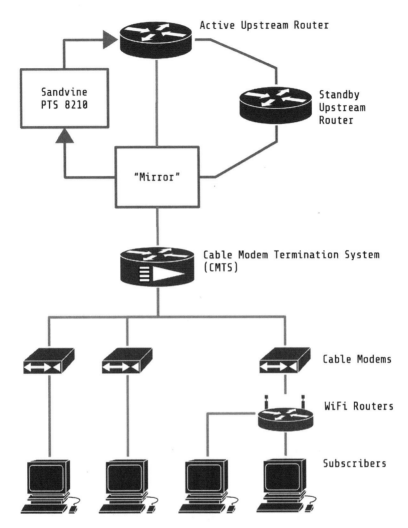

Figure 5. Network diagram submitted by Comcast to the Federal Communications Commission to explain its P2P traffic management (reproduction).

after Napster, attempted to further decentralize the network by treating every node as both a client and a server. All peers were equal, and no central index existed. A search, for example, passed between peers rather than queried from a central database like Napster. Ares Galaxy, a fork of Gnutella, brought back some centralization to provide greater reliability.

BitTorrent treated all peers as equal and even enforced a rule that users had to upload as much as they downloaded, but it also initially relied on some central servers to coordinate peers and locate files.

P2P networks, according to Comcast, caused congestion in their infrastructure. Much of this had to do with the design of internet service over coaxial cable. Along with the rest of the cable industry, Comcast had repurposed its cable network to provide internet service. The Cable Television Laboratories consortium invested heavily in research to develop the Data over Cable Service Interface Specification (DOCSIS).[94] The first version of DOCSIS was certified in 1999, and it guided cable companies as they upgraded their infrastructure to deliver broadband internet. DOCSIS specifies the entire provision of cable broadband internet, including the arrangement of cable modems and the CMTS. The specification requires that all data passed between cable modems and the CMTS be encrypted (using the Baseline Privacy Plus protocol).[95]

Daemons on a home user's cable modem put DOCSIS into practice, dealing with the messy realities of cables and wires. Daemons encoded digital packets as analog signals and sent them up the coaxial cable. A big part of their job was coordinating how to share the common coaxial cable. The shared wire of cable television, while fine for broadcasting fifty-seven channels, needed greater daemonic supervision to be used for multiple, bidirectional communications. Daemons communicated with the CMTS every two milliseconds to reserve time (or mini slots), upload data, and interpret signals sent downstream.[96] Thus, the cable network is like Selfridge's Pandemonium: full of daemons screaming at each other to coordinate resources.

Cable modems also managed transmission conditions for customers. Comcast (like many ISPs) had already begun to use its cable modems to tier its service. In June 2006, the company sold internet service in tiers that ranged from 4 Mbps download and 384 Kbps upload to 8 Mbps download and 768 Kbps (well below the DOCSIS 2.0 maximums of 43 Mbps download and 36 Mbps upload).[97] Comcast does not mention these tiers in its disclosure, but cable modems typically enforced service tiers. When a cable modem boots up and connects to the CMTS, it downloads a boot file that includes instructions for its Simple Network Management Protocol (SNMP) daemon. These instructions match the modem to a customer and configure the SNMP daemon to operate at the bandwidth limits set by the customer's service tier.[98] These daemons obey a vision of a network, ensuring that their transmission does not exceed the maximum download and upload bandwidth set by the CMTS. Given the responsibility delegated to the cable modem, it should be no surprise there was a healthy interest in cable modem hacking to bypass its security features and reconfigure the SNMP daemon to ignore upload and download limits set by the ISP.[99]

These idealistic P2P networks, however, put the cable modem in an awkward spot. From its inception, P2P posed a problem for the cable internet because it placed greater demand on the scarcest resource, upload capacity. DOCSIS provisioned more bandwidth for download throughput than upload throughput. Comcast had likely upgraded to DOCSIS 2.0 by 2006.[100] DOCSIS 2.0 allowed for a theoretical maximum of 42.88 megabits per second for download, versus 30.72 megabits per second for upload. Cable modems simply could not generate the complicated high frequency modulations needed to use more cable capacity. The lower frequency also meant that upstream traffic had to contend with greater interference from mobile phone traffic.

P2P developers knew their networks could be a nuisance and had taken measures to protect themselves in hostile environments. Developers had begun to design their networks to avoid detection. EMule, the P2P network that provoked the Comcast investigation, had implemented what it called "protocol obfuscation" by 2006. As the eMule project explained:

[Protocol Obfuscation is] a feature which causes eMule to obfuscate or "hide" its protocol when communicating with other clients or servers. Without obfuscation, each eMule communication has a given structure which can be easily recognized and identified as an eMule packet by any observer. If this feature is turned on, the whole eMule communication appears like random data on the first look and an automatic identification is no longer easily possible. This helps against situations where the eMule Protocol is unjustly discriminated or even completely blocked from a network by identifying its packets.[101]

Under protocol obfuscation, the packets' metadata did not inform daemons of the type of traffic, which effectively "hid" the network from the daemons' gaze and presumably from its traffic shaping. Protocol obfuscation broke with the internet protocols by deliberately evading packet classification. TCP/IP assumed the packet header to be accurate even though it preferred daemons to avoid looking at it in keeping with the E2E principle. By refusing to be accurate, eMule undermined trust in the suite.

Protocol obfuscation was one reason Comcast installed new DPI and traffic management middleboxes in their networks beginning in May 2005. Comcast also hoped to better manage P2P networks. In its submission to the FCC, the company made the rare gesture of disclosing the manufacturer and model of their network equipment: a Sandvine Policy Traffic Switch (PTS) 8210. Sandvine, the manufacturer of the device, was a leader in the DPI industry. Their brochure for the PTS 8210 describes an apparent answer to Comcast's congestion problems:

> Subscriber behavior has always been difficult to characterize. What applications are popular? How does usage vary by service? Are third-party services increasing? Sandvine Network Demographics reporting, without impinging on subscriber privacy, provides valuable insights into application behavior and trends.[102]

Sandvine could deliver on these promises because it had programmed (like its competitors) a new set of daemons to inspect and manage networks. Each PTS had a Policy Traffic Switch daemon (PTSd). As Sandvine explained: "PTSd is the daemon that holds or enforces the rules specified for processing the incoming traffic."[103] The introduction of the Sandvine PTS 8210 marked an important change in the network, a change that Comcast initially did not announce, leaving it to the public to discover. In fact, Comcast did not update its terms of service to disclose its traffic management until January 25, 2008.[104]

The PTSd wielded a much more powerful gaze into the network and thwarted P2P protocol obfuscation. The PTS 8210 "inspected and stored" all packets exchanged between two peers (technically a flow) for the duration of a session. Mislabeling packets no longer worked because the PTS daemon didn't look at the header to identify the packet. Sandvine elaborated: "There is no limit on how deep in the packet or flow the PTS can go," and its gaze "spans across multiple packets ensuring that TCP-based protocols are identified 100% of the time."[105] The PTS's daemons could then identify packets based on both patterns embedded within individual packets (like the OpenDPI code) and patterns in the flow itself even when it was obfuscated.

Not only could the PTS 8210 observe more of the network; it also included a built-in system of analytics and demographic reporting. (Well aware of privacy concerns, Comcast frequently highlighted in their disclosure that they did not read any content, even though the Sandvine PTSd could likely assemble parts of a message using its flow analysis.) These reports must have appealed to Comcast as it sought to make sense of the network's performance. The PTS's brochure promised "over 150 fully-customizable reports" useful for "marketing, operations, security, and support." The brochure included a few examples of reports that demonstrate that the device could track user behaviors such as protocols, bandwidth usage, or total minutes of VoIP conversation. The PTS could also track usage by class of activity, so an ISP could determine the popularity of streaming versus online gaming or the types of attacks taking place on its network.

The PTS 8210 offered numerous responses to a congested state. The device could manipulate packets themselves to alter the type-of-service bits in the header to enable DiffServ during routing. The PTS could also use Sandvine's FairShare policy management to "allocate equitable network resources during periods of congestion." What these technological solutions imply is that the network itself should fairly allocate bandwidth. However, in the same brochure, Sandvine also noted that the device could create new service tiers, for example gamers could buy a package that guaranteed a better in-game experience.[106] The influence of the PTS 8210 then could be said to modulate between guaranteeing a fair network and further stratifying the internet beyond speed and into different profiles of users.

FairShare was only one of many solutions to P2P congestion. Well before the Comcast affair, Sandvine, in a 2004 report, evaluated seven different solutions to manage P2P traffic and optimize the changing behavior of networks on their infrastructure. These different options describe the various ways daemons could manage P2P and help situate the unique features of the PTS 8210. First, an ISP could just buy more bandwidth, but Sandvine argued (as have ISPs subsequently in regulatory hearings) that "the increased amount of bandwidth actually encourages bandwidth abuses, as the offending subscribers have increased resources to consume."[107] Instead of adding bandwidth, an ISP could simply subtract or block P2P traffic from their network. The problem was, as Sandvine admitted:

> Blocking all P2P traffic is certain to lead to customer dissatisfaction and aggravate customer churn. In fact, some service providers are beginning to tout their high-speed services as "P2P Friendly," leveraging their P2P posi-

tion into a powerful marketing tool, capturing the interest—and wallets—of frustrated subscribers.[108]

Blocking was too risky a strategy because it was too overt and could potentially lead to customers' developing conscious animosity toward their ISP. Too much frustration (an issue discussed in the next chapter) could work too well, leading to a total drop in network traffic as customers quit Comcast's service. Interestingly, Sandvine also suggested the controversial approach of network caching (also known as "content distribution"), where ISPs store the contents of P2P networks closer to the customer. Caching appeared to be "a workable solution," but its legal ambiguity exposed the ISP to "a range of serious risks," and Sandvine warned that caching could result in "a host of legal issues and a mass of bad PR" due to the ambiguous, gray, or illegal contents of many P2P networks[109] (a calculation of risk that reiterates the commonalities between transmission and security). Bandwidth caps, Sandvine suggested, could also limit P2P traffic by introducing economic penalties for users who consume too much.[110] Today caps are almost universal, but at the time, Sandvine warned that caps were a "heavy-handed and imprecise approach to the P2P problem."[111]

Sandvine preferred to recommend more dynamic, or modulating, solutions to P2P. ISPs could throttle traffic to prevent P2P networks from using too much of the available bandwidth (as was done in Canada) or, even better, manage traffic depending on the current state of the network. Sandvine claimed, as its report turned into an advertisement, that its products were "essentially 'listening in' on the P2P conversations" so that they could "step in and facilitate a transfer among local subscribers, rather than allowing the P2P protocol to connect randomly to a client on an external network."[112] Controversially, Sandvine proposed that the ISP should interfere in the interactions between end daemons to push them to connect based on proximity. This solution, one that proposes a different type of collaboration, rather than antagonism, between P2P daemons and networks, might have solved bandwidth issues had it been adopted by Comcast. Instead, Comcast configured its daemons to interfere in P2P networks by reducing all upstream traffic.

To manage the congestion caused by P2P applications, Comcast installed Sandvine's PTS 8210 equipment next to every CMTS (though sometimes two CMTSs shared one Sandvine switch). The PTS monitored a *copy* of the upstream traffic that passed through the CMTS to the active upstream router that led to the general internet.[113] Comcast had installed the PTS 8210 on a duplicate network, or "out of line," to reduce points of failure. Traffic passed through a splitter—labeled as a "Mirror" in Figure 5—that passed a copy of traffic to the PTS 8210. (In contrast, an "inline" application installed the PTS in between the CMTS and the active upstream router. By being out of line, the PTS could fail without disrupting the operations of the CMTS.)

Sandvine daemons looked for a few troublesome networks. Comcast's prior testing had revealed that Ares, BitTorrent, eDonkey, FastTrack, and Gnutella "were generating disproportionate amounts of traffic."[114] Comcast configured the PTS 8210 to track and count packets related to those applications (likely using proprietary DPI by Sandvine, though it is not mentioned in the report). Sandvine daemons kept track of the overall number of upload sessions generated by each P2P network per CMTS (rather than per user). A "session" referred to a connection established between two peers in a P2P network. BitTorrent, for example, creates swarms where users download and upload parts of a file. Comcast focused on instances of "unidirectional" sessions, when a subscriber only sends information to a peer, not receiving another part from that peer, as opposed to what they called "bidirectional" sessions, when two peers exchange data.[115] In BitTorrent, this unidirectional flow was called "seeding." A user seeded a BitTorrent network when, having completed downloading a file, they left the BitTorrent client running to keep sharing the file with other users. Comcast explained, "the number of simultaneous unidirectional upload sessions of any particular P2P protocol at any given time serves as a useful *proxy* for determining the level of overall network congestion" (italics added).[116] It is reasonable to assume that Comcast had many ways to detect congestion in its infrastructure, so it is important to note their decision to pick simultaneous unidirectional upload sessions as its proxy.

Each PTS 8210 had a stateful awareness of its part of the Comcast network. Comcast configured the Sandvine PTS 8210 to observe the levels of unidirectional upstream traffic per application. When sessions exceeded a threshold, the device's daemons intervened. Thresholds differed by application. Through testing, Comcast decided that one CMTS tolerated up to one hundred fifty sessions for Ares networks, while another CMTS tolerated only eight BitTorrent sessions before intervening. These thresholds derived from estimates of how much bandwidth a session consumed. Comcast set a lower threshold for BitTorrent sessions than for

Ares because the former consumed more bandwidth per session than the latter. Thresholds also included a calculation of how well unidirectional sessions functioned as a proxy for overall activity. As Comcast explained, "the BitTorrent protocol more heavily promotes bidirectional uploads as compared to eDonkey, so, while they both may have the same total number of sessions, BitTorrent would have a much higher percentage of bidirectional sessions than eDonkey."[117] Comcast calculated a ratio of three bidirectional sessions for every one unidirectional session observed for eDonkey. BitTorrent had a ratio of twenty bidirectional sessions for every one unidirectional, and so BitTorrent had a lower threshold because unidirectional sessions implied a much larger amount of overall activity.

Comcast did not elect to use the PTS 8210 to create new service tiers, nor did they use FairShare to manage bandwidth. Exceeding the threshold caused the PTSd to try to diminish upstream traffic on its domain. As the PTS 8210 was "out of line," its daemons could not interact directly with the packets passing through the Comcast network. This fact limited the daemons' grasps since they could not reduce bandwidth or drop packets from the network. Instead, the daemons injected reset packets into downstream traffic. Reset packets are conventionally sent from receiver to sender to inform the sender that some error requires communication to be restarted. By injecting reset packets, the PTS 8210 caused daemons on the home computer to think the session had ended in error and to thus close the connection. Comcast used the technique to "delay unidirectional uploads for that particular P2P protocol in the geographic area."[118] The PTS 8210 continued to inject reset packets until unidirectional sessions fell below the threshold or when the proxy for congestion returned to an acceptable level. Importantly the technique broke IP conventions by having the server intervene in the control messages sent between two peers on the network, a violation of the E2E principle.[119]

Gauging the effects of the throttling on users is difficult. The court cases mostly focused on Comcast's false advertising. According to a class action suit that was eventually filed against the company, Comcast had: "(1) slowed, delayed or otherwise impeded peer-to-peer (P2P) transmission sent using its high-speed Internet service (HSIS) (even though it advertised 'unfettered' access) and (2) failed to disclose this practice to its subscribers."[120] Possible effects varied depending on the network. The EFF, in its response to the case, suggested that packet injection adversely affected BitTorrent's and Gnutella's networks. Reset packets "impair[ed] the node's ability to discover and establish proper communications with other parts of the Gnutella network."[121] The EFF also suggested that traffic management delayed Lotus Notes and Windows Remote Desktop networks. Comcast's filings do not mention these targets, so it is possible that reports were inaccurate or that the PTSd accidentally targeted these networks. If the latter explanation is true, it is an important reminder of a daemon's probabilistic gaze. Such probabilities include the possibility that daemons misclassified some packets.

Comcast's case is a specific example of the use of flow control against certain networks. Tim Wu calls this "broadband discrimination" in his original article on net neutrality.[122] The concept of flow control helps clarify this discrimination. Daemons discriminate by degrading transmission conditions for certain networks, in this case P2P, intentionally providing different conditions of transmission than what is considered best by the network. Faced with a fiber-coaxial infrastructure struggling to provide sufficient upload capacity, Comcast decided to selectively desynchronize the coordination of P2P networks, frustrating its users, to ensure the success of other networks. Amid growing adoption of P2P, which was not an unforeseeable change, given how the E2E principle championed end users, the network changed how it transmitted networks, forcing P2P networks to suffer so other networks could succeed.

2008: User-Centric Traffic Management

The Comcast case is not the last example of polychronous optimization. New polychronous optimizations have arisen even after net neutrality legislation. Some even claim to support the principle. Attention to daemons helps track these polychronous optimizations. Increasingly, daemons have turned their gaze to problem users. To be clear, this approach still manages networks, but only select parts: the nodes. Comcast modified their strategy in reaction to the public, legal, and regulatory response to its network management. The company made a number of changes in its infrastructure with the goal of targeting certain users. In other words, in response to concerns that its traffic management techniques discriminated against P2P, Comcast shifted focus to home users who use more than their "fair share" of bandwidth.

Comcast's new traffic management policy, diagrammed in Figure 6, reconfigured its cable modem and its infrastructure. Comcast installed three servers further upstream than the CMTS, near its regional network routers, although "the *exact* locations of various servers ha[d] not been

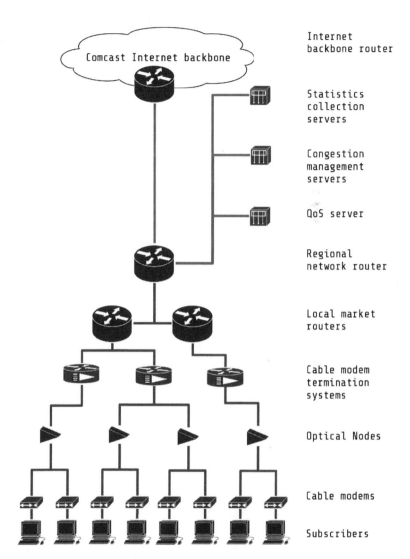

Figure 6. Network diagram submitted by Comcast to Federal Communications Commission to explain its user-centric traffic management (reproduction).

finalized."[123] Proximity to the regional network routers meant that these servers managed more than one CMTS at a time, serving an even wider geographic area. Comcast planned to install three kinds of servers to manage its users:

1. Sandvine Congestion Management FairShare servers designed to detect when a CMTS port was congested, similar to the way the PTSd had monitored for congestion;
2. Packetcable Multimedia servers manufactured by Camiant Technologies configured to manage the cable modems of Comcast customers;
3. and Internet Detailed Record Collector servers focused on monitoring the data sent and received by Comcast's customers (Comcast had not selected a vendor for these when it submitted its explanation to the FCC).

These servers enforced a two-step threshold for traffic management. Daemons on the Sandvine server monitored each CMTS port for congestion over fifteen-minute intervals. Based on lab tests, technical trials, and other simulations, Comcast set a first threshold at the CMTS level. Daemons classified a CMTS line as being in a near-congestion state "if an average of more than 70 percent of a port's upstream bandwidth capacity and more than 80 percent of a port's downstream bandwidth capacity is utilized" over the fifteen-minute period, and daemons responded if a line in the CMTS passed this threshold.[124] Sandvine daemons queried the Internet Detailed Record Collector servers for cable modems using more than 70 percent of their provisioned upstream or downstream bandwidth in that fifteen-minute period. If the search returned no results, the daemons did nothing. If it did return a list of customers using a lot of their bandwidth, then the daemons' traffic management targeted these customers. In other words, if a customer bought an 8-Mbps-down / 1-Mbps-up internet service package, they would be flagged if they used on average more than 5.6 Mbps down and 0.7 Mbps up in a fifteen-minute window. These two thresholds triggered Comcast's new congestion management techniques.

Comcast daemons managed perceived congestion by introducing a new label to prioritize all packets sent and received by cable modems. Comcast updated all the boot files of cable modems to flag packets as either Priority Best Efforts (PBE) or Best Efforts (BE). By default, a cable modem sent and received all packets as PBE. They all had, in other words, the same status unless a CMTS entered a near-congestion state. Any cable modems identified in an extended high-consumption state had their packets set to BE rather than PBE. Daemons at the CMTS prioritized PBE over BE when they sent bursts of packets up or down the shared lines. Comcast explained:

A rough analogy would be to buses that empty and fill up at incredibly fast speeds. As empty buses arrive at the figurative "bus stop"—every two milliseconds in this case—they fill up with as many packets as are waiting for "seats" on the bus, to the limits of the bus' capacity. During non-congested periods, the bus will usually have several empty seats, but, during congested periods, the bus will fill up and packets will have to wait for the next bus. It is in the congested periods that BE packets will be affected. If there is no congestion, packets from a user in a BE state should have little trouble getting on the bus when they arrive at the bus stop. If, on the other hand, there is congestion in a particular instance, the bus may become filled by packets in a PBE state before any BE packets can get on. In that situation, the BE packets would have to wait for the next bus that is not filled by PBE packets. In reality, this all takes place in two-millisecond increments, so even if the packets miss 50 "buses," the delay only will be about one-tenth of a second.[125]

A missed bus might not be a big inconvenience, but a change in one tenth of a second (or one hundred milliseconds) was enough to exceed the minimum requirements of networks like Xbox gaming. (This bus analogy takes on new meaning in the next chapter, as Comcast also uses a bus analogy in an ad campaign.) Comcast, at the end of its filings, promised to implement this new system by December 31, 2008. It is still running today, as far as I can tell.

Today, user-centric management has been positioned as a polychronous optimization that respects net neutrality regulations. Saisei, another player in the traffic-management industry, advertises its own user-centric traffic management product called "FlowCommand" as "the world's first 'Net Neutrality' enforcer." FlowCommand can "monitor and control every flow on an Internet Service Provider's broadband links—millions of concurrent data, voice and video sessions—in real time without impacting the performance of the network."[126] Much like Comcast, Saisei sidesteps accusations of meddling with networks by focusing on "rogue users." The problem, as the technical support joke goes, is between the chair and the keyboard. An administrator can tame rogue users:

> The "Host Equalization" tick box on the FlowCommand User Interface immediately implements this "policy," giving every host—user—on a link exactly the same percentage of the available bandwidth that every other user has, regardless of what application(s) they may be running. So,

aggressive applications, including P2P apps like BitTorrent or high volumes of YouTube traffic, that used to grab huge amounts of link bandwidth, will get the same percentage of a link's bandwidth as every other user on the network if that link approaches congestion.[127]

The daemon, in effect, becomes responsible for preserving net neutrality by consolidating the networks of every user into distinct, equitably provisioned flows. The FlowCommand's superior management allows infrastructures to eliminate the need for spare, emergency capacity. Comcast set the threshold for near-congestion at 70 to 80 percent, but since FlowCommand's host equalization allows links to run "close to [100 percent] utilization without ever stalling a session, there is far more bandwidth available for all."[128] Far from being just an instrument of optimization, the daemons are the optimal way of managing the internet: they are better than humans at Comcast at making decisions about what constitutes congestion.

Saisei's net neutrality enforcer raises important questions about the limits of the idea. If regulators were to make a pact with the devil, so to speak, they could ensure complete equity among users through persuasive optimization. Doing so goes well beyond the ideals of nonsynchronous optimization that seem to have informed net neutrality. Network equality could indeed be a more radical optimality than neutrality, one that sets the creation of common, equal conditions of transmission for all as its ideal.[129] Given the netscapes of power described by Winseck above, such a future is unlikely. Yet the promise of daemonic optimization looms large on the internet as it does in other parts of society.

2018: Future Optimizations

Future optimizations might not require any human oversight. New daemons promise to manage the network themselves. Aria Networks describes itself as "a provider of Artificial Intelligence (AI) driven planning and optimization software for networks"[130] and promises to create a self-optimizing network in which "the ultimate vision is a network that can respond to fluctuating demand in real time and deliver service levels immediately."[131] The possibility of the next generation of daemons to automatically optimize the internet raises questions akin to legal theorist Frank Pasquale's concerns over a black box society. In his investigations of financial credit systems and online data brokers, Pasquale questions the forms of social control manifest through opaque technical systems.[132] Like proponents of net neutrality, Pasquale worries that "the values and prerogatives that the encoded rules enact are hidden within black boxes."[133] In the case of the internet, daemons are part of the black box now operating in proprietary infrastructures within the depths of the infrastructure. Black boxes might operate with novel computational logics, but it is just as likely that optimization will reassert logics of capital. Both Winseck and Pasquale draw a close parallel between optimization and capital. Pasquale writes: "Power over money and new media rapidly concentrates in a handful of private companies."[134] Further research must trace this link to explore the ways the political economy of the internet drives daemonic development and programs the optimal.

Where future research should question who programs the next optimization, I wish to reflect on the optimism of autonomous daemonic optimization. Critiques of big data and algorithms have clearly demonstrated the capacity of automated computational systems to discriminate,[135] but software and algorithms endure as institutional solutions to human bias.[136] Why was the disclosure that Facebook used humans to manage their "news feed" a scandal?[137] Should not the clear biases of its algorithms be subject to the same scrutiny as human bias? (But it should be a scandal, since the leak demonstrated the glaring lack of public oversight over these new media empires.) These same debates over automation may well come to internet management (if they're not already here). Canadian and American net neutrality regulations allow for reasonable network management while preventing discrimination. What values and prerogatives will be drawn into the network due to this exception? Will this loophole be tolerated because daemons will be able to better "solve" the internet than humans?

Daemons, or at least their autonomous successors, might manage the internet better, but there are risks in that optimism. Louise Amoore, in her book discussing the politics of algorithmic regulation, warns about the loss of enchantment. Drawing on the work of Jane Bennett, Amoore writes, "for Bennett, enchantment 'can propel ethics,' at least in the sense that the magic of future potential, the promise of a life not yet lived, remains open."[138] The same might be said of the internet's metastability. Perhaps an enchanting internet is worth the risk of suboptimality. Amoore warns that systems like self-optimizing daemons might "actively annul the potential for the unanticipated," and instead she ponders what it means "to live with the unknowability of the future, even where it may contain dangers or risks."[139] The stakes of internet optimization, to be fair, are different from Amoore's interest in the security state, but they are not marginal. The internet is quickly becoming the de facto global communication system, if it has not already. Polychronous optimization promises a metastability for all these networks as if pure immanence can be solved by code.

A future where autonomous policy daemons automatically optimize the internet risks depoliticizing their influence. Amoore warns of the political consequences of this automation, writing, "if the decision were to be rendered easy, automated or preprogrammed, then not only would the decision be effaced, but politics itself is circumscribed."[140] Her words echo in the promises of Saisei Networks, whose FlowCommand makes optimal network management easy. The easy solution effaces its hidden values and politics. Amoore herself calls for a politics of possibility against these technical solutions. She writes that "the question for critique becomes how to sustain potentiality, how to keep open the indeterminate, the unexpected place and the unknowable subject."[141]

Perhaps what needs to be politicized is the optimism of the technological fix. Peter Galison, writing on cybernetics, comments that "perhaps disorganization, noise, and uncontrollability are not the greatest disasters to befall us. Perhaps our calamities are built largely from our efforts at superorganization, silence, and control."[142] Nonsynchronous optimization captures (at the expense of performance) a project of a network of networks that can never be adequately provisioned, whose control will also be partial. Perhaps it is a more apt foundation for the network of networks in that it begins with an admission of limits. Nonsynchronous optimization has a sense of a diversity that cannot be fully known nor solved; it embraces, to recall the words of Bennett, the internet as a "volatile mixture."[143]

CONCLUSION

The internet as Pandaemonium stretches from the microscale of daemons to the macroscales of internet governance and its political economy. In Pandaemonium, daemons enact flow control, working together across the infrastructure. Daemons collaborate to create flows for networks, but their collaborations differ. Nonsynchronous optimizations require daemons at the edges of the infrastructure to be responsible for key decisions during transmission. The center of the infrastructure is left unsettled without an attempt to create some internal metastability. Unruly P2P daemons have prompted internet service providers like Comcast to install new networking computers in their infrastructure. Comcast's decision exemplifies a new trend in networking, away from nonsynchronous communication and toward a polychronous internet.

With only so much space in the pipe, ISPs have invested in more sophisticated daemons able to prioritize larger volumes of traffic and "to ensure that P2P file sharing applications on the Internet do not impair the quality and value of [their] services."[144] More and more, ISPs leverage their flow control as a technological fix to attain a network optimality of managed temporalities. This polychronous optimization produces and assigns various temporalities that have comparative values. Like prime-time television, certain time slots have more value than others. However, the times of a tiered internet have less to do with the hour of the day than with the relations between times. File sharing is assigned less priority, and its forces of coordination and exchange cease to operate optimally. Polychronicity is driven by a profound new ability to remake itself always in service of the optimal.

These changing daemons illuminate the difficult relationship between net neutrality and the internet infrastructure industry. Regulation generally focuses on the ISPs without paying much attention to the industry developing the equipment that violates net neutrality. While these daemons have many legitimate uses in enterprise and private infrastructures, they become the virtualities of ISP infrastructures, the actual features not yet implemented. Regulation stops an ISP from enabling these features, but not from an industry developing them in the first place. Instead, these daemons become a source of what ISPs have described as service delivery innovation.[145] Daemons wait to be the next innovation.

To be effective, net neutrality regulation has to track this industry and encourage the development of daemons that abide by its rules. With daemons that have both many legitimate applications and some configurations that violate neutrality, their movements have to be tracked. The Citizen Lab, in comparison, has demonstrated how network censorship equipment often travels into authoritarian and repressive regimes.[146] Where the Citizen Lab has called for greater export controls of these technologies, internal regulatory agencies should also have a greater understanding of the equipment installed in public internet infrastructures.

Polychronous optimizations will continue to be a policy issue for years to come as it guides the design of new infrastructures. The transition to mobile, for example, has given the telecommunications industry an opportunity to rebuild infrastructure to better enact polychronous optimization. The Third Generation Partnership Project (3GPP) is an industry-initiated standards organization creating protocols and guidelines for mobile infrastructure. The group comprises regional telecommunications standards organizations from China, Europe, India, Japan, Korea, and the United States and is responsible for standardizing mobile wireless protocols such as Long-Term Evolution (LTE) and High-Speed Packet Access (HSPA).[147] These standards deal with the physical, or more accurately *spectrum,* issues necessary for packet-switched communications. The organization also provides guidelines for mobile internet infrastructures, including the Policy and Charging Control architecture (PCC). Started in 2005, the PCC standardized quality of service and the ways in which its members levy usage-based charges. As 3GPP members implement PCC, they install new daemons to apply its charging mechanisms and maintain its quality standards. DPI manufactures like Procera Networks sell products designed to implement these features.[148] These standards allow daemons to attach new metadata to messages, such as subscriber categories and service guarantees, to striate transmission conditions. The global scale of the 3GPP means that its complex logic of optimization extends far beyond any one infrastructure. Instead, it aims to establish these logics across infrastructures. TCP/IP, by contrast, had difficulty enforcing use of its type-of-service flag in the header.

If humans seem too absent for the discussion above, the next chapter moves from focusing on daemons to the feelings about them. What is the experience of having your communications delayed? How do we suffer from buffering? The next chapter describes these feelings through the analysis of five commercials by network providers that describe the various feelings imparted by flow control: frustration, isolation, exclusion, envy, and boredom. Comcast, for example, advertises to people riding the bus that it "owns faster," suggesting that people can pay to enjoy faster internet like paying for a car to avoid public transit. Moving beyond technical solutions, these marketing pleas demonstrate how ISPs describe an optimal internet and attempt to valorize the experience of priority and avoiding frustrating delays.

5 SUFFERING FROM BUFFERING?

Affects of Flow Control

WE SIT IN FRONT OF OUR COMPUTERS waiting for media to load. We stare at the familiar turning circle when a video buffers on YouTube. Buffering postpones the satisfaction of watching another cat play or learning how to assemble a new piece of furniture. At other times, bad connections cause our conversations to stutter into incomprehensible fragments. Distant friends and family cut out or suddenly speed up as the connection resynchronizes. Avatars perish in virtual worlds because of lag: a sudden pause, and we find ourselves staring up from the ground or floating above our digital corpses. Our communications online depend on responsive and reliable rates of transmission to such an extent that we suffer when we lose access. In our everyday internet use, we assume that transmission will be imperceptibly instantaneous. But common occurrences of waiting, frustration, and disconnection rupture this heedlessness, making us aware of transmission. Our cursors turn from a commanding arrow to a helpless circle spinning in an endless loop, so we have to wait a little longer. More packets need to arrive. There is too much "jitter." We wait a little more. For what? Optimal conditions of transmission and a return to blissful heedlessness.

We might wonder as we wait. What bedevils us? Does the browser have a few bad plug-ins? Microsoft's web browser Internet Explorer helps "enhance our experience" by ranking the delay introduced by its plug-ins, telling the user that, for example, a toolbar introduced a 0.07-second delay. Maybe the router should be restarted? New smart plugs allow you to power on and off your electronics remotely through a smartphone app or through Amazon Alexa voice commands. Should the internet service provider (ISP) be contacted to switch to a new service tier? Performance Internet can easily be upgraded to Internet Pro Plus for a fee. Diagnosis also turns inward. Did I cause the delay? What am I doing wrong? Did I download too much and blow the usage cap? Any or all of these worries and anxieties might run through one's mind while waiting.

In these moments, computer screens usually display icons: spinning circles, pinwheels, or tirelessly turning hourglasses. They are examples of what Nicole Starosielski calls the "aesthetics of lag."[1] These icons also resemble "sigils," an old word to describe symbols for demons. No sigil is perhaps more familiar than *ouroboros,* the snake forever eating its tail, now ubiquitous as the spinning loading circle. Staring at these sigils, users might wonder what bedevils their connection. The sigils give no answer. Buffering could be a by-product of a daemonic optimization. The affects of delay and buffering are a key influence of flow control, the power of daemons to create and distribute states of transmission. Such a result could be deliberate (in the case of The Pirate Bay discussed in the next chapter) or a mistake (as in the case of Rogers Internet discussed in chapter 7).

Where past chapters have explained the operation of flow control, this one analyzes the affective influence of daemons. "Affect" is a key concept for understanding media infrastructures, according to Starosielski and Lisa Parks.[2] Building on this approach, I draw a link between the technical workings of flow control and the experience of communication online. As is well understood, lag and buffering create moments when we come into contact with the infrastructure, an awareness of being connected. The causes of buffering and delay are multiple: physical distance, "buggy" routers, obsolete computers. Whatever the cause, buffer is, according to Neta Alexander, an experience "on three different levels: as a temporary emotional distress, as a disruption that triggers various bodily reactions, and as an enduring and unrecognized affective response of anxiety."[3] Prior chapters have explained how daemons create these states; this one studies how avoidance of these experiences of delay and buffering comes to be desirable. How do the technical workings of daemons, in other words, come to be meaningful to us?

In this chapter, I trace a link between unarticulated affect and the feelings associated with buffering. Media theorist Taina Bucher, for example, interviews people about their lay understandings of algorithms. Her work traces the affective influence of algorithms and their relationship to human meanings. She finds an algorithmic imaginary: the ways people understand algorithms.[4] Where her study captures a micropolitics of algorithmic control, I argue that larger systems of meaning for daemons circulate through advertising. Advertisements fill the silence left by sigils.

"Internet not performing well? Time to switch to the fastest Internet."
"Why wait?" These advertising messages give meaning to the a-semiotic work of daemons.

While there has been some illuminating work interviewing internet customers about their lay understandings of the network,[5] these advertisements succinctly articulate a range of feelings associated with flow control. In only thirty seconds or less, commercials appeal to popular feelings about internet use as a value proposition for why the public should pay for their services. These commercials cast optimization as something either frustrating or delightful. Advertisements distill feelings of speed, delay, being in sync, envy, and boredom. They also explain how these feelings exist in context, claiming that some customers feel superior because they do not experience delay like their neighbors. ISPs' advertisements offer a rich source for articulations of the affective influence of flow control. I have selected five commercials to analyze as key testimony about the affective states and feelings inspired by flow control. These selections are intended to work as a means to think through these concepts rather than as a complete catalog of emotions felt when communicating on the internet.

DAEMONS, AFFECT, AND MEANING

My interest in the felt experience of transmission resonates with what Patricia Clough has described as the "affective turn."[6] Affect has a much richer and contested history than can be discussed here,[7] but it can be defined as "pre-individual bodily forces augmenting or diminishing a body's capacity to act."[8] The use of "pre-individual" points to that which circulates before people have feelings or meanings. Affects then are a plurality of conditions, commonalities, and habits or events that are folded into the human experience. Infrastructures have affects. The internet has what Susanna Paasonen, Ken Hillis, and Michael Petit call "networked" affects related to the conditions of communication and being in communication. As they explain,

> Networked communications involve the circulation of data and information, but they equally entail a panoply of affective attachments: articulations of desire, seduction, trust, and memory; sharp jolts of anger and interest; political passions; investments of time, labor, and financial capital; and the frictions and pleasures of archival practices.[9]

Affects here are multiple and broader than just the circulation of data and information, but conditions of transmission have their own affective attachments.

Adrian Mackenzie captures this affective influence of transmission in his concept of "wirelessness":

> ["Wirelessness"] designates an experience toward entanglements with things, objects, gadgets, infrastructures and services and imbued with indistinct sensations and practices of network-associated change. Wirelessness affects how people arrive, depart and inhabit places, how they relate to others and indeed, how they embody change.[10]

Wirelessness is a kind of networked affect that preconditions how people relate to each other in connected spaces.[11] These entanglements—humans on their phones attached to public WiFi and connected to their personal networks—have to be in communication and are made possible by the invisible ether of wireless signals. Daemons also live in these entanglements, and it is their particular affective influence that interests this chapter.

Internet daemons are a unique object through which to study affect. They are at the locus of the conditions of circulation and affective attachments. Their flow control creates frictions and disrupts tempos that register affectively. Flow control is an affective influence. It involves modulations of transmission, leading some networks to entangle better than others, often subtly so. This augments or diminishes a network's capacity to be and a body's ability to be networked.

Daemons' influence is more communicative than informational. This distinguishes the influence of daemons from comparable studies of algorithms. Nick Diakopolous, in his foundational work on computational journalism, emphasizes how algorithms prioritize, classify, associate, and filter information.[12] These algorithmic activities dictate what appears on screen, whereas daemons influence the responsiveness of the screen. Flow control resembles what Tarleton Gillespie describes as a "cycle of anticipation" in his own review of the "relevance of algorithms." Social media anticipate user requests (for instance, autocompleting a search query) to ensure a better, by virtue of being more responsive, user experience.

Daemons' affective influence on networks is a kind of "priming," a concept developed by Brian Massumi, a major contributor to the theory of affect. Priming "orientat[es] a participant's entry into a situation."[13]

In other words, priming involves the preconditions of encounter, and online, these include the conditions of transmission: the waiting; the slight stutter; those moments spent wondering if the Wi-Fi router has to be reset, why the video chat cuts out, or how the last 10 percent of loading always takes longer than the first 90 percent. By modulating the conditions of transmission, internet daemons prime users for their experience on a network as being delayed, timely, or instantaneous. Their flow control assigns resources that enhance or degrade the act of networking.

Priming is felt, but not necessarily consciously. Individual feelings of frustration or delay articulate the broader affects of flow control. These articulations resemble Raymond Williams's concept, foreshadowing the affective turn, of "structures of feeling," which he describes as "a cultural hypothesis" that theorizes "a social experience which is still in process, often indeed not yet recognized as social but taken to be private, idiosyncratic, and even isolating, but in analysis (though rarely otherwise) has its emergent, connecting, and dominating characteristics."[14] Structures of feeling closely fit those individual experiences of staring at the familiar *ouroboros* loop when a video buffers on YouTube. Even though all internet users experience delay (the time taken to sit and wait for content), they often feel it as a unique personal experience. Where Williams focuses on the affective nature of "dominant systems of belief and education,"[15] this chapter follows his logic to analyze the common feelings that ensue from the affective influence of flow control.

I use advertisements to track the articulation of structures of feeling from the affects of flow control. Advertisements are one part of a "circuit from affect to subjectively felt emotional states."[16] Zizi Papacharissi argues that advertising "engages potential consumers through the suggestion of a possible affective attachment they might develop for a product . . . [and therefore] directs audiences to produce particular affects that align with the advertised product."[17] The same logic applies to ISPs advertising their services. Their advertisements give the work of daemons an emotional charge and foster tangible feelings associated with the daemons' influence: frustration at delay, angst from being out of sync, or delight in an otherwise heedless moment of uninterrupted surfing. Advertisements also connect daemons' polychronous optimizations to broader structures of feeling and affects. Fast internet service connects to a more general desire for speed. Conversely, delay exacerbates the anxiety of falling behind or out of touch in a moment of social acceleration. This chapter traces a circuit that begins with the affective priming of flow control that advertisements attach to other affects and articulate in known structures of feeling.

WE OWN FASTER: THE FAST AND THE NON-FASTER

Waiting for the next bus to arrive, commuters seek some modest protection from the rain or snow in small shelters. Marketers have noted the prime locations of these shelters on street corners in urban centers and have begun advertising on their walls. Smart campaigns, like Comcast's in 2007, take advantage of the shelters' unique locations to target commuters. The poster copy reads in big print: "Legal Notice." Below, a declaration also in bold, states "We Own Faster.™" Commuters, the ad continues, do not have to worry, because the bus, with "its many stops," is a "non-Faster form of transportation," so it does not infringe on Comcast's ownership of "speed and swiftness." The ad reminds commuters that their waiting can be avoided. You can pay your way out of the "non-Faster" internet by joining Comcast, just as you can buy a car and drive to work. The ad is particularly ironic given Comcast's use of a bus metaphor to describe packet prioritization in chapter 4. Some packets had to wait to get on the bus while other packets got on immediately. As much as Comcast attempted to use the bus as a neutral metaphor to describe its traffic management, their advertisement reveals the cultural and affective feelings attached to taking the bus. Priority, in its many forms, is a privilege of speed.

The ad affectively attaches internet speed to privilege. Certainly, speed functions as a kind of heedlessness about the conditions of transmission. "Fast" implies that the problems of transmission over a distance never intrude on the user's consciousness. The privilege of fast also allows users to enjoy the wider structure of feeling related to speed. By selling fast, Comcast aligns its internet service with a cultural "chronotopism," a term John Armitage and Joanne Roberts use to refer to the business literature around the turn of the millennium that embraced high speed as a kind of utopia.[18] Speed is valuable. Armitage and Phil Graham suggest high-speed networks have an economic necessity, since modern, or rather hypermodern, capitalism demands the negation of space and time so it can function on the global stage.[19] The growth of high-frequency trading or algorithmic trading, for example, depends on almost zero delay. The Hibernian Express, a network link between New York and London, is currently being built at a cost of $300 million solely to reduce delay by five to six milliseconds.[20] Chronotopism aligns with a widespread myth that political economist Vincent Mosco describes as the "digital sublime."[21] According to the proponents of this myth, the internet promised to annihilate time and space and would be fast enough to put the entire world in instant contact. This sublime feeling of speed, as Comcast reminds us, is not evenly distributed.

Though Comcast wants its customers to feel faster, not all internet users do. By contrasting the slow bus with the fast Comcast network, the ad signals the relationship between status and network performance. As Jonathan Crary notes in his work on the 24/7 society, "one of the superficial but piercing truisms about class society is that the rich never have to wait."[22] The rich (according to Crary) or the fast (according to Comcast) benefit from a faster internet in part because the slow suffer with annoying wait times and interrupted streaming. Comcast reminds those waiting for the bus that, if they had some extra income they could drive, just as those waiting for a download on its basic Economy Plus plan could upgrade for just sixty dollars a month to its Extreme 105 plan. Comcast claims that faster internet service will include faster loading of web pages (because "waiting for pages to load is an annoyance") and uninterrupted streaming, so that "one can stream media without interruptions and long gone are the days of reloading videos or movies in the middle of watching."[23]

These different tiers of speed serve as a reminder that the existence of Fast depends on the existence of "non-Faster." Inequity distinguishes speed, a logic that Paul Virilio considers in his *dromology*, or "study of the logic of speed."[24] For Virilio, speed functions as a new kind of class.[25] Forms of incarceration like the poorhouse, prison, or shantytowns "solve a problem less of enclosure or exclusion than of traffic."[26] By containing their subjects, prisons move slowly, whereas highways and private boulevards afford faster forms of circulation. These two different speeds stratify society like classes. Comcast, similarly, implicitly divides users of the internet into two classes: the Fast and the non-Fast. By positioning itself as "Owning Faster," the company appoints itself the governor of speeds, deciding who gets to luxuriate in fastness and who suffers in non-fastness.

The idea of "owning faster" can also suggest to users a need to accept polychronous optimization as necessary and accept that Comcast knows how best to optimize for speed. With the passing of the FCC Restoring Internet Freedom Order, these types of speed tiers might become more common. New incentives for marketplace innovation likely will lead to even better daemons to stratify bandwidth into ever more granular tiers and classes. In contrast to the United States, in other countries, flow control has become more regulated in recent years (as will be discussed in chapter 7). These network neutrality regulations still allow for reasonable network management. In Canada, ISPs cannot discriminate, but they still can manage transmission on their networks. Cathy Avgiris, executive vice president and general manager of communications and data services at Comcast Cable, explained in a company press release announcing its decision to end usage caps that Comcast is "committed to manage data usage on our network with a clear set of important principles designed to maximize the benefits of using our *high-speed data service* to access the Internet for all of our customers" (italics added).[27] By associating itself with speed, Comcast self-justifies its network optimization as the best way to achieve fastness, essentially inventing its own standard for accountability. In its advertising, Comcast sends a clear signal that it knows how to ensure the broadest possible feeling of speed.

Differences in network performance, however, cannot be described by the feeling of fastness alone.[28] Indeed, fast versus slow oversimplifies the affective influence of flow control. What is the inverse? If the Fast necessitates the non-Fast, what feelings manifest from unprioritized networks? The following two examples focus on the negative side of speed: the feelings of frustration and isolation due to delay. These feelings, as well as fastness and slowness, become part of complex network optimizations that draw on the affective influence of flow control.

SUFFERING FROM BUFFERING? FRUSTRATING ATTENTION

A video of a snowboarder approaching a jump begins to play on a Rogers Internet sales page; it stops just before the snowboarder launches off. A loading bar appears indicating that data must be buffered to provide smooth video playback. The bar appears for only a second before Rogers reveals the twist: the video has been loaded the whole time. Above the loading bar, the snowboarder turns to the viewer (breaking the fourth wall) and explains that customers of Rogers Internet no longer have to wait. Rogers's high-speed internet is the cure for anyone "suffering from buffering." But unlike other companies, Rogers Internet sells both the poison and the cure.

Figure 7. Screenshot of Rogers SpeedBoost web advertisement.

What does it mean to suffer from buffering? The malady, as diagnosed by Rogers, results from the awareness of delay, that feeling of frustration while waiting for the snowboarder to complete the jump, as much as from the delay itself. The loading bar symbolizes delayed gratification. The hoax's power comes from acknowledging that delayed transmissions frustrate users in the same way any unresponsive system would. The snowboarder breaks the fourth wall just at the moment when the viewer expects the pay-off. The ad then knows the moment of peak attention, that emotionally charged time of anticipation, and uses it to deliver its message. In doing so, the ad tries to articulate these affective conditions of waiting as a meaningful emotion to viewers. It articulates the affects of transmission as feelings related to delay and frustrations of cultural expectations around computer use in addition to reasserting its impor- tant role in distributing these attachments through its internet service.

For as long as user experience has been measured in computing, delay causes frustration. Robert B. Miller,[29] a pioneer in human–computer inter- action, found that users disliked a gap between entering their command and receiving the response. He measured frustration by asking how long people would wait for a response from a computer. How quickly did com- puters need to respond to not frustrate users? He found users expected a System Response Time (SRT) of one tenth of a second, meaning that a user expected some response in less than the blink of an eye after enter- ing a command. At the time, a response meant an acknowledgment of an input, rather than the actual output, for example the sound of a click when a mouse selects an object on screen. Users would wait a little longer for new information such as a next page or new frame. As Miller wrote:

The user—and his attention—is captive to the terminal until he receives a response. If he is a busy man, captivity of more than [fifteen] seconds, even for information essential to him, may be more than an annoyance or a disruption. It can readily become a demoralizer—that is a reducer of work pace and of motivation to work.[30]

As computers developed, SRT became a measure of usability. A functional system, one that does not demoralize its users, lessened delay and met users' response expectations.

Researchers in human–computer interaction continued to explore responsiveness long after Miller conducted his studies in the late 1960s.[31] Compaq Computers interviewed over 1,250 workers about their experiences using computers in 1999. A quarter of those surveyed admitted to experiencing daily frustration with their machines (and three quarters admitted to swearing at their computers).[32] Another study asked a class of thirty-seven students what about using computers caused them frustration, and delay online was a common cause. Frustration defined a significant portion of their computer experience. As much as "one third to one half of the time spent in front of the computer was lost due to frustrating experiences" caused by "error messages, timed out/dropped/refused connections, freezes, long download time, and missing/hard-to-find features."[33] Frustration led to anxiety, stress, and discomfort. These studies, while focused on computer use in general, demonstrate that computers affectively charge life on screen and that these affective attachments manifest in feelings or even physical outbursts (such as the Compaq study's finding that 25 percent of workers under the age of twenty-five would occasionally kick their computers).

Delay still frustrates users today.[34] In many ways, internet users may have become more impatient as the technology has accelerated.[35] As a participant stated in a study of internet experience: "You get a bit spoiled I guess once you're used to the quickness, then you want it all the time."[36] Contemporary networks certainly perform faster than early computers did. In 2014, the average latency (or round-trip time) between a command and its response was 0.04025 seconds in the United States and 0.0406 seconds in Canada, according to data from Measurement Lab (M-Lab). Deviation from responsiveness influences user behavior. Research conducted in 2006 found that viewers abandoned videos after four seconds of loading time.[37] In 2009, users would not wait more than two seconds for a shopping website to load.[38] In 2012, users began abandoning a video if it did not load in two seconds.[39] User impatience concerns cloud computing services as well. Google Drive, Dropbox, and BitTorrent Sync have all been evaluated and ranked by their responsiveness. BitTorrent claimed when it launched its new Sync cloud service that it was sixteen times faster than its competitors. Sync took forty-one seconds to upload a 1.36-gigabyte video file, as opposed to DropBox, which took eleven minutes.[40] While the results could be contested, BitTorrent's performance of the test demonstrates the belief that delay threatens user satisfaction with cloud computing. How long is someone willing to wait to access a file in the cloud?

Through delay, flow control functions as a subtle influence on internet use by drawing on cultural expectations of responsiveness. This influence is reminiscent of Gillespie's description of the effects of Digital-Rights-Management (DRM) technologies as a kind of "effective frustration."[41] He suggests that DRM has a certain power as a control technology that does not prevent unauthorized uses but makes transgressions frustrating enough to deter them probabilistically. Digital locks are not unbreakable, but they introduce enough of a delay to sway people from circumventing copyright law. Frigging around, so to speak, with a piece of software becomes a waste of time after a while. Effective frustration depends on digital media being valued because they save time. To put it another way, digital media work when users are in control, not staring at a pinwheel, rebooting the "damn thing" after it crashes, or wasting an hour only to realize it was never going to work in the first place. DRM needs to add only a little bit of frustration in order to discourage certain uses.

Where DRM frustrates users away from authorized use, flow control might frustrate users enough to switch from piracy to legitimate channels of content consumption. Flow control might delay certain networks as a way to discipline user behavior. (Discipline is not always necessary, as internet daemons can forever manage certain users or traffic without a need to modify behavior). Delay frustrates users away from illicit networks, perhaps toward more profitable ones that behave reliably. This relatively gentle pushing is an example of "nudge theory," a popular application of behavioral psychology in which indirect cues reinforce certain behaviors. In the case of flow control, the effects of delay subtly guide users away from networks deemed too costly or risky by internet service providers.[42] Enigmax, a writer for the news blog *TorrentFreak*, which is dedicated to covering Peer-to-Peer (P2P) and piracy issues, accused the cyber-locker RapidShare of using delay to deter pirates.[43] Anyone using the site without a paid account (an unattractive option for someone accustomed to getting content for free) would experience reduced download speeds. Verizon, under investigation by the Federal Communications Commission (FCC) for its throttling of mobile users with unlimited data plans, admitted they used traffic management to "ensure that this small group of customers [who download large amounts of data] do not disadvantage all others."[44] Delay, in other words, affectively influences users to stop being so active without telling them to stop.[45]

The Rogers ad also primes users toward feeling frustrated during the work of watching.[46] Dallas Smythe argues that audiences work for their over-the-air television programs by performing the labor of paying attention to advertisements.[47] Television channels sold advertisers audience commodities: aggregates of attention tied to specific demographics. While Smythe's premise focuses his model on the broadcasting era, J. Macgregor Wise introduces the broader term of "attention assemblage."[48] Attention is not given, but assembled through a multiplicity of sociotechnical practices. Watching videos online involves an attention assemblage that is different from prime-time, popcorn, and a couch. Videos may capture attention either virally, "as a clip that spreads to the masses via digital word-of-mouth mechanisms without significant change," or mimetically, in a form "that lures extensive creative user engagement in the form of parody, pastiche, mash-ups or other derivative work."[49] These distinct modes of attending (either as watching or as manipulating and remixing) require reliable transmission to ensure the appropriate information arrives at the appropriate moment of attention.

The commercial by Rogers Internet reminds viewers of the company's influence over the distribution of delay. Disrupting the attention assemblage is a powerful influence, as considerable effort goes into capturing attention online. Netflix, in its 2012 annual report, acknowledges that their "reputation and ability to attract, retain and serve [their] subscribers is dependent upon the reliable performance of [their] computer systems," and delay is a symptom of unreliability.[50] If it is an ordeal to actually watch the show, if video always buffers, has the network negatively primed the user? By increasing commitment to its public stance in favor of net neutrality, one might conclude that Netflix worried that vertically integrated ISPs like Comcast or Verizon would compete with Netflix by delaying its traffic to frustrate its customers.[51] With its repeal in the United States, Netflix vulnerability might be a new profit center for ISPs.

These few examples, far from being exhaustive, demonstrate the ability of delay and lag to disrupt the attention assemblage of the web.

The commercial draws a link between the affective capacity of flow control to delay and the ensuing feelings of frustration. Internet daemons cause networks to be delayed (intentionally or not). Delay manifests as individual feelings of frustration and impatience that prime internet users: it both disrupts attention assemblages and alters the preferred networks of internet users. But delay causes feelings other than frustration as well: it can isolate and exclude certain users from being in communication with one another. These feelings can be discussed better in relation to the next advertisement.

DANCING BY MYSELF: FEELING LEFT OUT

A man dressed in a trench coat walks to the center of Grand Central Station. Commuters pass by as he stares at its iconic clock. All the noise of human commotion seems to pause as the clock strikes noon. The man pulls off his coat to reveal an all-black outfit. He begins to dance. His moves appear choreographed though no one else joins him. The longer he dances, the more he appears out of sync with the busy station. He begins to search for eye contact only to discover the glares of a small crowd in matching outfits, his peers. He stops and checks his cellphone, which displays a loading bar for a second then a message informing him that the "flash mob" has been pushed back to 12:30 p.m. "Don't be the last to know," an announcer warns before the AT&T logo appears. To put it another way, don't embarrass yourself by dancing like a fool in public because you're behind the times. AT&T's reliable and fast mobile internet promises to keep you better in touch with your fellow dancers.

AT&T plays on such common experiences of disconnection and isolation to remind viewers that reliable transmission ensures better adherence to social tempos. A difference of a second past noon is long enough to distinguish a hipster in a flash mob from a fool dancing alone.[52] "Information," as Virilio writes, "is only of value if it is delivered fast."[53] Social coordination and cooperation depend on certain rates of transmission so that, for example, the flash mob can dance in formation. Temporalities, as stated above, are manifolds of past, future, and present. The ad assumes the dancer is part of one temporality. The scene in Grand Central presumably happened after a shared meeting to discuss the plan, set a time, and synchronize their watches. Up until the event,

Figure 8. AT&T "Dancing Alone" commercial.

the dancers likely practiced their moves on their own in preparation for the event. They converged in the station, all in sync, but an email informs most of the participants of a delay. They adjust accordingly, except for the protagonist, who falls out of sync with his peers. He is behind the times just enough that his future entails dancing alone in front of his unamused friends. The public humiliation and regret of being the lone dancer stands in for the many real anxieties caused by being disconnected from social temporalities. The AT&T ad whispers subtextually that you need a fast network to keep up with the times.

These concerns are quite real. In the United Kingdom, for example, ISP TalkTalk misclassified the OnLive gaming service as P2P traffic.[54] As a result, gamers experienced random disconnections and delay. They suffered, in other words, from being unable to participate in a virtual community, a subtle isolation caused by flow control. Though delays to BitTorrent and other P2P file-sharing networks have been well documented, concerns have also been raised that some ISPs shape internet telephone, or Voice over Internet Protocol (VoIP), traffic. A joint investigation by the Body of European Regulators of Electronic Communications (BEREC) and the European Commission (EC) found at least one ISP that managed VoIP traffic on wired networks and twenty-seven mobile operators that restricted VoIP traffic to varying levels.[55] To the end user, these disruptions may be both mysterious and frustrating when just trying to catch up with friends.

While the commercial expresses the anxiety of being disconnected, flow control might also create anxiety causing people to disconnect. Packet inspection daemons increasingly count usage, charging users a fee for transmitting data above these limits.[56] Feelings manifest as a result of these caps. Participants in one study of bandwidth caps "struggled with understanding what mysterious processes or applications and websites were using up bandwidth."[57] Users worry that they will "go over their cap" and "have to pay more." The threat of a high bill with overage charges compels users subject to a cap on their bandwidth to regulate their use accordingly. As one participant of the study put it: "I think [my daughter] is actually very sweet when she said she won't have Facebook and all that because Facebook would suck [bandwidth]. And I used to Skype full time with my friends in the UK [but] now [I] stopped doing that."[58] These anxieties speak to how an awareness of overage might function as another disciplinary force on users. Fear that their ISPs watch their bandwidth consumption (no matter the accuracy of these charges[59]) leads to an economization of internet usage in which users internalize the costs of bandwidth and regulate their behavior.

ISPs have devised a cure for these worries: zero rating, a technique used by ISPs to exclude certain services like their own movie stores, sponsored content, or internet telephony services from the data cap. Comcast offered an internet telephony service without a cap so users can talk away without worrying about overages.[60] Naturally, its competitors' VoIP services are not exempt from the cap. In Canada, mobile internet providers had tried to offer their own television streaming, charging by the hour rather than the megabyte, so subscribers to Bell Mobility can enjoy Bell Mobile TV for ten hours, but they have to worry about exceeding their data limit if they watch too much Netflix.[61]

So far, advertisements have connected the affects of flow control with broader structures of feeling related to acceleration or feelings of being delayed. The AT&T commercial suggests another "digital divide." Generally, divides exist between those who can afford access and those who cannot, the information "haves" and "have-nots."[62] AT&T draws a divide between those who can ignore the conditions of transmission and those who must be constantly aware, those who have to worry about whether they will receive the update about the flash mob in time and those who take the network for granted. These divides suggest how flow control has a relational influence. Experiences of delay and other network effects are always comparable. Slow permits the fast. Frustration makes relief all the more appealing. The next section analyzes how network optimization creates a broader structure of feeling that includes both the delayed and the accelerated.

YOU CAN'T GET THIS WITH THE OTHER GUYS: THE OPTIMIZED AND THE DISOPTIMIZED

Two men, a host and his guest, sit in front of a modern iMac computer. Something has prompted them to use the internet, though their motivations for going online, like the computer screen, are hidden from the audience. The action begins with the guest's reaction to the speed of his host's computer connection. "This is awesome," he exclaims, as the scene cuts to an angle showing the computer screen playing a music video. When the guest protests, "but I have the exact same computer and mine is never this fast," the host turns to the camera to explain: "The difference is I have Rogers Internet with their SpeedBoost technology. It detects when there is available bandwidth and it automatically turbocharges stuff so it loads way faster." As he finishes his pitch, his wife brings the two men cups of coffee. She has no speaking role and does not even acknowledge the guest. For approximately five of the scene's twenty-three seconds, she lovingly caresses her husband and then walks off. All the while, the guest looks at them both, appearing jealous not only of the host's wife but also of his superior internet. "That's just not fair," he laments, and the host agrees, "No, it is not fair." The advertisement aims to convince Canadian consumers to subscribe to Rogers Internet because its SpeedBoost technology is something "you can't get with the other guy's network."[63]

The commercial further connects those feelings caused by delay with a broader social trend called "social acceleration." This trend is a long-term and historic process distinct from, though related to, economic change (i.e., capitalism) and noneconomic factors by which people experience a loss or decline of the amount of time available for perception and decision making.[64] (Concern over the fast pace of life dates at least as far back as Montesquieu commenting on the hurry of France and Alex de Tocqueville's concerns over the restless American character.[65]) Social acceleration includes accelerations in the rate of technological devel-

Figure 9. Rogers "Not Fair" commercial.

opment, social change, and the pace of life.[66] Less time is allowed for decision or reflection. Since these cycles of acceleration cause a loss, they provoke anxiety that there is no longer time to think, deliberate, or relax.[67] Instead, people have to constantly react to keep up with the times. Crary describes this contemporary anxiety to keep up as "near irresistible because of the portent of social and economic failure—the fear of falling behind, of being deemed outdated."[68] Social acceleration might be seen to intensify those feelings of anxiety and isolation when desynchronized from the fast pace of society. Any moment spent doing anything other than interacting is wasted time.

Yet social acceleration is not an even process (not everyone accelerates). The Rogers commercial gestures toward this uneven distribution of acceleration. The ad articulates a sense of flow control as a process of uneven modulations that distribute feelings of delay, anxiety, and speed that closely relate to class and privilege. A future not evenly distributed. Some users feel frustration, and others exuberance. Some applications seem delayed, and others seem prompt and reliable. It is not just fast and slow, for as seen in the commercial, uneven flow control opens up a field of difference that allows a person to act smug and privileged. These commercials sell their services as providing privileged access to these feelings while reminding viewers that ending delay and isolation might be just a service tier away.

This tiered system resembles what Sarah Sharma, in her writings on time and power, theorizes as a "bio-political economy of time," which she explains as "concerned with the multiplicity of time, the interdependent and inequitable relations of temporal difference that are compressed deep within the social fabric."[69] She gives the example of air travel, a relevant example here, since communication and transportation have been separate only since the electric telegraph. Air travel has its own economy of time, the time spent in a plane's seats. Passengers can pay to travel first class and enjoy the trip in spacious seats or be forced to endure the constant innovations in economy-class seat design. Yet, this luxury can be justified only amid the demands of an overreaching work life. As Sharma writes, first class participates in the "normalizing of overwork by making it more palatable."[70] In other words, first-class travel makes overwork luxurious.[71] By referring to these relations as an economy, Sharma emphasizes the relative values of different feelings, which resemble the different costs attached to service tiers by Rogers Internet. By seating them next to each other, Rogers draws a comparison between the host and the guest as symbols of different connection statuses. "The other guys" refers to those suffering from buffering, feeling out of touch and slow. Conversely, Rogers customers experience a lot more than fast: an attractive feeling for affluent households with no time to lose. The optimized and the disoptimized are on display.

In the commercial, Rogers Internet sells an accelerated temporality known as SpeedBoost, part of its broader polychronous optimization. SpeedBoost is a branded name for a quality-of-service configuration that accelerates short bursts of data, resulting in faster speeds for specific applications like YouTube.[72] Faster, but contextually faster. Users pay to access boosted speeds to avoid waiting for videos or short bursts of data. SpeedBoost depends on daemons to choose these opportunities and select applications for boosting. Users experience a contextually faster internet with certain boosted applications chosen by configured algorithms and delayed applications like P2P file sharing.

Feelings of flow control, then, include moments of exuberance, and of the sublime, but also of frustration. While the guest character likely will return home to the disappointment of a slow internet, he experiences a moment of joy at being able to *use* a fast internet connection. He notices that awesome feeling that the host experiences every day. Suddenly the internet actually behaves according to cultural expectations of computing and chronotopism: everything is fast and users can be heedless of the conditions of transmission.

Rogers Internet further blends the value of boosted speed with male fantasies of being in the driver's seat and being an object of desire. The lingering touch of the host's wife serves to remind the audience of the inadequacy of the other guy. To the targeted masculine audience, a fast internet is a status symbol just like an attractive, subservient wife. The ad depends on convincing its audience that access to this boosted temporality is valuable enough to switch to Rogers and situates the wife as another object of desire as part of this status. The guest embodies "the other guy," as he lacks the status of both speed and an attractive wife, but his exclusion is necessary because the value of a boosted temporality depends on the existence of an "other guy" who moves slowly and lacks status. Rogers attempts social stratification through describing the value of the boost in its advertisement and by enacting a less frustrating internet experience with its SpeedBoost technology. This stratification exemplifies one form of network optimization that regularizes relations and hierarchies within internet communications.

What can be done to resist this uneven distribution? Not much, apart from switching providers, according to these four advertisements. Each lacks any representation of audience reception and/or resistance to flow control. How do people respond to delay other than with frustration? Getting up out of the chair or doing something else seems like a more plausible response than passively waiting. A penultimate video suggests how a broader desire for speed may override such tactical responses. Perhaps it is easier to wait a little longer than it is to come to terms with the real issue. Desire for heedless transmission necessitated by capitalism, assumed by social acceleration, or mythologized by the internet may fold into home internet users' willingness to wait a little longer rather than admit to being one of the non-Fast.

WHAT DO WE DO WHILE WAITING?

A finger pushes down on a mouse, tapping out a rhythm to match the boredom of a man waiting in front of his computer. The commercial cuts to his computer screen showing another loading bar. Where the other commercials have alluded to the frustration of delay or have condensed it, this commercial dwells on delay for its entirety. The man has to find ways to pass the time until his download finishes. He bounces a ball then tries some stretches until eventually crying out to his offscreen partner to ask if their internet is slow. "Yes," a voice replies back, and then the commercial turns back to the man's face to show he has grown a thick beard whose length gives a very obvious cue to the viewers about how much time has been wasted. The screen goes black, and again an ISP, this time RoadRunner Internet, reminds its audience not to waste their time and to get faster service. The beard is a reminder that time spent waiting can never be regained. "Speed is time saved in the most absolute sense of the word," according to Virilio, "since it becomes human time."[73] Each second spent waiting is lost, dead forever. Though the commercial never suggests an answer, the question is still: Why suffer from buffering? Could waiting be something other than a waste of time? Why wait longer? Why not get up and leave?

The protagonist comes close to unplugging but never does. Instead, he exemplifies what Linda Stone popularly called "continuous partial attention."[74] Stone devised the term to refer to the phenomenon of users paying attention to multiple media at once. The protagonist demonstrates this experience as he exercises and stretches but never stops partially attending to his computer. If he left the computer altogether, he would have rejected the tempo of the internet. Instead, he shows a much more troublesome aspect of how flow control folds with other social desires to enforce its influence.

The emotions described above help understand why we do not look away.[75] Digital culture developed with a promise of both responsive machines and a better ability to manage society.[76] Delay frustrates the desires of various computer cultures for users to feel in control. Perhaps responsiveness isn't the issue: perhaps users simply seek the satisfaction of finishing a job, the work of attending. Or do the demands of capitalism compel users to endure waiting because the threat of leaving may be too costly? Do users wait in order to sustain the myth of the obliteration of time and space? Chronotopism has woven a strong desire for speed into society. Perhaps waiting is an extension of a technological fetish that David Harvey describes as when "we endow technologies—mere things—with powers they do not have (e.g., the ability to solve social problems, to keep the economy vibrant, or to provide us with a superior life)."[77] The fetish creates a desire to wait in order to attain this superior life, and turning away might represent too painful an acknowledgment that it is a fantasy. All these possibilities represent only the start of a catalog of the desires imbricated with flow control, augmenting its influence.

The familiar *ouroboros* sigil seems to reinforce the desire to keep staring. Web design techniques, for example, attempt to extend the user's patience by avoiding any indication of wait time. Most loading indicators mimic the *ouroboros* sigil rather than a more informative progress bar. The first browsers, like Mosaic or Netscape, set the trend by using a "throbber" animation at the top right of the screen to indicate a page's loading. The throbber pulses, spins, or shows a dancing dragon until the page loads, but unlike a progress bar, it does not indicate wait time. If experimental research suggests that a progress bar lessens the frustration of delay,[78] then why not substitute it for a throbber? Too difficult technically? Possibly, but a progress bar might also be too much of an admission of failure to be responsive for a firm like Netscape then, or Netflix now, to accept. Or perhaps adding a loading bar would disrupt the user's attention too much (by allowing a glance away or another momentary tactic) to be permitted by the attention assemblage. If one knew the amount of time to wait, one could leave and do other tasks. A progress bar allows you to slack off or step away. Instead, the sigil eschews even the estimation of an outcome, and the uncertain delay of the throbber tempts the user to keep waiting, as a response could be a moment away.

Chronotopism and a need for speed translate into unattainable definitions of the optimal. A good network is a fast network even though a fast network cannot be good to all its customers. The realities of shared infrastructure imply that not everyone can be fast. Instead, daemons are programmed or have to manage bandwidth inequitably in order to maintain the status of speed, instant contact, and no waiting for those who can pay for these feelings. The challenge in a polychromous optimization is to find new ways to stratify users, to create value through the modulations of transmission.

Could other emotions be a speculative basis for another optimization? Could delay and lag be seen as a common, rather than individual, feeling? Instead of trying to one-up our neighbors, the limits of bandwidth could be treated as a shared concern and delay could become a cause for inclusion rather than isolation. Crary notes that waiting has a social dimension, as seen in the last moments of the Soviet Union as documented in the film *D'Est* by Chantal Akerman. The film includes long scenes of waiting, a common experience in this forgotten time. This waiting is a very different way to deal with issues of scarcity from what these five commercials propose. Crary writes, "mixed in with the annoyances and frustrations is the humble and artless dignity of waiting, of being patient as deference to others, as a tactic of acceptance of time shared in common."[79] Waiting, while frustrating, also becomes a moment of common connection and sharing time, a very different form of queue management. Of all the concepts discussed so far, perhaps these feelings remain the most abstract for today's society. Perhaps the performance lost in nonsynchronous optimization might not be so bad after all.

CONCLUSION

The future of internet daemons might resemble one last commercial depicting people playing ping-pong and wearing virtual reality (VR) headsets. Imagine if a video feed from a camera strapped to the front of the headset replaced a player's regular vision. Could people play ping-pong mediated through this apparatus? Would the feed be responsive enough for people to react in time? Or would it be a game of two people, each in solitude, swinging into the air and connecting with neither the ball nor each other? These questions are not far off from an emergent future of autonomous cars, augmented reality, cloud computing, and the Internet of Things (IoT). These devices all require constant, instant communication, and the slightest delay might cause these interactions to fall out of sync. All these activities require daemons. These augmented realities—from ping-pong to smart phones—only increase their influence in mediating digital communication.

An augmented-reality ping-pong match is one of a few scenarios imagined by the Swedish internet service provider ume.net, part of Umeå Energi. The scenario figures in the company's "Living with Lag" marketing campaign promoting its new gigabit internet service. Two commercials depict the ping-pong match and other attempts to perform everyday tasks while wearing a VR headset.[80] In the ping-pong scenario, one player serves the ball, which bounces across the table toward the other player wearing the headset. The wearer swings late, well after the ball has bounced off the table. Whether these people succeed in their tasks largely depends on the state of the headset. The commercial explains that the headset's video feed is delayed either by a third of a second in normal mode or by three seconds in lag mode. Wearers know they are in lag mode when a loading sigil appears in their video feed. The audience knows too. The commercial's point of view switches to the video feed seen from inside the VR headset. During the ping-pong match, the sigil arrives to indicate lag mode, the steady bounce cuts out, and the player swings too late. These videos serve as a reminder that internet communication is not simply about sending messages, but about the ability to interact and take part in society, participation that suffers affectively because of slight lag or delay.

The "Living with Lag" commercial ends with a simple question: "You wouldn't accept lag offline, so why do it online?" As always, the solution is ume.net's faster gigabit service. This depiction of "lag mode," like so many ISP commercials, articulates the affective influence of transmission, priming the player's reaction to the ball. The ISP's daemons coordinate to avoid lag mode or to relegate some networks to it. While I have largely focused on daemons' relations to P2P networks and cloud computing, it is not difficult to imagine the work of daemons that would be required to enable and optimize the mediated experience of augmented reality networks. The internet daemons of tomorrow might optimize a world in which some people are more present due to the priority of their network connection while others seem out of touch.

The uneven influence of daemons will continue to demand critical attention, since they likely will not be in the service of everyone equally. As daemons become more intelligent, big data and the standing reserve of bits[81] will offer new insights to include in their calculations. Currently the packet provides a tangible unit by which to understand daemonic calculations, but how will future daemons make decisions? For example, the ISP Cable One used customers' credit scores to decide which service level to provide them.[82] Will daemons optimize for physical location? Could service plans be based on lifestyle choices, for example a musical commuter or a late-night clubber? What other metadata might expand their gaze?

The affective influence of flow control provides a better understanding of the influence of control than the usual concerns about a nonneutral internet. Often, these concerns are framed as a cableization of the internet in which users pay for access to certain walled gardens (as in: do you enjoy social media? Access is another five dollars per month).[83] Such warnings overlook the flexibility of flow control. It is a much more subtle influence that maintains an open internet while shaping, controlling, and disciplining use through uneven feelings of network performance. Flow control works through distinctions of experience, not in blocks or restrictions. ISPs use the affective influence of flow control to create a structure of feeling that might vary across their network or per application: some applications and users benefit from a boosted internet; the other guys sit and suffer and wait.

Perhaps the most unsettling aspect of considering the implications of "Living with Lag" is the idea that an outside view will continue to exist at all. The advertisement's punch line relies on the ability of the audience to objectively watch, from their secure position in real time, a person struggle to live in lag mode. Manuel Castells warned about a timeless time when the local, natural sequence of time would be disrupted.[84] While this notion takes the naturalness of time too much for granted, it does provoke questions about what temporalities might be called public? What times are shared? A polychronous internet might replace a default transmission experience, a minimum download speed for example, with an economy of transmission. In such an internet, there would be no objective experience by which to gauge whether a connection is fast or slow, no viewpoint outside the headset.

For now, the feelings wrought by the affective influence of flow control and captured in these five commercials include the pleasure of speed and instant communication, but also anxiety, frustration, isolation, and the boredom of waiting for the device to load. These feelings articulate the intentional and unintentional affective influence of flow control. Daemonically managed latency, prioritization, and congestion affectively charge online communication, which can lead to tangible feelings of exuberance or frustration. While these feelings seem so personal when we experience them, ISPs sell their services based on reliably delivering them. So often, internet use is a reminder of working within the confines and limits of a technology, rather than actualizing myths of freedom like the blue skies of Windows, the galaxies of Apple, or the instant world of the information superhighway. Could a shared acknowledgment that a common internet means a little waiting for *everyone* lessen the influence of flow control? Could there even be a pleasure in waiting together?

Polychronous optimization has not gone unchallenged, nor does it operate with absolute certainty. A key struggle over the internet now unfolds over the conditions of transmission. Internet hackers and pirates flaunt attempts to optimize the internet by enlisting their own algorithms to cloak or elude traffic management. The next chapter considers one reaction to flow control: the activism of The Pirate Bay (TPB). Since 2003, TPB's website has been one of the most public symbols of a free and unmanaged internet—for better or worse. Part of their multifaceted struggle includes the elusion of flow control.

6 THE DISOPTIMIZED

The Ambiguous Tactics of The Pirate Bay

ON JANUARY 31, 2008, Swedish authorities filed charges against the three administrators of the infamous site "The Pirate Bay" (TPB): Fredrik Neij, Gottfrid Svartholm Warg, and Peter Sunde. The trial of the site's administrators was one front in a long battle to remove TPB from the internet. The website had served as the homepage for internet piracy since its launch in 2003 and belonged to a broader propiracy, anticopyright movement in Sweden.[1] This informal movement included political parties and think tanks, while the TPB team coordinated an easy-to-find and politically vocal website that facilitated mass piracy. The website acted mostly as a search engine for BitTorrent files, allowing people to search for legal and illegal content shared online and had also acted as a tracker that coordinated this Peer-to-Peer (P2P) file sharing for a time. As it was one of the most popular websites in the world, TPB's web traffic gave its administrators political influence that they leveraged to become critics of copyright and proponents of free copying. Jonas Andersson Schwarz, who has written an in-depth history of the group and its relationship to online file sharing, describes their politics as "a publicly visible stance, supportive of unrestricted file-sharing."[2]

The events that led to the TPB trial and eventually jail time for its administrators began two years earlier. Police forces raided TPB, confiscated its fifteen servers, and arrested three people on May 31, 2006.[3] Reports later indicated that international groups, specifically the Motion Picture Association of America (MPAA), pressured the Swedish government and police into action.[4] After the raid, the MPAA released a statement celebrating the end of the site. The Pirate Bay countered by bringing the site back online three days later with their usual logo replaced by a phoenix rising to celebrate its resurrection.

TPB's political and practical support of copyright infringement made them a key target of Hollywood's war on online piracy. Hollywood, to be fair, was just one copyright holder antagonized by The Pirate Bay's admins. With sly, offensive, and rude remarks, the "Legal Threats" page on their website cataloged their responses to the frequent requests by media firms and rights holders to remove infringing torrents. In their various replies, administrators explained that they kept the site as open as possible; TPB did not censor any of the torrents on their server. As spokesperson for TPB, Sunde explained in an interview: "We have created an empty site where the only condition was that you cannot upload something where content doesn't match the description or if it blatantly is criminal in Sweden."[5] Elsewhere he says, "we have a strong policy at TPB that we do not censor anything."[6] As court cases shuttered other P2P networks, TPB endured as a global symbol of online piracy. Nonetheless, keeping the site online had not been easy. It had faced numerous challenges, including constant legal threats, police raids, and domain seizures, and now the administrators faced jail time.

Ultimately, the trial was as much about securing infrastructure as it was about copyright. The pirates popularized BitTorrent and pushed to make BitTorrent networks more difficult to manage. These tactics undermined the work of daemons, especially the use of Deep-Packet-Inspection (DPI) technologies to protect copyright. While there has been much discussion of the legal maneuvers of the group and its trial,[7] there has been less focus on the group's infrastructural tactics. Behind the symbol of a phoenix rising that appeared on the relaunched website was a lot of technical work. Following police questioning, TPB's admins and volunteers had quickly rebuilt the servers and other infrastructure needed to keep the site online. The relaunch ended up being one of the many ways that the advocacy of TPB turned to matters of internet infrastructure, and ultimately to the work of daemons.

Where hexes and wards repel demons, P2P and "dark" networks ("darknets," anonymous networks) repel internet daemons. In their struggles to stay online, TPB admins tried to discover the limitations of daemonic control and then undermine it. This conflict happened deep within the internet's infrastructure, largely outside public view. TPB relied on new developments in the BitTorrent protocol to become more difficult to shut down. Eventually, they tried to shield against the watchful gazes of daemons by launching a virtual private network (VPN) that encrypted its customers' packets. These tactics help not only to define the limits of flow control but also to introduce an alternative to polychronous optimization. For all the antics on the TPB website, its admins and its broader movement are primarily motivated by a desire for even greater decentralization of internet control.

This chapter explores these strategies and tactics developed by TPB admins to elude flow control. My use of "elude" is deliberate. The word comes from Martin Joughin's English translation of a conversation between Antonio Negri and Gilles Deleuze from the French journal *Future Antérieur,* which appears in the book *Negotiations.*[8] Joughin translates the original French phrase "pour échapper au contrôle" as "so we can elude control." He substitutes "elude" for the French verb *échapper,* which can also translate as "escape," "dodge," or "run away."[9] TPB's case resonates with multiple of these meanings of *échapper*: its use of BitTorrent enacts *elusion* as a kind of *running away,* whereas darknets are an attempt to *dodge.* TPB's case, then, illustrates the elusion of flow control, building on the limits of control discussed in chapter 1.

PIRATBYRÅN, ACCELERATIONISM, AND ESCALATIONISM

The Piratbyrån, or "Piracy Bureau," started TPB. The bureau was, by its own admission, "a cluster with fuzzy borders."[10] From 2003 to its end in 2010, Piratbyrån was a think tank, an alternative news site, an artists' movement, and a hacktivist project. Schwarz explains: "Part of the hazy nature of Piratbyrån was that they avoided making formal decisions, instead organizing in real time on IRC [Internet Relay Chat]."[11] The name of the cluster parodied the Swedish Anti-Piracy Bureau, a government initiative to thwart copyright infringement. As the Anti-Piracy Bureau tried to find ways to eliminate piracy, the Piratbyrån sought to proliferate it and to embrace piracy not simply as anticopyright, but as a different kind of politics altogether.

This propiracy movement, I have argued elsewhere, has a centrifugal politics.[12] Pirates desire networks without centers, a kind of rhizomatic communication always in flux. This strategy can be witnessed in many of the group's tactics and in the P2P networks described in chapter 4. Take Kopimism, a concept popularized by the Piratbyrån and now a religion that celebrates the copy.[13] Unlike Creative Commons (its clear inspiration), a Kopimi logo indicates that its creators want people to copy it. In their manifesto, "POwr, xxxx, Broccoli and KOPIMI," the Piratbyrån offered 100 slogans. Though the absurd, controversial, and political tone of the manifesto resists any *one* reading, it clearly embraces Kopimism, encouraging its readers to "/join #kopimi," to "upload," to "invent or misuse Kopimi," and to "share files with anyone who wants."[14] Like a rhizome, Kopimism wants every licensed object to be generative. "To be rhizomorphous," according to Gilles Deleuze and Félix Guattari, "is to produce stems and filaments that seem to be roots, or better yet connect with them by penetrating the trunk, but put them to strange new uses."[15] Kopimism captures this rhizomatics that seeks to create not only networks without centers, but networks that undermine central authorities. This centrifugal approach fits within the long history of piracy. In its many forms, piracy has been a form of communication and, earlier still, of transportation that resists central authority and has undermined the authorized movement of goods, whether under the dominion of queen or capital. In his history of piracy from the high seas to the hackers and phreakers of the late twentieth century, Adrian Johns concludes that piracy is deeply embedded in modernity and in the history of property regimes, so specific manifestations of piracy resist historically specific property regimes.[16] And Piratbyrån's interest in centrifuge, while not discussed in Johns's book, contests the mechanism of security and authority necessary for the *intellectual* property regime.

This centrifugal politics has manifested in confrontations with culture industries, with governments, and with internet daemons. Where the first two confrontations occur in courtrooms and ballot boxes, Piratbyrån's opposition to daemons occurs in the infrastructure of the internet. To contest daemons, TPB became something like a war machine, a vehicle propelled to stay out of the reach of control. Deleuze and Guattari introduce the "war machine" to describe something outside the state: "It is not enough to affirm the war machine is external to the apparatus. It is necessary to reach the point of conceiving the war machine as itself a pure form of exteriority, whereas the State apparatus constitutes the form of interiority we habitually take as a model."[17] Like a war machine, TPB had to invent new tactics to elude being captured and itself integrated into the circuits of optimization online.

Rasmus Fleischer, one of the key members of the group and now a prominent academic, reflected on these tactics in a 2010 blog post. His reflections are worth quoting at length:

In 2005, we arranged with Piratbyrån a May Day celebration. It was, if I remember it right, just at the time when Sweden was about to implement harsher copyright laws, and even politicians began to realize that the regulation of file-sharing activity was actually becoming political. The celebration, however, was not in a mood of sadness or protest, but rather a joyful affirmation of the openness of P2P networks. One of the slogans: "Welfare begins at 100 mbit." Accelerating digital communications and enabling access was fresh strategies which produced a kind of politics which did not fit into the Swedish party system. This accelerationism also enabled a certain political transversality and new alliances between hackers, artists and intellectuals, and it could quite easily be underpinned by a mainstream deleuzianism and/or benjaminism. All this while entertainment industries kept clinging on to the model of selling "units" (cd, dvd).[18]

The freshness of piracy certainly inspired political tactics, such as the rise of the Swedish and later European pirate parties (though they are largely unaffiliated with the Piratbyrån), but it also inspired the cultivation of new tactics to thwart attempts to control the internet. He characterized these tactics as "accelerationism." The term reflects some of the unpredicted success the group had just experienced. Two years earlier, the Piratbyrån had launched TPB. The public website became a phenomenon, as will be discussed later, actualizing a popular embrace of copying and sharing. The success, however, did not last.

In the same blog post, Fleischer noted an emerging turn away from these tactics: "We certainly do not call for accelerated communications any more." Political interest had shifted, and the movement had begun to turn back from its prior strategy: Fleischer now suggested a switch from growth to hiding. He called, tentatively, for an "escalationism" characterized by adopting tactics such as encryption, darknets, and tunneling. His comment resonated with a turn to tunneling by TPB with the launch of its IPREDator VPN discussed later on.

Accelerationism and escalationism are two strategies developed by the Piratbyrån that eluded control. Accelerationism eluded control by moving faster than or outrunning the modulations of daemons, tactics that stay ahead of a daemon's gaze or grow faster than can be contained. Escalationism, conversely, dodged control; it is fatalistic, in contrast to the optimism of accelerationism. Escalationism tried to be hidden, though not unknown, to control—at least for a time. Both these tactics raise important questions for the study of flow control.

Fleischer's use of accelerationism predates the recent academic interest in accelerationism, particularly the attempt to create a progressive accelerationism in light of its dark interpretation by Nick Land.[19] Land's accelerationism interpreted a passage by Deleuze and Guattari that a revolutionary path might not "withdraw from the process, but to go further, to 'accelerate the process.'"[20] Land, who has been called a Deleuzian Thatcherite by a foremost theorist on accelerationism, Benjamin Noys,[21] interpreted the quote as a call to turn toward capitalism, to accelerate its tendencies, in order to bring about its end. This suicidal turn, depoliticized by antihumanist themes in Land's thought and subsequent speculative realist work, has been further marred by Land's participation in the "neoreactionary," "Dark Enlightenment" movement, which embraces the market so fully it jettisons democracy, diversity, and equality.[22] The concept, however, has moved past these bleak origins. Nick Srnicek and Alex Williams have called for a "left-wing" accelerationism that frees the concept from capitalism and looks to technology and automation as engines of human progress.[23]

Accelerationism has a polysemy: it is capable of being both a call for fully automated luxury communism and a faith that capitalism is a machine sent from the future to destroy humanity. The piratical position to these various meanings is not entirely clear. The embrace of welfare, postscarcity, and high technology advocated by pirates resonates with a positive accelerationism. Yet, there is a degree of fatalism in Fleischer's later discussion of escalationism as a way to avoid a darker future by triggering a confrontation now. Similar to Deleuze and Guattari's discussion of acceleration and capitalism, escalationism entertains the possibility of disaster. My ensuing discussion of the Piratbyrån has an unsettled relationship with accelerationism, which requires more critical reflection, especially in reference to critiques of the idea.[24] Such a project is well beyond a discussion of infrastructural politics on the internet, but the ambiguous position of accelerationism in this chapter should serve as a reminder to treat these concepts with caution even as they clarify TPB's strategies.[25]

COPY AND PASTE: ACCELERATIONISM AND THE PIRATE BAY

A difference in tactics between TPB's admins and the hacker collective Anonymous illustrates the accelerationist approach. In 2012, TPB's website faced being banned within the United Kingdom. The British courts ordered local ISPs to block the website.[26] In line with other instances of internet censorship, the block altered TPB's local domain name systems to prevent customers from locating their servers. Pirates, hackers, and free-speech advocates quickly responded by launching new websites with lists of proxy servers and alternative domain names that allowed Britons to circumvent the block. UKAnonymous2012, a part of the hacktivist group Anonymous, responded in typical fashion by launching a Distributed Denial of Service (DDoS) attack called #OpTPB. The operation targeted Virgin Media, one of the ISPs participating in the block. DDoS is a core tactic for Anonymous and others engaged in politically motivated hacking or hacktivism.[27] TPB admins responded to the DDoS attacks in a Facebook post:

> Seems like some random Anonymous groups have run a DDoS campaign against Virgin media and some other sites. We'd like to be clear about our view on this: We do NOT encourage these actions. We believe in the open and free internets, where anyone can express their views. Even if we strongly disagree with them and even if they hate us. So don't fight them using their ugly methods. DDoS and blocks are both forms of censorship.[28]

Instead of DDoS attacks, TPB's Facebook post suggested that "if you want to help: start a tracker, arrange a manifestation, join or start a pirate party, teach your friends the art of bittorrent, set up a proxy, write your political representatives, develop a new p2p protocol."[29] Where UKAnonymous2012 created a spectacle through its DDoS campaign, TPB admins encouraged their users to copy and paste. In the face of threats, TPB's posts called for more copying; the accelerationist solution was to grow, expand, and intensify P2P networking.

The Pirate Bay website can be considered an accelerationist tactic carried out by the Piratbyrån, who started TPB on November 21, 2003.[30] Rasmus Fleischer recalled: "It started off as just a little part of the site. Our forum was more important. Even the links were more important than the [torrent] tracker."[31] The tracker site became so popular, however, that the Piratbyrån decided to split it into a separate organization in October 2004.[32] Piratbyrån handed administration to three men in their twenties: Warg (aka: Anakata), Neij (aka: TiAMO), and Sunde (aka: brokep). Their participation was political. Warg stated: "I see the Pirate Bay as a sort of organized civil disobedience to force the change of current copyright laws and the copyright climate."[33] The three administrators worked in their spare time to run the site and serve as its public representatives. In addition, Mikael Viborg, a prominent lawyer in Sweden, provided legal assistance to the site.[34] And Carl Lundström, a controversial Swedish businessman, helped to fund the site's launch.[35] This strange mix is further proof of Fleischer's claim that accelerationism did not conform to conventional Swedish politics.

TPB accelerated the growth of piracy simply by staying online. The website has been among the top five BitTorrent sites on the internet, and as of this writing, it remains online, unlike most sites of its contemporaries.[36] TPB rose to prominence by enduring a series of contractions of mass piracy beginning with the demise of Napster in 2001.[37] P2P file sharing suffered setbacks due to legal actions and attempts to commercialize on the part of some of the platforms themselves. Court cases shuttered the leading P2P applications, beginning with KaZaa, Morpheus, and Grokster in 2005, and then Limewire in 2010.[38] Numerous search engines that were started to help users find BitTorrent swarms disappeared due to legal pressure and court rulings.[39] While many of these applications succumbed to legal actions, it is important to note that commercial and community pressures also led to contractions in the size of mass piracy. KaZaa, for example, bundled its ostensibly free software with obtrusive spyware and adware. Limewire, on the other hand, sold a "professional" version of its software that promised faster downloads and searches. All these networks disappeared, but TPB survived and kept attracting users.

Given the popularity of other file-sharing protocols in 2003, the Piratbyrån's decision to use the BitTorrent protocol appears to be a tactical choice. At the time, the protocol was relatively unknown, having been released only in 2001.[40] Bram Cohen, the developer of BitTorrent, announced the new network on a mailing list dedicated to decentralization and the implications of the End-to-End principle (E2E). To be clear, there is no formal link between the idea of accelerationism and BitTorrent. Rather, the protocol has tendencies emphasized by the Piratbyrån. Some technical explanation clarifies this point. BitTorrent networks break files down into pieces. BitTorrent daemons frantically exchange pieces of the file, making sure that every peer has a copy. Pieces do not have to be sent sequentially. Instead, a daemon collects one piece from one peer, another from a different peer, and so on. Through constant exchange of these pieces, a network ensures each user receives a complete copy of the data being shared.[41] There is no client or server; rather, daemons simultaneously upload and download data. Continual exchange between peers means that multiple copies of a piece exist in the swarm, ensuring the decentralization of the file into the network.

The BitTorrent protocol encourages symmetrical uploading and downloading (as Comcast discovered, described in chapter 4). The more one shares, the more one receives. Users who do not share are choked: daemons will stop sending data to them. In this way, BitTorrent programs collectively organize their networks to ensure all nodes contribute data to the network. This strategy is reflected in how the network treats new users. New users do not have anything to share, so they start already choked. As such, new users are three times more likely to benefit from a feature known as "optimistic unchoking," in which a node decides to send pieces to a user even if that user has been classified as choked. Typically, programs will attempt to share the rarest piece of a torrent. Once a node has pieces and starts sharing them, other nodes recognize that it is sharing and unchoke the connection to send it more files.

Canadian ISPs provide a good description of BitTorrent's consequences to infrastructure, but their comments need some context. In 2009, the Canadian Radio-Television and Telecommunications Commission (CRTC), a key regulatory institution of the Canadian internet, held hearings on the use of DPI and traffic management techniques. The hearings summoned manufacturers, ISPs, and public-interest groups to debate a framework eventually referred to as Canada's Network Neutrality Rules. (The ruling, discussed later, remains contentious.) Bell Canada, one of Canada's biggest ISPs, claimed in their filings to the hearing that P2P file sharing was a corrosive technology that uses a disproportionate amount of bandwidth compared to other types of traffic.[42] Their assertion that file sharing is disproportionate reflects BitTorrent's accelerationism, as it grows by constantly creating more and more connections between peers. This growth conflicted with Bell's expectations that one computer establish a limited number of connections to other hosts, from a node to a major server. In contrast, BitTorrent creates a swarm of connections between many users. BitTorrent traffic expands between peers, establishing hundreds of connections to share different bits of the same file. The increase in connections between peers strains the capacity of infrastructural resources.

As much as BitTorrent (at least in 2009) congested infrastructure, the internet traffic management practices hearings revealed just how much BitTorrent disrupted ISPs' optimization. Another large Canadian ISP, Rogers Communications, argued: "[P2P file sharing is] the least effective method of transmitting data. The cost of bandwidth on the last mile access network to the home is much greater than the cost of bandwidth in a traditional file server."[43] In other words, P2P is suboptimal, and its traffic shaping reflected that opinion. Rogers disclosed their use of DPI to limit all P2P file-sharing uploading to a maximum of eighty kbps.[44] Bell stated that they throttled BitTorrent, Gnutella, Limewire, Kazaa, eDonkey, eMule, and WinMX traffic on residential networks. Throttling limited download speed to 512 kbps from 4:30 p.m. to 6:00 p.m. daily and reduced it further to 256 kbps after 6:00 p.m. The caps rose at 1:00 a.m. back to 512 kbps before being turned off after 2:00 a.m.[45] Since their optimal internet clearly favored hubs, it should come as no surprise that both Rogers and Bell started numerous video-on-demand services that relied on the traditional client–server relationship with central servers delivering multimedia content. While there is no explicit link between degrading P2P and promoting comparable video-on-demand services, the ISPs' attitude reveals a trajectory for network development in which the owners have more control over the priorities of the network. To be fair, their activities are not sinister, but they do constitute a network optimization in conflict with the Piratbyrån's centrifugal desires.

While the BitTorrent protocol decentralizes P2P networking, it does require some central index of torrent swarms and, in the past, a tracker to coordinate sharing. A number of websites arrived to fill this void, including TPB, but in doing so, became easy targets for copyright enforcement agencies. To be more difficult to take offline, TPB adopted developments in the BitTorrent protocol that reduced potential chokepoints, as well as legal accountability. First, TPB stopped coordinating the activities of its peers (technically it stopped running a tracker) in November 2009.[46] Instead, users took on the role of coordination through a technical innovation known as Distributed Hash Tables (DHTs). Second, its admins announced in January 2012 that they would cease hosting any torrent files in favor of Magnet links.[47] The Magnet uniform resource identifier scheme gives directions on how an application might find content on the internet without specifying a location. Client applications search DHTs and peer exchanges using the Magnet link metadata to locate and then start sharing a file.[48] As a result of this change, TPB shrunk down to ninety megabytes and could, therefore, be easily backed up and transported.[49] At the time, TPB admins joked about putting its small index on autonomous drones and sending them out through the city as a distributed network. Finally, the group announced that it had stopped running on its own servers in favor of hosting the entire service on shared servers distributed across the globe (similar to the approach used by WikiLeaks until it was shut down by Amazon). Although TPB admins had toyed with moving their servers offshore or into secure bunkers,[50] they still relied on a centralized cluster of servers hosted in Sweden until October 17, 2012, when they moved to cloud servers.

With the rise of advanced traffic management came a need to rethink the tactic of accelerationism. As early as 2006, one of its members, Neij, suggested "the Pirate Bay will outlive its usefulness."[51] Accelerationism now seems of a time when the internet might grow to become a digital commons faster than it could be shut down. TPB fit within a general optimism about free knowledge, sharing, and excess. For pirates, this optimism period ended, along with accelerationism as a strategy.

Pirates turned to escalationism. Fleischer, reflecting on the end of a politics of acceleration wrote, "in 2010, we are tunneling communications."[52] By "tunneling communication," he meant both an analogy to tunneling underground to avoid detection and a technical term that refers to routing communications through encrypted or obscure channels. Constructing darknets—private, obscure networks on the internet—exemplified the escalationism tactic.

Escalationism might also be understood as an interpretation of Deleuze's own speculations on new weapons in a control society. In an interview with Negri, Deleuze suggests that:

> Maybe speech and communication have been corrupted. They're thoroughly permeated by money—and not by accident but by their very nature. We've got to hijack speech. Creating has always been something different from communicating. The key thing may be to create vacuoles of noncommunication, circuit breakers, so we can elude control.[53]

The idea of noncommunication might not mean simply to stop communicating, but to question the very expression of communication. Elsewhere, Deleuze defines communication as the transmission of information or order-words.[54] To stop communicating would not be to stop talking, but to stop the widespread distribution of an information system or, to borrow from Deleuze, a "system of control." Given the ubiquity of flow control, fleeing no longer seems viable. Accelerating assumes a free horizon, whereas Deleuze suggests the creation of a "vacuole," a term from the Latin *vacuus,* meaning an empty or open space. This method requires tactical meaninglessness, or at least meaningless to daemons. The next section explores the tactic of escalation as a way to obfuscate traffic from the daemon's gaze.

TPB's admins' foray into escalationism happened in response to changes in Swedish law. On April 1, 2009, the Swedish government ratified Directive 2004/48/EC of the European Parliament and of the Council of April 29, 2004, on the Enforcement of Intellectual Property Rights (also known as the Intellectual Property Rights Enforcement Directive, or IPRED). The introduction of IPRED closed the loopholes that allowed TPB to operate legally in Sweden. The directive further allowed for greater police monitoring of the internet, in part through the packet inspection daemons of national ISPs.[55] IPRED's introduction led to a change in tactics associated with TPB.

TPB launched a VPN service mockingly named IPREDator. They announced the service on the homepage, an important and oft-used tactic by TPB. Like Google's "doodles," TPB changes the logo on their front page to publicize events, campaigns, and issues.[56] In this case, TPB's admins posted a screenshot from the Nintendo video game *Mike Tyson's Punch-Out* that depicted the game's protagonist, Little Mac, fighting Glass Joe, an early opponent who is easily defeated due to his characteristic glass jaw. Below the image, a headline announced "IPREDator IS ONLINE" and "Sign up Now for Multiplying Combo."

Their IPREDator service is an example of what Finn Brunton and Helen Nissenbaum call "cooperative obfuscation," a tactic that seeks to collectively obfuscate data collection. The Onion Router (TOR) exemplifies this practice. TOR is a distributed network formed by home computers volunteering to route the data of their peers anonymously. The relays anonymize and encrypt data and disrupt the tempo of packet transmission to prevent the kind of flow inspection discussed earlier. The collective efforts of nodes thereby enable a darknet. Another example is the Invisible Internet Project (I2P), which also promises traffic anonymity and security through a similar distributed network. These tactics are also called "circumvention" technologies. Anonymous and Telecomix, both prominent hacktivist groups, have developed secure tunnels and network connections for dissidents in nation-states with censorious regimes, most recently in Egypt and Syria.[57] Their efforts continue a long history of developing anticensorship proxy services like the Citizen Lab spin-off Psiphon and proxy servers.

IPREDator was a privacy-oriented VPN service. Today, such services are popular, but at the time, a consumer markets for VPNs was nascent.

IPREDator, in other words, helped popularize VPNs as a privacy enhancing technology. Sunde explained that IPREDator sought "to hide from what the government does in the form of giving companies police powers."[58] He meant that governments had mandated ISPs to watch for copyright infringement and security threats. Well before the recent popularization of VPNs to avoid geo-blocking (e.g., blocking Canadians from accessing Netflix's larger American catalogue) and the rise of other similar services, IPREDator provided a VPN that tunneled subscriber communications through trusted servers in Sweden. The tunnel is a secure and encrypted link between the home user and the IPREDator's servers. This arrangement protects subscribers' traffic from being monitored by their local ISP, and it allows subscribers to anonymously connect to the internet. The IPREDator servers anonymize traffic. Outside servers know only that they have a connection from the IPREDator servers, rather than from specific customers. The service initially cost a flat five euros per month and did not charge by usage.

IPREDator appropriated VPNs from their traditional business uses. VPN technology started as a way for businesses to maintain a private network on the common internet. Researchers at AT&T in the United States and the United Kingdom proposed VPNs in 1988 as a way to use public networks privately. This meant creating autonomous and encrypted networks running on public infrastructures.[59] A number of VPN protocols developed, including Point-to-Point Tunneling Protocol (PPTP), Internet Protocol Security (IPSec), Point-to-Point Protocol over Ethernet (PPPoE), OpenVPN, and Layer 2 Tunneling Protocol (L2TP).[60] While IPREDator currently uses the GNU Public License OpenVPN, it started with PPTP, which establishes a direct link between a client server and a VPN server. All traffic from the client (a request to a website, for example) flows from the client to the VPN server, out to the internet, and back to the VPN server, where it returns the information to the client. PPTP emerged out of research conducted by a consortium of companies, including Microsoft and 3Com, that led to Request for Comments (RFC) 2637, posted in July 1999.[61] While the protocol does not outline any encryption for its tunneling, IPREDator uses 128-bit encryption using Microsoft Point-to-Point Encryption for traffic and the Microsoft Challenge Handshake Authentication Protocol to log into the VPN.[62] This encryption prevents daemons from looking into the packet to see its contents.

Trygghetsbolaget i Lund AB, a firm that had worked with the Pirate Party in the past to create political VPNs, handled their VPN services.

IPREDator operates as a "pre-paid flat-rate service" because this business model, they claimed, has the lowest reporting requirements, since they do not have to log and charge for usage. IPREDator does not keep logs of users, since IPRED does not mandate data retention.[63] IPREDator's security page claims that they would cooperate with Swedish authorities only in the event that a user may be facing jail time and that, furthermore, for "inquires from other parties than Swedish authorities IPREDator will never hand over any kind of information."[64] Given that their service attracts international customers, they again appear to be playing international laws to their advantage, forcing international legal cooperation before releasing any data to an international user's local authorities.

The Packeteer PacketShaper 8500

How IPREDator obfuscates traffic warrants some more technical explanation. To do so, I use a lab environment to simulate detection and obfuscation tactics (a common practice in computer science). To perform the simulation, I gained access to a used Packeteer PacketShaper 8500 connected to the internet. Access to traffic management equipment like the PacketShapter 8500 is difficult, and so the following section offers a rare window into the management of these middleboxes. In the lab, I connected a stock Windows computer to the PacketShaper, which was, in turn, connected to the internet, not unlike a home user passing through an ISP's infrastructure to connect to the general internet. The Windows computer had to connect to the internet through the PacketShaper. I had direct access to both devices, allowing for both the simulation of traffic on the lab computer and direct configuration of a foundational DPI appliance.

Packeteer led the field in advanced traffic management from its founding in 1996 until its acquisition by BlueCoat in 2008.[65] The most robust appliance in their product line circa 2002, the PacketShaper 8500 handles 200 megabits per second to delineate a maximum of 500,000 IP flows into over 5000 classes, partitions, or policies. Since many networks routinely use more than 200 mbps, the software clearly has its limits. More recent DPI devices are able to handle much higher loads of traffic.

A pamphlet for the product suggests that it is "the answer to service providers' demands for a high-capacity solution that delivers differentiated services, ensures fair and equal access, enforces user policies and improves profit margins through various co-location services."[66] A review of the newly launched project stated that "the largest demographic for peer-to-peer file sharing is college students" and that the PacketShaper is a serious asset "in a university environment, where protocols such as those associated with Kazaa and Gnutella are clogging up the pipes"; however, P2P protocols "disguise themselves via HTTP tunneling or using multiple ports" (a phenomenon previously discussed in chapter 4 as "port spoofing"). To compensate, the review continued: "[The PacketShaper] looks at more than just port number. Instead, it examines application signatures."[67] Comcast faced an identical problem, as P2P networks also used port spoofing to avoid detection.

The PacketShaper 8500 is administered through a web interface. The interface includes ways to classify and manage networks, like other DPI appliances discussed earlier. Its class-based perspective consists of a tree of traffic classes grouped into inbound and outbound.[68] The order of the tree determines the match. Like a hand moving down a list, the PacketShaper runs through the tree from top to bottom, matching information in a packet to patterns in classes. For HTTP (HyperText Transfer Protocol), FTP (File Transfer Protocol), and NNTP (Network News Transfer Protocol) networks in particular, the Packeteer 8500 allows for even more granular classification. Like other DPI boxes, the PacketShaper could target Firefox clients browsing TPB while allowing all other HTTP traffic to flow normally. It could match FTP packets based on file names or extensions. Also, the PacketShaper could identify the binary groups that were havens for pirated content on newsgroups (NNTP).

The tree changes when Packeteer releases an update, when administrators add classes, or when the PacketShaper discovers new patterns on its own. Most vendors release updates that add new classes based on their own monitoring of traffic pattern trends (as exemplified by Arbor Network's ATLAS program, discussed in chapter 4). Each traffic class includes a list of rules for the PacketShaper to follow to identify a packet. Does its header contain a declaration of being part of a BitTorrent network? Do the packet contents include commands associated with FTP? In addition to these prepackaged classes, the PacketShaper also automatically adds classes when set to "traffic discovery" mode. The automated mode searches for repeating traffic patterns and creates new classes once it recognizes the same pattern three times. A network administrator might leave the appliance in discovery mode for a week or so to generate a list of popular applications before turning it on and letting it run.

The PacketShaper manages classes through policies and partitions. Policies, according to the manual, manage individual flows, while partitions manage aggregated flows (similar to classes and policy maps in Cisco's Internetwork Operating System, or IOS). A difference, in other words, of granularity, where a policy allows a network to "to manage bandwidth on a flow-by-flow basis" and a partition groups packets "so that all of the flows for the class are controlled together as one."[69] A policy could apply to HTTP, where HTTP could also be part of a partition that includes FTP and email. The manual suggests creating rules that protect "mission-critical" traffic while shaping "aggressive traffic." Policies and partitions set the modulations of daemons to guarantee a bit rate, set the priority in the queue, pass the traffic through the network, impose DiffServ or MPLS (Multi-Protocol Label Switching), or block traffic altogether. Policies can simultaneously block malicious content, ignore normal activities so packets travel according to best efforts, and guarantee bitrates for value-added traffic. The most common function would be to guarantee a minimum and maximum bitrate to ensure proper application functionality. Along with guarantees, a policy might also allow a flow to burst—that is, to temporarily send more bits than it rates—according to a priority and a limit. A partition, like a slice of pie, divides the available bandwidth into sections that have a fixed capacity.

IPREDator eludes the PacketShaper by avoiding its gaze. As part of the experiment, seen in Figure 10, I monitored the real-time graph included in the PacketShaper's web interface to interpret the daemon's gaze. The graph plots the network's bandwidth consumption over time. To test this gaze, I attempted to duplicate the experience of an IPREDator user seeking to avoid traffic management targeted at BitTorrent. I downloaded a torrent of the Ubuntu Linux distribution using version 5.2.2 of the BitTorrent client from roughly 2009. While the lab computer opened and connected to the Ubuntu torrent's network, the PacketShaper monitored BitTorrent (labeled Outbound/BitTorrent and Inbound/BitTorrent) and VPN traffic (labelled Outbound/GRE and Inbound/GRE). As the download began, Inbound/BitTorrent traffic spiked upward. Since the PacketShaper easily recognizes BitTorrent traffic, it can just as easily throttle it. Under the "manage" tab, one can select policies or partitions to limit the flow of BitTorrent traffic. For this experiment, I set a partition of fifty kilobytes per second. After one minute, shaping kicked in. The Inbound/BitTorrent

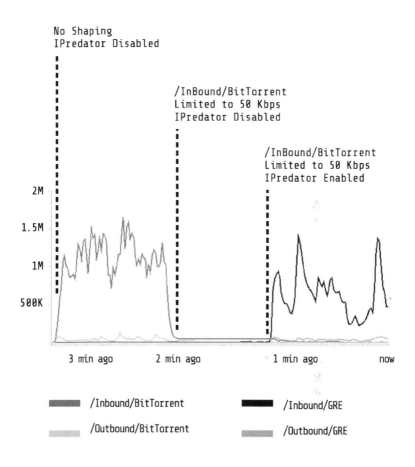

No Shaping
IPredator Disabled

/InBound/BitTorrent
Limited to 50 Kbps
IPredator Disabled

/InBound/BitTorrent
Limited to 50 Kbps
IPredator Enabled

2M
1.5M
1M
500K

3 min ago   2 min ago   1 min ago   now

/Inbound/BitTorrent   /Inbound/GRE
/Outbound/BitTorrent   /Outbound/GRE

Application rate activity in bits per second

Figure 10. BitTorrent performance with and without IPREDator virtual private network enabled.

line dropped until it plateaued at the set limit. On the lab computer, the download slowed down too. If the application of the PacketShaper to the BitTorrent traffic exemplifies the daemon's reach, then IPREDator attempts to loosen its grip. Logging on to IPREDator completely alters the flow of packets. Repeating the test from above, when a shaped BitTorrent exchange logs into IPREDator, its traffic drops as it changes addresses on the internet; however, as its location stabilizes and the client reestablishes

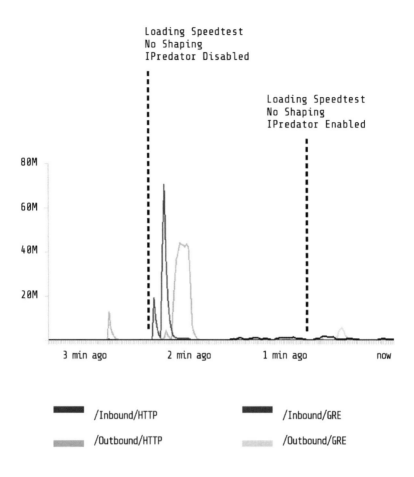

Loading Speedtest
No Shaping
IPredator Disabled

Loading Speedtest
No Shaping
IPredator Enabled

80M

60M

40M

20M

3 min ago   2 min ago   1 min ago   now

▬▬▬▬ /Inbound/HTTP   ▬▬▬▬ /Inbound/GRE

▬▬▬▬ /Outbound/HTTP   ▬▬▬▬ /Outbound/GRE

Application rate activity in bits per second

Figure 11. SpeedTest performance with and without IPREDator virtual private network enabled.

contact, the traffic stabilizes and climbs past the set limit of fifty kilobytes per second to communicate at the same rate as before.

The results distinguish accelerationist and escalationist tactics. IPREDator, in contrast to TPB, is slow; it actually degrades performance. Figure 11 depicts the results of another experiment using a popular internet performance test called SpeedTest. I performed the test with and without IPREDator enabled and monitored the results using the same

PacketShaper interface. Without IPREDator, download speeds reached 80,000 kbps and upload speeds reached 40,000 kbps. Though hard to see at the far right of the graph, tests using IPREDator reached a mere 5,000 kbps download, and upload speed was even slower. Importantly, the delay was not a result of the Swedish traffic having to connect to the United States, a longer distance to travel. SpeedTest has testing servers located in Sweden, so when I ran the IPREDator-enabled test, it connected to a Swedish testing server. The advantages of IPREDator are obscurity and autonomy, not speed.

IPREDator illustrates the second tactic of TPB related to escalationism. IPREDator privately transmits BitTorrent packets, but publicly they appear as VPN traffic (specifically Inbound/GRE and Outbound/GRE, according to the PacketShaper). The service hides contraband traffic among the more desirable corporate traffic of the internet. IPREDator is a tool of escalationism not because it hides the traffic perfectly, but because it obfuscates it. This camouflage makes it more difficult for daemons and blurs their gaze. While the PacketShaper can simply add a new filter to manage GRE traffic, it does so at the risk of also affecting commercial VPN traffic. Most VPN traffic comes from corporations who use it to secure communication between an employee in the field and company servers. In a sense, IPREDator hides BitTorrent networks among corporate ones, taking advantage of the fact that ISPs cannot manage VPN traffic too greatly without the risk of alienating business customers.

Escalationism is now a larger tactic employed by pirates, hacktivists, and P2P developers to struggle against, but not escape, control. Escalationism hides from advertising, social media profile tracking, and state surveillance. Tactics include various forms of obfuscation that produce "misleading, false or ambiguous data to make data gathering less reliable and therefore less valuable," as Brunton and Nissenbaum describe them, including time-based obfuscations that temporally disrupt surveillance, selective obfuscations that jam data mining by specific sites like Facebook, and ambiguating obfuscations that "render an individual's data permanently dubious and untrustworthy as a subject of analysis."[70] The BitTorrent extension Hydra, for example, injects dummy requests and other misinformation to confuse analysis of its traffic, and so the user's activities are never apparent to those watching. Darknets created by TOR or I2P encrypt traffic and route messages between peers to be less attributable to the source. New private channels like Slack and Discord create communities hidden from search engines but easy to find. VPNs like IPREDator are just one of many forms of escalationism today.

THE MOST DISASTROUS ESCALATIONS?
RECKONING WITH THE PIRATE BAY

Accelerationism and escalationism were both strategies invented by TPB, but they function as more general concepts to understand resistance to daemonic optimization. These strategies function like a war machine. Deleuze and Guattari write that "the war machine invents speed and secrecy."[71] The Piratbyrån chanced upon BitTorrent as a radical speed, an accelerationist speed. The website became something independent from them, not necessarily under their command. It grew rapidly and globally. Escalationism, in turn, deals in secrecy. Both strategies endure online, with hackers looking for new proliferate kinds of rapid networking or better ways to go dark. Speed and secrecy might be seen as the new weapons about which Deleuze speculates in his discussion of elusion and control. While these tactics might elude daemons, I wonder about the effectiveness of the overall strategy of invention.

Daemons are never idle. Deleuze and Guattari, in the same quote above, suggest that "there is a certain speed and a certain secrecy that pertains to the State, relatively, secondarily."[72] That is to say, the war machine is not defined by the state, but it does inspire a response from the state apparatus. The worry is that these strategies function as a reason to improve flow control precisely because they attempt to elude it. Control grows through its opposition. Deleuze and Guattari describe the same dynamic for the war machine, that it propels the state by defining its limits, by being what it cannot capture:

[The war machine] is a kind of rhizome, with its gaps, detours, subterranean passages, stems, openings, traits, holes, etc. On the other side, the sedentary assemblages and State apparatuses effect a capture of the phylum, put the traits of expression into a form or a code, make the holes resonate together, plug the lines of flights, subordinate the technological operation to the work model, impose upon the connections a whole regime of arborescent conjunctions.[73]

Plugging holes and imposing connections are all a kind of productivity. These responses show the risk of these tactics. Far from eluding control, they might make it even worse. Remember that Packeteer sold its PacketShaper as a solution to out-of-control piracy on academic networks in the quotes above. Piracy justified an investment in control.

Even more unsettling is that these moves might have been anticipated by the Piratbyrån. Fleischer explains that the motivation for escalation was not escape. Fleischer's goal was to escalate the activities of the daemons toward some sort of greater confrontation. By contrast, Brunton and Nissenbaum list six reasons for obfuscation, from buying time to expressing protest. The underlying strategy of escalationism was to provoke, to trigger a confrontation. Fleischer compared tunneling to concerns about wiretapping that "would only escalate encryption and tunneling—which, in its turn, will surely provoke legislators to attack darknets, and so on, as a positive feedback loop out of control."[74] Darknets, encryption, and protocol obfuscation all provoke daemons. To Fleischer, at the time, that was the point:

> However, we could say that escalationism does not have escalation as its object, any more than the war machine has war as its object. It might even have more to do with preventing the most disastrous escalations. One way to do it might be to let the escalation happen before it becomes disastrous. But it is in the nature of escalationism that there is no subject that can judge the right timing, before the whole thing has escalated into something else.[75]

Escalationism hopes to provoke a confrontation sooner rather than later, hoping that the conformation is on better terms. Less abstractly, the goal of going dark now is to provoke questions about daemons now, rather than allow more capable daemons to be developed in the future. Escalationism may be seen as a strategy of secrecy and publicity. Will they be better or more disastrous? Fleischer ends without clarifying what he means by a disastrous escalation, but the intent is clear. Escalationism is a risky path that might provoke something far worse than present flow control. Yet, the ways this strategy hoped to make public and mobilize around the confrontation remained unclear.

The ambiguity of accelerationism and escalationism does not imply that piracy has exhausted itself. Perhaps the propiracy movement could offer more of an intervention in media policy than an elusion of flow control. What would an accelerationist optimization be? The radical sharing of BitTorrent could inspire a new form of traffic management in which performance is common to users. What would happen if infrastructures abandoned service tiers and accelerated networks? In keeping with the accelerationist spirit, that might mean an embrace of artificial intelligence and an intelligent infrastructure. It might involve taking Saisei's FlowCommand at its word. Mentioned in chapter 4 as an example of a fully autonomous policy daemon, FlowCommand promises to be "the world's first 'Net Neutrality' enforcer."[76] Could such an intelligent daemon impose fair bandwidth for all users? Maybe an iso-synchronization in which all nodes have equal bandwidth?

Further, what would an escalationist optimization be? An infrastructure that is unknown or unknowable? Could pirates undermine the growing concentration of data? At a time when the internet has become a standing reserve of data on demand for surveillance agencies and corporations alike,[77] could escalationist optimization create networks without concentrations of knowledge, without aggregations of data that tempt marketers, corporations, law enforcement, and surveillance agencies? The outcome might be a much more disconnected internet, like the kinds of mesh wireless infrastructures being installed in cities such as Barcelona, Kansas City, and Montreal. These infrastructures can be local pockets of connectivity with bounded limits on the circulation of information.[78] An escalationist optimization could valorize these borders, creating points beyond which data will never aggregate.

CONCLUSION

Risky infrastructural tactics were not the only interventions by TPB's administrators. They also influenced internet culture and cultivated global opposition to increased copyright enforcement. The raid catalyzed the Swedish community around the group and fostered the nascent pirate movement. Swedish youth who grew up with computers and digital networks began to engage politically in response to the raid. The police raid inspired a growth in membership in the Swedish Pirate Party as young Swedes expressed their outrage and pushed the party into the public spotlight. Pirate parties spread throughout Europe and North America.[79] TPB's administrators, for their part, continued their infrastructural struggles within the legal system. The police proceeded with their case and filed charges on January 31, 2008, two years after the raid. The trial began a year later in February 2009 and ended in April that same year. TPB appealed, and the court case truly ended only when the group lost their final appeal in 2012. The Swedish court found them guilty. The three administrators were sentenced to roughly a year of jail time and fines totalling $6.5 million.[80] Losing the court cases did not shut down the website, as the Swedish Pirate Party began to host the site.[81] Even though the site administration has changed since, TPB (as of this writing) is still online. Current administrators keep a lower profile, although they continue to post on the site's blog and in its Facebook group (aptly named "The Pirate Bay War Machine").[82] TPB continues to be one of the top BitTorrent sites in the world.[83]

If, at the end of this chapter, elusion seems a fraught response to daemons, what are other ways to confront them? In the final chapter, I turn from these more theoretical questions to examine policy matters that relate to daemons. Policy makers, as much as pirates, have attempted to respond to the issues raised by flow control. Usually their approach to the matter draws on the concept of net neutrality. Making flow control matter to policy makers offers a new set of challenges that help further elaborate the concept. What does the concept of flow control reveal? How does it reconceptualize the internet in contrast to net neutrality? What normative approaches does it offer that could lead to sound policy? The next chapter delves into the relationship between the public and flow control through a review of an important network neutrality enforcement case in Canada.

7 A CRESCENDO OF ONLINE INTERACTIVE DEBUGGING?

Gamers, Publics, and Daemons

RENÉ DESCARTES AND COMPUTER GAMERS faced a similar problem. A mischievous creature haunted both of them. Symptoms varied. Descartes worried that some malicious demon was manipulating him, generating illusions that meant he could not trust his hands, eyes, flesh, and blood. Everything his senses detected might be one of these illusions caused by an evil demon (or evil genius in other interpretations).[1] Canadian gamers had less existential woes. Beginning in 2010, gamers who subscribed to Rogers Internet experienced trouble enjoying online games like *World of Warcraft* and *Call of Duty*. The *ouroboros* symbol of lag haunted their games until, suddenly, something broke their connection to these virtual worlds. Neither Descartes nor these gamers had proof of their suspicions. Where Descartes adopted a philosophical approach, gamers, specifically customers of Rogers Internet in Canada, had to develop their own methods to explain their connection issues. How could gamers identify the true cause from among the possibilities? Could it be their modems or their home routers? Or maybe a problem with a recent update to the game? These questions led the gamers deep into the infrastructure of their internet service provider (ISP) and into a Pandaemonium, that home of its daemons, named for the capital city of hell in John Milton's *Paradise Lost.*

The *World of Warcraft* gamers discussed in this chapter faced a situation common to many caught up in the distributive agency of infrastructure. What is their relation to a technical infrastructure? What is the proper response when it fails? Reflecting on the subject's position in these assemblages, Jane Bennett writes: "Perhaps the ethical responsibility of an individual now resides in one's response to the assemblages in which one finds oneself participating: Do I attempt to extricate myself from assemblages whose trajectory is likely to do harm? Do I enter into the proximity of assemblages whose conglomerate effectively tends toward the enactment of nobler ends?"[2] Gamers could easily switch to a better ISP (though media concentration limits their choices). They could have extracted themselves from the assemblage, to borrow Bennett's phrasing. But they had another option: to fix Rogers. This choice did not so much address harm (beyond the frustration of losing in the game), but rather involved making an infrastructure accountable, specifically to Canada's regulations for net neutrality if a violation of the neutrality principle proved to be the cause of their connection issues.

By choosing to address the issue, Canadian gamers exemplified how publics address the influence of daemons in the internet. As we have seen, "daemons" refers to those programs running in the internet's infrastructures that control communication. "Publics" refers to strangers bound together by a common issue, and they are a vital force that keeps the internet running and accountable. Chris Kelty stresses the importance of internet-focused recursive publics in creating the internet's critical infrastructure.[3] The free software movement, as Gabriella Coleman compellingly argues, is vital to preserving internet freedom.[4] Publics have also had an important role in internet regulation, as was seen in the Comcast case discussed in the introduction. Canadian gamers have had a role too. Before net-neutrality legislation had even passed in the United States and the European Union, Canadian gamers had prompted an early case of net-neutrality enforcement.

The two-year struggle between Rogers Internet and Canadian gamers presents a critical case through which the role of publics in revealing the operations of daemons and holding them accountable can be understood. The obstacles these gamers faced exemplify the challenges of rendering daemons public. Gamers lacked proof of a problem; only a sense that something unusual was happening prompted them to investigate. This feeling of being affected is a critical step in the formation and resolution of problems by publics. Daemons, however, thwart the development of publics. Their intangibility and the invisibility of their operations make wider reflection difficult. Publics affected by daemons have to bootstrap their own convention through *mediators* and reflexive apparatuses. In other words, the public comes to know itself and its unifying issue only through a cycle of positive feedback in which research leads to a better, wider definition of the public. This chapter and the appendix give special attention to internet measurement. Since ARPANET, researchers have had to find tools to study the internet's running code. These tools enable a sort of public research into distributed systems like the internet (or what might be called an early algorithmic audit[5]). The appendix elaborates the history and technologies of internet measurement that help to reveal the work of daemons, whereas this chapter reflects more on the role of finding mediators for daemons. The story of these mediators, together with the work of publics, provides a fitting end to the book, revealing how advocacy and public engagement offer perhaps the only enduring response to the influence of daemons.

"HOW DOES THIS AFFECT YOU?"
ROGERS INTERNET AND WORLD OF WARCRAFT

Canadians were having a hard time playing *World of Warcraft* (WoW) in 2010. The Massive-Multiplayer-Online (MMO) game was at the height of its popularity. The fantasy game had just released its third expansion, "Cataclysm," with a fire-breathing dragon named Deathwing the Destroyer gracing its box cover. But daemons, not dragons, were bothering gamers. Lag, disconnections, and difficulty joining a game plagued gamers from sea to sea. Explanations were scattered across blogs and internet news websites, as well as in the support forums for the game and for local ISPs. In the WoW forums, a gamer using the alias "Shifthead" started a thread on December 18, 2010, entitled "Rogers ISP, WoW, and you!" Shifthead frequently suffered from high latency, the time a packet takes to reach its destination (usually measured in milliseconds). The post asked "How does this affect you?" Shifthead's post generated twenty-three pages of replies and discussion lasted until late 2011.[6]

No one believed that the disconnection issues were random. Shifthead blamed Rogers Internet and linked to stories from consumer-oriented internet news sites *Torrentfreak* and *DSLReports*.[7] These websites reported that Rogers Internet had changed its internet traffic management practices sometime after September 2010. Customers had reported numerous connection issues that adversely affected WoW and other applications. Replies to Shifthead's post echoed these stories.

Gamers had a reason to suspect Rogers Internet. Investigations by eMule and Vuze users into Comcast mentioned in the introduction had also discovered that Rogers, like most Canadian ISPs, actively managed Peer-to-Peer (P2P) traffic. Gamers knew that Rogers continued to manage upstream traffic, stopping BitTorrent networks from consuming too much of its limited capacity, and so they suspected that WoW traffic was mistakenly being throttled.

By the time of Shifhead's post, these practices were common knowledge, thanks in part to a public inquiry. In 2009, citizen and industry concern prompted the Canadian regulator, the Canadian Radio-Television and Telecommunications Commission (CRTC), to enact one of the first net-neutrality rules. The rulings resulted from a complaint by internet resellers who bought wholesale internet access from Canada's established players, a practice that was a national policy meant to promote competition in the market. The Canadian Association of Internet Providers (CAIP), an association of fifty-five small ISPs in Canada, submitted a complaint that Bell had begun throttling their wholesale internet connections.[8] Even though they denied CAIP's initial request to stop Bell, the CRTC launched formal regulatory hearings on throttling and other internet traffic management practices in April 2008. The commission heard from ISP representatives, telecommunications experts, and public-interest groups over the summer of 2009. During the hearings, Canadian ISPs disclosed that they did manage P2P applications, configuring their daemons to find and limit these networks.

The CRTC released its policy on internet-traffic management practices on October 21, 2009. The Telecom Regulatory Policy CRTC 2009-657 permitted traffic management so long as it met four conditions. First, all practices had to be publicly disclosed (ISPs could comply by simply stating their practices on their websites). Second, the traffic management had to meet a defined need. Traffic management was a fundamental tool for ISPs, but it had to be used properly. The last two conditions concerned fairness and competitive neutrality. The CRTC prevented ISPs from using traffic management practices uncompetitively or preferentially. This included prohibiting ISPs from using Deep Packet Inspection for anything other than traffic management. Prominent advocates of net neutrality, such as Michael Geist, Canada Research Chair of Internet and E-commerce Law at the University of Ottawa, and Milton Mueller, scholar of internet governance, cautiously embraced the framework.[9]

WoW gamers knew that, if Rogers Internet had deliberately throttled WoW, then it had broken these new rules. No one suspected that Rogers was throttling WoW traffic for anti-competitive reasons. Posters in Shifhead's thread speculated about numerous explanations, including the throttling being the result of error. This would be an acceptable excuse, but posters debated whether Rogers Internet knew about the issue. If the company did know that WoW had connection issues, then why had it not released a statement? Why had it not updated its traffic management disclosure? Gamers debated how best to bring the issue to the attention of Rogers Internet. Could they find some evidence to convince Rogers or to justify a complaint to the CRTC?

These puzzled gamers revealed a common criticism of the CRTC's traffic-management policy, and indeed of net-neutrality legislation in general. While regulations limited the work of daemons, they lacked oversight. The onus rested on the complainant to provide evidence of violations of these principles (a common problem for ex post facto rules). As WoW gamers were learning, finding answers was difficult. In a blog post about the same issues affecting WoW gamers, Christopher Parsons, an expert in telecommunications and privacy now at the University of Toronto's Citizen Lab, called for third-party oversight to watch for misapplications of traffic management and to alert the public.[10] Without such a third party in place, WoW gamers were left discussing the problem with each other, guessing at explanations.

BEDEVILED PUBLICS

These affected gamers offer a first step toward understanding a public response to flow control and to daemonic media. As the WoW gamers replied to each other, they formed part of a public dedicated to proving daemonic effects. "Publics" is a term used by the pragmatists Walter Lippmann and John Dewey. Publics, to Dewey, are "all those who are affected by the indirect consequences of transactions to such an extent that it is deemed necessary to have those consequences systematically cared for."[11] Though Dewey predates affect theory, it is telling that he defined publics as the affected, a suggestion that publics initially did not know exactly what was bothering them. No sense of being a public or knowledge of their problems prefigures the transaction, but once formed, publics function both as a means to acquire knowledge and as a political resolution (not unlike the advertisements discussed in chapter 5). Indirect consequences demand a response. Affected strangers become drawn into participating in a collective understanding. As people become more aware of the consequences, they become more aware of their problem and their role in a solution. Democracy, to Dewey, succeeds in resolving the complexities of life through this process of affected persons systematically caring for the indirect consequences of transactions that got them involved in the first place.

Publics are a conceptual and normative way to address technical controversies and open black boxes, such as through the work of Noortje Marres and Bruno Latour, as well as that of Jane Bennett, on whom I draw more frequently. According to Bennett, a public "is a contingent and temporary formation" that forms after being "provoked to do so by a problem, that is, by the 'indirect, serious and enduring' consequences of 'conjoint action.'"[12] There are many problems that could cause people to form a public: scientific controversies, events, debates, and problems like the disconnection issues in WoW. To those studying infrastructure, problems might be seen as an outcome of infrastructural inversion: when the system breaks, its workings become more apparent.[13] Digital technology, however, has often been seen to complicate the formation of publics. In his studies of networked-information algorithms, Mike Ananny argues that algorithmic sorting convenes publics, though these computational associations are rarely apparent to those affected.[14] Ananny gives the example of computational analysis of Facebook data sorting people by sexual orientation. Targeted advertising also aggregates people into fluid and self-correcting probable categories. As John Cheney-Lippold argues, these algorithmic calculations of relevance become a feedback loop in which people come to identify with their calculated demographics.[15] Daemons also convene publics, as WoW gamers were learning.

WORLD OF WARCRAFT GAMERS AND THEIR PROBLEMS

Posters in Shifthead's thread tried to solve the problem. Respondents tried to find some proof connecting their issues to Rogers's traffic management practices. In doing so, these publics formed affective bonds and relationships similar to Zizi Papacharissi's descriptions of "networked structures of feeling."[16] Gamers had difficulty finding answers linking their connection issues to Rogers Internet's infrastructure. The only evidence was a post by a Rogers employee in a *DSLReports* forum on October 28, 2009. The employee, using the handle "RogersKeith," admitted that changes in its traffic management had disrupted some non-P2P networks, but he did not directly mention WoW. RogersKeith promised to respond to the issue as quickly as possible.[17] No updates had been made to Rogers's traffic management disclosure on their website.

Conversations in the thread turned to discussions of how best to raise

awareness of the problem. While niche-oriented, internet-focused out-
lets had covered the news of Rogers traffic management in 2010, coverage had been largely absent since. Posters in the thread believed they
made up only a small portion of those affected by Rogers Internet's throttling. Other games and other gamers might also be affected. Furthermore,
their experience of being throttled was only one aspect of the wider problem of violations of net neutrality that affected all of Rogers's customers.
Could those other, regular internet users be enlisted in the cause? The
WoW posters, for their part, cited issues like net neutrality and privacy
that implicitly connected their own concerns with a larger, more inclusive public.

The gamers debated how to address this lack of publicity. A poster by
the name of "Demonomania" suggested creating a petition. Other posts
linked to different forums where, it turned out, others were discussing the
issues as well. To troubleshoot similar issues, "Goldmonger" then opened
a thread on the game's forums on January 26, 2011. He asked people to
run a test (technically a traceroute) and post the results, including their
location, operating system, and ISP, on the thread. He hoped that a running list of this technical information would help the game's owners and
the Canadian ISPs fix the issue.[18] On the Rogers support forums, a customer using the alias "Ressy" asked Rogers to explain the issue. Her post
generated fifty-eight pages of replies. She posted a link to Shifthead's
thread.[19] These threads pointed both to the scope of the issue and to the
fragmentation of these affected strangers.

These threads illustrate the convening of a public. If publics begin as
"a relation among strangers," according to Michael Warner, then some
aspects of the transaction must cause people to think they might be
affected by a common issue.[20] He calls this cause the reflexive apparatus,
and it plays a crucial part in the forming of a public by allowing people to
think of themselves as part of something collective. Looking at climate-
change activism, for example, Marres contends that domestic appliances
have the potential for "dramatizing connections between practices in
here and changing climates out there."[21] A new dishwasher arriving in
the home, Marres suggests, brings with it a political opportunity for its
users to reflect on water use and its consequences for the environment.
Drawing these kinds of connections suggests an approach to climate-
change activism that seeks to raise awareness of the links from the private space of the home out to the environment, instead of attempting
to inject an environmental awareness into a detached domestic sphere.

The reflexive apparatus is usually obvious. Traditional media have prominent reflexive apparatuses. Benedict Anderson suggests that newspapers created reading publics integral to early nationalism.[22] As he writes, "the date at the top of the newspaper, the single most important emblem on it, provides the essential connection—the steady onward clocking of homogeneous empty time."[23] The date allowed the public to imagine they existed in a common time, and thus could relate to issues as nations rather than as mere individuals or families. Newspapers and television programs, Warner argues, similarly to Anderson, have a punctual temporality of circulation that produces a routine capable of fostering a subjectivity, or publicness, from its audience of strangers. The reflexive apparatus allows the possibility of systematically caring about an issue.

What WoW gamers were learning is that daemons frustrate the convening of publics. As forum poster "Haakonii" noted, traffic management "is transparent, undetectable and beyond the technical comprehension of the man-on-the-street."[24] Daemons leave little trace of their influence. Screens depict only the outputs of calculations. Ganaele Langlois argues that the web includes both what users see represented on screen and a-semiotic encodings "that work through the transformation of human input (meaningful content and behavior) into information that can then be further channeled through other informational processes and transformed, for instance, into a value-added service."[25] Much of the internet (algorithms and software processes) functions a-semiotically, or without signification. Daemons, like algorithms and software, also function in the microtemporalities of computing, a scale imperceptible to humans.[26] Calculations occur too quickly for a user to notice, and daemons, by default, do not leave a record. Moments of reflection evaporate even though their implications endure.

However, it is more than just that daemons are unrepresented and untraceable; often, difference is the only commonality of daemonic publics. Daemons function dynamically, which often privatizes affects by network or by user. A user experiences a particular array of affects composed through their own way of being online. Gilles Deleuze describes this type of subjectivity as "dividuality." He writes: "We no longer find ourselves dealing with the mass/individual pair. Individuals are 'dividuals,' and masses, samples, data, markets, or 'banks.'"[27] Individuals dissolve into a variety of profiles and network classes. One user might have some of their traffic throttled while others experience acceleration. These experiences appear unique or individual, a product of targeting and redlining.[28] Dividuality increases differences and fragmentation as it dissects users into dividuals. The body public, in other words, is ever thus dissected and reassembled constantly. Marco Deseriis expresses this condition well:

> By breaking down the continuity of the social bios into dividual sessions and transactions, the engineer of control produces what Franco Berardi calls a "cellularized" info-time, an abstract time that is no longer attached to the body of any specific individual but generated by the automated recombination of dividual fragments of time in the network.[29]

People remain dividualized. Daemons seemingly destabilize the traditional subjectivity of media and publics. This suggests that publics simply cannot form because the myriad of dividual sessions thwarts the necessary reflexive apparatus. Gamers, then, faced an uphill battle in trying to convene a public out of these desperate experiences of disconnection and lag.

WILL THIS PROBLEM FIX ITSELF?

Posters did find solutions. Some tried contacting Rogers. One poster described the results of such efforts: "Just called Rogers, complained, and they said 'we do not throttle people.' Called back, got a different service rep, and he said 'we have not had other complaints about this issue.'"[30] Through calls and posts, gamers began to compose themselves as they assembled more and more evidence about this public problem. By the second page of the thread, comments had begun to discuss Deep Packet Inspection (DPI), concerns about this technology raised by the Canadian privacy commissioner, and the role of the CRTC in regulating internet traffic management practices. Although posts did not solve the issue, they did help these gamers understand themselves as a public.

But this nascent public had difficulty finding a resolution. Some posters suggested avoiding the problem rather than solving it. One user experienced better connections by tunneling to WoW servers using a paid service called WoWtunnels. Not unlike IPREDator, discussed in the previous chapter, subscribers paid $3.95 (USD) per month to connect directly to WoWtunnels' server, which was located closer to the WoW servers.[31] WoWtunnels extricated gamers from the problem (to recall Bennett's question of what public should do with broken infrastructures, mentioned at the start of the chapter). But this solution carried a risk:

Blizzard, the game's manufacturer, was forever looking to stop cheaters and banned players with suspicious account activity. One replier, seemingly frustrated, summed up the issue: "So wait, are we Rogers users all SOL from now on or will this fix itself?"[32] Did gamers actually have a way to resolve their affliction?

Customers weren't out of luck, Shifthead replied. People needed to raise the issue. Shifthead posted, "if more people call in about it, the better the chance Rogers will revert the changes."[33] Calling in, to Shifthead, meant talking with Rogers and contacting the CRTC. Indeed, Shifthead wrote that the CRTC had already received one complaint. Could others write more? How could they provide evidence of the issue? How could they enlist others to help them prove it? Shifthead was calling for those in the forum to systematically care for the issue. The challenge, however, was to find ways to investigate the hidden world of daemons. His call can be heard as part of a larger refrain on the internet: how can publics embrace their daemons?

THE DEMOS AND THE DAEMON

According to Dewey, publics are an "immense intelligence."[34] This intelligence is active; it comes from members of the public being participants rather than spectators: "If we see that knowing is not the act of an outside spectator but of a participator inside the natural and social scene, then the true object of knowledge resides in the consequences of directed action."[35] One cannot see without being an active part of the world. Yaron Ezrahi quotes the above passage from a commentary on Dewey and adds that "seeing is always an aspect of acting and interacting, of coping with problems and trying to adapt and improve, rather than just contemplate, mirror, or record."[36] Ezrahi's interpretation inverts the relationship between publics and information, positing that publics do not just receive information, but produce it. Knowledge results from experience and process, not just witness and spectacle. Through the stories and conversation found in venues like the WoW forums, people come to know themselves as forming a public. These formational moments offer an opportunity to create new knowledge about the world, creating the possibility of publics becoming aware, becoming engaged, and developing into a tangible political force capable of addressing the provoking issue.

Public research works as a kind of recursion. Douglas Engelbart, ARPA researcher and early architect of personal computing, adapting the term "bootstrapping" (generally meaning developing something without assistance), describes it here as a form of positive feedback and uses it to describe a loop or recursion in which scientists, through their research, improve their ability to do research. Building a computer was both research and a better way to do research, as the computer could aid future research.[37] Geoffrey Bowker later uses bootstrapping to describe how infrastructure needs to exist in order to exist.[38] Chris Kelty describes a process like bootstrapping in his work on recursive publics, which are "publics concerned with the ability to build, control, modify and maintain the infrastructure that allows them to come into being in the first place."[39] Bootstrapping emphasizes this recursive move when publics come to know themselves, the issues, and the solution simultaneously.

Research helps a public understand its relation to daemons. Though Dewey emphasized the human side of publics, Bennett argues that the conjoint action of a public includes more than humans: "For is it not the case that some of the initiatives that conjoin and cause harm started from (or later became conjoined with) the vibrant bodies of animals, plants, metals, or machines?"[40] Could daemons not be added? The formation of a public then involves seeing itself as part of a larger system. Bennett gestures to Latour's idea of a parliament of things as a way to imagine a heterogeneous public putting daemons and demos (demographics) on equal footing, although she rejects his tendency for horizontalism. The forming of a public, then, involves more than just humans becoming aware; it requires a new sense of the world.

Such a task is well-stated by Michel Callon, Pierre Lascoumes, and Yannick Barthe in their writings on sociotechnical democracy. They argue that publics, through their formation, compose a common world. Publics begin as what they call "uncertainties of groupings" that lack a collective understanding. "Composition" designates a collective that seemingly creates a new grouping, but it also casts the identity of its members in flux. Embracing daemons is not an orientation to reality, but a composition of a common world that involves new understandings of the issues and senses of self. It is a recursive process similar to bootstrapping, or as they write, compositions "simultaneously define (or redefine) the significant entities."[41] Controversies like the nascent one facing WoW gamers are "powerful apparatuses for exploring and learning about possible worlds."[42] The challenge is to develop methods to compose the world that are inclusive of both gamers and daemons.

In what ways could the gamer publics better understand their relation to daemons and their larger infrastructures? The challenge involved a kind of public research, finding methods that could reveal the work of daemons. Shifthead began: "Are there any definitive tests that can prove this is happening to you?" In other words, what tools might be able to translate the effects of flow control or the feelings of frustration into something more tangible. Shifthead did not have an answer and dispelled hopes that simple measures could detect the issue: "I'm afraid not. Because the throttling is only dropping certain packets, pings and [traceroutes] are completely unaffected." Pings and traceroutes are popular—and very old—tools for internet measurement, as discussed in the appendix. These tools might be some of the first tools for public research of flow control. They were not the only ones.

On the third page of the thread, "Haakonii" mentions a tool named "Glasnost" that was created by one of the leading internet-measurement projects, the Measurement Lab (M-Lab). The tool simulates different packet flows (Flash, BitTorrent, and HTTP) and compares their performance. Hypothetically, all flows should perform equally. If not, then the Glasnost results provide some evidence of traffic management. Glasnost, however, lacked the ability to simulate WoW packets, and Shifthead replied, "this test is fairly useless for the type of throttling Rogers does." A fair point, but one that did not solve the public's inability to understand their problem.

Shifthead and others were searching for what I call "mediators," a term borrowed from Deleuze and by which I mean tools and methods to include daemons in publics. Deleuze writes:

> [Mediators are] not so much a matter of winning arguments as of being open about things. Being open is setting out the "facts," not only of a situation but of a problem. Making visible things that would otherwise remain hidden.[43]

Note his use of "making [the French *rendre*, to render, to make, or to return] visible," as opposed to "finding" or "revealing."[44] Broadly speaking, internet-measurement tools can function as a mediator: they return the hidden work of daemons to the public. Mediators help publics know the transaction that caused them to be affected. Mediators in this sense are both dynamic, in that they become active projects to observe flow control, and static, since they endure as databases and logs of evidence. In doing so, mediators help publics better understand themselves and their problems. Mediators function to bootstrap the reflexive apparatus and convening of publics. By revealing the modulations of flow control, internet measurements publicize the dividual effects and allow daemons to be part of the conjoint action of publics. I discuss more mediators in the appendix.

Not all mediators are technical or simply concern daemons. As mentioned earlier, blog posts and forum threads also help publics understand themselves. What the posters sought were ways to convene those members of the public not already reflexively aware of their association. Mediators, from blog posts to forums to internet measurements, become a way to convene these publics. This process of bootstrapping leads to a bigger public, more capable of composing a common world.

CATACLYSM: TERESA MURPHY AND ROGERS INTERNET

Publics did eventually convene to resolve the WoW controversy. The desperate threads and theories began to connect through the work of Teresa Murphy. She had been a WoW gamer since 2006 and noticed a strange issue when visiting her sister: Murphy could not connect to the game from her sister's Rogers Internet connection. She told the blog *The Torontoist*: "Mostly, I thought it was weird . . . you just couldn't see a cause for the problem."[45] Her attempts to diagnose the problem using internet-measurement tools failed. She could connect to the internet, but something between her and the WoW servers disrupted that connection. Using her alias "Ressy," she started a thread on the Rogers Internet technical support forums on January 17, 2011. Her initial post explained the issue and asked "Who can I talk to [in order] to get this fixed?" That turned out to be complicated.

Rogers employees replied two days after Murphy's first post, assuring her that an investigation was under way. Her first replies to the support agent were hopeful, as she expected the matter to be fixed soon. Her tone deteriorated as a week passed without any resolution. Ten days after her first post, she claimed to have heard from a WoW employee who claimed they had not been contacted by Rogers Internet. Rogers support staff continued to post in the forum to state that the matter was still being resolved. The official replies ignored new evidence posted in the thread.

As Murphy waited for a clear answer from Rogers, she began to connect the threads between the WoW forums and the Rogers forums.[46] She actively posted in Shifthead's threads in the WoW forum, as well as others dedicated to the Rogers issue. She responded to questions from other gamers, helping them understand the issue and correcting rumors. In her posts, she explained her conversations with both Blizzard and Rogers Internet. She also learned what others discovered in their own complaints and investigations. One poster in the Rogers forum shared a link to another thread on *DSLReports*. Another poster shared the news that *Starcraft 2* players were also experiencing problems and posted a copy of a chat log with Rogers Internet technical support.[47] Another poster using the alias "irix" posted that Rogers uses Cisco SCE traffic management devices. Irix explained that these devices use "a combination of packet content inspection, number of connections, connection establishment / teardown rate, packet size and other traffic characteristics to classify traffic." Irix continued, writing that changes in WoW's code meant that "the SCE can sometimes, especially under higher traffic conditions in WoW, mis-categorize WoW traffic and cause it to be rate limited / throttled." Irix's post proved to be a decisive comment offering a clear technical and alternative explanation to the problem.[48] Technical support did not reply to these comments.

Murphy's activities culminated on February 14, 2011. She posted on the Rogers Internet forum that she had sent a complaint to the CRTC outlining the problem affecting WoW gamers and her difficulties getting a response from Rogers. The CRTC responded to Murphy's letter on February 23, 2011. She wrote to her fellow WoW gamers: "I think I love the CRTC. They accepted my complaint against Rogers throttling gaming, stating it's P2P traffic."[49] The CRTC addressed their letter to both Murphy and Rogers Internet and asked Rogers to explain the issue. Thus, the burden of evidence shifted to Rogers, but only briefly. The complaint remained unresolved for the rest of 2011.

Rogers responded on March 22, 2011. Their letter admitted that an update to its traffic management practices interfered with WoW traffic, but they claimed that the issue occurred only when a customer connected to a P2P network while playing the game. This meant that if a P2P network was running on any connected device (say, another computer in a household sharing a connection among a few computers), WoW gamers might experience connection issues. Rogers also claimed that they had known about the issue and tried to fix it. Their initial solution did not work, but they promised a new one by June. Until then, Rogers suggested gamers turn off any P2P applications while running the game, including disabling the official P2P network that Blizzard used to share updates for the game.

Murphy rejected Rogers's explanation, drawing on what she learned in the forums. P2P had nothing to do with WoW disconnection issues. The theory had already been rejected in the forum threads. Two months before Rogers's reply, on February 9 to be precise, when Murphy responded to one poster to explain that she had used P2P only during patching processes, an activity infrequent enough that it alone could not completely explain the issue. Brianl, a WoW employee, replied the same day to corroborate Murphy's explanation:

> Your game connection is not on p2p, so . . . you're welcome? :)
>
> If your ISP thinks that is what is causing the issues, I humbly request that you ask them to contact us directly. We will be more than happy to speak with them and discuss why their customers may be seeing these issues.[50]

Furthermore, irix's post citing issues with the Cisco SCE appliance cast doubt on Rogers Internet's explanation. These competing explanations marked a point of collision between two worlds: Rogers Internet's public face and the gamer publics.

Murphy responded to Rogers Internet via a letter to the CRTC on March 29, 2011. No better record of the controversy likely exists than her letter. It included data collected by gamers, records of interactions with Rogers, and complaints posted in the threads mentioned above. She asked, drawing on her knowledge of Rogers Internet, why WoW traffic suffered even when no P2P networks were running. The letter documented her concerns that Rogers had misinformed its customers of the issue. Murphy also explained the technical side of WoW patching and provided a timeline that raised questions about why Rogers had not admitted the error sooner. Murphy offered a competing explanation of the issue: she argued that Rogers Internet used Cisco devices to shape traffic and that these devices misapplied rate limits to WoW traffic (similar to irix's claim).

Murphy also mentioned that similar issues with WoW connection had been reported and resolved quickly in the United States. Indeed, "Brianl," the same technical support officer helping Shifthead and others, had addressed similar disconnection issues in a thread from November 2010, explaining that Blizzard "changed [its] traffic pattern, and this is what is triggering traffic management systems to throttle individual connections."[51] Later, on November 18, Brianl explained that Cisco had to change its policy maps (discussed in chapter 5) to correctly classify WoW traffic and expected a patch in late November.[52] His comments corroborate the belief among WoW gamers that their connection issues had nothing to do with P2P networks. The questions for Murphy (and, by extension, the CRTC) were why Rogers Internet had not applied these patches and why it cited P2P traffic as the cause of the misclassification.

For all my previous talk of publics, this public response to flow control was initially something of a one-person operation. Teresa Murphy had been the sole representative of the WoW gamers to the CRTC for most of this complaint process. Her submissions alone had kept the CRTC connected to the discussions happening on WoW forums. Her letters passed on the complaints and findings of her gaming peers. She also provided an important counterargument to Rogers Internet's descriptions of their infrastructure, which conflicted with the explanations refined in the discussion threads. Like her peers in the forums, she still had difficulty publicizing the issue. Her activity had attracted no mainstream press attention and only scant coverage in sympathetic blogs up until late July. OpenMedia, Canada's digital policy advocacy group, had blogged about her case back in March.[53] Geist, Canada's foremost internet law expert, had blogged multiple times, mostly to update his readers about the status of the complaint.[54] Yet, she had also been making connections with her peers that led to a change in tactics.

Through Twitter, Murphy met another concerned party, Jason Koblovsky. He had participated in the CRTC internet-traffic-management hearings. Koblovsky mentioned to Murphy that he wanted to create an organization to represent Canadian gamers.[55] Together they cofounded the Canadian Gamers Organization (CGO) on July 26, 2011. In many ways, the group became a mediator both for gamers to understand their common issues and for the wider public concerned with the state of the internet in general. Indeed, OpenMedia allowed the group to guest blog on its website, connecting these gamers with one of the largest internet-oriented advocacy lists in Canada. This attention proved an important push to increase pressure on Rogers Internet and the CRTC to resolve the issue.

It also helped that CGO filed a new complaint with the CRTC on July 31, 2011, claiming that Rogers Internet interfered with another popular online game, *Call of Duty: Black Ops*. Their press release included a description of another test—a mediator—that showed the game suffered due to traffic management by Rogers Internet. The advocacy group also expanded their policy intervention by filing complaints with the Ontario Ministry of Consumer and Business Affairs. Their advocacy soon attracted more press attention, with the *Huffington Post* running a story on the issue on August 22, 2011.[56]

More than just expanding concern beyond a single game, CGO sustained the issue long enough for it to be resolved. On September 2, Rogers admitted that the issue affected non-WoW gamers but downplayed the problem, again claiming that it rarely happened and could be avoided if gamers turned off P2P networking. This time, Rogers Internet's response attracted more attention. The Canadian Broadcasting Corporation (CBC) reported on the issue.[57] Internet throttling again became of interest to the press.

A different mediator also made a timely intervention in Canadian media coverage. Milton Mueller, a leading expert on internet governance, used the Glasnost internet measurement project, the same tool Shifthead dismissed in the forums, to gather data about the global use of traffic management. Canada and Rogers appeared at the top of the list.[58] Though Glasnost did not help gamers solve their problem, it helped journalists understand the matter. The CBC subsequently reported that "Rogers throttles file-sharing traffic from BitTorrent more than any other Internet provider in North America."[59] Mueller's findings reinforced a narrative in Canadian press coverage that Canadian ISPs had a problematic relationship with internet traffic management.

As much as the work of publics led to the enforcement of the CRTC's net neutrality framework, the complaint was resolved outside of public purview. The CRTC passed the complaint on to its Compliance and Enforcement Sector on October 27, 2011, which meant that the company finally accepted that there was an issue that warranted penalties. Gamers did not hear from the CRTC until the next year. On January 20, 2012, Andrea Rosen, Chief Compliance and Enforcement Officer, wrote to Rogers Internet to explain that its investigation had found that its Cisco equipment "applied a technical ITMP to unidentified traffic using default peer-to-peer ('P2P') ports."[60] The CRTC, in other words, found that Rogers Internet was wrong, though not entirely. P2P networks might interfere with WoW traffic, but only because Rogers daemons misclassified game-related packets. More importantly, the CRTC found Rogers Internet had implemented a controversial policy to throttle any unknown traffic on P2P ports. Just as had been warned by net neutrality advocates, Rogers's polychronous optimization had foreclosed the unknown or the unpredictable. The perceived need for a manageable network outweighed the risk of unknown applications causing upstream congestion.

The CRTC ended its letter by asking Rogers either to rebut its evidence or to explain how it planned to comply with its regulation. The conversation ended in February 2012 when Rogers agreed to phase out any use of internet traffic management for P2P applications. This effectively ended the company's attempt to optimize its infrastructure. Today, Rogers Internet's traffic management policy simply states: "Rogers uses a variety of network management techniques. These techniques have evolved as the Internet has changed. We continue to manage the network to limit spam, viruses and other security threats."[61] It remains for the next public to hold that statement accountable.

DAEMONIC MEDIA POLICY

The controversy above raises important questions for policy and regulatory responses to daemons. This response will require reconsideration of each party's role in the affair and the matter of accountability for distributive agency. Bennett, in her own study of infrastructural failure in the North American blackout of 2003, wonders how to assign blame after breakdowns caused by distributive agency. Formulating a policy response to the blackout was frustrating, as there was nobody to blame. Her theory of agency "does not posit a subject as the root cause of an effect" because "there are instead always a swarm of vitalities at play."[62] With this in mind, what should be done? How should Rogers Internet respond to their unruly daemons? What could the regulator do to acknowledge this distributive agency? Were gamer publics essential to the complaints success or merely spectacle? Answers to these questions require regulatory and policy principles concerning the accountability and management of optimizations. These concerns have their closest affinities to the emerging debates around regulating algorithms and bots.

Certainly a daemonic media policy would mean a reorientation of accountability in internet infrastructures. Ethical debates about algorithms frame the problem as an accountability gap between "the designer's control and algorithm's behaviour."[63] Rogers discovered this gap when its daemons misclassified WoW traffic. This gap is even wider in an optimization enforced by many daemons working in tandem, and in these ethical debates, "insufficient attention has been given to distributed responsibility, or responsibility as shared across a network of human and algorithmic actors simultaneously."[64] In the case above, accusations of fault could be made against Rogers Internet, Cisco Systems, and perhaps Blizzard. All three parties faced the dilemma of discovering the problem and assigning blame. This is called a problem of "traceability."[65] Forum posts, technical reports, and independent audits all had to identify the culprit. These lines of investigation collectively pulled the Cisco router into public view—for a time.

Distributed agency should not lead to an abdication of accountability. Bennett, for her part, plays with that idea, finding two political possibilities: "It is ultimately a matter of political judgment what is more needed today: should we acknowledge the power of human-nonhuman agencies and resist a politics of blame? Or should we persist with a strategic understatement of material agency in the hopes of enhancing the accountability of specific humans?"[66] Rogers Internet, to her point, could be seen either as at fault or as a smaller player in a bigger system. They were accountable, but not necessarily to blame. They were slow to respond, but without clear intent. The ISP's unexpected or ill-advised network management policy caused as much trouble for the company as gamers. Their daemons simply did not behave the way they planned. Is internet regulation now hopeless?

Perhaps it is more a matter of responsibility than of blame. No matter how distributed the agency, Rogers Internet remains the responsible party. The company's daemons malfunctioned, and they had the authority to fix them. The resolution of the issue ultimately depended on them. Though their motivations seem ambiguous, their responsibility is clear. My point reflects one of Bennett's comments about the electrical blackout she uses to discuss distributive agency:

> Though it would give me great pleasure to assert that deregulation and corporate greed are the real culprits in the blackout, the most I can honestly affirm is that corporations are one of the sites at which human efforts at reform can be honestly applied, that corporate regulation is one place where intentions might initiate a cascade of effects.[67]

Given the humanism of media policy, a response must apply to Rogers first, before daemons, if only to ensure a cascade of effect to resolve gamers' issues. Beyond this case, more thought should be given to the traceability problem in distributed systems as called for in algorithm studies. Perhaps causality should be abandoned in favor of probability (a nod to the roots of the daemon). What if there was a threshold of traceability, an indication that a certain party has a majority or large stake in the matter. Such a turn might require a reconsideration of accountability, and perhaps a sense of forgiveness for mischievous daemons.

ISPs could also be more proactive in minimizing complexity in their infrastructures. Rogers Internet installed a daemon that they did not fully understand or control. That might hold a warning to network administrators when they install new daemons in the future. Do they know all that a daemon may do? ISPs need to better acknowledge which daemons they allow to share their infrastructure. Perhaps ISPs should aim to limit the unforeseen consequences of complexity by removing daemons. Lessened complexity might also be an added benefit of network neutrality rules that restrict the types of daemons that can be installed on a network.

In any case, ISPs need to admit they are not the only ones to speak on behalf of their daemons. Instead, they should listen more to others who understand and interpret their networks. That could be difficult for a company accustomed to representing its infrastructure, but Murphy and her fellow gamers knew a different side of that infrastructure. They too represented it publicly in the end. It is unclear how an ISP could admit not fully understanding its infrastructure in a regulatory context. Perhaps a trade-off could be made between responsibility and culpability in which ISPs are allowed to listen and admit mistakes with lower penalties. That might require more of a change in the ISPs' public relations than in the regulatory context. Even now, the consequences of violating Canadian telecommunication law are low enough to allow domestic ISPs to be more publicly engaged.

The unruly daemons of Rogers Internet pose some new challenges for traditional media regulators. They can no longer avoid studying the deep materiality of infrastructure. The CRTC, for its part, prefers to be technologically neutral, avoiding infrastructural detail in its decisions. But daemons demand more attention, and not just their active configuration but their possible uses as well. Regulations might require an ISP to disable a daemon's more advanced packet inspection features now, but once installed, these capabilities are ready to be used in the future. Reckoning with daemons might require drawing on new areas such as robot law.[68] Sandra Braman, writing about the development of the internet through a review of the Requests for Comments (RFCs) archive, reflects:

To those responsible for ensuring a network that offers all the capacities the Internet offers when unconstrained, the first pass at building a network (while simultaneously conceptualizing and reconceptualizing just what that network should be) very quickly yielded a keen sense of the importance of both daemon and human citizens; further research, conceptualization and theorization in this area would be helpful for those currently building out the domain of robot law and in other areas of the law in which machinic liability is a matter of concern.[69]

Braman's reference to robot law highlights one important pathway to daemonic media policy. Machinic liability might offer another way to frame the net neutrality debate as a question of daemonic autonomy and the risk of out-of-control daemons.

Regulators, journalists, and academics all have an important role in the formation of publics that could speak for and with daemons. The WoW gamers succeeded in large part because the CRTC responded to and validated their concerns. Institutions can be mediators for publics. Hearings by the U.S. Federal Communications Commission (FCC) and the Canadian CRTC convene publics around a shared issue and give them a chance to speak for themselves. However, the formality of the complaint process at the CRTC clearly created barriers for participation. Murphy succeeded in spite of the formal complaint letters she was asked to produce. How could regulators clarify their expectations for public participation? Policy scholar Jonathan Obar has argued that form petitions and other tools created by advocacy groups enable better public participation. Though often accused of being a kind of astroturfing or faked grassroots support, these tools help translate public opinion into a language more accessible to the regulator.[70]

Regulators might look to validating mediators (like those discussed in the appendix) that help the public diagnose and document issues. Such a task differs from calls for greater transparency or more data. Calls for transparency often assume that seeing how things work inevitably leads to understanding, trust, and regulatory outcomes.[71] But data can be obtuse, and critiques have been made against open data that are similar to those made against a lack of data. The idea of openness often stands in for the type of participation and accountability it hopes to inspire.[72] Open data, further, requires intermediaries and experts to actually use it.[73] Indeed, the CRTC already required ISPs to disclose their traffic-management practices on their websites and submit information for their annual monitoring reports, but neither effort had any bearing on the WoW complaint. By engaging more in the field of internet measurement, regulators could at least legitimate new mediators for publics to diagnose their issues. Or regulators could be even more involved by creating their own tools or by creating legislative conditions for effective disclosure. Could policy be created to facilitate Freedom of Information Act requests about daemons (similar to calls for an FDA for algorithms)?[74]

Internet measurement tools do not simply provide only data about the internet: they provide means for improving and encouraging public participation. Mediators, in this case, provide what Jennifer Gabrys, Helen Pritchard, and Benjamin Barratt call "good enough data":

> [This data] might fall outside of the usual practices of legitimation and validation that characterise scientific data (which also has its own processes for determining if data is good enough). However, it could be just good enough to initiate conversations with environmental regulators, to make claims about polluting processes, or to argue for more resources to be invested in regulatory-standard monitoring infrastructure.[75]

Internet measurement tools and other mediators might not conclusively diagnose a problem (a formidable challenge in a distributed system), but they might indicate enough symptoms to warrant further investigation.

By improving channels of public feedback, a regulator acts as an important check on the public's legitimacy. Some publics have recently taken a darker turn.[76] Conspiracies, racism, and a deep suspicion of public institutions have affectively charged online publics. The story of the 2013 subreddit about the bombing of the Boston Marathon may mark a key turning point. An attempt to crowdsource the investigation ended with two people being falsely accused and Reddit apologizing for "online witch hunts and dangerous speculation."[77] What's more troubling is that Reddit had already banned disclosing personal information on the site in part to prevent false and racialized allegations in the aftermath of the bombing. Community standards were ignored. Moderation could not keep up. The threat of these witch hunts and conspiracies will continue to haunt the legitimacy of publics. Reddit witch hunts are a reminder that publics do not necessarily act in the public interest. The effects of indirect consequences, to recall Dewey's phrase, vary by person and by class, race, and gender (terms noticeably absent from Dewey's writing).[78] The freedom to feel upset or frustrated can be a privilege not afforded to all. Regulators and corporations might act as a check on publics, holding their public-mindedness accountable.

The success of Murphy, CGO, and OpenMedia is an important reminder that media advocacy can translate popular concerns into regulatory change.[79] Groups like OpenMedia and CGO might be seen as an example of what Danny Kimball calls "wonkish populism." They employ a discursive strategy that "entails public participation in arcane administrative procedures, with rhetoric antagonistic to establishment structures, but steeped in policy minutia."[80] Part of this activism involves finding new means of public participation.

Murphy deserves the most credit for collecting and making sense of all the forum posts. Her work is like a "data story" that composed data and experience into a narrative that could be read by the CRTC.[81] Gabrys, Prichard, and Barratt suggest these data stories might be another source of "good enough data," in the Rogers case, helping publics engage with environmental problems. Murphy's intervention might be seen as one data story generated by the WoW gamers.

As they tell their stories, publics have to question how much to adopt regulatory and corporate discourses about an issue like the internet. As much as checks and balances might address accountability and equity questions with publics, they create problems about formulating the scope of the public and its means of systematically caring for something. Publics risk forming themselves around institutions unwilling or unable to address the issue. Some matters might not translate into demands easily heard by regulators. Publics then have to be aware of that which cannot translate.[82] The WoW gamers succeeded, in part, by turning the international conversations happening on forums into a national issue. This national formation perhaps limited a broader global public concerned with internet optimizations.

Publics finally need to be more aware of themselves. Becoming upset about game performance is a privilege, one not possible for anyone living in rural and remote communities with less reliable internet access.[83] Relying on customer complaints for regulation creates blindspots based on who has the privilege to complain. Big data sets in public life create similar biases. Who has the luxury to generate data?[84] Publics face a test of whether caring for their indirect consequences leads to greater public benefit. Dewey, in some ways, signals this need. An indirect consequence must be *systematically* cared for. Systematic care, in the case of the WoW gamers, meant drawing out the issue beyond their game performance, out to being about the rights of all Canadians to internet service without accidental or undisclosed discrimination. Indeed, calls for communication rights[85] or a right to internet service might be one way for publics, especially ones with the privilege of being prioritized, to demand that their experience be universal.

CONCLUSION

"Now you have seen the temporal and the eternal fire, and you have reached the place where on my own I can discern no further."
VIRGIL'S LAST WORDS TO DANTE IN THE *PURGATORIO*

THIS JOURNEY THROUGH PANDAEMONIUM NOW ENDS. Through the book, I have explored the history of internet daemons, their present work, and the conflicts between them and against them. Though contested, they are a constant presence online. Daemons run on the switches, routers, gateways, and other middleboxes that the internet's infrastructure comprises. Networking happens through their constant work. Daemons inspect, queue, route, and coordinate the sending of packets across the internet. Their distributive agency enacts what I have called "flow control." Through this control, daemons realize the conditions of transmission that govern networks online, enacting a certain optimization.

Internet daemons have come to antagonize pirates, hackers, and gamers, as well as regulators and publics. This book also has focused on the limits of daemonic control. Pirates elude daemons through cunning tactics that outrun and hide from their pattern recognition and control. Publics, conversely, try to reveal how daemons malfunction, bringing their unruly behavior to account. Yet, daemons continue to confound both pirates and publics.

Within these conflicts are two very different visions for communication. The internet has many kinds of optimization, but this book has focused on two: nonsynchronous and polychronous. The latter is currently more prominent. The goal of polychronous optimization is to consolidate authority in the infrastructure in hopes of achieving an optimal metastability for the network of networks. As a result, the unruly daemons of the early internet now fall increasingly under the tempo of a common conductor creating a stable, predictable optimization. Thus far, these optimizations have favored networks that are predictable, knowable, and desirable, as seen in the many advertisements that celebrate speed and reliable performance.

These optimizations reflect the early divides between Claude Shannon and Norbert Wiener over entropy. To recall the discussion from chapter 1, Shannon had a more positive view of entropy than Wiener. Shannon believed that entropy could contribute to information, whereas Wiener sought to avoid it altogether. Seventy years later, this debate plays out in these two optimalities. Wiener's concerns resemble those of a daemonic desire for order and managed networks. Allot Communications, a prominent supplier of internet equipment, contrasts managed and unmanaged infrastructure in a sales video for its "Smart Pipe" service. "When the pipe is unmanaged," the video explains, "bandwidth allocation is chaotic." Managed and unmanaged easily stand in for polychronous and nonsynchronous optimization. By providing a managed service, "Allot Solutions allows service providers to gain full visibility and control of their broadband networks." Greater flow control allows an ISP to structure traffic into tiers. The video continues: "For example, basic service plans give low-volume broadband consumers a package tuned to their needs and their budget. Advanced subscribers make up the majority of consumers who use internet services regularly but not excessively, while premium subscribers get the throughput quota priority and optimization services they need." The managed service, which is the polychronous optimization, translates messy uncertainty and disorder into a known, organized internet. That might not be an optimal outcome in the end. Reflecting on the history of cybernetics, Katherine Hayles ends with a provocation: "As chaos theory has taught us, disorder is not necessarily bad, and the void is not always empty."[1] Shannon's optimism about entropy might be the better choice when the alternative is to "optimize, monetize, personalize with pipes managed by Allot."[2]

These optimizations matter because the internet hosts a collision of political visions, alters the circulation of cultures, and sparks ruptures of production such as free software and user-generated content. The internet facilitates new forms of social coordination and cooperation as networks. The stakes of flow control are more than sending and receiving, more than faster or slower. Flow control keeps people and software in communication, allowing the possibility of being networked together in cultures, economies, and political movements, but also frustrating the success of networks in achieving efficiency. Too often, the definitions of the optimal remain concerned with efficiency, cost, and reliability without considering the diversity of the internet (as Allot exemplifies). My history hopefully has raised questions about the *governance of the governance* of bandwidth. As much as daemons have become more intelligent and more capable, they have not become more governable. Instead, definitions of the optimal remain calculations best left to economics or engineering. Though daemons are vital to the proper functioning of the internet, ignoring the risks of optimization leaves flow control unchecked. The future of flow control threatens network diversity as internet service providers (ISPs) optimize their networks to remove disruptions and inefficiencies, even at the expense of creative and democratic expression.

Matters of optimization and its intents exceed this book, but I hope my book offers a beginning for studies of other daemonic media. My intent has been both to analyze the daemonic internet and to guide studies of other daemonic media. In what follows, I would like to summarize some questions and approaches that arose on my journey through Pandaemonium. Finally, I offer some speculation on what I discern on the horizon and how daemonic media studies might be put in service of understanding even larger problems in media theory.

LESSONS FOR OTHER DAEMONIC MEDIA STUDIES

Throughout the book, I have shared my fascination with daemons. My many technical descriptions delight in their workings. My study offers some key questions for other daemonic media studies. What daemons inhabit other infrastructures? How do they acquire information? What are their gazes? How do they work? What are their grasps? How do these daemons coordinate? There was no one clear path to find answer to these questions: I have relied on historical documents, technical manuals, hacks, experimental observation, and policy proceedings. Each method offers a unique insight into the daemon, from being able to situate its development in a larger technical history to understanding how daemons function (and malfunction). Future daemonic media studies might find these pathways useful, but it is likely that new methods will also have to be found to study daemons hidden in proprietary code, purposefully obfuscated or simply obtuse. Intersections between computer science and media studies, discussed in the appendix, provide a good foundation for developing these new methods.

In tandem with studies of daemons themselves, I use the concept of the diagram to explore their arrangements. In chapter 3, I described a few of the diagrams associated with various states of the internet. These diagrams prefigure the daemons that come to be in their hubs and spokes. Diagrams also illustrate the actual work of daemons and their flow control. Comcast's submission to the Federal Communications Commission (FCC), discussed in chapter 4, included a diagram that elaborated how it managed Peer-to-Peer (P2P) networks. With the rise of software-defined networking and AI, new diagrams will better elaborate the changing ways daemons enact flow control. Where else can diagrams be found? How might a search for diagrams inform other studies of media infrastructure?

Finally, daemonic media studies question optimization. The internet is one great Pandaemonium, filled with daemons from its core to the end user, where one daemon provides the input for another to form patterns of continuous variation and control. Daemons cooperate to realize programmed optimalities. I have shown a particular distributive way to enact the optimal, but I believe this to be only one kind of optimization at work today. Future studies must first understand the techniques of optimization, how things other than daemons and diagrams manage social and communicative practices. Future research will also have to balance the intents of programmers with the unruliness of daemons. What is the optimal? Who (or what) defines it? When is an optimization working according to plan? When have daemons done something unexpected? Discovering optimizations as practices and goals will be difficult, but a necessary project of daemonic media studies.

DAEMONS AND OPERATING SYSTEMS

With these contributions of daemons in mind, I wish to return to one lingering question. What of the UNIX purist who complains that the daemon is a term best reserved for operating systems alone? Should the term daemon be reserved for programs managing printer queues? Do my internet daemons muddle clear technical language? To this hypothetical objection, I say that my expanded vision of daemons might be the first step to understanding the operating systems at work today. "Operating system" typically refers to the basic program that puts a computer in use, such as Windows or Apple OS.

My expansion of the term "daemon" is perhaps a symptom of a declining interest in formal research into operating systems.[3] In many ways, operating systems have been overshadowed by the term "platform," a concept used early on by Scott Lash and Adrian Mackenzie to think about operating systems as modes of participation and coordination in digital society.[4] Platforms, Lash writes, allow people to "participate in various forms of technological life."[5] While the platform highlights the user agency found on today's internet, I wonder the value of returning to the operating system and the daemon as a way to capture the scale and function of the distributive agency that coordinates social media, apps, or ubiquitous internet access.

Indeed, daemons inspired now forgotten, but much more ambitious, operating systems.[6] After Bell Labs developed UNIX, researchers there continued to work on other operating systems. Started in the late 1980s, Plan 9, Bell Labs' next operating system, attempted to move beyond the desktop to create a hybrid of a centralized time-sharing system and a decentralized personal computer. The operating system, in short, was bigger than one computer. The goal of Plan 9 was "to build a system that was centrally administered and cost-effective using cheap modern microcomputers as its computing elements":

> The idea was to build a time-sharing system out of workstations, but in a novel way. Different computers would handle different tasks: small, cheap machines in people's offices would serve as terminals providing access to large, central, shared resources such as computing servers and file servers.[7]

Plan 9 was not an operating system in today's conventional sense, since it was not located on *a* device, but rather *across* devices. In contemporary media studies, Plan 9 seems to resemble a platform, a kind of technological phenomenon operating on a massive scale, distributed across many devices.

Comparing Plan 9 to a platform is not far off from its own development. Java was the primary competitor to Plan 9. Java's designers attempted to turn the internet into one universal platform by writing code that could run on any computer no matter its local operating system, as Mackenzie presciently analyzed.[8] This possibility of a universal platform inspired Bell Labs to shift its work on Plan 9 to focus on a new competitor to Java, Inferno. The metaphor of the daemon once reserved for UNIX became the speculative foundation for a new way to imagine operating systems.

Dante's famous work inspired not only Inferno's name but also the names of its programming language, LIMBO, and its communication protocol, STYX. I cannot tell if Dante name-inspired the actual design as well, but Inferno did use a number of layers to isolate its different processes and daemons, not unlike the rings of Dante's hell. The engineers at then Lucent Labs imagined Inferno as creating a vast interconnected system of many devices, platforms, and locations not unlike the vast, interconnected cosmos toured in Dante's *Inferno, Purgatorio,* and *Paradiso.* It extended the operating system well beyond the desktop, much like the daemons encountered in this book. The operating system was

designed to be used in a variety of network environments—for example, those supporting advanced telephones, handheld devices, TV set-top boxes attached to cable or satellite systems, and inexpensive Internet computers— but also in conjunction with traditional computing systems.[9]

Inferno could be run across these different systems, uniting different technologies, devices, and users into one system. Where Java aimed to be a universal platform for development, Inferno sought to create order in a world in which "entertainment, telecommunications, and computing industries converge and interconnect."[10] With Inferno, the idea of the operating system was abstracted from the lone desktop computer or the central time-sharing system. Inferno was a "network operating system for this new world."[11]

Inferno was used in some smart telephone terminals and some of Lucent firewalls, but it never replaced Java. In turn, Java never succeeded in creating a universal platform. These failures, however, should not have us forget the scope of these pervasive systems. What if Inferno signals an overlooked change in operating systems from being local to being networked? What if the operating system now operates at a much larger scale, across many computers, phones locations, and tablets? Where I have used Pandaemonium as a concept to analyze the internet, perhaps it is Inferno that might inspire studies of global networked operating systems.

In the next part of this conclusion, I would imagine internet daemons along with other daemons and mechanisms of control at work in these networked operating systems. The internet might be seen as a place of competing operating systems, host to a few global overlapping heterogeneous systems comprised of wires, devices, and protocols, as well as daemons. Google, Apple, Facebook, Amazon, and Microsoft likely control these operating systems. While the nature and the logics of these operating systems are beyond what I can speculate here, a daemonic media studies helps explore the operation of these systems. Daemonic flow control is one of five controls in my estimation. Other daemons and controls include connecting, standardizing, mediating, securing, and transmitting. Connecting gives an infrastructure its space, creating a shared physical connection. Standards and protocols constitute a language for the computational components of networks and, at times, their human coders. Platforms and websites are mediators that enable access to digital life and the circulation of shared desires, feelings, relations, and labor. Securing, perhaps the most secret control, assesses the risks and threats in network behavior. Amid these other potential daemons and other controls, internet daemons control the flows of information within these operating systems. The following section introduces these different controls and gives examples of their operation and their limits.

CONNECTING: A NETWORK OF NETWORKS

Operating systems vary in their connectivity, depending on where they connect, whom they connect with, and how they filter their connections. As evidenced by metaphors like "cloud computing," the internet usually appears in the popular imagination as ephemeral, but these out-of-sight, buried physical connections can have profound effects on our digital lives. Homes have "tails" (slang for a fiber connection) or connect over repurposed coaxial cable or twisted-wire copper lines. These media alter how networks can send signals and the amount of available bandwidth. Comcast daemons, as discussed in chapter 4, had to make do with shared cable lines. Mediums of communication have a spatial influence on networks. Fiber backbone often follows long-established rights-of-way along railway lines. These fiber lines frequently converge at Internet Exchange Points and Carrier Hotels that establish the physical connections between autonomous infrastructures. Often, these data centers are strategically located near to cheap water to reduce cooling costs.[12] Undersea cables wind around the globe, connecting nations and corporations. For example, internet access degraded in all of eastern Africa after a boat anchor dropped off the coast of Kenya accidentally cut the East African Marine Systems cable.[13] Global connectivity depends largely on these kinds of international, often undersea cables.[14] These cables determine the routes packets take as they travel internationally.

Points of infrastructure function as important points of control.

When President Hosni Mubarak faced popular unrest, his regime tried to disconnect Egypt by turning off these sites of interconnection.[15] These interconnection points may also be monitored or filtered by daemons to prevent particular connections without completely disconnecting from the internet, such as the frequent bans of domains related to the Falun Gong in China, the blocks of The Pirate Bay (TPB) by the United Kingdom, and the CleanFeed program in Canada, which aims to block child pornography.[16]

Interconnection involves a control that influences who or what might be in communication. Robert Latham describes this control as the network relations or logics "whereby computer networks would form and then connect or not connect (and the consequences of such formation and connection)."[17] Network relations attend to the consequences of connection and disconnection and to the forces driving connections in and between networks. Who can talk to whom? Which systems connect?[18] Which nodes connect first or are avoided altogether?

The political economy of internet peering perhaps best demonstrates the control exerted by mechanisms of connecting.[19] "Peering" refers to how different infrastructures on the internet connect to one another. Few networks now exchange data without economic compensation. These few, known as "Tier 1," have agreed to settlement-free interconnections across which data passes unconditionally. This form of interconnection is closest in spirit to the internet engineers and "netheads" who valued free interconnection as a way to create a global or even intergalactic computer network.[20] However, networks now increasingly agree to settlement-based innterconnections that attach cost recovery for data exchanged. Settlement-based interconnections, known as "Tier 2" and "Tier 3," create asymmetrical data flows, with one network paying to send its traffic to the other. Recently in the United States, ISPs Verizon and Comcast has been in disputes with content-distribution networks Level 3 and Netflix over who should pay to upgrade the links between their networks.[21] Who should be responsible for maintaining peering links? Should the distribution networks bear the cost, since they send the bulk of the traffic, or should ISPs be the ones to ante up because their business model is founded on connecting to the internet?

Canada provides a good example of the political consequences of peering. Most major ISPs in Canada peer outside of the country. As a result, traffic between Canadians often travels through the United States in a process of "boomerang routing," in which data exits Canada, travels on American networks, and then returns to its final, Canadian destination. Boomerang routing has been accused of undermining Canada's information sovereignty, since many network decisions happen outside its borders, which means that Canadian data might be lawfully intercepted by American surveillance agencies.[22]

Connectivity as a control has its own limits and exploits. As much as states or other network administrators hope to control connectivity, the intense complexity of the system creates opportunities to elude this control. If their network blocks a location online, users might connect to a *proxy*, a server that acts as an intermediary between blocked content and affected user. Often, networks cannot physically disconnect a problematic site and instead block its domain. The U.S. Department of Homeland Security has taken to seizing the domain names of piracy websites whose servers reside outside the country. In other words, they prevent the domain name from locating the server when they cannot disconnect the server itself.[23] Seizing the domain name, however, does not disconnect the site from the internet, and affected users can circumvent this maneuver by using an alternative domain name server or connecting to a proxy server that connects to the internet from a different location. When the United Kingdom blocked TPB's domain, the pirates enlisted hundreds of servers to act as proxies to forward traffic to their servers without having to rely on the blocked domain names.[24] These examples demonstrate the limits of connectivity as a control, though with less optimism than when John Gilmore claimed, "the Net interprets censorship as damage and routes around it."[25]

Gilmore's optimism seems ever more dated to me amid the growing reality that the internet infrastructure increasingly relies on centralized players administering a few international content-distribution networks. The online circulation of videos, websites, and apps largely depends on a physical infrastructure of servers mirroring data. Akamai, Amazon, Google, Level 3, and Netflix are all major players in the business of content distribution. These companies own servers near consumer ISPs, or even, as in the case of Netflix's OpenConnect program or Google's Cache, *within* an ISP's infrastructure. Proximity and local peering lower connection and transit costs while boosting performance, a clear win for those with the economic power to participate in this infrastructural competition. Josh Braun calls for a distribution studies to explore the infrastructures that enable online video streaming.[26] Others have called for new internet policy to address the growing influence of these privatized infrastructures.[27]

With the rise of content-distribution networks, daemons' flow control may at first seem to have a waning influence, but these networks actually increase the importance of local daemonic optimizations. Capitalizing on local installations of content-distribution networks requires daemons able to route and prioritize them. Indeed, "zero-rating" programs proposed by ISPs in Canada and the United States leverage daemons to increase the discoverability of certain networks by advertising that its packets do not count toward their customers' data caps. If these trends continue, ISPs will increasingly use a combination of zero-rating and content-distribution networking to privilege networks with low transit costs or those with a working relationship with the ISP. Daemons, in short, are vital to managing the interconnections between parts of a networked operating system.

STANDARDIZING: DISTRIBUTION OF CONDUCT

Moving from connecting to the next set of controls that may be part of networked operating systems, standardizing, it is helpful to remember the Domain Name System (DNS) used to disconnect TPB from the British internet. The DNS acts as a bridge between the mechanisms related to connecting, on the one side, and those related to standardizing, on the other. As the de facto standard for addressing, the DNS has the power to connect and disconnect different parts of the internet.[28] The DNS wields this tremendous influence because the daemons of the internet have mutually agreed to use it to locate resources.

DNS is just one standard used to interconnect technical systems. Protocols, standards, and formats make up the second mechanism of control that allows parts of the internet, particularly daemons, to understand each other. Generally speaking, "standards" refers to agreements about measurement, quality, or safety, but digital media depend on a variety of standards to ensure technical compatibility and interoperability.[29] Different hardwares can *interoperate* so long as they abide by common standards (not a small feat, as anyone who grew up trying to share floppy disks between Macintosh and IBM computers can attest). International organizations like the Internet Corporation for Assigned Names and Numbers (ICANN), the Internet Engineering Task Force (IETF), and the International Telecommunications Union (ITU) develop, debate, and administer protocols.[30] Information also circulates through shared, standardized file formats, such as a Microsoft Word document or a HyperText-Markup-Language (HTML) file, that specify how to store information.

Standards are mechanisms of control precisely because they regulate the conduct of communication: free communication through strict standards. Alexander Galloway describes this control as "protocological"[31] and argues that it functions by distributing and embedding the same rules across the network, regulating the conduct of communication at the node. To join a network, nodes must obey the rules of a protocol. By defining the rules of networking at the nodes, protocols maintain control in decentralized networks and keep conduct consistent among diverse and dispersed nodes.

Standards have political and economic ramifications.[32] The unforeseen consequences of protocols have also had significant impacts in the domains of intellectual property and ownership. For example, competing hypertext formats widely differed in their approach to attribution: the world wide web provided far less than the fabled Xanadu Hypertext System.[33] The former allowed for rapid growth, but since no formal rules were established to attribute original sources, situations such as spammers repurposing Wikipedia content as their own easily arose.[34] Formats matter too. The small sizes of the MP3 audio format and the DIVX video format facilitated online file sharing and an explosion in piracy.[35]

Formats, standards, and protocols all exemplify the ways daemons communicate. Most often these standards are human-readable as well as machine-readable, but that might not be the case in the future. Google recently conducted a machine-learning, or "deep learning," experiment in which neural networks developed their own encrypted language.[36] While only an experiment, it points to a time when daemonic language might be entirely unintelligible to humans. This scenario presents a different kind of problem than the question of open standards.[37] Some outputs of deep learning are difficult for even their programmers to understand; the output is effectively a black box. Where proprietary, closed standards might at least be human-readable to those with access, daemons could someday create network patterns and optimizations that will be impossible for human network engineers and administrators to fully comprehend.

This matter of legibility might play out in the protocols of the Internet of Things (IoT), one term used to describe the expansion of the internet.

The future of the digital communication has at least two discernible courses ahead of it today: operating systems using Internet Protocol version 6 (IPv6) or ones filled with daemons speaking in tongues foreign to any human mind. The former would perpetuate some public oversight through standards, whereas the latter would turn the protocols of the internet into proprietary code. The laws of cyberspace might be compiled into a private language, finally breaking with the social imaginary that once dreamed of an open internet. Moves like Google developing its embedded operating system Brillo suggest that the internet is probably headed toward a fragmentation such that what I see as overlapping operating systems today disaggregate into even more distinct systems.[38]

MEDIATING: PARTICIPATION IN TECHNOLOGICAL FORMS OF LIFE

Operating systems may also control the points of entry for users, what is often called "platforms" (in a much narrower sense than discussed above with, e.g., Bell Labs' Plan 9 platform). Where protocols emphasize the conduct of the network, platforms emphasize the integration of protocols and standards.[39] Platforms are a "convergence of different technical systems, protocols and networks that enable specific user practices and connect users in different and particular ways."[40] The concept of the platform helps explore the operations of control in heterogeneous systems with horizontal and vertical factors. The next section discusses the ways platforms *mediate* as a third mechanism of control and their daemons mediate inputs in global operating systems.[41]

The platform is a particular technological stage on or from which the user can operate, a stage shared by a common user base across the web. We tweet, check in, or pin depending on the affordances and functions of platforms.[42] Facebook's website and apps allow participation in its virtual community; its technical work simplifies converting a text entry into a "status" update distributed to friends. Web browsers (often overlooked as platforms) dictate website functionality depending on how they implement web standards. The linguistic dimensions of platforms also influence user behavior and its technical functions. The term "platform" itself "fits neatly with the egalitarian and populist appeal to ordinary users and grassroots creativity, offering all of us a 'raised, level surface.'"[43] Platforms encourage users to participate in the internet only after agreeing to terms of use, privacy policies, and codes of conduct. These legal documents attempt to control user behavior with threats of legal action while also granting platforms broad access to use uploaded data. The breadth of the work that platforms do complicates their influence. YouTube's economic interest in becoming a professional streaming video platform conflicts with the demands of its users, so it has to "play host to amateur video culture and provide content owners the tools to criminalize it."[44]

Platforms mediate user input.[45] Mediation is a kind of control in its purest form, since it processes user input toward particular outputs. This influence varies from Twitter limiting all messages to 140 characters to Facebook's much more subtle forms of mood manipulation. All across the internet, web developers run constant experiments on platform users to discover the optimal layout and ensure that surfers click the right button (or donate the right amount in political campaigns).[46] Platforms also influence user behavior by reflecting their activities back in particular ways and providing personalized vantage points into the digital world, what Eli Pariser calls "filter bubbles."[47] How Netflix recommends movies influences film culture,[48] just as news apps reconfigure the work of newspaper editing through their dynamic promotion of content.[49] Facebook conducted trials that promoted content using sentiment analysis to vary the mood of a user's "news feed": a positive news feed led to a somewhat increased probability of happier posts.[50] Google News has also admitted to favoring positive stories, so when disappointed Brazilians visited the site after it lost in the 2014 World Cup, they found fewer stories that mocked their team's poor showing.[51]

Mediation often influences user behavior to maximize an operating system's profit. Most social media companies depend on user-generated content to create commodities such as data profiles, usage behavior, or simply viewers.[52] Twitter has developed a secondary business of selling access to its data firehose, the flow of users' activity.[53] Since social media depends on advertising, its platforms encourage users to post more content to create better profiles and cybernetic commodities to sell to advertisers. Facebook's news feed algorithms score users' posts to encourage them to share more and more often. Inactivity diminishes the score (at least in its 2012 iteration): the lower a score, the less likely a post will be seen by others.[54] More activity drives traffic, which leads to increased advertisement views and more advertisement sales, and in turn, those ads can be better-targeted using the profiles Facebook has built from user activity.

Users find their own use of platforms' affordances. Cultural adoption recontextualizes platforms' features in a fashion similar to Andrew

Feenberg's model of the two-stage process of technological influence from its design to its actual use.[55] MySpace, one of the early social networks, gave users the ability to pin their top eight friends to their profile page. The feature created great social conflict, as users suddenly had to justify which friends appeared in the list. Platforms' mediating constraints can be maneuvered around, or "gamed," in many ways, especially when platforms can provide revenue for users.[56] Some female content producers on YouTube earn income by gaming its recommendation algorithms. "Reply girls," as they are known, create videos in response to other highly popular videos. They edit their response so that YouTube selects a sexually suggestive thumbnail when recommending what to watch next for users. Reply girls appeal to a viewer's erotic curiosity. A link is clicked and the reply girl receives another view.[57] As a result, YouTube has adjusted its recommendation system to cut down on the success of reply girls.[58] Mechanisms of control on a platform then have to be seen as constantly being reconfigured through systems of feedback to ensure the effectiveness of its controls against these unruly mis-users.[59]

My interest in daemons complements studies of social media platforms that have questioned the role of algorithms and bots in creating, ranking, editing, and moderating content online.[60] Algorithms and bots resemble daemons in their infrastructural role. Like a daemon, algorithms run as the background processes of platforms. Likewise, on mobile phones, background algorithms communicate the device's location to advertisers in new programs like Facebook's Local Awareness[61] or Rogers Alerts[62] that enable geographically targeted ads. These are just a few examples, but they link the intelligence in the internet's infrastructure with broader trends in technology and society.

AI, bots, and daemons also operate in the production of content on platforms, more so than daemons that influence the transmission and circulation of this content. Wikipedia depends on bots to protect against vandalism.[63] Political bots on Twitter engage in what communications scholars Sam Woolley and Phillip N. Howard call computational "propaganda."[64] The political sphere as mediated by social media platforms has failed the Turing test with bots tweeting to amplify political messages, demobilize supporters, and artificially inflate the numbers of followers online.[65] These political bots are a few machines of everyday life. Most mobile operating systems have on-demand artificial intelligence companions like Apple's Siri or Microsoft's Cortana. While distinct from the daemons encountered in this book, a daemonic media studies will help analyze these new programs.

Flow control further can help to understand the influence of platforms by emphasizing the subtle nudge of responsiveness. Programs like Google's AMP (Accelerated Mobile Page) and Facebook's Instant Articles exemplify the emerging power of platforms. Both programs aim to improve how third-party stories load on their respective platforms. Facebook hosts Instant Articles so that the content of their program partners loads faster than other stories on its platform. Google's AMP sets standards for web code. The project includes specifications for a webpage's HTML code, known as AMP HTML, a new AMP JavaScript library, and a Google-owned content delivery network that "is a cache of validated AMP documents published to the web."[66] For coding to AMP standards, content creators are promised their pages will load more quickly, presumably when accessed from Google Search. These slight boosts in page-loading time promise to have a familiar affective influence—a nudge, so to speak—that might be another way platforms function as gatekeepers. Nothing will be as simple as "normal" versus "lag" mode, but rather a diverse ecosystem of content designed to nudge users into keeping within the boundaries of an operating system. These ensuing and subtle differences in performance will need the same attention as questions about trending and popularity.

BANDWIDTHS OF THE ACCEPTABLE: SECURITIZATION OF THE INTERNET

Operating systems have also become involved in a fourth control: securitization. Just as desktop operating systems have been secured, networked operating systems likely will require greater investment in security. Mechanisms of security may be understood through Michel Foucault's more historical writings on security. He discusses security as a means to influence "a reality in such a way that this response cancels out the reality to which it responds—nullifies it, or limits, checks, or regulates it."[67] Securitization has three parts: a gaze, a calculation of risk, and mechanisms of intervention. This calculation evaluates reality between "an average considered as optimal on the one hand, and, on the other, a bandwidth of the acceptable that must not be exceeded."[68] "Bandwidth of the acceptable" is a particularly apt term for examining network securitization. Certain activities on the network might exceed a limit of acceptable risk, requiring mechanisms of security to mitigate the probability of some outcomes and ensure the perpetuation of other realities. Intellectual property requires much of this investment in security. Unauthorized copying is one symptom of a technological problem that Tarleton Gillespie explains as "how to control the way that someone uses something that is freely handed to them."[69] How do you stop a user from actually using that record button? Copying music sheets, home-taping, and bootlegging each represent the vulnerability of open technologies when it comes to the security of intellectual property.[70] Where copyright has long attempted to regulate behavior, Digital Rights Management (DRM), filtering software, and trusted computing embed restrictions into computers and other platforms to prevent unauthorized uses.[71] As platforms have moved from the desktop to the web, they have developed new mechanisms to secure their content and user activity. YouTube, for example, has to check seventy-two hours of uploaded video per minute for infringement. Not unlike Charon, YouTube has developed its own guard to manage this data flow. The company's ContentID system automatically monitors uploaded videos and compares them to a database of known copyrighted works (or references files). A match causes ContentID either to block the video or to keep it up but redirect its revenue to the copyright holder.[72] Platforms' attempts to protect intellectual property point both to the influence of platforms when mediating user input and to the next mechanisms related to security that will attempt to neutralize threats, risks, and unacceptable behavior.

Mechanisms of security imbricate with the three prior mechanisms discussed above. America's National Security Agency (NSA) programs like FAIRVIEW and STORMBREW partner with major internet backbone providers to tap submarine cables.[73] Commercial ISPs worry about the health of the network and filter out threats using devices similar to those used to monitor interconnection. Network security appliances scan for bugs, worms, and viruses and stop these threats from circulating on their networks—a kind of inoculation. New security protocols like DNS-SEC secure the DNS by creating an international system of distributed trust to authenticate domain names and prevent man-in-the-middle attacks that allow a rogue server to hijack a legitimate domain name.[74] Platforms, as discussed above, also work to prevent risks. Google, for example, removed 345 million links at the request of copyright holders in 2014.[75]

Mechanisms of security have often relied on surveillance to elicit self-censorship in a population,[76] but more advanced programs have tended to avoid public attention altogether. Singapore, early in its adoption of the internet, opted for a "light-touch regulatory approach" using symbolic bans of websites to cultivate self-discipline in internet users.[77] Unfortunately, these national security measures pale in comparison to the covert militarization of cyberspace by the Five Eyes intelligence agencies.[78] Leaks from Edward Snowden and Mark Klein revealed that these agencies inspect most internet traffic through interception points installed in key locations of the internet backbone. Mark Klein described NSA "splitter rooms" installed in AT&T's network to siphon data.[79] In these rooms, a Deep-Packet-Inspection (DPI) device built by a Narus (the STA 6400 traffic analyzer) inspected AT&T customers' packet streams.[80]

Snowden, among his many leaks, disclosed how Five Eyes collects most internet traffic through upstream programs such as FAIRVIEW[81] and TEMPORA[82] that tap major undersea data cables through targeted programs such as PRISM, which collects data from major firms like Apple, Facebook, and Google,[83] or through LEVITATION, which mines data on 102 cyberlockers like SendSpace and MegaUpload.[84] Analysts then use programs such as XKEYSCORE to query the vast quantity of data collected.[85] Their efforts construct a data flow to inform their vision of reality, calculate the bandwidth of the acceptable, and regulate or nullify possible futures. These robust efforts align more with Foucault's concept of security than with his panoptic model of surveillance.[86] Five Eyes seems to prefer to clandestinely observe and intervene, rather than discipline internet users with the threat of being watched. In fact, the Five Eyes agencies could be said to encourage, rather than suppress, so that they can better identify possible threats. Able to respond when necessary without a need for spectacle, the Five Eyes have an array of cyberweapons to disable and disrupt online threats (best seen in the leaks related to the Cyber Activity Spectrum of the Communications Security Establishment of Canada, or CSEC),[87] as well as offline weapons to discredit and destroy threats.[88]

While calculations of the bandwidth of the acceptable might be difficult to observe deep in the headquarters of the Five Eyes, the industry of human commercial content moderation demonstrates how all threats require a certain degree of deliberation. Dick pics, beheading videos, and images of animal cruelty clog the inputs of user-generated content. All social media platforms require users to abide by terms of service that regulate conduct, but automating acceptable use has proven more difficult. Instead, up to 100,000 human content moderators patrol social media platforms. These low-paid laborers, usually in the global South, watch all flagged content and decide whether it violates the acceptable use policies.[89] Facebook has a "user operations" team that monitors behavior, a "safety" team that watches for self-harm, and an "authenticity" team looking for fake accounts. No matter the content, a response requires calculation. Moderators have a few moments to decide if the content is inappropriate. Guidelines, habit, and acceptable use policies inform how a moderator judges the content and how, in turn, to respond. Many firms are located in the Philippines because its colonial history provides moderators with better sensitivities to American values.[90] Bots and algorithms (mentioned above) have also begun to automate this work of securing the platform. Google and Facebook, for example, have begun to automate the human work of content moderation with new algorithms designed to flag and remove extremist videos.[91]

Throughout this book, internet daemons have had a close relation to processes of securitization. The traffic-management industry discussed in chapter 4 does double duty as a way to both manage bandwidth and secure infrastructures, and it is sometimes called the cybersecurity industry. Arbor Network's ATLAS program (Active Threat Level Analysis System), a global system of observation and detection of threats, exemplifies how daemons are tasked with solving the problem of cybersecurity. Yet, the reach of daemons also polices bandwidth. Andrea Kuehn and Stephanie Michelle Santoso join internet-governance expert Milton Mueller in arguing that DPI is increasingly used for copyright enforcement.[92] Indeed, copyright protection drives the production of new daemons to manage copyright better within infrastructures. As online piracy has moved to streaming sites and cyberlockers, Cisco Systems intends to sell a new device that inspects packets for copyrighted content and blocks them.[93] This control does not occur within the platform or in the protocol, but during transmission through the work of internet daemons. Thus, networked operating systems may be able to use daemons to nullify certain possibilities in addition to controlling the flows of information.

Together these daemons and other mechanisms of control create an ecology of control that coordinates new Infernos—networked operating systems. This broad overview contextualizes the internet daemons of this book. Flow control coordinates with mechanisms of connecting, standardizing, mediating, and securing. For networked operating systems to function, they require internet daemons to coordinate their data flows and systems of feedback across their vast distributed operations.

Daemonic media studies should prove helpful to understanding these new Infernos and their daemons as they become the internets and as they become embedded more into everyday life, expanding to connect more infrastructures, more devices, and more people. The term "Internet of Things" has been popularized to capture this expansive vision of the internet's reach. Phil Howard, in his book on the concept, argues for the term to be broadened from marketing lingo to an understanding that "nation-states, polities, and governments need to be thought of as socio-technical systems, not representative systems."[94] A renewed interest in operating systems might be a means to analyzing this wider theorization of the IoT that draws on my daemonic media studies.

LIVING WITH OUR DAEMONS

As daemons multiply, it helps to remember their mythic origins and the optimism therein. Dante, in his journey through heaven and hell in the *Divine Comedy,* encountered the demon Charon, who ferried souls across the river Styx into hell: "Charon the demon, with eyes of glowing coal, beckoning them, collects them all; smites with his oar whoever lingers."[95] Charon hints at the power of the daemon as a mythical spirit whose presence explains how something works, who repeats a task endlessly toward a goal. James Clerk Maxwell thought of his demon as being capable of what was impossible for mortals. His demon was conjured out of hope for a technical solution to human fallibility. Such optimism endures in the internet today as Maxwell's descendants champion artificial intelligence, which promises to solve what humans cannot and conceive of new optimizations to resolve issues mired in politics and policy.

This daemonic optimism raises a final question. What do daemons desire? What futures do they hope for? Rendering these daemonic desires public might be the primary task of a daemonic media studies. Only through coming to terms with our daemons will future studies be possible. Daemonic media studies embrace the volatile mixture of lively daemons, bots, and algorithms, of wires, cables, and processors, and of a multitude of humans. Daemonic media studies are fascinated by daemons because they are presently important to media policy and power. Daemons allow the internet to be a multimedia medium by managing its various networks. Where I have argued that daemonic flow control guides the operation of the internet and underlies key policy debates like net neutrality, future studies must look to other instances of daemonic influence. In an era of algorithms, AI, and bots, I expect their manifestations to be legion.

ACKNOWLEDGMENTS

Acknowledgments have always been my favorite part of a book, a glimpse into all the people connected to the final manuscript. My own book is no different. It is the product of countless interactions, moments of generosity and friendship. In writing these last words, I am happy to remember all the people who made this book possible and stayed with me on the long journey to its completion. To all those below (and to those I erroneously omitted), thank you for being part of this project.

This book started to take shape under the supervision of Greg Elmer at Ryerson University. A friend and mentor, Greg has been the most constant and supporting part of my academic career. At Ryerson, I had the privilege of working with Robert Latham, who helped me understand interdisciplinary research, and Barbara Crow, who taught me the rigor of critical thought. My home at Ryerson was always the Infoscape Center for the Study of Social Media, or "the Lab." Thanks to all members, past and present, including Paul Goodrick, Peter Ryan, Steven James May, Joanna Redden, Yukari Seko, Paul Vet, Erika Biddle, Brady Curlew, and Zachary Devereaux. A special thanks goes to Ganaele Langlois for being so influential on my thinking and theoretical approach. Many members of the Lab have helped shape this project long after my time at Ryerson. Thanks to Kenneth C. Werbin and Isabel Pedersen for the continued friendship, Matthew Tiessen for sharing a love of Harmony Lunch restaurant and Deleuze, as well as to Alessandra Renzi, who helped shape the style of the project through her brilliance and friendship.

This project really began at the Department of Communications at the University of Washington. Even though I had only one month of summer in Seattle, I miss the city and my friends there. Thanks to Phil N. Howard for giving me an opportunity to work in the Department of Communication and for the feedback as I refined this research agenda. Special thanks goes to Katy Pearce for being such an inspiring colleague and to Jessica Beyer for being a kind, most generous friend. Our conversations over beers and chips at the College Inn Pub are some of my fondest memories in Seattle, and I am so happy we have been able to continue talking about piracy and the weird internet long after I left Seattle. I am grateful to the department and David Domke for the chance to present my work before the faculty as part of its colloquia series.

Though writing is truly a lonely craft, research is not. I am so grateful for all those colleagues with whom I have had the chance to discuss common interests—so many great people. I thank Mike Ananny, Mark Andrejevic, Solon Barocas, Geneviève Bonin, Finn Brunton, Taina Bucher, Dave Choffnes, Nick Couldry, Kate Crawford, Laura DeNardis, Nicholas Diakopoulos, Joan Donovan, Kevin Driscoll, Elizabeth Dubois, Robert Gehl, Tarleton Gillespie, Alison Hearn, Tero Karppi, Tim Markham, Phil Mirowski, Milton Mueller, Taylor Owen, Frank Pasquale, Ben Peters, John Durham Peters, Jeff Pooley, Alison Powell, Sarah T. Roberts, Scott Rodgers, Nick Seaver, Tom Streeter, Lana Swartz, and Fred Turner for their feedback and comments on iterations of this project. I am so grateful to know and to have learned from so many of you. A special thanks to Robyn Caplan, danah boyd, and the great people at Data + Society for giving me a chance to attend many of their events and be a part of their community. I also thank Daniel Kriess, Dave Karpf, and C. W. Anderson for being scholars who inspire me and who have taught me so much about the field of communications. Sincere thanks to Dave Berry, Jennifer Gabrys, and especially Stephanie Schulte for their support and feedback at critical times in this book's development. One final thank you to Daniel Paré, who, in his own subtle way, contributed greatly to this project.

I completed this book in the Department of Communication Studies at Concordia University. From nuclear waste to newspapers, from games to visions of God, I never want for new ideas and ways to challenge my own thinking. Special thanks to Charles Acland, Bill Buxton, Maurice Charland, Mia Consalvo, Liz Miller, and Peter van Wyck for their feedback and insights that helped form this project. I have also had the room to succeed thanks to the dedication of my past two chairs, Monika Kin Gagnon and especially Sandra Gabriele. A few of my classes read earlier drafts of this book. Much respect goes to Roxanne, Olivier, Lindsay, Nicholas, Ramatoulaye, Maxim, Will, Harris, Tyler, Matthew, Simon, Christina, Margaret, Matthew, Quentin, Gavin, Anaïse, Adi, Krystal, Harleen, Bianca,

Nicholas, and Amanda, all students of my Perspectives on the Information Society class that read a draft in its entirety.

Outside the department, I have been welcomed as a member of the Milieux Institute and the Media History Research Center thanks to Bart Simon and Darren Wershler. Concordia is home to many colleagues whom I count as good friends. Thanks to Joshua Neves for all the opportunities to share my work. I greatly benefited from a chance to speak in his Piracy class in the Global Emergent Media Lab and from being a participant at the fantastic 2017 Seminar in Media and Political Theory: CAPTURE. Thanks especially to Jeremy Clark, Martin French, Lisa Lynch, and Elena Razlogova for being such good friends and colleagues. I would also like to acknowledge my colleagues at McGill—Gabriella Coleman, Darin Barney, Marc Raboy, Becky Lentz, and Jonathan Sterne—who have made Montreal a much richer community.

Throughout this book, I have been welcomed into the small but vital area of Canadian media policy. In the depths of writing about the ARPANET's history, I relied on this group to find meaning relevant to my own scholarship. A special thanks goes to my academic colleagues who inspire me in their engaged scholarship: Reza Rajabiun, Dwayne Winseck, Catherine Middleton, Ben Klass, David Skinner, Charles Davies, and Leslie Regan Shade. Thanks to past and present members of OpenMedia, especially Steve Anderson and Josh Tabish. I would also like to thank Hyman Glustein, Cynthia Khoo, JF Mezei, Lex Gill, and Tamir Israel for being so patient and generous with their profound knowledge of media policy. The field is now a big part of my life, and I am thankful to share this interest with such great people.

Though mentioned only in brief, my interest in internet measurement coincided with the launch of Canada's first open, public internet-measurement system. I am proud to have played a small part in the project led by the Canadian Internet Registration Authority. Thank you to Jacques Latour, Rock Chantigny, Allan MacGillivray, and Don Slaunwhite for letting me feel a part of the project and for their commitment to building the best internet for Canadians. My own knowledge of internet measurement would be greatly wanting without the advice and insights of the Measurement Lab Consortium and the Open Technology Institute. Chris Ritzo and Colin Anderson have answered countless emails, offering constant support and in-depth knowledge of the internet.

I have had a few chances to present chapters from this book or discuss my research in depth. These are institutions, reflecting on it now, that have had a profound impact on this project. I made a major step forward in the concept of internet daemons thanks to Valerie Belair-Gagnon and Colin Agur, then at the Yale Information Society Project. In addition to your friendship, the opportunity to present gave me an important push to start piecing the final project together. I also had the chance to present an early draft of what are now chapters 1 and 2 at the "Bits, Bots, and Bytes" reading group led by Gabriella Coleman. The reading group has been the site of some of my favorite discussions in Montreal. Thanks to key members, including Sophie Toupin, Christina Haralanova, and especially Gabriella Coleman for her truly generous comments. Finally, I thank the Citizen Lab for allowing me to participate in its Summer Institute. Ronald Deibert, Christopher Parsons, and Masashi Nishihata are scholars whose impact and dedication motivate me to do better, more engaged research.

I cannot begin to describe the support and guidance offered by Rob Hunt as he suffered through my desire to write in sentence fragments. His editing and support made this book possible. I cannot imagine it being completed without him. Also thanks to Margaret Macdonald for her enthusiasm and for help in the late stages of this project.

Thanks to the entire team at the University of Minnesota Press for seeing this project through to its completion.

A final thank you goes to my friends and family for supporting me through this project. I've been lucky to count David Mason, Jeremy Shtern, and Evan Light as friends willing to indulge my own daemonic obsession. A big thanks goes to Luke Simcoe, for being great and for also appreciating the dread (now a Spotify playlist called "Internet Daemons").

This book has been written through the love and support of my partner Jillian, who not only has listened to countless discussions of internet policy but reminds me every day of the joy in life and the awesome unknown. Finally, a last thank you to Wallace, my own demon of writing, whom I love without end.

This book has been graciously supported by the Social Sciences and Humanities Research Council in addition to the Open Access Fund and the Aid to Research-Related Event grant from Concordia University.

APPENDIX

Internet Measurement and Mediators

The field of internet measurement offers rich resources for finding new mediators for publics and regulators. Internet measurement is a research agenda in computer science. It refers to the development and use of software for analyzing the operation of computer networks, including the internet. As much as the internet can be taken for granted, these tools often reveal how it performs in unexpected ways. And not just for researchers either: most internet measurements are publicly available, meaning that anyone can run and use them. In this appendix, I describe a bit more of the field to those unfamiliar with approaches found in computer science.

Internet measurement is as old as the Advanced Research Projects Agency's ARPANET. Interface Message Processors (IMPs) had the ability to send a "trace" bit, or what today might be called a "traceroute." Trace bits helped ARPANET researchers map how IMPs routed packets. IMPs were required to handle trace bits distinctly and log a report that detailed how they handled packets. Collecting reports allowed ARPANET researchers to understand how packets traveled across the experimental system. Data aggregated at the Network Measurement Center (NMC) run by Leonard Kleinrock at the University of California, Los Angeles. The center was the first node in ARPANET; it collected IMP data and used the Network Measurement Program to "format and print out the measurement statistics generated by the IMPs."[1]

These early internet measurements illustrate an important lesson: studying the operation of ARPANET meant analyzing both running code and written code.[2] There is an allure in thinking of written code as the constitution of "cyberspace," a metaphor encouraged by the work of Lawrence Lessig,[3] but ARPANET had to be understood through observation. Even in the early ARPANET proposal from 1968, researchers cited a need to observe the network's operation, although they had access to all its design documents and ran simulations of its performance. As a simulation made real, ARPANET had to run in order for how it worked to be understood. Through NMC, ARPANET researchers discovered lockups, points of congestion, and other errors in IMP programs not predicted in the source code.

The NMC was one way ARPANET designers understood their daemons, and it gave way to a number of different initiatives to study internet performance. Many of the first measurement tools studied the internet through the protocological responses of daemons. Mike Muuss developed the ping tool to measure the time taken to communicate between two nodes of the network (or "round-trip" time). Muuss's tool repurposed the echo request feature of the Internet Control Message Protocol. Daemons had to reply to these requests, so ping worked by sending a request and then measuring the time taken to receive a response.[4] Ping in turn inspired the modern successor to the trace bit. Developed in 1987, traceroutes repurposed the echo request packets sent by ping to measure the different hops encountered by a packet.

While pings and traceroutes were simple, freely available tools, the growing size of the early internet required more sophisticated methods. Vinton Cerf provided a major catalyst for research in internet measurement. His RFC (Request for Comments) 1262 from October 1991 encouraged and provided guidelines for the development of tools for measuring the internet. The bulk of the short RFC stressed the need to ensure measurement did not interfere with network performance or violate privacy, but underlying these concerns was a belief that "data is vital to research and engineering planning activities, as well as to ensure the continued development of the operational infrastructure."[5] Cerf acknowledged that the task of measuring the internet was now a vital task, but no longer a small one.

Internet measurement gradually emerged as a field of research, but not overnight. As Robert E. Molyneux and Robert V. Williams wrote eight years after Cerf's RFC, internet measurement was "dispersed, fragmentary, fugitive, and rarely scholarly."[6] The Cooperative Association for Internet Data Analysis (CAIDA) was a key center of early research and remains one of the biggest initiatives dedicated to internet measurement. CAIDA began in 1997 as a project of the University of California, San Diego, and the San Diego Supercomputer Center, where it still runs today. Research in computer science did not translate into media studies except for Martin Dodge and Rob Kitchin, whose geography of cyberspace research included a discussion of the National Science Foundation Network (NSFNET) mapping efforts.[7]

Internet measurements developed into two varieties. Passive measurements "capture data in the normal working of the Internet," whereas active measurements "introduce traffic in order to test network behavior."[8] Tools measure passively because they adopt the standpoint of an observer of the network, monitoring and recording behavior. A test becomes active when it generates control traffic to measure network activity. Both methods have their supporters and critics. Passive monitoring observes actual network performance, but the approach raises privacy concerns, as it monitors usage and it may interfere with the performance of the machine, thereby skewing results. Many middlebox manufacturers, like Sandvine, have looked to sell their measurement as a new source of audience insights. Active measurement, by contrast, does not require direct access to the logs. Instead, a third party can generate its own data with active measurement. The distinction can be a benefit to some testing initiatives that seek to provide an outside perspective on performance. Many of the major internet measurement initiatives are by independent third parties and, as a result, use active measurement.

The field of active internet measurement changed significantly with the introduction of Ookla's Speedtest in 2006. For the first time, the tool crowdsourced internet measurement at scale by asking the public to test their connection and then pooling this data to make claims about the nature of connectivity in general. Speedtest started as a side project of popular internet-hosting service SpeakEasy and offered its users a simple and interactive tool to test the upload and download speeds of their home internet connection.[9] On May 25, 2010, Ookla launched NetIndex, a website that aggregated the 1.5 billion tests conducted into an interactive global map of internet speeds.

Crowdsourcing, at its best, offers a novel solution to the study of distributed systems like the internet. No one test, or even tests from one location, accurately describes the internet. Given the inability of any one vantage point to objectively assess the system's performance, crowdsourcing observes systems at scale, turning to the public to study a public thing. To scale, its tools must be run easily on home computers while adhering to standards that ensure tests (scattered across the globe) measure roughly the same part of the infrastructure. Their popularity has been their strength, and many crowdsourced internet measurements have proven useful in understanding this changing infrastructure.

The Measurement Lab (M-Lab) is perhaps the best example of a crowd-sourced internet measurement. M-Lab is an international infrastructure of testing servers located in standardized locations worldwide. The project has deployed over 130 servers located in core internet exchange points in major cities. Every server is located off-net, meaning it is run independently from an ISP. More than servers, M-Lab is an open platform for anyone to deploy measurement tools so long as they agree to release the code and the data to the public. The platform enables many kinds of crowdsourced tests, from tools to measure speed to censorship. Data is open to the public, making the project one of the few sources of public domain measurement data. In this way, M-Lab exemplifies the best practices by developing testing standards for infrastructure, maintaining an open platform to encourage new tests, and making its data open to independent analysis.[10]

Around 2003, another important measurement tool, SamKnows, was developed in the United Kingdom by Sam Crawford. SamKnows has built a testing infrastructure similar to M-Lab, actually often using M-Lab testing servers, but it has also standardized the locations of the home testing points. SamKnows has developed its own whitebox, a small computer that runs at a customer's premises and automatically tests the connection. Whiteboxes provided a more stable testbed though it is more costly to implement. Today, SamKnows is used by regulators in Canada, Europe, the United States, and the United Kingdom. The success of SamKnows is an example of how regulators can deploy their own mediators for the internet.

These are just a few approaches to internet measurement. Given the size of the field, all the approaches or tools available cannot be listed here. A few examples, however, illustrate what kinds of tools could be used to study daemons' packet inspection, routing, and queuing.

1. Packet inspection: A "frankenflow" is a technique to analyze packet inspection, specifically how daemons classify packets. Frankenflows resemble a regular flow of packets and are constructed by copying an application's packet flow and then changing data in the application layer of the copied packets. By changing specific parts of the packets, frankenflows reveal which bits a daemons reads to classify the packet. Studies using this technique have found that mobile carrier T-Mobile uses the host header in HyperText Transfer Protocol (HTTP) traffic to zero-rate video traffic for certain American customers. Understanding these detection techniques

allows for a better understanding of the types of daemons at work in a commercial infrastructure and whether Internet Service Providers (ISPs) are being forthright when describing their practices to the public.[11]

2. Queuing: Glasnost, mentioned in chapter 7, uses techniques similar to frankenflows to detect how ISPs might vary transmission conditions for different networks. Glasnost sends samples of packets associated with different networks—such as Peer-to-Peer (P2P) networks like BitTorrent and eMule, Flash video, and more traditional networks like email and HTTP—and then compares the results. By comparing performance, Glasnost reveals whether an ISP gives preferential treatment to one network over another.[12] This detection tends to compare the performance per protocol, whereas newer measurement tools can compare performance between apps. WeHe, developed by researchers at Northeastern University, University of Massachusetts, and Stony Brook University, builds on the prior work on frankenflows. It detects violations of network neutrality if one app performs better than another app. Available for both Android and Apple phones, the app allows any user to detect whether their mobile service provider might be throttling Amazon, Netflix, Skype, Spotify, or YouTube.[13]

3. Routing: The traceroute remains an important technique for testing local routing conditions, but it has also been productively used in crowdsourcing projects to understand larger patterns of internet routing. The IXmaps project asks the public to run traceroutes and upload them to its common database. Researchers then aggregate and map these traceroutes to track how packets move across international borders and whether they pass through known surveillance points of the U.S. National Security Agency (NSA). IXmaps uses popular and government websites as the destinations for its traceroutes, so the results also reveal what services might have a probability of being collected by bulk surveillance.[14]

These different internet-measurement techniques represent a few of the tools that exist to reveal the hidden work of daemons. As of this writing, I have found no clear example of how to study policy management by daemons or the distribution of rules between then.

These tools have yet to be widely adopted in any regulatory contexts. Instead, most national broadband-measurement programs tend to focus on measuring broadband speed (download and upload capacity, as well as latency). These studies provide important details about the digital divide, giving important insights into the differences between peak and off-peak performance, as well as between different ISPs and different regions. However, these programs tend to use HTTP performance as a proxy for overall web performance. Assuming HTTP exemplifies average use might become untenable with the turn toward better traffic differentiation. In response, reporting might have to provide per-protocol or per-application breakdowns. Further, the influx of new daemons in post-network neutrality regulatory contexts will require newer tools like WeHe, capable of understanding the changing modulations of flow control.

Beyond the telecommunications context, these tools may guide the study of other daemonic systems. Internet measurement could be a source of inspiration for other kinds of algorithmic audits and studies of black-box systems. In every case, mediators have to be developed that negotiate the problems of studying distributed and dynamic systems. The crowdsourcing approach, particularly M-Lab, offers a good course of action when done in the public interest.

NOTES

Introduction

1 EMule, "Disappearing Uploaders."

2 The official website is offline, but a copy is archived at Wayback Machine, https://web.archive.org/web/20060818203724/http://www.filesharingweb.de/mediaWiki/index.php/English:List_of_Bandwidth_throttling_ISPs.

3 Vuze, "Bad ISPs."

4 Roth, "The Dark Lord of Broadband Tries to Fix Comcast's Image."

5 Topolski ("FunChords"), "Comcast Is Using Sandvine to Manage P2P Connections."

6 Schoen, "EFF Tests Agree with AP"; Schoen, "Comcast and BitTorrent"; Svensson, "Comcast Blocks Some Internet Traffic."

7 Wu, "Network Neutrality, Broadband Discrimination."

8 The harm, in other words, was a contractual issue, rather than emotional.

9 For those interested in following the legal, policy, and regulatory responses to net neutrality, see Marsden, *Network Neutrality.*

10 Bastian, Klieber, Livingood, Mills, Woundy, and Comcast, "RFC 6057: Comcast's Protocol-Agnostic Congestion Management System."

11 Beniger, *The Control Revolution,* 44–48.

12 Wiener, *Cybernetics or, Control and Communication in the Animal and the Machine,* 58–59.

13 Raymond, *The New Hacker's Dictionary,* 141.

14 Eeten and Mueller, "Where Is the Governance in Internet Governance?"; Goldsmith and Wu, *Who Controls the Internet?*

15 The origin of the quote has been difficult to trace. Garson O'Toole of *Quote Investigator* (blog) found the first mention in 1992 ("The Future Has Arrived — It's Just Not Evenly Distributed Yet," http://quoteinvestigator.com/2012/01/24/future-has-arrived/).

16 Cloud services were estimated to grow from $41 billion in 2011 to $148.8 billion by 2014; Valentino-DeVries, "More Predictions on the Huge Growth of 'Cloud Computing.'" Sony's Playstation 4, a definitive media device, will stream games off cloud servers rather than requiring gamers to download copies of the game to their console.

17 CBC News, "ISPs Limit Access to CBC Download, Users Say."

18 Van Schewick, "Network Neutrality and Quality of Service: What a Non-Discrimination Rule Should Look Like."

19 BEREC and EC, *A View of Traffic Management.*

20 Hookway, *Pandemonium.*

21 Braman, "Posthuman Law."

22 Suarez, *DAEMON.*

23 Boczkowski and Lievrouw, "Bridging STS and Communication Studies," 951.

24 Wendy Hui Kyong Chun, "On 'Sourcery,'" 320.

25 Chun, "On 'Sourcery,'" 305.

26 Braman, "Posthuman Law." See also Hookway, *Pandemonium.*

27 Braman, "From the Modern to the Postmodern," 109.

28 Bennett, *Vibrant Matter,* 25.

29 Bennett, *Vibrant Matter,* 24.

30 Bennett, *Vibrant Matter,* 20.

31 Boden, *Mind As Machine,* 898–99.

32 Crevier, *AI,* 40–41.

33 Selfridge, "Pandemonium," 521.

34 Pandemonium was actually more than a proposal. Gerald Dinneen, a colleague of Selfridge, programmed a working version of Selfridge's program to recognize Morse code. It could be considered one of the first artificial intelligence programs. See: Boden, *Mind as Machine,* 705; Selfridge and Neisser, "Pattern Recognition by Machine."

35 Crevier, *AI,* 40.

36 Selfridge, "Pandemonium," 516.

37 Selfridge, "Pandemonium," 516.

38 Selfridge, "Pandemonium," 516.

39 Selfridge, "Pandemonium," 516.

40 Bennett, *Vibrant Matter,* 31.

41 Boden, *Mind as Machine,* 902.

42 Quoted in Berry, *Critical Theory and the Digital,* 122.

43 Berry, *Critical Theory and the Digital,* 121–48.

44 Cormen, Leiserson, and Rivest, *Introduction to Algorithms,* 5.

45 Selfridge, "Pandemonium," 520.

46 Kleinrock, *Communication Nets.*

47 Ford and Fulkerson, "Maximal Flow through a Network," 399.

48 D. N. Rodowick, as quoted in Elmer, "A Diagram of Panoptic Surveillance," 238.

49 Deleuze and Guattari, *A Thousand Plateaus,* 141.

50 Bennett, *Vibrant Matter,* 24.

51 Roderick, "(Out of) Control Demons."

52 Elmer, "Panopticon—Discipline—Control."

53 While machines fill Deleuze's writing, "Postscript on the Societies of Control" specifically uses the term *mécanisme/mecanism* alongside the French *machine* used

for English terms like "war machine." I use the term "mechanism" to refer to the application or processes of control.

54 Deleuze, "Postscript on the Societies of Control," 6.
55 Galloway, *Protocol*.
56 Lash, "Power after Hegemony," 71.
57 Kaplan, *Wiley Electrical and Electronics Engineering Dictionary*, 536.
58 Gucnin, Köncmann, and Tuncel, *A Gentle Introduction to Optimization*.
59 Chinneck, "Practical Optimization."
60 Beniger, *The Control Revolution*, 296.
61 Haraway, *Simians, Cyborgs and Women*, 164.
62 Kleinrock, "Principles and Lessons in Packet Communications," 1320.
63 Selfridge was vague about whether Pandemonium had supervised or unsupervised learning.
64 Kleinrock, "On Flow Control in Computer Networks."
65 Federal Communications Commission, *Report and Order on Remand, Declaratory Ruling, and Order*, 53.
66 Parks, "Infrastructure," 106.
67 Sandvig, "The Internet as Infrastructure," 100 (a nod to Harold Innis at the end).
68 Mirowski, *Machine Dreams*; Hayles, "Self-Reflexive Metaphors in Maxwell's Demon and Shannon's Choice." See also Leff and Rex, *Maxwell's Demon*.
69 Mirowski, *Machine Dreams*, 4–7.
70 Edwards, *The Closed World*; Hayles, *How We Became Posthuman*; Edwards, "Some Say the Internet Should Never Have Happened"; Mirowski, *Machine Dreams*; Pickering, "Cyborg History and the World War II Regime"; Galison, "The Ontology of the Enemy."
71 For an excellent summary of the net-neutrality literature, see Löblich and Musiani, "Network Neutrality and Communication Research."
72 For example, for possibilities of racial bias, see Pasquale, *The Black Box Society*, 40.
73 Striphas, *The Late Age of Print*.
74 Bucher, "Want to Be on the Top?"; Gillespie, "The Relevance of Algorithms."
75 Ananny and Crawford, "A Liminal Press"; Anderson, "Towards a Sociology of Computational and Algorithmic Journalism"; Diakopoulos, "Algorithmic Accountability: On the Investigation of Black Boxes."
76 Kushner, "The Freelance Translation Machine."
77 Beer, "Power through the Algorithm?"; Lash, "Power after Hegemony."
78 Gillespie, "The Relevance of Algorithms," 167.
79 Bucher, "A Technicity of Attention"; Mager, "Algorithmic Ideology."
80 Feuz, Fuller, and Stalder, "Personal Web Searching in the Age of Semantic Capitalism."
81 For a more elaborate discussion on media and infrastructure that informs my own writing, see Parks and Starosielski, "Introduction."

1. The Devil We Know

1 Haraway, "Manifesto for Cyborgs."
2 Hayles, *How We Became Posthuman*, xiii–xiv.

3 For a proper discussion of his influence, see Waldrop, *The Dream Machine*.

4 Mayr, *The Origins of Feedback Control*; Galison, "The Ontology of the Enemy," 261–62.

5 Mirowski, *Machine Dreams*, 46–54; Earman and Norton, "Exorcist XIV"; Georgescu-Roegen, "Entropy."

6 Maxwell, *Theory of Heat*, 338.

7 Maxwell, *Theory of Heat*.

8 Hayles, "Self-Reflexive Metaphors," 219.

9 I am particularly inspired by the first two chapters of Mirowski, *Machine Dreams*.

10 Hayles, "Self-Reflexive Metaphors," 216.

11 Wiener, *Cybernetics*, 57.

12 Wiener, *Cybernetics*, 58.

13 Earman and Norton, "Exorcist XIV," 455.

14 Mirowski, *Machine Dreams*, ch. 2.

15 Hayles, *How We Became Posthuman*, 12–13.

16 Wiener, *Cybernetics*, 125–26.

17 Hayles, "Print Is Flat, Code Is Deep," 225.

18 Shannon, "A Mathematical Theory of Communication."

19 Or the seas, in the case of John Cunningham Lilly; see Peters, *The Marvelous Clouds*, 64–65.

20 Artificial companionship is an old idea. Long before IBM's Deep Blue became the world chess champion, a chess-playing automaton known as the Turk enchanted Europe and the United States in the late seventeenth century (before it was revealed that a human had been secretly moving the chess pieces; see Wood, *Edison's Eve*. Before long, it would be computers treating people just like pawns in chess. In the 1820s, Charles Babbage developed mechanical machines to replace the mathematical work of calculating logarithmic tables then done by human computers, and these thinking machines could be seen to anticipate and later inspire the first digital computers; see Schaffer, "Babagge's Intelligence." However, Babbage's difficulty in gaining attention meant the idea of artificial intelligence developed for a while in theoretical physics.

21 Turing, "Computing Machinery and Intelligence."

22 Shannon, "Programming a Computer for Playing Chess."

23 Galison, "The Ontology of the Enemy."

24 Turing, "Computing Machinery and Intelligence."

25 Kittler, *Gramophone, Film, Typewriter*, 17.

26 Wiener, *Cybernetics*, 58.

27 Shannon, "Programming a Computer for Playing Chess," 256.

28 Hayles, "Self-Reflexive Metaphors," 215–16; Mirowski, *Machine Dreams*, 28–29.

29 Hayles, "Self-Reflexive Metaphors," 224.

30 Wiener, *Cybernetics*, 62.

31 Wiener, *Cybernetics*; Wiener, *The Human Use of Human Beings*.

32 Mirowski, *Machine Dreams*, 58–68.

33 Wiener, *Cybernetics*, 58.

34 Oxford English Dictionary, "Metastable."

35 Wiener, *Cybernetics*, 58.

36 Abbate, *Recoding Gender;* Light, "When Computers Were Women"; Hicks, *Programmed Inequity.*

37 Waldrop, *The Dream Machine.*

38 Kita, "J.C.R. Licklider's Vision for the IPTO"; Lukasik, "Why the ARPANET Was Built"; Waldrop, *The Dream Machine.*

39 The IRE was the predecessor to the Institute of Electrical and Electronics Engineers (IEEE). The IRE merged with the American Institute of Electrical Engineers in 1963 to become the IEEE. *Transactions on Information Theory* became part of the *IEEE Transactions on Information Theory* journal, still published today. It remains high ranking among the IEEE journals and has published groundbreaking work, such as an early description of Google's PageRank algorithm.

40 Licklider, "Man-Computer Symbiosis," 4.

41 Light, "When Computers Were Women"; Schaffer, "Babagge's Intelligence."

42 Simon, "Reflections on Time Sharing," 43.

43 Wiener, *Cybernetics*, 44.

44 Licklider, "Man-Computer Symbiosis," 5.

45 Licklider, "Man-Computer Symbiosis," 3.

46 Licklider, "Man-Computer Symbiosis," 7.

47 Licklider, "Man-Computer Symbiosis," 7.

48 Licklider, "Man-Computer Symbiosis," 4–5.

49 For a more comprehensive history, see: Aspray, "An Annotated Bibliography of Secondary Sources on the History of Software"; Campbell-Kelly and Aspray, *Computer;* Ceruzzi, *A History of Modern Computing;* Randell, "An Annotated Bibliography of the Origins of Digital Computers."

50 Edwards, *The Closed World;* Jacobs, "SAGE Overview"; Norberg and O'Neill, *Transforming Computer Technology;* Redmond and Smith, *From Whirlwind to MITRE;* Valley, "How the SAGE Development Began."

51 Conventional thinking at the time would have used electromechanical computers to run the SAGE programs. Digital computers, as Paul Edwards makes clear in *The Closed World,* were not a logical next step for defense research. Electromechanical computers had been battle tested during World War II. Scientists and engineers sold their experimental research on digital computing to the U.S. Air Force with the promise that adaptable machines would be able to track and intercept incoming enemy missiles in a complex battleground. Researchers at MIT positioned digital computing as the answer to the real-time problem. Engineers argued digital computing could be reprogrammed to adapt to varied inputs and situations, whereas the physical encoding of a program in the gears and switches of an analog machine prevents easy adaptation. Digital researchers became convinced that these analog machines operated with too much imprecision and delay for a real-time defense system. Digital computing, in contrast, offered the needed precision and instant response time. The campaign proved successful, and SAGE move forward into digital computers, foreclosing electromechanical research.

Digital computing soon eclipsed electromechanical systems as the dominant trajectory in computing.

52   Edwards, *The Closed World,* 104.

53   Jacobs, "SAGE Overview"; Valley, "How the SAGE Development Began."

54   Campbell-Kelly, *From Airline Reservations to Sonic the Hedgehog,* 41–45; Ceruzzi, *A History of Modern Computing,* 250; Copeland, Mason, and Mckenney, "SABRE."

55   Simon, "Reflections on Time Sharing," 43–44.

56   Ceruzzi, *A History of Modern Computing,* 154–58.

57   Lee, "Claims to the Term 'Time-Sharing.'"

58   In early 1959, the computer would have been called an IBM 709, but later in the year, the model number changed to 7090. The number here refers to the later model number, though both versions of the number have been used in descriptions of the CTSS.

59   Norberg and O'Neill, *Transforming Computer Technology,* 76–98.

60   Lee, McCarthy, and Licklider, "The Beginnings at MIT."

61   Though the internet and the telephone, especially AT&T, are often historically pitted against one another, the Supervisor can be seen as a digital solution to earlier electromechanical attempts to intensify the multiple messages that could be carried by one telegraph wire. Alexander Graham Bell invented the telephone while trying to create a harmonic multiplexer for telegram signals.

62   Corbato et al., *Compatible Time-Sharing System.*

63   Fevolden, "The Best of Both Worlds?"

64   Beranek, "Roots of the Internet," 56–60; Norberg and O'Neill, *Transforming Computer Technology,* 86.

65   Norberg and O'Neill, *Transforming Computer Technology,* 104–8.

66   Parks and Starosielski, "Introduction," 4.

67   Edwards, "Infrastructure and Modernity," 187.

68   Castells, *The Rise of the Network Society,* 412.

69   Galloway and Thacker, "Protocol, Control, and Networks."

70   Numerous perspectives have attempted to describe the current temporal conditions and how these conditions endure through practices or technologies. A few in-depth reviews do exist on approaches to time and society: Adam, *Time and Social Theory*; Adam, "Time"; Abbott, *Time Matters*; May and Thrift, *TimeSpace*; Brose, "An Introduction towards a Culture of Non-Simultaneity?"; Hörning, Ahrens, and Gerhard, "Do Technologies Have Time?"

71   See Williams, *Gilles Deleuze's Philosophy of Time.*

72   Mumford, *Technics and Civilization,* 14.

73   Carey, *Communication as Culture,* 157.

74   Carey, *Communication as Culture,* 168.

75   Lewis, *Flash Boys.*

76   Sharma, *In the Meantime,* 9.

77   Corbato et al., *Compatible Time-Sharing System.*

78   Take Our Word for It, "Sez You."

79   Edwards, "Infrastructure and Modernity," 188.

80 Foucault, "Truth and Power," 133.

81 Massumi, "Translator's Note"; Negri, *The Savage Anomaly.*

82 Williams, *Keywords*, 72.

83 Acland, *Swift Viewing*; Jowett, Jarvie, and Fuller, *Children and the Movies*; Lippmann, *Public Opinion.*

84 Beniger, *The Control Revolution*; Yates, *Control through Communication.*

85 Edwards, "Infrastructure and Modernity"; Star, "The Ethnography of Infrastructure"; Winner, *The Whale and the Reactor.*

86 Carey, *Communication as Culture*; Innis, *The Bias of Communication.*

87 Yates, *Control through Communication*, xvi.

88 Cf. Guillory, "The Memo and Modernity."

89 Beniger, *The Control Revolution*, 8.

90 Quoted in Guins, *Edited Clean Version*, 6.

91 Guins, *Edited Clean Version*, 7.

92 Zittrain, *The Future of the Internet and How to Stop It.*

93 Deleuze, "Postscript on the Societies of Control," 4.

94 Burroughs, "The Limits of Control," 38.

95 Beniger, *The Control Revolution*; Carey, *Communication as Culture.*

96 Galloway and Thacker, *The Exploit.*

97 McCormick, "4.6 Million Snapchat Phone Numbers and Usernames Leaked"; Wortham, "Snapchat."

98 Deleuze, "Postscript on the Societies of Control," 4.

99 Deleuze, "On Gilbert Simondon," 87.

100 Non-synchronous communication resembles what Manuel Castells calls "timeless time," which he problematizes as a global force that perturbs local times (*The Rise of the Network Society*, 464–68).

2. Possessing Infrastructure

1 Davies, "Report on a Visit to USA," 7.

2 Abbate, *Inventing the Internet*; Waldrop, *The Dream Machine*; Norberg and O'Neill, *Transforming Computer Technology.*

3 Greenberger, *Computers and the World of the Future*, 236.

4 Hu, *A Prehistory of the Cloud.*

5 Lukasik, "Why the ARPANET Was Built," 4–6.

6 Kita, "J. C. R. Licklider's Vision for the IPTO"; Norberg and O'Neill, *Transforming Computer Technology*, 26–29.

7 Licklider, "Memorandum."

8 Kleinrock, "An Early History of the ARPANET"; Leiner et al., "The Past and Future History of the Internet"; Roberts, "The Evolution of Packet Switching."

9 See Wiener's comments in Greenberger, *Computers and the World of the Future*, 21–26.

10 Turner, *From Counterculture to Cyberculture*, 1–2.

11 O'Neill, "The Role of ARPA in the Development of the ARPANET, 1961–1972," 77.

12 Frank, Kahn, and Kleinrock, "Computer Communication Network Design," 255.

13 Waldrop, *The Dream Machine*, 223–24.

14 Licklider, "Memorandum."

15 Licklider, "Memorandum."

16 Kleinrock, "An Early History of the ARPANET," 28.

17 Marill and Roberts, "Toward a Cooperative Network," 426.

18 Marill and Roberts, "Toward a Cooperative Network," 426.

19 Paulsen, "When Switches Became Programs."

20 Greene and Brown, "Route Control in AUTOVON Electronic Switching Centers."

21 Galison, "War against the Center."

22 Marill and Roberts, "Toward a Cooperative Network," 428.

23 Norberg and O'Neill, *Transforming Computer*, 163–68.

24 Roberts, "Multiple Computer Networks and Intercomputer Communication," 2.

25 I can find no evidence connecting the term "IMP" with the mythical imp.

26 Norberg and O'Neill, *Transforming Computer Technology*, 164.

27 Roberts, "Multiple Computer Networks and Intercomputer Communication," 4.

28 Kleinrock, "Principles and Lessons in Packet Communications," 1328.

29 See Chun, "Programmability."

30 Roberts, "Multiple Computer Networks and Intercomputer Communication," 4.

31 Abbate, *Inventing the Internet*, 37–38; O'Neill, "The Role of ARPA in the Development of the ARPANET," 78.

32 Abbate, *Inventing the Internet*, 23.

33 Davies, "Report on a Visit to USA."

34 Davies, "Interview," 3.

35 Davies, "Proposal for a Digital Communication Network," 3.

36 Davies, "Proposal for a Digital Communication Network," 13.

37 Davies et al., "A Digital Communication Network for Computers Giving Rapid Response at Remote Terminals," 1.

38 Davies, "Proposal for a Digital Communication Network," 1–2.

39 Davies, "Proposal for a Digital Communication Network," 5.

40 Davies, "Proposal for a Digital Communication Network," 9.

41 Davies, "Proposal for a Digital Communication Network," 8.

42 Davies et al., "A Digital Communication Network for Computers Giving Rapid Response at Remote Terminals," 3.

43 Here is another example of how packet-switching communication operationalized the breakdown between humans and machines. Packets were the standard unit of digital information for either humans or machines.

44 Davies et al., "A Digital Communication Network for Computers Giving Rapid Response at Remote Terminals," 8.

45 Mirowski and Nik-Khah, *The Knowledge We Have Lost in Information*.

46 Licklider, "Man-Computer Symbiosis," 5.

47 Mirowski, *Machine Dreams*.

48 Norberg and O'Neill, *Transforming Computer Technology*, 167.

49 Hafner and Lyon, *Where Wizards Stay Up Late*, 80–81.

50 U.S. Army, "Request for Quotations—DAHC15 69 Q 0002," 27.

51 Kleinrock, *Communication Nets*, 4–9; Kleinrock, "Optimum Bribing for Queue Position."

52 Kleinrock, "An Early History of the ARPANET," 26–28.

53 Kleinrock, *Communication Nets*, 91–94. It is unclear how much Kleinrock's theory informed the responses to the RFQ. ARPANET's design tended to be framed as a matter of system engineering (Kahn, "Interview"). Packets also did not necessarily follow the same stochastic model, since they were explicitly designed to increase network activity. Kleinrock, for his part, would continue to administer ARPANET's Network Measurement Center (NMC) and used this vantage point to research new forms of flow control in the new digital network.

54 Davies, "Report on a Visit to USA," 3.

55 Kleinrock, "On Flow Control in Computer Networks," 1.

56 Dantzig, Fulkerson, and Johnson, "Solution of a Large-Scale Traveling-Salesman Problem."

57 Wilkinson, "Theories for Toll Traffic Engineering in the U.S.A."

58 U.S. Army, "Request for Quotations—DAHC15 69 Q 0002," 22.

59 Kleinrock, "Principles and Lessons in Packet Communications."

60 U.S. Army, "Request for Quotations—DAHC15 69 Q 0002," 34.

61 Frank, Kahn, and Kleinrock, "Computer Communication Network Design," 5.

62 Bolt, Beranek, and Newman Inc., *Report No. 1763: Initial Design for Interface Message Processors for the ARPA Computer Network*, 1–2.

63 Norberg and O'Neill, *Transforming Computer Technology*, 172–76.

64 Bolt, Beranek, and Newman Inc., *Report No. 1763*, III-30.

65 All without visiting a pipeline. Frank commented: "I had heard the word pipeline and I had seen pipes maybe on TV or certainly in the movies. I had never actually visited an oil field or anything like that" ("Interview," 3–4).

66 Frank compares ARPANET's topological problem to other known problems in computer science, including the Traveling Salesman problem, survivability, the design of telephone networks, and pipelines.

67 Frank and NAC, *First Annual Report*, 4.

68 The model assumed a traffic requirement of five hundred bits per second for all nodes, with an additional five hundred bits per second added to high-traffic nodes at the University of Illinois, the computer graphics research at the University of Utah, the RAND Corporation, the Lawrence Radiation Laboratory, Princeton, and atmospheric research at the National Center for Atmospheric Research and the National Weather Service.

69 Frank and NAC, *First Annual Report*, 3.

70 Davies, "The Control of Congestion in Packet-Switching Networks."

71 Price, "Simulation of Packet-Switching Networks Controlled on Isarithmic Principles," 44.

72 Davies, "The Control of Congestion in Packet-Switching Networks," 548.

73 Davies also criticized an early version of end-to-end congestion control employed by ARPANET: refusing connections to high-volume connections or at times of congestion. Davies found that this managed the wrong part of the problem, focusing

on the link and not the data rate. Blocking a connection, I suppose, seemed a crude solution and one that avoided the more complex questions of active flow control that intrigued Davies in the paper.

74 Cohen-Almagor, *Confronting the Internet's Dark Side*, 21n18.

75 Cerf and Kahn, "A Protocol for Packet Network Intercommunication"; Kleinrock, "Principles and Lessons in Packet Communications"; Kleinrock, "An Early History of the ARPANET"; Leiner et al., "The Past and Future History of the Internet"; Abbate, *Inventing the Internet*; Waldrop, *The Dream Machine*; Russell and Schafer, "In the Shadow of ARPANET and Internet"; Russell, *Open Standards and the Digital Age*.

76 Braman, "Laying the Path"; Braman, *The Framing Years*; Braman, "The Geopolitical vs. the Network Political."

77 Braman, "Laying the Path," 70.

78 Braman, "Laying the Path," 79.

79 Braman, "The Framing Years."

80 Frank, "Interview," 14.

81 Kleinrock, "An Early History of the ARPANET," 30.

82 Sharma, *In the Meantime*, 9.

83 Mackenzie, *Transductions*, 123.

84 Gerovitch, "InterNyet."

85 Acland, "Harold Innis, Cultural Policy, and Residual Media," 177.

3. IMPs, OLIVERs, and Gateways

1 See, for example, Abbate, *Inventing the Internet*; Norberg and O'Neill, *Transforming Computer Technology*; Salus, *Casting the Net*; Waldrop, *The Dream Machine*; Russell, *Open Standards and the Digital Age*; Russell and Schafer, "In the Shadow of ARPANET and Internet"; Mailland and Driscoll, *Minitel*.

2 Licklider and Taylor, "The Computer as a Communication Device," 37.

3 Licklider and Taylor, "The Computer as a Communication Device," 37.

4 Elmer, "A Diagram of Panoptic Surveillance."

5 Deleuze and Guattari, *A Thousand Plateaus*, 141.

6 Galloway, *Protocol*, 32–33.

7 Galloway, *Protocol*, 39.

8 Galloway, *Protocol*, 30.

9 Walden, "The Arpanet IMP Program," 29.

10 Brim and Carpenter, "Middleboxes."

11 Bellovin and Cheswick, "Network Firewalls," 50.

12 Orman, "The Morris Worm."

13 Avolio, "Firewalls and Internet Security"; Ingham and Forrest, "Network Firewalls."

14 Abbate, *Inventing the Internet*, 83–90.

15 Abbate, *Inventing the Internet*, 66–68.

16 Carr, Crocker, and Cerf, "HOST-HOST Communication Protocol in the ARPA Network."

17 Abbate, *Inventing the Internet*, 78–81.

18 Carr, Crocker, and Cerf, "HOST-HOST Communication Protocol in the ARPA Network," 592.

19 Carr, Crocker, and Cerf, "HOST-HOST Communication Protocol in the ARPA Network," 592.

20 Norberg and O'Neill, *Transforming Computer Technology*, 183–85.

21 Cerf and Kahn, "A Protocol for Packet Network Intercommunication," 646.

22 Gillespie, "Engineering a Principle."

23 Campbell-Kelly, "Data Communications at the National Physical Laboratory (1965–1975)."

24 Russell and Schafer, "In the Shadow of ARPANET and Internet."

25 Abbate, *Inventing the Internet*, 124.

26 Rybczynski, "Commercialization of Packet Switching."

27 Mathison, Roberts, and Walker, "The History of Telenet."

28 Cerf and Kahn, "A Protocol for Packet Network Intercommunication," 641.

29 Mills, "The Fuzzball," 115.

30 Mills, "The Fuzzball."

31 Tanenbaum, *Computer Networks*, 17.

32 Tanenbaum, *Computer Networks*, 41–46.

33 Dourish, "Protocols, Packets, and Proximity."

34 A CIDR report that Geoff Huston maintains (http://www.cidr-report.org/as2.0/) produced this count of autonomous systems on March 13, 2018.

35 Dix, "Router Man."

36 Bunnell and Brate, *Making the Cisco Connection*, 2–7; Carey, "A Start-Up's True Tale."

37 Synergy Research Group, *Cisco's Dominant Share of Switching & Routers Holds Steady*.

38 Murphy, "A Critical History of the Internet"; Driscoll, "Hobbyist Inter-Networking and the Popular Internet Imaginary"; Carey and Elton, "The Other Path to the Web"; Kelty, *Two Bits*.

39 Licklider and Taylor, "The Computer as a Communication Device," 22.

40 Licklider and Taylor, "The Computer as a Communication Device," 22.

41 Licklider and Taylor, "The Computer as a Communication Device," 26.

42 Licklider and Taylor, "The Computer as a Communication Device," 37.

43 Licklider and Taylor, "The Computer as a Communication Device," 39.

44 Mansell, *Imagining the Internet*.

45 Quarterman and Hoskins, "Notable Computer Networks," 958.

46 Grier and Campbell, "A Social History of Bitnet and Listserv"; Quarterman and Hoskins, "Notable Computer Networks," 953–54; Shade, "Computer Networking in Canada."

47 Ceruzzi, *A History of Modern Computing*, 298–99.

48 Farrand and Carrapico, "Networked Governance and the Regulation of Expression on the Internet"; Gillespie, "The Relevance of Algorithms"; Pfaffenberger, "If I Want It, It's OK."

49 Driscoll, "Hobbyist Inter-Networking and the Popular Internet Imaginary"; Driscoll, "Social Media's Dial-Up Ancestor."

50 Ceruzzi, *A History of Modern Computing*, 298.

51 Murphy, "A Critical History of the Internet"; Senft, "Bulletin-Board Systems"; Shade, "Roughing It in the Electronic Bush"; Scott, *BBS: The Documentary*; Lungu and Stachniak, "Following TRACE."

52 Turner, *From Counterculture to Cyberculture*.

53 Quoted in Sterling, *The Hacker Crackdown*. 300.

54 Barbrook and Cameron, "Californian Ideology."

55 Rheingold, *The Virtual Community*, xx.

56 Turner, *From Counterculture to Cyberculture*.

57 Beyer and McKelvey, "You Are Not Welcome among Us"; Dyer-Witheford, "E-Capital and the Many-headed Hydra."

58 Turner, *From Counterculture to Cyberculture*, 56–68.

59 Land, "Flying the Black Flag," 186.

60 Sterling, *The Hacker Crackdown*, 77.

61 Kline, Dyer-Witheford, and de Peuter, *Digital Play*, 209–17; Tetzlaff, "Yo-Ho-Ho and a Server of Warez."

62 Bush, "FidoNet"; Murphy, "A Critical History of the Internet," 35–36; Shade, "Roughing It in the Electronic Bush."

63 Gehl, "Power/Freedom on the Dark Web."

64 For a few examples see: Abbate, *Inventing the Internet*; Abbate, "Privatizing the Internet"; Ceruzzi, "The Internet before Commercialization"; Latham, "Networks, Information, and the Rise of the Global Internet"; Moschovitis, *History of the Internet*; Murphy, "A Critical History of the Internet"; Norberg and O'Neill, *Transforming Computer Technology*; Salus, *Casting the Net*.

65 For a detailed discussion, see Russell, *Open Standards and the Digital Age*.

66 Day, *Patterns in Network Architecture*, xix.

67 The National Science Foundation had already begun to commercialize portions of its network operations. Janet Abbate wrote that the "NSF saw commercial operation of the Internet as a means to an end: a robust, high-speed, economically sustainable information infrastructure for scientists" (Abbate, "Privatizing the Internet," 10). NSFNET contracted out network service to MERIT, a consortium of the State of Michigan Strategic Fund, IBM, and MCI. IBM and MCI asked for a commercial service to recuperate their investment in the NSF backbone (Cook, "NSFnet Privatization"). The NSF agreed, and in June 1990, the newly formed Advanced Network Services (ANS) began providing the network backbone for the internet, subcontracted by MERIT. The move merged the commercial traffic that took place on ANS with the academic traffic of ARPA.

68 Shah and Kesan, "The Privatization of the Internet's Backbone Network," 96–103.

69 Turner, *From Counterculture to Cyberculture*, 154.

70 Peters, *How Not to Network a Nation*.

71 Gillespie, *Wired Shut*.

4. Pandaemonium

1 Cisco Systems, *Cisco SCE 8000 Service Control Engine.*

2 Synergy Research Group, *Cisco's Dominant Share of Switching & Routers Holds Steady.*

3 Grand View Research, *Deep Packet Inspection (DPI) Market Analysis.*

4 Grand View Research, *Global Software Defined Networking (SDN) Market Analysis.*

5 Dave Walden, a computer scientist who worked on the Interface Message Processor (IMP) at Bolt, Beranek, and Newman Inc. (BBN), has taken great steps to preserve the history of the IMP's development and even digitize its code. Walden listed at least fourteen different major updates of the IMP code from 1969 to 1989. He has also released an important archive of BBN documents used throughout this book. I'm hopeful that others will follow Walden's lead and elaborate the history of BBN and its IMPs. I thank him for clarifying the operations of the IMP to me. See Walden, "The Arpanet IMP Program."

6 Heart et al., "The Interface Message Processor," 559.

7 DeNardis, *Protocol Politics,* 6.

8 Braman, "Laying the Path."

9 DeNardis, *Protocol Politics.*

10 Bendrath, "The End of the Net as We Know It?" 4; DeNardis, "A History of Internet Security"; Ingham and Forrest, "Network Firewalls."

11 Julkunen and Chow, "Enhance Network Security with Dynamic Packet Filter," 269.

12 Elmer and Opel, "Pre-Empting Panoptic Surveillance"; Massumi, "Potential Politics and the Primacy of Preemption."

13 ISC8 Inc., "ISC8 Acquires Key Assets of Bivio Networks."

14 Finnie and Heavy Reading, *ISP Traffic Management Technologies.*

15 Parsons, *Deep Packet Inspection in Perspective*; Bendrath and Mueller, "The End of the Net as We Know It?"

16 Grand View Research, *Deep Packet Inspection (DPI) Market Analysis.*

17 Van Dijck, "Datafication, Dataism and Dataveillance."

18 Finnie and Heavy Reading, *ISP Traffic Management Technologies,* 8.

19 Cisco Systems, *Administration Guide vA1(7).*

20 Bell Aliant, "Reply Comments on Public Notice 2008-19."

21 Ingham and Forrest, "Network Firewalls," 33.

22 Kaiser, "HTML5 and Video Streaming."

23 Kafka, "How One Company Figured Out How Many People Watch Netflix's New Shows."

24 Goodin, "It Wasn't Easy."

25 Fichtner, "Bye Bye OpenDPI."

26 Finnie and Heavy Reading, *ISP Traffic Management Technologies.*

27 Anderson, "Encrypted and Obfuscated?"

28 Le and But, *Bittorrent Traffic Classification,* 3.

29 Williamson, "A Revolutionary New Approach."

30 Heart et al., "The Interface Message Processor," 551.

31 Saisei Networks, "Products."

32 Sprenger, *The Politics of Micro-Decisions.*

33 Sandvig, "Network Neutrality Is the New Common Carriage."

34 Tanenbaum, *Computer Networks*, 397–408.

35 Finnie and Heavy Reading, *ISP Traffic Management Technologies*, 6.

36 Electronic Privacy Information Center, "Deep Packet Inspection and Privacy"; Federal Trade Commission, *Protecting Consumer Privacy in an Era of Rapid Change*; Office of the Privacy Commissioner of Canada, *Deep Packet Inspection Essay Project*; European Commission, "Telecoms"; Parsons, "The Politics of Deep Packet Inspection."

37 McStay, "Profiling Phorm"; Kuehn and Mueller, *Profiling the Profilers.*

38 Paul, "Canadian ISP Tests Injecting Content into Web Pages."

39 Mayer, "How Verizon's Advertising Header Works."

40 Varadhan, *Request for Comments.*

41 Heart et al., "The Interface Message Processor," 555.

42 Tanenbaum, *Computer Networks*, 355.

43 Heart et al., "The Interface Message Processor," 555.

44 McQuillan, "The Birth of Link-State Routing," 68.

45 McQuillan, "The Birth of Link-State Routing," 69.

46 McQuillan, "The Birth of Link-State Routing," 69.

47 McQuillan, "The Birth of Link-State Routing," 70.

48 McQuillan, "The Birth of Link-State Routing," 69.

49 McQuillan, "The Birth of Link-State Routing"; McQuillan et al., "Improvements in the Design and Performance of the ARPA Network."

50 Tanenbaum, *Computer Networks*, 430.

51 Tanenbaum, *Computer Networks*, 428.

52 Cisco Systems, *What Is Administrative Distance?*

53 BIRD describes itself as "a non-interactive program running on background which does the dynamic part of Internet routing, that is it communicates with other routers, calculates routing tables and send[s] them to the [operating system] which does the actual packet forwarding" (Filip et al., "The BIRD Internet Routing Daemon Project"). It is beginning to be installed in the internet. A 2016 crowd-funding campaign, for example, raised 857 percent over its goal, netting $1,139,344 to build a high-performance home router that uses BIRD (CZ.NIC, "Turris Omnia").

54 Tanenbaum, *Computer Networks*, 429.

55 Kleinrock, *Communication Nets.*

56 Davies, "Proposal for a Digital Communication Network," 7–8.

57 Heart et al., "The Interface Message Processor," 560.

58 Van Schewick, *Internet Architecture and Innovation*, 85.

59 Kleinrock, "An Early History of the ARPANET," 34–35.

60 Kleinrock, *Communication Nets*, 7.

61 Tanenbaum, *Computer Networks*, 402.

62 Duffy, "Cisco's IOS vs. Juniper's JUNOS."

63 Cisco Systems, *Cisco IOS Quality of Service Solutions Configuration Guide, Release 12.2.*

64 Cisco Systems, *Cisco Wide Area Application Services Configuration Guide (Software Version 5.0.1)*, Appendix A: "Predefined Optimization Policy."

65 Cisco Systems, *Cisco Wide Area Application Services Configuration Guide (Software Version 5.0.1)*, Appendix A: "Predefined Optimization Policy."

66 Allot Communications, "VideoClass."

67 Openwave Mobility, "Openwave Mobility First to Use Quality-Aware Optimization."

68 Huston, *ISP Survival Guide*; Tanenbaum, *Computer Networks*, 424.

69 Tanenbaum, *Computer Networks*, 409–11.

70 Marques et al., "An Analysis of Quality of Service Architectures," 17.

71 Tanenbaum, *Computer Networks*, 412–14.

72 Paterson, "Bandwidth Is Political," 185–89; Tanenbaum, *Computer Networks*, 415–17; Paterson, "End User Privacy and Policy-Based Networking."

73 Rosen, Viswanathan, and Callon, *RFC 3031*.

74 Finnie and Heavy Reading, *ISP Traffic Management Technologies*, 12.

75 Grand View Research, *Global Software Defined Networking (SDN) Market Analysis.*

76 Feamster, Rexford, and Zegura, "The Road to SDN."

77 Juniper Networks, "NorthStar WAN SDN Network Controller."

78 Juniper Networks, "NorthStar Controller Web User Interface Guide," 58.

79 Van Schewick, *Internet Architecture and Innovation.*

80 This ambiguity has led to the existence of both broad and narrow versions of the E2E principle, according to Barbara van Schewick. The narrow definition allows for IMPs and their descendants to have some influence over networking, including, for example, some error control between internet daemons. The broad definition is a reinterpretation of the principle expressed by the authors in an article from 1998. There they state that "specific application-level functions usually cannot and preferably should not, be built into the lower levels of the system—the core of the network" (Reed, Saltzer, and Clark, quoted in van Schewick, *Internet Architecture and Innovation*, 67). Van Schewick points out that both definitions compromise on network functionality. The design rules of the broad version, van Schewick writes, "reflect the decision to prioritize long-term system evolvability, application autonomy and reliability over short-term performance optimizations" (*Internet Architecture and Innovation*, 79). Encoding functions in the core prevented the system from adapting due to the cost and difficulty of changing core networking software. However, this flexibility degrades network performance since daemons lack the intelligence to optimize traffic and control for errors. Therefore, the network has less intelligence but more adaptability.

81 Saltzer, Reed, and Clark, "End-to-End Arguments in System Design," 287.

82 Saltzer, Reed, and Clark, "End-to-End Arguments in System Design," 284–85.

83 Isenberg, "The Dawn of the 'Stupid Network.'"

84 Benkler, *The Wealth of Networks*; van Schewick, *Internet Architecture and Innovation*; Zittrain, *The Future of the Internet and How to Stop It.*

85 Zittrain, *The Future of the Internet and How to Stop It*, 31.

86 Winseck, "Netscapes of Power," 805.

87 For a comparative review of this case, see Mueller and Asghari, "Deep Packet In-spection and Bandwidth Management."

88 Van Schewick, *Internet Architecture and Innovation*, 260–61.

89 Dyer-Witheford, "E-Capital and the Many-headed Hydra."

90 Gillespie, "Engineering a Principle"; Sandvig, "Shaping Infrastructure and Innovation on the Internet."

91 Gillespie, "Engineering a Principle," 443.

92 Wu, "When Code Isn't Law."

93 Oram, *Peer-to-Peer*; Beyer and McKelvey, "You Are Not Welcome among Us."

94 DerEngel, *Hacking the Cable Modem*, 36–37.

95 Van Beijnum, "Meet DOCSIS, Part 1."

96 Cisco Systems, *Cisco IOS CMTS Cable Software Configuration Guide, Release 12.2SC*.

97 These numbers come from the internet archive's records for Comcast. The link is available at The Wayback Machine Internet Archive: https://web.archive.org/web/20060621113235/http://www.comcast.com/Benefits/CHSIDetails/Slot3PageOne.asp.

98 DerEngel, *Hacking the Cable Modem*, 66–68.

99 DerEngel, *Hacking the Cable Modem*.

100 Comcast mentions only that it had not yet adopted DOCSIS 3.0.

101 Emule, "Protocol Obfuscation."

102 Comcast included a copy of its brochure as part of its submission to the FCC.

103 Sandvine Inc., *Sandvine Essentials Training (SET): Module 1*, 49.

104 Bangeman, "Comcast Tweaks Terms of Service in Wake of Throttling Uproar."

105 Sandvine Inc., *Sandvine Policy Traffic Switch (PTS 8210)*, 1.

106 Sandvine also mentioned that its PTS 8210 could provide advertising solutions. Though Sandvine does not elaborate, the link between DPI and advertising resembles the behavioral advertising discussed by Andrew McStay in "Profiling Phorm."

107 Sandvine Inc., *Meeting the Challenge of Today's Evasive P2P Traffic*, 4.

108 Sandvine Inc., *Meeting the Challenge of Today's Evasive P2P Traffic*, 6.

109 Sandvine Inc., *Meeting the Challenge of Today's Evasive P2P Traffic*, 7.

110 In Canada, these are known as economic traffic management practices.

111 Sandvine Inc., *Meeting the Challenge of Today's Evasive P2P Traffic*, 7.

112 Sandvine Inc., *Meeting the Challenge of Today's Evasive P2P Traffic*, 12.

113 The diagram also included a standby router, presumably as a fail-safe, though it is not discussed in the filing.

114 Comcast, *Attachment A*, 8.

115 Comcast language closely resembles a report prepared by Sandvine in 2004 about the BitTorrent protocol. Sandvine described unidirectional activity as "seeding" and recommended managing this type of traffic as an effective way to cope with the popularity of BitTorrent (Sandvine Inc., *Session Management: BitTorrent Protocol*).

116 Comcast, *Attachment A*, 8.

117 Comcast, *Attachment A*, 9–10.

118 Comcast, *Attachment A*, 10.

119 Eckersley, von Lohmann, and Schoen, "Packet Forgery by ISPs"; Schoen, "Detecting Packet Injection."

120 United States Judicial Panel on Multidistrict Litigation, In re: Comcast Peer-to-Peer (P2P) Transmission Contract Legislation, Case No. 2:08-md-01992 (E.D. Pa., 2008).

121 Eckersley, von Lohmann, and Schoen, "Packet Forgery by ISPs."

122 Wu, "Network Neutrality, Broadband Discrimination."

123 Comcast, *Attachment B*, 14.

124 Comcast, *Attachment B*, 8.

125 Comcast, *Attachment B*, 12.

126 Paine, "50 Shades of Net Neutrality Is Here."

127 Paine, "50 Shades of Net Neutrality Is Here."

128 Paine, "50 Shades of Net Neutrality Is Here."

129 Taylor, *The People's Platform*.

130 Aria Networks, "Aria Networks and TierOne Announce OEM Partnership."

131 Aria Networks, "Self-Optimising Networks."

132 Pasquale, *The Black Box Society*.

133 Pasquale, *The Black Box Society*, 8.

134 Pasquale, *The Black Box Society*, 9.

135 Bucher, "Want to Be on the Top?"; Gillespie, "The Relevance of Algorithms"; Barocas, Hood, and Ziewitz, "Governing Algorithms"; Boyd and Crawford, "Critical Questions for Big Data."

136 Pasquale, *The Black Box Society*; Poon, "From New Deal Institutions to Capital Markets."

137 Gillespie, "Algorithms, Clickworkers, and the Befuddled Fury around Facebook Trends"; Manjoo, "Facebook's Bias Is Built-In, and Bears Watching."

138 Amoore, *The Politics of Possibility*, 169.

139 Amoore, *The Politics of Possibility*, 169.

140 Amoore, *The Politics of Possibility*, 169.

141 Amoore, *The Politics of Possibility*, 156.

142 Galison, "The Ontology of the Enemy," 266.

143 Bennett, *Vibrant Matter*, 25.

144 Rogers Communications, *Comment on Public Notice 2008–19*.

145 McKelvey, "Ends and Ways"; van Schewick, *Internet Architecture and Innovation*.

146 Marquis-Boire et al., *Planet Blue Coat*; Senft et al., *Internet Filtering in a Failed State*.

147 Third Generation Partnership Project (3GPP), "Partners."

148 Procera Networks, *PacketLogic Policy and Charging Control*.

5. Suffering from Buffering?

1 Starosielski, "Fixed Flow."

2 Parks and Starosielski, *Signal Traffic*.

3 Alexander, "Rage against the Machine," 19.

4 Bucher, "The Algorithmic Imaginary."

5 Marshini Chetty et al., "You're Capped."
6 Clough, "The Affective Turn."
7 See Gregg and Seigworth, *The Affect Theory Reader*; Hillis, Paasonen, and Petit, *Networked Affect*.
8 Clough, "The Affective Turn," 1.
9 Paasonen, Hillis, and Petit, "Introduction: Networks of Transmission," 1.
10 Mackenzie, *Wirelessness*, 5.
11 However, Mackenzie stepped back from linking these feelings with control, as he argued wirelessness brings "something irreducible to systems of control" (*Wirelessness*, 213).
12 Diakopoulos, "Algorithmic Accountability."
13 Massumi, *The Power at the End of the Economy*, 29.
14 Williams, *Marxism and Literature*, 132.
15 Williams, *Marxism and Literature*, 132.
16 Clough, "The Affective Turn," 2.
17 Papacharissi, *Affective Publics*, 21.
18 Armitage and Roberts, "Chronotopia."
19 Armitage and Graham, "Dromoeconomics."
20 Tiessen, "High-Frequency Trading and the Centering of the (Financial) Periphery."
21 Mosco, *The Digital Sublime*.
22 Crary, *24/7*, 124.
23 Comcast, "The Advantages of High Speed Internet."
24 Armitage and Graham, "Dromoeconomics," 112.
25 Crogan, "Theory of State," 144.
26 Virilio, *Speed & Politics*, 33.
27 Avgiris, "Comcast to Replace Usage Cap."
28 The move beyond speed draws on Gilles Deleuze and Félix Guattari. Though clearly influenced by Virilio, they questioned how he assimilated three distinct speeds (nomadic, regulated, and speed of nuclear proliferation) into one "fascist" character of speed. They argued in favor of the multiplicity of speeds, rather than overall tendency of speed (Crogan, "Theory of State," 141–43).
29 Miller, "Response Time."
30 Miller, "Response Time," 277.
31 Lazar, Jones, and Shneiderman, "Workplace User Frustration with Computers"; Shneiderman and Plaisant, *Designing the User Interface*.
32 Wakefield, "Rage against the Machine—Survey."
33 Ceaparu et al., "Determining Causes and Severity of End-User Frustration," 345.
34 Egger et al., "Waiting Times"; Hossfeld et al., "Initial Delay vs. Interruptions"; Ryan and Valverde, "Waiting Online."
35 Ceaparu et al., "Determining Causes and Severity of End-User Frustration."
36 Quoted in Bouch, Kuchinsky, and Bhatti, "Quality Is in the Eye of the Beholder," 8.
37 Akamai, "Akamai and JupiterResearch Identify '4 Seconds.'"
38 Lohr, "Impatient Web Users Flee Slow-loading Sites."
39 Krishnan and Sitaraman, "Video Stream Quality Impacts Viewer Behavior."

40 Protalinski, "BitTorrent Performance Test."

41 Gillespie, "Designed to 'Effectively Frustrate.'"

42 Yeung, "'Hypernudge'"; Thaler and Sunstein, *Nudge*.

43 Enigmax, "RapidShare Slows Download Speeds to Drive Away Pirates."

44 Quoted in Brodkin, "Verizon."

45 The discipline of transmission could also be seen as a kind of teaching through infrastructure. Susan Leigh Star suggested knowledge of infrastructures is "learned as part of membership" ("The Ethnography of Infrastructure," 381). Flow control teaches user behavior through moments of frustration, isolation, exclusion, envy, and boredom. It bothers as well as delights. Though never blocked, it frustrates certain uses or experiences of networks while simplifying others, all teaching the user how to participate in the system.

46 Beller, *The Cinematic Mode of Production*; Crary, *Suspensions of Perception*; Smythe, *Dependency Road*; Terranova, *Network Culture*.

47 Smythe, *Dependency Road*.

48 Wise, "Attention and Assemblage in a Clickable World."

49 Shifman, "An Anatomy of a YouTube Meme," 190.

50 Netflix, *2012 Annual Report*, 11.

51 Brodkin, "Netflix Performance."

52 It's worth noting that AT&T's advertisement was a slight against its rival T-Mobile, who staged a flash mob in London's Liverpool station. See: http://www.adweek.com/news/advertising-branding/ad-day-att-131843.

53 Virilio, *The Art of the Motor*, 140.

54 Ernesto, "TalkTalk's P2P Throttling Kills OnLive Games."

55 BEREC and EC, *A View of Traffic Management*, 15.

56 Rogers Communications, "Hi-Speed Internet."

57 Chetty et al., "You're Capped," 4.

58 Chetty et al., "You're Capped," 4–6.

59 See Higginbotham, "More Bad News about Broadband Caps."

60 Van Schewick, "Network Neutrality and Quality of Service," 46.

61 Stastna, "Bell's Discounting of Mobile TV against the Rules."

62 Barzilai-Nahon, "Gaps and Bits"; Mansell, "From Digital Divides to Digital Entitlements"; Norris, *Digital Divide*.

63 Rogers Internet, "Rogers Commercial."

64 Hassan, *Empires of Speed*; Rosa, "Social Acceleration"; Rosa and Scheuerman, *High-Speed Society*; Scheuerman, "Liberal Democracy and the Empire of Speed"; Scheuerman, *Liberal Democracy*; Wajcman, "Life in the Fast Lane?"

65 Scheuerman, *Liberal Democracy*, 5–6.

66 Rosa, "Social Acceleration"; Scheuerman, *Liberal Democracy*; Wajcman, "Life in the Fast Lane?"

67 Menzies, *No Time*; Rosenberg and Feldman, *No Time to Think*; Wolin, "What Time Is It?"

68 Crary, *24/7*, 46.

69 Sharma, "It Changes Space and Time," 66.

70 Sharma, "The Biopolitical Economy of Time," 73.

71 As one high-frequency stock trader explained to the University at Albany: "It's not just enough to fly in first class; I have to know my friends are flying in coach" (Lewis, "The Wolf Hunters of Wall Street:").

72 See Bauer, Clark, and Lehr, "Powerboost."

73 Virilio, *Speed & Politics*, 46.

74 Levy, "(Some) Attention Must Be Paid!"

75 Alexander, reflecting on the same issue, suggests that waiting might be a "nascent manifestation of masochism" ("Rage against the Machine," 22).

76 Edwards, *The Closed World*; Turkle, *Life on the Screen*.

77 Harvey, "The Fetish of Technology," 3.

78 Cao, Ritz, and Raad, "How Much Longer to Go?"

79 Crary, *24/7*, 123.

80 Umeaenergi, "Living with Lag—an Oculus Rift Experiment"; Umeaenergi, "Living with Lag—Lag View."

81 Barney, *Prometheus Wired*.

82 Bode, "CableOne Brags."

83 Aaron, "A Scary Picture."

84 Castells, *The Rise of the Network Society*.

6. The Disoptimized

1 For a longer discussion see Burkart, *Pirate Politics*.

2 Schwarz, "For the Good of the Net," 66.

3 One of these servers now resides in the Swedish National Museum of Science and Technology (http://www.tekniskamuseet.se/1/259_en.html).

4 Daly, "Pirates of the Multiplex"; Moya, "Swedish Prosecutor."

5 Jones, "The Pirate Bay in the Hot Seat," np.

6 Sunde, "The Pirate Bay Interview."

7 Touloumis, "Buccaneers and Bucks"; Burkart, *Pirate Politics*; Schwarz, *Online File Sharing*.

8 Deleuze, "Control and Becoming."

9 Thanks to Ganaele Langlois for help with my own translation work here.

10 Eriksson, "Speech for Piratbyrån @ Bzoom Festival in Brno, Czech Rep."

11 Schwarz, *Online File Sharing*, 127.

12 McKelvey, "We Like Copies"; Beyer and McKelvey, "You Are Not Welcome among Us."

13 Sinnreich, "Sharing in Spirit."

14 The Pirate Bay, "POwr, xxxx, Broccoli and KOPIMI."

15 Deleuze and Guattari, *A Thousand Plateaus*, 15.

16 Johns, *Piracy*.

17 Deleuze and Guattari, *A Thousand Plateaus*, 354.

18 Fleischer, "Pirate Politics,"

19 Mackay and Avanessian, *#Accelerate*; Noys, *Malign Velocities*; Beckett, "Accelerationism."

20 Deleuze and Guattari, *Anti-Oedipus*, 238–39.

21 Noys, *Malign Velocities*.

22 Frank, "Come with Us If You Want to Live."

23 Srnicek and Williams, *Inventing the Future*. See also Cunningham, "A Marxist Heresy?"

24 Berry, *Critical Theory and the Digital*; Cunningham, "A Marxist Heresy?"; Noys, *Malign Velocities*.

25 Thanks to David Berry for inspiring this reflection.

26 Halliday, "British ISPs Will Block The Pirate Bay within Weeks."

27 Sauter, *The Coming Swarm*; Wray, "Electronic Civil Disobedience."

28 Quoted in Protalinski, "The Pirate Bay Criticizes Anonymous for DDoS Attack."

29 Quoted in Protalinski, "The Pirate Bay Criticizes Anonymous for DDoS Attack."

30 Ernesto, "The Pirate Bay Turns 10 Years Old: The History."

31 Daly, "Pirates of the Multiplex."

32 Ernesto, "The Pirate Bay Turns 10 Years Old: The History."

33 Kurs, "Yo Ho Ho."

34 Norton, "Secrets of the Pirate Bay."

35 For more details about the founding of the group, see Simon Klose's 2013 documentary *TPB AFK: The Pirate Bay Away from Keyboard*.

36 Ernesto, "Pirate Bay Is the King of Torrents Once Again."

37 Schwarz, "For the Good of the Net."

38 Austin, "Importing Kazza—Exporting Grokster"; Plambeck, "Court Rules That LimeWire Infringed on Copyrights."

39 Wikipedia keeps an excellent list of BitTorrent sites that have shuttered over the years (http://en.wikipedia.org/wiki/Legal_issues_with_BitTorrent).

40 Cohen, "Decentralization [BitTorrent release announcement]."

41 Legout, Urvoy-Keller, and Michiardi, "Understanding Bittorrent."

42 Chung, "Bell Reveals Internet Throttling Details to CRTC."

43 Rogers Communications, *Comment on Public Notice 2008–19*.

44 Rogers Communications, "Rogers Network Management Policy."

45 Chung, "Bell Reveals Internet Throttling Details to CRTC."

46 Anderson, "Pirate Bay Moves to Decentralized DHT Protocol, Kills Tracker."

47 Geere, "Pirate Bay to Abandon .torrent Files for Magnet Links."

48 Ernesto, "BitTorrent's Future."

49 Ernesto, "Download a Copy of The Pirate Bay."

50 Ernesto, "The Pirate Bay Ships New Servers to Mountain Complex"; Libbenga, "The Pirate Bay Plans to Buy Sealand."

51 Norton, "Secrets of the Pirate Bay."

52 Fleischer, "Pirate Politics."

53 Deleuze, "Control and Becoming," 175.

54 Deleuze, "Having an Idea in Cinema."

55 Burkart, *Pirate Politics*, 87–92.

56 McKelvey, "We Like Copies."

57 Greenberg, "Meet Telecomix."

58 Tay, "Pirate Bay's IPREDator Not a Place to Hide."

59 Wood et al., "Virtual Private Networks."

60 Snader, *VPNs Illustrated.*

61 Hamzeh et al., "RFC 2637."

62 Patoway, "Security Flaw Makes PPTP VPN Useless for Hiding IP on BitTorrent."

63 Tay, "Pirate Bay's IPREDator Not a Place to Hide."

64 Quoted from the IPREDator "Legal" page: https://www.ipredator.se/page/legal. The page does not provide an author or date, but more information about IPREDator can be found at https://ipredator.se/page/about.

65 Lawson, "Blue Coat to Acquire Packeteer for $268 Million."

66 Packeteer Inc., *Packeteer's PacketShaper/ISP.*

67 DeMaria, "PacketShaper 8500."

68 Packeteer Inc., *Packetshaper Packetseeker Getting Started Guide.*

69 Packeteer Inc., *Packetshaper Packetseeker Getting Started Guide.*

70 Brunton and Nissenbaum, "Vernacular Resistance to Data Collection and Analysis."

71 Deleuze and Guattari, *A Thousand Plateaus,* 354.

72 Deleuze and Guattari, *A Thousand Plateaus,* 354.

73 Deleuze and Guattari, *A Thousand Plateaus,* 415.

74 Fleischer, "Piratbyran's Speech at Reboot."

75 Fleischer, "Pirate Politics."

76 Paine, "50 Shades of Net Neutrality Is Here."

77 McKelvey, Tiessen, and Simcoe, "A Consensual Hallucination No More?"

78 Haralanova and Light, "Enmeshed Lives?"

79 Burkart, "Cultural Environmentalism and Collective Action"; Miegel and Olsson, "From Pirates to Politician."

80 Ernesto, "The Pirate Bay Appeal Verdict"; Kiss, "The Pirate Bay Trial."

81 Lindgren and Linde, "The Subpolitics of Online Piracy," 148–49.

82 The page is accessible at https://www.facebook.com/ThePirateBayWarMachine/.

83 Ernesto, "Top 10 Most Popular Torrent Sites of 2016."

7. A Crescendo of Online Interactive Debugging?

1 Bouwsma, "Descartes' Evil Genius."

2 Bennett, *Vibrant Matter,* 37–38.

3 Kelty, *Two Bits.*

4 Coleman, *Coding Freedom.*

5 Sandvig et al., "An Algorithm Audit."

6 Shifthead, "Rogers ISP, WoW, and You!"

7 Ernesto, "Rogers' BitTorrent Throttling Experiment Goes Horribly Wrong."

8 Anderson, "Canadian ISPs Furious about Bell Canada's Traffic Throttling"; Nowak, "CRTC Opens Net Neutrality Debate to Public."

9 Bendrath and Mueller, "The End of the Net as We Know It?"; Geist, "CRTC Sets Net Neutrality Framework."

10 Parsons, "Rogers, Network Failures, and Third-Party Oversight."

11 Dewey, *The Public and Its Problems,* 15–16.

12 Bennett, *Vibrant Matter,* 100.

13 Edwards et al., "Introduction."

14 Ananny, "Toward an Ethics."

15 Cheney-Lippold, "A New Algorithmic Identity"; Elmer, *Profiling Machines*.

16 Papacharissi, *Affective Publics*.

17 RogersKeith, Comment on Vindari, "[Extreme Plus] Utorrent Settings and Rogers."

18 Goldmonger, "Canada ISP Latency Issues."

19 Ressy, "Rogers Throttling/Deprioritizing World of Warcraft."

20 Warner, "Publics and Counterpublics," 55.

21 Marres, "Front-Staging Nonhumans," 204.

22 Anderson, *Imagined Communities*.

23 Anderson, *Imagined Communities*, 33.

24 Haakonii, Comment on Shifthead, "Rogers ISP, WoW, and You!"

25 Langlois, "Meaning, Semiotechnologies and Participatory Media," 22.

26 Gehl, "The Archive and the Processor."

27 Deleuze, "Postscript on the Societies of Control," 5.

28 See Sandvig, "Network Neutrality Is the New Common Carriage."

29 Deseriis, "The General, the Watchman, and the Engineer of Control," 392.

30 Fault, Comment on Shifthead, "Rogers ISP, WoW, and You!"

31 WoWtunnels is now defunct, but the Internet Archive has a copy of their website: https://web.archive.org/web/20080605055306/http://www.wowtunnels.com/.

32 Winderans, Comment on Shifthead, "Rogers ISP, WoW, and You!"

33 Shifthead, "Rogers ISP, WoW, and You!"

34 Dewey, *The Public and Its Problems*, 219.

35 Dewey as quoted in Ezrahi, "Dewey's Critique," 318.

36 Dewey as quoted in Ezrahi, "Dewey's Critique," 322.

37 Bardini, *Bootstrapping*, 23–24.

38 Bowker, "The History of Information Infrastructures."

39 Kelty, *Two Bits*, 7.

40 Bennett, *Vibrant Matter*, 102.

41 Callon, Lascoumes, and Barthe, *Acting in an Uncertain World*, 132.

42 Callon, Lascoumes, and Barthe, *Acting in an Uncertain World*, 28.

43 Deleuze, "Mediators," 127.

44 See Latham, "Border Formations."

45 Kupferman, "How World of Warcraft Players Got Rogers to Admit It Was Wrong."

46 Ressy also wrote a detailed log of the interactions between gamers and the CRTC, but the link to it has gone dead.

47 KingNerd, Comment on Ressy, "Rogers Throttling/Deprioritizing World of Warcraft."

48 Irix, Comment on Ressy, "Rogers Throttling/Deprioritizing World of Warcraft."

49 Ressie, Comment on Goldmonger, "Canada ISP Latency Issues."

50 Brianl, Comment on Goldmonger, "Canada ISP Latency Issues."

51 Brianl, Comment 1 on Tachion, "Outrageous Latency & Constant DC."

52 Brianl, Comment 2 on Tachion, "Outrageous Latency & Constant DC."

53 Webb, "Gamers vs. Rogers."

54 Geist, "Rogers Faces More Questions"; Geist, "CRTC Issues Warning to Rogers."

55 Ellis, "Why Is the CRTC Auditing the Gamers Instead of Rogers?"

56 Tencer, "Gamers' Group."

57 CBC News, "Rogers Admits It May Be Throttling Games."

58 Mueller and Asghari, "Deep Packet Inspection and Bandwidth Management"; Asghari, van Eeten, and Mueller, *Internet Measurements and Public Policy.*

59 Chung, "Rogers Throttling May Breach Net Neutrality Rules."

60 Canadian Radio-Television and Telecommunications Commission (CRTC), Archived email.

61 Rogers Internet, "Rogers Network Management Policy."

62 Bennett, *Vibrant Matter,* 31–32.

63 Mittelstadt et al., "The Ethics of Algorithms," 11.

64 Mittelstadt et al., "The Ethics of Algorithms," 12.

65 Mittelstadt et al., "The Ethics of Algorithms," 5.

66 Bennett, *Vibrant Matter,* 38.

67 Bennett, *Vibrant Matter,* 37.

68 Calo, Froomkin, and Kerr, *Robot Law.*

69 Braman, "The Geopolitical vs. the Network Political," 291.

70 Obar, "Closing the Technocratic Divide?"

71 Flyverbom, "Transparency"; Ananny and Crawford, "Seeing without Knowing."

72 McKelvey, "Openness Compromised?"; Tkacz, *Wikipedia and the Politics of Openness.*

73 Schrock and Shaffer, "Data Ideologies of an Interested Public."

74 Tutt, "An FDA for Algorithms."

75 Gabrys, Pritchard, and Barratt, "Just Good Enough Data," 2.

76 Brabham, "The Boston Marathon Bombings"; Nhan, Huey, and Broll, "Digilantism"; Schneider and Trottier, "The 2011 Vancouver Riot."

77 Reddit, "Reflections on the Recent Boston Crisis."

78 Margonis, "John Dewey's Racialized Visions of the Student and Classroom Community."

79 Shade, "Public Interest Activism in Canadian ICT Policy."

80 Kimball, "Wonkish Populism."

81 Gabrys, Pritchard, and Barratt, "Just Good Enough Data."

82 Neilson and Rossiter, "Precarity as a Political Concept," 64–67.

83 McMahon et al., "Making Information Technologies Work at the End of the Road."

84 Crawford, "The Hidden Biases in Big Data."

85 Raboy and Shtern, *Media Divides.*

Conclusion

1 Hayles, *How We Became Posthuman,* 232.

2 Allot Communications, "Allot Smart Pipe Management."

3 Pike, *Systems Software Research Is Irrelevant.*

4 Mackenzie, "Java"; Lash, *Critique of Information.*

5 Lash, *Critique of Information,* 24.

6 Thanks to David Mason for all the conversation and the casual aside about Inferno from Bell Labs that inspired this section.

7 Pike et al., "Plan 9 from Bell Labs," 222.

8 Mackenzie, "Java."

9 Dorward et al., "The Inferno Operating System," 5.

10 Dorward et al., "The Inferno Operating System," 5.

11 Dorward ct al., "The Inferno Operating System," 5.

12 Hogan, "Data Flows and Water Woes."

13 Parnell, "Epic Net Outage in Africa as FOUR Undersea Cables Chopped."

14 Starosielski, *The Undersea Network.*

15 Kurra, "Egypt Shut Down Its Net with a Series of Phone Calls."

16 Deibert et al., *Access Denied.*

17 Latham, "Networks, Information, and the Rise of the Global Internet," 149.

18 The problem of network relations is a familiar one within telecommunications, since it resembles the disputes between regional telephone companies over how to connect to one another when providing long-distance services (see Noam, *Interconnecting the Network of Networks*). The economics of connection manifest in calls to different regions or countries having specific long-distance rates (and in the bewildering choices of long-distance plans and calling cards).

19 See DeNardis, *The Global War for Internet Governance*, chapter 5.

20 Crawford, "Internet Think."

21 Anderson, "Peering Problems"; Brodkin, "Netflix Packets Being Dropped."

22 Clement, Paterson, and Phillips, "IXmaps."

23 Geist, "All Your Internets Belong to US, Continued."

24 Halsall, "The Pirate Bay Proxy."

25 Barlow, "A Declaration of the Independence of Cyberspace."

26 Braun, "Transparent Intermediaries."

27 Holt, "Regulating Connected Viewing"; Stevenson, *The Master Switch and the Hyper Giant.*

28 Mueller, *Ruling the Root.*

29 Busch, *Standards*; Lampland and Star, *Standards and Their Stories*; Russell, *Open Standards and the Digital Age.*

30 DeNardis, *Protocol Politics*; DeNardis, *Opening Standards.*

31 Galloway, *Protocol.*

32 The externalities of standards have become sites of political, economic, and social struggle. The U.S. National Security Agency (NSA) and the Communications Security Establishment of Canada (CSEC) have actively undermined security protocols to ensure interception (see Ball, Borger, and Greenwald, "Revealed"). Document formats such as the Open Document Format (ODF) attempt to wrest control from the dominant Word file format and the influence of Microsoft (see Rens, "Open Document Standards for Government"). Developers of the HTML5 web standard are currently debating whether to include Digital Rights Management (DRM), normalizing an important control to secure digital content (see Schrock, "HTML5 and Openness in Mobile Platforms"). English continues to be the de facto

language on the web in part because character encoding standards lack international characters. It was only in 2010 that the Internet Corporation for Assigned Names and Numbers (ICANN) started to allow international characters with some national domain names (so the town of Hörby might finally have a proper domain name; see ICANN, "First IDN CcTLDs Available," and Pargman and Palme, "ASCII Imperialism").

33 Rosenzweig, "The Road to Xanadu."

34 Langlois and Elmer, "Wikipedia Leeches?"

35 Leyshon, "Time—Space (and Digital) Compression"; Spilker and Hoier, "Technologies of Piracy?"; Sterne, *MP3*.

36 Anthony, "Google Teaches 'AIs' to Invent Their Own Crypto."

37 Russell, *Open Standards and the Digital Age.*

38 Mansell, *Imagining the Internet*; Kelty, *Two Bits.*

39 Elmer, "The Vertical (Layered) Net."

40 Langlois et al., "Networked Publics," 419.

41 I use the term "mediation" deliberately. Nick Couldry describes mediation as "capturing a variety of dynamics within media flows," elaborating, "by 'media flows' I mean flows of production, circulation, interpretation or reception and recirculation, as interpretations flow back into production or outwards into general social and cultural life" ("Mediatization or Mediation?" 9).

42 Nagy and Neff, "Imagined Affordances."

43 Gillespie, "The Politics of 'Platforms,'" 358.

44 Gillespie, "The Politics of 'Platforms,'" 359.

45 Van Dijck, *The Culture of Connectivity*; Gillespie, "The Politics of 'Platforms'"; Langlois et al., "Mapping Commercial Web 2.0 Worlds."

46 Karpf, *The MoveOn Effect*; Kreiss, *Taking Our Country Back.*

47 Pariser, *The Filter Bubble.*

48 Hallinan and Striphas, "Recommended for You."

49 Ananny and Crawford, "A Liminal Press."

50 Meyer, "Everything We Know About Facebook's Secret Mood Manipulation Experiment."

51 Shahani, "In Google Newsroom, Brazil Defeat Is Not a Headline."

52 Cote and Pybus, "Learning to Immaterial Labour 2.0"; Elmer, *Profiling Machines*; Mosco, *The Political Economy of Communication*; Terranova, *Network Culture.*

53 Helmond, "Adding the Bling."

54 Bucher, "Want to Be on the Top?"

55 Feenberg, *Questioning Technology.*

56 Consalvo, *Cheating.*

57 Stuart, "Megan Lee Heart and Reply Girls Game the System."

58 O'Neill, "YouTube Responds to Reply Girls."

59 Söderberg, "Misuser Inventions and the Invention of the Misuser."

60 Diakopoulos, "Algorithmic Accountability"; Ananny, "Toward an Ethics"; Gillespie, "The Relevance of Algorithms"; Crawford and Lumby, "Networks of Governance."

61 Chen, "Facebook Will Start Tracking Which Stores You Walk Into."

62 Krashinsky, "Rogers to Offer Promotional Ads by Text."

63 Reagle, *Good Faith Collaboration*, 84–86.

64 Woolley and Howard, "Political Communication, Computational Propaganda, and Autonomous Agents."

65 Woolley, "Automating Power."

66 Google, "Load AMP Pages Quickly with Google AMP Cache."

67 Foucault, *Security, Territory, Population*, 47.

68 Foucault, *Security, Territory, Population*, 47.

69 Gillespie, *Wired Shut*, 652.

70 Johns, *Piracy*.

71 While they predate the popularity of platforms, Raiford Guins details simple software logics functioning in "device control" to regulate the interactions of the household. These devices offered a variety of mechanisms of control: they "block, filter, sanitize, clean and patch" digital information to allow open circulation while embedding certain limits within this freedom. Guins focuses on the developments in media technologies that facilitate a "control at a distance." Control embeds in DVD players, televisions, and computer games that can manage the circulation of content on the fly (see *Edited Clean Version*).

72 Dayal, "The Algorithmic Copyright Cops"; YouTube Help, "How Content ID Works."

73 Angwin et al., "NSA Spying."

74 Kuerbis and Mueller, "Securing the Root."

75 Vincent, "Google Received More than 345 Million Link Takedown Requests Last Year."

76 The development of self-censorship can be much more complicated than the cultural influence of state surveillance, as seen in Azerbaijan, where an honor culture and fear of state monitoring guide online impression management (Pearce and Vitak, "Performing Honor Online.").

77 Lee, "Internet Control and Auto-Regulation in Singapore."

78 "The Five Eyes" refers to the international intelligence alliance between Australia, Canada, New Zealand, the United Kingdom, and the United States. This cooperation includes both human intelligence (popularly seen as the work of spies and covert operations) and signals intelligence or SIGINT. Cooperation in SIGINT occurs between Canada's CSEC, America's NSA, the Australian Signals Directorate (ASD), New Zealand's Government Communications Security Bureau (GCSB), and the Government Communications Headquarters (GCHQ) of the United Kingdom.

79 Bamford, *The Shadow Factory*.

80 Anderson, "AT&T Engineer."

81 Timberg, "NSA Slide Shows Surveillance of Undersea Cables."

82 MacAskill et al., "GCHQ Taps Fibre-Optic Cables."

83 Greenwald and MacAskill, "NSA Prism Program Taps in to User Data of Apple, Google and Others."

84 Hildebrandt, Pereira, and Seglins, "CSE Tracks Millions of Downloads Daily."

85 Lee, "Report."

86 The leaks may have done little to change American public opinion. As of 2013,

Americans care more about avoiding the watch of criminals (33 percent) or advertisers (28 percent) than about avoiding that of the government (5 percent) or law enforcement (4 percent) (see Rainie et al., "Anonymity, Privacy, and Security Online"). In 2015, Pew found that 30 percent of American adults had heard about the surveillance programs. Of those aware, 34 percent had modified their behavior to protect their information from the government (see Rainie and Madden, "Americans' Privacy Strategies Post-Snowden").

87 Hildebrandt, Pereira, and Seglins, "CSE Tracks Millions of Downloads Daily."

88 Greenwald, "How Covert Agents Infiltrate the Internet."

89 Crawford and Gillespie, "What Is a Flag For?"; Roberts, "Behind the Screen."

90 Bazelon, "How to Stop the Bullies"; Chen, "The Laborers Who Keep Dick Pics and Beheadings Out of Your Facebook Feed."

91 Menn and Volz, "Google, Facebook Quietly Move toward Automatic Blocking."

92 Mueller, Kuehn, and Santoso, "Policing the Network."

93 Andy, "Cisco Develops System to Automatically Cut-Off Pirate Video Streams."

94 Howard, *Pax Technica*, xxi.

95 Dante, *Divine Comedy: The Inferno*, 41.

Appendix

1 Karas, "Network Measurement Program (NMP)," 1.

2 McKelvey, "A Programmable Platform?"

3 Lessig, *Code*.

4 Muuss, "The Story of the PING Program."

5 Cerf, *Guidelines for Internet Measurement Activities*.

6 Molyneux and Williams, "Measuring the Internet," 288.

7 Dodge and Kitchin, *Mapping Cyberspace*.

8 Molyneux and Williams, "Measuring the Internet," 300.

9 Peterson, "Speakeasy Founder Leaves for New Venture."

10 Dovrolis et al., "Measurement Lab."

11 Li et al., "Classifiers Unclassified"; Kakhki et al., "BingeOn Under the Microscope."

12 Dischinger et al., "Glasnost."

13 More details about WeHe are available at its website: https://dd.meddle.mobi /index.html.

14 Clement, Paterson, and Phillips, "IXmaps."

BIBLIOGRAPHY

Aaron, Craig. "A Scary Picture for the Future of the Wireless Web." *The Huffington Post.* December 15, 2010. http://www.huffingtonpost.com/craig-aaron/a-scary-picture -for-the-f_b_796990.html.

Abbate, Janet. *Inventing the Internet.* Cambridge, Mass.: MIT Press, 1999.

Abbate, Janet. "Privatizing the Internet: Competing Visions and Chaotic Events, 1987– 1995." *IEEE Annals of the History of Computing* 32, no. 1 (2010): 10–22.

Abbate, Janet. *Recoding Gender: Women's Changing Participation in Computing.* Cambridge, Mass.: MIT Press, 2012.

Abbott, Andrew. *Time Matters: On Theory and Method.* Chicago: University of Chicago Press, 2001.

Acland, Charles R. *Swift Viewing: The Popular Life of Subliminal Influence.* Durham, N.C.: Duke University Press, 2012.

Acland, Charles R. "Harold Innis, Cultural Policy, and Residual Media." *International Journal of Cultural Policy* 12, no. 2 (2006): 171–85.

Adam, Barbara. "Time." *Theory, Culture & Society* 23, no. 2–3 (2006): 119–26.

Adam, Barbara. *Time and Social Theory.* Cambridge, UK: Polity Press, 1990.

Akamai Technologies. "Akamai and JupiterResearch Identify '4 Seconds' as the New Threshold of Acceptability for Retail Web Page Response Times." *Akamai,* November 6, 2006. http://www.akamai.com/html/about/press/releases/2006/press _110606.html.

Alexander, Neta. "Rage against the Machine: Buffering, Noise, and Perpetual Anxiety in the Age of Connected Viewing." *Cinema Journal* 56, no. 2 (2017): 1–24. DOI: 10.1353 /cj.2017.0000.

Allot Communications. "VideoClass." http://www.allotworks.com/datasheets/DS _VideoClass_rev2.1_A4_12-2013.pdf.

Allot Communications. "Allot Smart Pipe Management." YouTube video, 1:01. June 29, 2011. https://www.youtube.com/watch?v=PpqdSnH8Tqg.

Amoore, Louise. *The Politics of Possibility: Risk and Security beyond Probability.* Durham, N.C.: Duke University Press, 2013.

Ananny, Mike. "Toward an Ethics of Algorithms Convening, Observation, Probability, and Timeliness." *Science, Technology & Human Values* 41, no. 1 (2016): 93–117. DOI: 10.1177/0162243915606523.

Ananny, Mike, and Kate Crawford. "A Liminal Press: Situating News App Designers within a Field of Networked News Production." *Digital Journalism* 3, no. 2 (March 4, 2015): 192–208. DOI: 10.1080/21670811.2014.922322.

Ananny, Mike, and Kate Crawford. "Seeing without Knowing: Limitations of the Transparency Ideal and Its Application to Algorithmic Accountability." *New Media & Society*, December 13, 2016. DOI: 10.1177/1461444816676645.

Anderson, Benedict. *Imagined Communities: Reflections on the Origin and Spread of Nationalism.* New York: Verso, 1991.

Anderson, C. W. "Towards a Sociology of Computational and Algorithmic Journalism." *New Media & Society* 15, no. 7 (November 1, 2013): 1005–21. DOI: 10.1177/1461444812465137.

Anderson, Nate. "AT&T Engineer: NSA Built Secret Rooms in Our Facilities." *Ars Technica*, April 12, 2006. http://arstechnica.com/uncategorized/2006/04/6585-2/.

Anderson, Nate. "Canadian ISPs Furious about Bell Canada's Traffic Throttling." *Ars Technica*, March 26, 2008. http://arstechnica.com/uncategorized/2008/03/canadian-isps-furious-about-bell-canadas-traffic-throttling/.

Anderson, Nate. "Encrypted and Obfuscated? Your P2P Protocol Can Still Be IDed." *Ars Technica*, August 25, 2010. http://arstechnica.com/tech-policy/news/2010/08/encrypted-and-obfuscated-your-p2p-protocol-can-still-be-ided.ars.

Anderson, Nate. "Peering Problems: Digging into the Comcast/Level 3 Grudgematch." *Ars Technica*, December 9, 2010. http://arstechnica.com/tech-policy/news/2010/12/comcastlevel3.ars/.

Anderson, Nate. "Pirate Bay Moves to Decentralized DHT Protocol, Kills Tracker." *Ars Technica*, November 17, 2009. http://arstechnica.com/tech-policy/news/2009/11/pirate-bay-kills-its-own-bittorrent-tracker.ars.

Andy. "Cisco Develops System to Automatically Cut-Off Pirate Video Streams." *TorrentFreak*, October 21, 2016. https://torrentfreak.com/cisco-develops-system-automatically-cut-off-pirate-video-streams-161021/.

Angwin, Julia, Jeff Larson, Charlie Savage, James Risen, Henrik Moltke, and Laura Poitras. "NSA Spying Relies on AT&T's 'Extreme Willingness to Help.'" *ProPublica*, August 15, 2015. https://www.propublica.org/article/nsa-spying-relies-on-atts-extreme-willingness-to-help.

Anthony, Sebastian. "Google Teaches 'AIs' to Invent Their Own Crypto and Avoid Eavesdropping." *Ars Technica*, October 28, 2016. http://arstechnica.com/information-technology/2016/10/google-ai-neural-network-cryptography/.

Aria Networks. "Aria Networks and TierOne Announce OEM Partnership." *Aria Networks Blog*, March 22, 2016. http://www.aria-networks.com/news/aria-networks-tierone-announce-oem-partnership/.

Aria Networks. "Self-Optimising Networks." *Aria Networks.* Accessed July 21, 2016. http://www.aria-networks.com/solutions/self-optimising-networks-son/.

Armitage, John, and Phil Graham. "Dromoeconomics: Towards a Political Economy of Speed." *Parallax* 7, no. 1 (2001): 111–23.

Armitage, John, and Joanne Roberts. "Chronotopia." In *Living with Cyberspace: Technology and Society in the 21st Century,* edited by John Armitage and Joanne Roberts, 43–56. New York: Continuum, 2002.

Asghari, Hadi, Michel van Eeten, and Milton Mueller. *Internet Measurements and Public Policy: Mind the Gap.* Rochester, N.Y.: Social Science Research Network, 2013. http://papers.ssrn.com/abstract=2294456.

Aspray, William. "An Annotated Bibliography of Secondary Sources on the History of Software." *Annals of the History of Computing* 9, no. 3/4 (1988): 291–343.

Austin, Graeme W. "Importing Kazza—Exporting Grokster." *Santa Clara Computer & High Technology Law Journal* 22 (2006): 577.

Avgiris, Cathy. "Comcast to Replace Usage Cap with Improved Data Usage Management Approaches." *Comcast,* May 17, 2012. http://corporate.comcast.com/comcast-voices/comcast-to-replace-usage-cap-with-improved-data-usage-management-approaches.

Avolio, Frederick. "Firewalls and Internet Security." *The Internet Protocol Journal* 2, no. 2 (1999). http://www.cisco.com/web/about/ac123/ac147/ac174/ac200/about_cisco_ipj_archive_article09186a00800c85ae.html.

Ball, James, Julian Borger, and Glenn Greenwald. "Revealed: How US and UK Spy Agencies Defeat Internet Privacy and Security." U.S. News, *The Guardian,* September 6, 2013. http://www.theguardian.com/world/2013/sep/05/nsa-gchq-encryption-codes-security.

Bamford, James. *The Shadow Factory: The Ultra-Secret NSA from 9/11 to the Eavesdropping on America.* New York: Doubleday, 2008.

Bangeman, Eric. "Comcast Tweaks Terms of Service in Wake of Throttling Uproar." *Ars Technica,* February 7, 2008. http://arstechnica.com/uncategorized/2008/02/comcast-tweaks-terms-of-service-in-wake-of-throttling-uproar/.

Barbrook, Richard, and Andy Cameron. "Californian Ideology." In *Crypto Anarchy, Cyberstates, and Pirate Utopias,* edited by Peter Ludlow, 363–88. Cambridge, Mass.: MIT Press, 2001.

Bardini, Thierry. *Bootstrapping: Douglas Engelbart, Coevolution, and the Origins of Personal Computing.* Stanford, Calif.: Stanford University Press, 2000.

Barlow, John Perry. "A Declaration of the Independence of Cyberspace." *Electronic Frontier Foundation,* February 8, 1996. https://www.eff.org/cyberspace-independence.

Barney, Darin. *Prometheus Wired: The Hope for Democracy in the Age of Network Technology.* Chicago: University of Chicago Press, 2000.

Barocas, Solon, Sophie Hood, and Malte Ziewitz. *Governing Algorithms: A Provocation Piece.* Rochester, N.Y.: Social Science Research Network, 2013. http://papers.ssrn.com/abstract=2245322.

Barzilai-Nahon, Karine. "Gaps and Bits: Conceptualizing Measurements for Digital Divide/S." *The Information Society* 22, no. 5 (2006): 269–78. DOI: 10.1080/01972240600903953.

Bastian, C., T. Klieber, J. Livingood, J. Mills, R. Woundy, and Comcast. "RFC 6057: Comcast's Protocol-Agnostic Congestion Management System." *Internet Engineering*

Task Force. Last updated October 14, 2015. http://datatracker.ietf.org/doc/rfc6057/?include_text=1.

Bauer, Steve, David D. Clark, and William H. Lehr. "Powerboost." Toronto, 2011. http://mitas.csail.mit.edu/papers/homenets-bauer-2011.pdf.

Bazelon, Emily. "How to Stop the Bullies." *The Atlantic,* February 20, 2013. http://www.theatlantic.com/magazine/archive/2013/03/how-to-stop-bullies/309217/.

Beckett, Andy. "Accelerationism: How a Fringe Philosophy Predicted the Future We Live In." World News, *The Guardian,* May 11, 2017 https://www.theguardian.com/world/2017/may/11/accelerationism-how-a-fringe-philosophy-predicted-the-future-we-live-in.

Beer, David. "Power through the Algorithm? Participatory Web Cultures and the Technological Unconscious." *New Media & Society* 11, no. 6 (September 1, 2009): 985–1002.

Bell Aliant. "Reply Comments on Public Notice 2008-19: Review of the Internet Traffic Management Practices of Internet Service Providers, Bell Aliant Regional Communications, Limited Partnership, and Bell Canada." February 23, 2009. http://www.crtc.gc.ca/public/partvii/2008/8646/c12_200815400/1029804.zip.

Beller, Jonathan. *The Cinematic Mode of Production: Attention Economy and the Society of the Spectacle.* Lebanon, N.H.: Dartmouth College Press, 2006.

Bellovin, S. M., and W. R Cheswick. "Network Firewalls." *Communications Magazine, IEEE* 32, no. 9 (1994): 50–57. https://crypto.stanford.edu/cs155old/cs155-spring09/papers/bellovin-cheswick.pdf.

Bendrath, Ralf, and Milton Mueller. "The End of the Net as We Know It? Deep Packet Inspection and Internet Governance." *New Media & Society* 13, no. 7 (November 1, 2011): 1142–60.

Beniger, James R. *The Control Revolution: Technological and Economic Origins of the Information Society.* Cambridge, Mass.: Harvard University Press, 1986.

Benkler, Yochai. *The Wealth of Networks: How Social Production Transforms Markets and Freedom.* New Haven, Conn.: Yale University Press, 2006.

Bennett, Jane. *Vibrant Matter: A Political Ecology of Things.* Durham, N.C.: Duke University Press, 2010.

Bennett, W. Lance. "Communicating Global Activism: Strengths and Vulnerabilities of Networked Politics." *Information, Communication, and Society* 6, no. 2 (2003): 143–68.

Beranek, Leo. "Roots of the Internet: A Personal History." *Massachusetts Historical Review* 2 (January 1, 2000): 55–75.

BEREC (Body of European Regulators of Electronic Communications), and EC (the European Commission). *A View of Traffic Management and Other Practices Resulting in Restrictions to the Open Internet in Europe: Findings from BEREC's and the European Commission's Joint Investigation.* May 29, 2012. http://ec.europa.eu/digital-agenda/sites/digital-agenda/files/Traffic%20Management%20Investigation%20BEREC_2.pdf.

Berry, David M. *Critical Theory and the Digital.* Critical Theory and Contemporary Society. New York: Bloomsbury Academic, 2014.

Beyer, Jessica L., and Fenwick McKelvey. "You Are Not Welcome among Us: Pirates and the State." *International Journal of Communication* 9 (March 26, 2015): 890–908.

Boczkowski, Pablo, and Leah A. Lievrouw. "Bridging STS and Communication Studies: Scholarship on Media and Information Technologies." In *The Handbook of Science and Technology Studies,* edited by Edward J. Hackett, Olga Amsterdamska, Michael E. Lynch, Judy Wajcman, and Wiebe E Bijker, 3rd ed., 951–77. Cambridge, Mass.: MIT Press, 2008.

Bode, Karl. "CableOne Brags It Provides Worse Service to Bad Credit Customers." *DSLReports,* May 27, 2016. http://www.dslreports.com/shownews/CableOne-Brags-It-Provides-Worse-Service-to-Bad-Credit-Customers-137070.

Boden, Margaret. *Mind as Machine: A History of Cognitive Science.* New York: Oxford University Press, 2006.

Bolt, Beranek, and Newman Inc. (BBN). *Report No. 1763: Initial Design for Interface Message Processors for the ARPA Computer Network.* January 1969. Sponsored by Advanced Research Projects Agency, Department of Defense: ARPA Order No. 1260. http://www.dtic.mil/dtic/tr/fulltext/u2/682905.pdf.

Bouch, Anna, Allan Kuchinsky, and Nina Bhatti. "Quality Is in the Eye of the Beholder: Meeting Users' Requirements for Internet Quality of Service." In *Proceedings of the SIGCHI Conference on Human Factors in Computing Systems,* 297–304. New York: Association for Computing Machinery, 2000. http://dl.acm.org/citation.cfm?id=332447.

Bouwsma, O. K. "Descartes' Evil Genius." *Philosophical Review* 58, no. 2 (1949): 141–51. DOI: 10.2307/2181388.

Bowker, Geoffrey C. "The History of Information Infrastructures: The Case of the International Classification of Diseases." *Information Processing & Management* 32, no. 1 (1996): 49–61.

boyd, danah, and Kate Crawford. "Critical Questions for Big Data: Provocations for a Cultural, Technological, and Scholarly Phenomenon." *Information, Communication & Society* 15, no. 5 (June 2012): 662–79. DOI: 10.1080/1369118X.2012.678878.

Brabham, Daren C. "The Boston Marathon Bombings, 4Chan's Think Tank, and a Modest Proposal for an Emergency Crowdsourced Investigation Platform." *Culture Digitally,* April 17, 2013. http://culturedigitally.org/2013/04/boston-marathon-bombing-and-emergency-crowdsourced-investigation/.

Braman, Sandra. "Laying the Path: Governance in Early Internet Design." *Info* 15, no. 6 (September 23, 2013): 63–83. DOI: 10.1108/info-07-2013–0043.

Braman, Sandra. "Posthuman Law: Information Policy and the Machinic World." *First Monday* 7, no. 12 (December 2, 2002). http://firstmonday.org/ojs/index.php/fm/article/view/1011/932.

Braman, Sandra. "From the Modern to the Postmodern: The Future of Global Communications Theory and Research in a Pandemonic Age." In *International and Development Communication: A 21st-Century Perspective,* edited by Bella Mody, 109–24. Thousand Oaks, Calif.: Sage, 2003.

Braman, Sandra. "The Framing Years: Policy Fundamentals in the Internet Design Process, 1969–1979." Paper presented at the TPRC conference, 2010. Rochester, N.Y.: Social Science Research, 2012.

Braman, Sandra. "The Geopolitical vs. the Network Political: Internet Designers and

Governance." *International Journal of Media & Cultural Politics* 9, no. 3 (2013): 277–96. DOI: 10.1386/macp.9.3.277_1

Braun, Joshua. "Transparent Intermediaries: Building the Infrastructures of Connected Viewing." In Holts and Sanson, *Connected Viewing: Selling, Streaming, and Sharing Media in the Digital Age,* edited by Jennifer Holt and Kevin Sanson, 121–43. New York: Routledge, 2014.

Brianl. Comment on Goldmonger, "Canada ISP Latency Issues." *World of Warcraft Forums,* February 9, 2011. http://us.battle.net/forums/en/wow/topic/1965838937?page=29#post-573.

Brianl. Comment 1 on Tachion, "Outrageous Latency & Constant DC—Pre 4.0.3." *World of Warcraft Forums,* November 16, 2011. http://us.battle.net/forums/en/wow/topic/1021053250?page=3#post-46.

Brianl. Comment 2 on Tachion, "Outrageous Latency & Constant DC—Pre 4.0.3." *World of Warcraft Forums,* November 18, 2011. http://us.battle.net/forums/en/wow/topic/1021053250?page=10#post-188.

Brim, Scott W., and Brian E. Carpenter. "Middleboxes: Taxonomy and Issues." Request for Comments 3234. Network Managing Group, 2002. https://tools.ietf.org/html/rfc3234.

Brodkin, Jon. "Netflix Packets Being Dropped Every Day Because Verizon Wants More Money." *Ars Technica,* February 21, 2014. http://arstechnica.com/information-technology/2014/02/netflix-packets-being-dropped-every-day-because-verizon-wants-more-money/.

Brodkin, Jon. "Netflix Performance on Verizon and Comcast Has Been Dropping for Months." *Ars Technica,* February 10, 2014. http://arstechnica.com/information-technology/2014/02/netflix-performance-on-verizon-and-comcast-has-been-dropping-for-months/.

Brodkin, Jon. "Verizon: We Throttle Unlimited Data to Provide an 'Incentive to Limit Usage.'" *Ars Technica,* August 5, 2014. http://arstechnica.com/business/2014/08/verizon-we-throttle-unlimited-data-to-provide-an-incentive-to-limit-usage/.

Brose, Hanns-Georg. "An Introduction towards a Culture of Non-Simultaneity?" *Time & Society* 13, no. 1 (March 1, 2004): 5–26. DOI: 10.1177/0961463X04040740.

Brunton, Finn, and Helen Nissenbaum. "Vernacular Resistance to Data Collection and Analysis: A Political Theory of Obfuscation." *First Monday* 16, no. 5 (2011). http://firstmonday.org/htbin/cgiwrap/bin/ojs/index.php/fm/article/view/3493/2955.

Bucher, Taina. "A Technicity of Attention: How Software 'Makes Sense.'" *Culture Machine* 13 (2012): 1–13.

Bucher, Taina. "The Algorithmic Imaginary: Exploring the Ordinary Affects of Facebook Algorithms." *Information, Communication & Society,* February 25, 2016, 1–15. DOI: 10.1080/1369118X.2016.1154086.

Bucher, Taina. "Want to Be on the Top? Algorithmic Power and the Threat of Invisibility on Facebook." *New Media & Society* 14, no. 7 (November 1, 2012): 1164–80. DOI: 10.1177/1461444812440159.

Bunnell, David, and Adam Brate. *Making the Cisco Connection: The Story behind the Real Internet Superpower.* New York: John Wiley and Sons, 2000.

Burkart, Patrick. "Cultural Environmentalism and Collective Action: The Case of the Swedish Pirate Party." Paper presented at the International Communication Association Conference, Phoenix, Ariz., May 2012.

Burkart, Patrick. *Pirate Politics: The New Information Policy Contests*. Cambridge, Mass.: MIT Press, 2014.

Burroughs, William S. "The Limits of Control." *Semiotext(e): Schizo-Culture* 3, no. 2 (1978): 38–42.

Busch, Lawrence. *Standards: Recipes for Reality*. Cambridge, Mass.: MIT Press, 2011.

Bush, Randy. "FidoNet: Technology, Tools, and History." *Communications of the ACM* 36, no. 8 (1993): 31–35.

Callon, Michel, Pierre Lascoumes, and Yannick Barthe. *Acting in an Uncertain World: An Essay on Technical Democracy*. Cambridge, Mass.: MIT Press, 2009.

Calo, M. Ryan, Michael Froomkin, and Ian Kerr, eds. *Robot Law*. Cheltenham, UK: Edward Elgar, 2016.

Campbell-Kelly, Martin. "Data Communications at the National Physical Laboratory (1965–1975)." *IEEE Annals of the History of Computing* 9, no. 3/4 (1988): 221–47.

Campbell-Kelly, Martin. *From Airline Reservations to Sonic the Hedgehog: A History of the Software Industry*. Cambridge, Mass.: MIT Press, 2003.

Campbell-Kelly, Martin, and William Aspray. *Computer: A History of the Information Machine*. Boulder, Colo.: Westview Press, 2004.

Canadian Radio-Television and Telecommunications Commission (CRTC). Archived email from Andrea Rosen, CRTC Chief Compliance and Enforcement Officer, to Ken Englehart, Senior Vice President Regulatory, Rogers Communications Inc. "SUBJECT: File #545613, Internet Traffic Management Practices ('ITMPs'), Section 36 of the Telecommunications Act, S.C.1993, c.38, as amended ('Act') and Paragraphs 126 and 127 of Telecom Regulatory Policy CRTC 2009-657 ('TRP CRTC 2009-657')." CRTC archive #545613. June 28, 2012. http://www.crtc.gc.ca/eng/archive/2012/lt120628.htm.

Cao, Yi, Christian Ritz, and Raad Raad. "How Much Longer to Go? The Influence of Waiting Time and Progress Indicators on Quality of Experience for Mobile Visual Search Applied to Print Media." In *Fifth International Workshop on Quality of Multimedia Experience (QoMEX), 2013*, 112–17. New York: IEEE, 2013. http://ieeexplore.ieee.org/xpls/abs_all.jsp?arnumber=6603220.

Carey, James W. *Communication as Culture: Essays on Media and Society*. Revised edition. New York: Routledge, 2009.

Carey, John, and Martin C. J. Elton. "The Other Path to the Web: The Forgotten Role of Videotex and Other Early Online Services." *New Media & Society* 11, no. 1–2 (February 1, 2009): 241–60.

Carey, Pete. "A Start-up's True Tale." *San Jose Mercury News*, December 1, 2001. http://pdp10.nocrew.org/docs/cisco.html.

Carr, C. Stephen, Stephen D. Crocker, and Vinton G. Cerf. "HOST-HOST Communication Protocol in the ARPA Network." In *Proceedings of the May 5–7, 1970, Spring Joint Computer Conference*, 589–97. New York: Association for Computing Machines, 1970. http://dl.acm.org/citation.cfm?id=1477024.

Castells, Manuel. *The Rise of the Network Society*. Cambridge, UK: Blackwell, 1996.

CBC News. "ISPs Limit Access to CBC Download, Users Say." *CBC News*, March 26, 2008. http://www.cbc.ca/news/arts/tv/story/2008/03/26/bittorrent-cbc.html.

CBC News. "Rogers Admits It May Be Throttling Games." *CBC News*, September 6, 2011. http://www.cbc.ca/news/technology/rogers-admits-it-may-be-throttling-games -1.1057354.

Ceaparu, Irina, Jonathan Lazar, Katie Bessiere, John Robinson, and Ben Shneiderman. "Determining Causes and Severity of End-User Frustration." *International Journal of Human-Computer Interaction* 17, no. 3 (2004): 333–56.

Cerf, Vinton G. *Guidelines for Internet Measurement Activities*. Internet Activities Board, October 1991. https://tools.ietf.org/pdf/rfc1262.pdf.

Cerf, Vinton G., and Robert E. Kahn. "A Protocol for Packet Network Intercommunication." *IEEE Transactions on Communications* 22, no. 5 (May 1974): 637–48. DOI: 10.1109/TCOM.1974.1092259.

Ceruzzi, Paul E. *A History of Modern Computing*. Cambridge, Mass.: MIT Press, 1998.

Ceruzzi, Paul E. "The Internet before Commercialization." In *The Internet and American Business*, edited by William Aspray and Paul E. Ceruzzi, 9–42. Cambridge, Mass.: MIT Press, 2008.

Chen, Adrian. "The Laborers Who Keep Dick Pics and Beheadings Out of Your Facebook Feed." *Wired*, October 23, 2014. http://www.wired.com/2014/10/content -moderation/.

Chen, Angela. "Facebook Will Start Tracking Which Stores You Walk Into." *Gizmodo*, June 15, 2016. http://gizmodo.com/facebook-will-start-tracking-which-stores-you -walk-into-1782022591.

Cheney-Lippold, J. "A New Algorithmic Identity: Soft Biopolitics and the Modulation of Control." *Theory, Culture & Society* 28, no. 6 (November 1, 2011): 164–81. DOI: 10.1177/0263276411424420.

Chetty, Marshini, Richard Banks, A. J. Brush, Jonathan Donner, and Rebecca Grinter. "You're Capped: Understanding the Effects of Bandwidth Caps on Broadband Use in the Home." In *Proceedings of the 2012 ACM Annual Conference on Human Factors in Computing Systems*, 3021–30. New York: Association for Computing Machines, 2012. http://dl.acm.org/citation.cfm?id=2208714.

Chinneck, John W. "Practical Optimization: A Gentle Introduction." Carleton University Faculty Page, December 16, 2015. http://www.sce.carleton.ca/faculty/chinneck/po .html.

Chun, Wendy Hui Kyong. "On 'Sourcery,' or Code as Fetish." *Configurations* 16, no. 3 (2008): 299–324. DOI: 10.1353/con.0.0064.

Chung, Emily. "Rogers Throttling May Breach Net Neutrality Rules." *CBC News*, October 25, 2011. http://www.cbc.ca/news/technology/rogers-throttling-may-breach -net-neutrality-rules-1.1055349.

Chung, Emily. "Bell Reveals Internet Throttling Details to CRTC." *CBC News*, July 14, 2009. http://www.cbc.ca/news/technology/bell-reveals-internet-throttling-details-to -crtc-1.806898.

Cisco Systems. *Cisco SCE 8000 Service Control Engine*. August 28, 2008. http://www

.cisco.com/c/en/us/products/collateral/service-exchange/sce-8000-series
-service-control-engine/data_sheet_c78-492987.html.

Cisco Systems. *Administration Guide VA1(7), Cisco ACE 4700 Series Application Control Engine Appliance—Configuring Class Maps and Policy Maps [Cisco ACE 4700 Series Application Control Engine Appliances]*. 2007. http://www.cisco.com/c/en /us/td/docs/app_ntwk_services/data_center_app_services/ace_appliances/vA1 _7_/configuration/administration/guide/admgd/mapolcy.html.

Cisco Systems. *Cisco IOS CMTS Cable Software Configuration Guide, Release 12.2SC*. February 15, 2015. http://www.cisco.com/web/techdoc/cable/Config/Sw_conf .html.

Cisco Systems. *Cisco IOS Quality of Service Solutions Configuration Guide, Release 12.2: Configuring Class-Based Shaping [Cisco IOS Software Release 12.2]*. January 30, 2014. http://www.cisco.com/c/en/us/td/docs/ios/12_2/qos/configuration /guide/fqos_c/qcfcbshp.html.

Cisco Systems. *Cisco Wide Area Application Services Configuration Guide (Software Version 5.0.1)*. March 25, 2015. http://www.cisco.com/c/en/us/td/docs/app_ntwk _services/waas/waas/v501/configuration/guide/cnfg/servicescontroller.html.

Cisco Systems. *What Is Administrative Distance?* May 8, 2013. http://www.cisco.com/c /en/us/support/docs/ip/border-gateway-protocol-bgp/15986-admin-distance .html.

Clement, Andrew, Nancy Paterson, and David J. Phillips. "IXmaps: Interactively Mapping NSA Surveillance Points in the Internet 'Cloud.'" Paper presented at "A Global Surveillance Society?" conference, City University, London, June 30, 2010. http:// www.ixmaps.ca/documents/interactively_mapping_paper.pdf.

Clough, Patricia T. "The Affective Turn: Political Economy, Biomedia and Bodies." *Theory, Culture & Society* 25, no. 1 (January 1, 2008): 1–22. DOI: 10.1177/0263276407085156.

Cohen, Bram. "Decentralization: Implications of the End-to-End Principle" [BitTorrent release announcement]. Yahoo group message, *Yahoo Groups: P2P Talk*, July 2, 2001. https://groups.yahoo.com/neo/groups/decentralization/conversations/topics /3160.

Cohen, Bram. "The BitTorrent Protocol Specification." BitTorrent.org, 2008. http://www .bittorrent.org/beps/bep_0003.html.

Cohen-Almagor, Raphael. *Confronting the Internet's Dark Side: Moral and Social Responsibility on the Free Highway*. New York: Cambridge University Press, 2015.

Coleman, Gabriella. *Coding Freedom: The Ethics and Aesthetics of Hacking*. Princeton, N.J.: Princeton University Press, 2013.

Comcast. *Attachment A: Comcast Corporation Description of Current Network Management Practices*. September 19, 2008. https://downloads.comcast.net/docs /Attachment_A_Current_Practices.pdf.

Comcast. *Attachment B: Comcast Corporation Description of Planned Network Management Practices to Be Deployed Following the Termination of Current Practices*. September 19, 2008. http://downloads.comcast.net/docs/Attachment_B_Future _Practices.pdf.

Comcast. "The Advantages of High Speed Internet: Why Invest in Faster Speed."

XFINITY Discovery Hub, July 6, 2017. https://www.xfinity.com/hub/internet/the-advantages-of-high-speed-internet.

Consalvo, Mia. *Cheating: Gaining Advantage in Videogames*. Cambridge, Mass.: MIT Press, 2009.

Cook, Gordon. "NSFnet Privatization: Policy Making in a Public Interest Vacuum." *Internet Research* 3, no. 1 (1993): 3–8.

Copeland, Duncan G., Richard O. Mason, and James L. Mckenney. "SABRE: The Development of Information-Based Competence and Execution of Information-Based Competition." *Annals of the History of Computing* 17, no. 3 (1995): 30–56.

Corbato, F. J., M. M. Daggett, R. C. Daley, R. J. Creasy, J. D. Hellwig, R. H. Orenstein, and L. K. Korn. *Compatible Time-Sharing System: A Programmer's Guide*. 2nd edition. Cambridge, Mass.: MIT Press, 1963.

Cormen, Thomas H., Charles E. Leiserson, and Ronald L. Rivest. *Introduction to Algorithms*. 3rd ed. Cambridge, Mass.: MIT Press, 1990.

Cote, Mark, and Jennifer Pybus. "Learning to Immaterial Labour 2.0: MySpace and Social Networks." *Ephemera: Theory and Politics in Organization* 7, no. 1 (2007): 88–106. http://ualresearchonline.arts.ac.uk/9014/1/7-1cote-pybus.pdf.

Couldry, Nick. "Mediatization or Mediation? Alternative Understandings of the Emergent Space of Digital Storytelling." *New Media & Society* 10, no. 3 (June 1, 2008): 373–91. DOI: 10.1177/1461444808089414.

Crary, Jonathan. *24/7: Late Capitalism and the Ends of Sleep*. New York: Verso, 2013.

Crary, Jonathan. *Suspensions of Perception: Attention, Spectacle, and Modern Culture*. Cambridge, Mass.: MIT Press, 1999.

Crawford, Kate. "The Hidden Biases in Big Data." *Harvard Business Review*, April 1, 2013. https://hbr.org/2013/04/the-hidden-biases-in-big-data.

Crawford, Kate, and Tarleton L. Gillespie. "What Is a Flag For? Social Media Reporting Tools and the Vocabulary of Complaint." *New Media & Society* 18, no. 3 (March 1, 2016): 410–28. http://papers.ssrn.com/abstract=2476464.

Crawford, Kate, and Catharine Lumby. "Networks of Governance: Users, Platforms, and the Challenges of Networked Media Regulation." *International Journal of Technology Policy and Law* 2, no. 1 (2013): 270–82. https://papers.ssrn.com/sol3/papers.cfm?abstract_id=2246772.

Crawford, Susan P. "Internet Think." *Journal on Telecommunications and High Technology Law* 5, no. 2 (2007): 467–86.

Crevier, Daniel. *AI: The Tumultuous History of the Search for Artificial Intelligence*. New York: Basic Books, 1993.

Crogan, Patrick. "Theory of State: Deleuze, Guattari and Virilio on the State, Technology and Speed." *Angelaki* 4, no. 2 (1999): 137–48.

Cunningham, David. "A Marxist Heresy? Accelerationism and Its Discontents." *Radical Philosophy* 191 (May/June 2015): 29–38.

CZ.NIC. "Turris Omnia: Hi-Performance & Open-Source Router." Embedded YouTube video 4:29. *Indiegogo*. Accessed August 9, 2016. https://www.indiegogo.com/projects/1313392.

Daly, Steven. "Pirates of the Multiplex." *Vanity Fair*, February 12, 2007. http://www
.vanityfair.com/ontheweb/features/2007/03/piratebay200703.

Dante (Alighieri). *Divine Comedy: The Inferno*. New York: Harper & Brothers Publishers,
1851. http://books.google.ca/books?id=m5Sl7EpZsC8C.

Dantzig, George, Delbert Fulkerson, and Selmer Johnson, "Solution of a Large-Scale
Traveling-Salesman Problem." In *50 Years of Integer Programming 1958–2008*,
edited by M. Junger et al., 7–9. Berlin: Springer, 2010. http://citeseerx.ist.psu.edu
/viewdoc/download?doi=10.1.1.606.2752&rep=rep1&type=pdf.

Davies, Donald Watts. "Proposal for a Digital Communication Network." National Physical Laboratory, 1966. http://www.dcs.gla.ac.uk/~wpc/grcs/Davies05.pdf.

Davies, Donald Watts. "Report on a Visit to USA in May 1965." The National Museum of
Computing archives. http://www.tnmoc.org/explore/archive.

Davies, Donald Watts. "The Control of Congestion in Packet-Switching Networks."
IEEE Transactions on Communications 22, no. 3 (June 1972): 546–50. https://pdfs
.semanticscholar.org/99ad/0c4ca20ae6289196441954cd266d0d3dd0c9.pdf.

Davies, Donald Watts. "Interview by M. Campbell-Kelly." March 17, 1986. Oral History
series. Charles Babbage Institute, Center for Information Processing, University of
Minnesota. https://conservancy.umn.edu/handle/11299/107241.

Davies, Donald Watts, K. A. Bartlett, R. A. Scantlebury, and P. T. Wilkins. "A Digital Communication Network for Computers Giving Rapid Response at Remote Terminals."
In *Proceedings of the First ACM Symposium on Operating System Principles, 1967*,
2.1–2.7. New York: Association for Computing Machines, 1967.

Day, John D. *Patterns in Network Architecture: A Return to Fundamentals*. Upper Saddle
River, N.J.: Prentice Hall, 2008.

Dayal, Geeta. "The Algorithmic Copyright Cops: Streaming Video's Robotic Overlords."
Wired, September 9, 2012. http://www.wired.com/threatlevel/2012/09/streaming
-videos-robotic-overlords-algorithmic-copyright-cops/.

Deibert, Ronald, John Palfrey, Rafal Rohozinski, and Jonathan Zittrain, eds. *Access Denied: The Practice and Policy of Global Internet Filtering*. The Information Revolution and Global Politics. Cambridge, Mass.: MIT Press, 2008.

Deleuze, Gilles. "Control and Becoming [interview with Antonio Negri]." In *Negotiations,
1972–1990*, translated by Martin Joughin, 169–77. New York: Columbia University Press, 1995. Originally "Le devenir révolutionnaire et les créateurs politiques."
Futur Antérieur, no. 1 (1990): 100–107.

Deleuze, Gilles. "Having an Idea in Cinema (On the Cinema of Straub-Huillet)." In
Deleuze & Guattari: New Mappings in Politics, Philosophy, and Culture, edited by
Eleanor Kaufman and Kevin Jon Heller, 14–19. Minneapolis: University of Minne-
sota Press, 1998.

Deleuze, Gilles. "Mediators." In *Negotiations, 1972–1990*, translated by Martin Joughin,
121–34. New York: Columbia University Press, 1995.

Deleuze, Gilles. "On Gilbert Simondon." In *Desert Islands and Other Texts: 1953–1974*,
edited by David Lapoujade, translated by Michael Taormina, 86–89. New York:
Semiotext(e), 2004.

Deleuze, Gilles. "Postscript on the Societies of Control." *October* 59, no. 1 (1992): 3–7.

Deleuze, Gilles, and Félix Guattari. *A Thousand Plateaus: Capitalism and Schizophrenia*. Translated by Brian Massumi. Minneapolis: University of Minnesota Press, 1987.

Deleuze, Gilles, and Félix Guattari. *Anti-Oedipus: Capitalism and Schizophrenia*. Translated by Robert Hurley, Mark Seem, and Helen R. Lane. Minneapolis: University of Minnesota Press, 1983.

DeMaria, Michael J. "PacketShaper 8500: Traffic Management Gets Smart." *Network Computing*, January 21, 2002.

DeNardis, Laura. "A History of Internet Security." In *The History of Information Security: A Comprehensive Handbook*, edited by Karl de Leeuw and Jan Bergstra, 681–704. Amsterdam: Elsevier, 2007.

DeNardis, Laura, ed. *Opening Standards: The Global Politics of Interoperability*. The Information Society Series. Cambridge, Mass.: MIT Press, 2011.

DeNardis, Laura. *Protocol Politics: The Globalization of Internet Governance*. Cambridge, Mass.: MIT Press, 2009.

DeNardis, Laura. *The Global War for Internet Governance*. New Haven, Conn.: Yale University Press, 2014.

DerEngel (Ryan Harris). *Hacking the Cable Modem: What Cable Companies Don't Want You to Know*. San Francisco, Calif.: No Starch Press, 2006.

Deseriis, Marco. "The General, the Watchman, and the Engineer of Control." *Journal of Communication Inquiry* 35, no. 4 (October 1, 2011): 387–94. DOI: 10.1177/0196859911415677.

Dewey, John. *The Public and Its Problems*. Denver, Colo.: Swallow Press, 1927.

Diakopoulos, Nicholas. "Algorithmic Accountability: On the Investigation of Black Boxes." *Tow Center for Digital Journalism*, December 3, 2014. https://towcenter.org/research/algorithmic-accountability-on-the-investigation-of-black-boxes-2/.

Dischinger, M., M. Marcon, S. Guha, K. P. Gummadi, R. Mahajan, and S. Saroiu. "Glasnost: Enabling End Users to Detect Traffic Differentiation." In *Proceedings of the 7th USENIX Conference on Networked Systems Design and Implementation*. Berkeley, Calif.: USENIX Association, 2010.

Dix, John. "Router Man." *Network World*, March 27, 2006. http://www.networkworld.com/article/2309917/lan-wan/lan-wan-router-man.html.

Doctorow, Cory. "'Poor Internet for Poor People': India's Activists Fight Facebook Connection Plan." Technology, *The Guardian*, January 15, 2016. https://www.theguardian.com/world/2016/jan/15/india-net-neutrality-activists-facebook-free-basics.

Dodge, Martin, and Rob Kitchin. *Mapping Cyberspace*. New York: Routledge, 2001.

Dorward, Sean M., Rob Pike, Dave L. Presotto, D. M. Ritchie, Howard W. Trickey, and Phil Winterbottom. "The Inferno Operating System." *Bell Labs Technical Journal* 2, no. 1 (Winter 1997): 5–18. DOI: 10.1002/bltj.2028.

Dourish, Paul. "Protocols, Packets, and Proximity: The Materiality of Internet Routing." In Parks and Starosielski, *Signal Traffic*, 183–204.

Dovrolis, Constantine, Krishna Gummadi, Aleksandar Kuzmanovic, and Sascha D. Meinrath. "Measurement Lab: Overview and an Invitation to the Research Community." *ACM SIGCOMM Computer Communication Review* 40, no. 3 (2010): 53–56.

Driscoll, Kevin. "Hobbyist Inter-Networking and the Popular Internet Imaginary: Forgotten Histories of Networked Personal Computing, 1978–1998." PhD diss., University of Southern California, 2014. http://digitallibrary.usc.edu/cdm/compoundobject/collection/p15799coll3/id/444362/rec/.

Driscoll, Kevin. "Social Media's Dial-Up Ancestor: The Bulletin Board System." *IEEE Spectrum: Technology, Engineering, and Science News,* October 24, 2016. http://spectrum.ieee.org/computing/networks/social-medias-dialup-ancestor-the-bulletin-board-system.

Duffy, Jim. "Cisco's IOS vs. Juniper's JUNOS." *Network World,* April 17, 2008. https://www.networkworld.com/article/2278150/data-center/cisco-s-ios-vs--juniper-s-junos.html.

Dyer-Witheford, Nick. "E-Capital and the Many-headed Hydra." In Elmer, *Critical Perspectives on the Internet,* 129–64.

Earman, John, and John D. Norton. "Exorcist XIV: The Wrath of Maxwell's Demon Part I, From Maxwell to Szilard." *Studies in History and Philosophy of Science Part B: Studies in History and Philosophy of Modern Physics* 29, no. 4 (1998): 435–71.

Eckersley, Peter, Fred von Lohmann, and Seth Schoen. "Packet Forgery by ISPs: A Report on the Comcast Affair." *Electronic Frontier Foundation,* November 2007. https://www.eff.org/wp/packet-forgery-isps-report-comcast-affair.

Edwards, Paul N. "Infrastructure and Modernity: Force, Time, and Social Organization in the History of Sociotechnical Systems." In *Technology and Modernity: The Empirical Turn,* edited by Thomas J. Misa, Philip Brey, and Andrew Feenberg, 185–226. Cambridge, Mass.: MIT Press, 2003.

Edwards, Paul N. "Some Say the Internet Should Never Have Happened." In *Media, Technology, and Society: Theories of Media Evolution,* edited by W. Russell Neuman, 141–60. Ann Arbor: University of Michigan Press, 2010. http://pne.people.si.umich.edu/PDF/Edwards2010InternetShouldNeverHaveHappened.pdf.

Edwards, Paul N. *The Closed World: Computers and the Politics of Discourse in Cold War America.* Cambridge, Mass.: MIT Press, 1997.

Edwards, Paul N., Geoffrey C. Bowker, Steve J. Jackson, and Robin Williams. "Introduction: An Agenda for Infrastructure Studies." *Journal of the Association for Information Systems* 10, no. 5 (2009): 364–74.

Egger, Sebastian, Tobias Hossfeld, Raimund Schatz, and Markus Fiedler. "Waiting Times in Quality of Experience for Web Based Services." In *Fourth International Workshop on Quality of Multimedia Experience (QoMEX), 2012,* 86–96. New York: IEEE, 2012. http://ieeexplore.ieee.org/xpls/abs_all.jsp?arnumber=6263888.

Electronic Privacy Information Center (EPIC). "Deep Packet Inspection and Privacy." Accessed July 5, 2016. https://epic.org/privacy/dpi/.

Ellis, David. "Why Is the CRTC Auditing the Gamers Instead of Rogers? (4)." *Life on the Broadband Internet* (blog), October 6, 2011. http://www.davidellis.ca/why-is-the-crtc-auditing-the-gamers-instead-of-rogers-4/.

Elmer, Greg. "A Diagram of Panoptic Surveillance." *New Media & Society* 5, no. 2 (June 1, 2003): 231–47.

Elmer, Greg. "Panopticon—Discipline—Control." In *Routledge Handbook of Surveillance*

Studies, edited by Kirstie Ball, Kevin Haggerty, and David Lyon, 21–29. New York: Routledge, 2012.

Elmer, Greg. *Profiling Machines: Mapping the Personal Information Economy*. Cambridge, Mass.: MIT Press, 2004.

Elmer, Greg. "The Vertical (Layered) Net." In *Critical Cyberculture Studies: New Directions*, edited by A. Massanari and D. Silver, 159–67. New York: New York University Press, 2006.

Elmer, Greg, ed. *Critical Perspectives on the Internet*. Lanham, Md.: Rowman & Littlefield, 2002.

Elmer, Greg, and Andy Opel. "Pre-Empting Panoptic Surveillance: Surviving the Inevitable War on Terror." In *Theorizing Surveillance: The Panopticon and Beyond*, edited by David Lyon, 139–60. Cullompton, UK: Willan, 2006. http://www.loc.gov/catdir /toc/fy0710/2007270291.html.

EMule. "Protocol Obfuscation." *EMule-Project.Net*, September 16, 2006. http://www .emule-project.net/home/perl/help.cgi?l=1&rm=show_topic&topic_id=848.

EMule. "Disappearing Uploaders." Official EMule-Board. Accessed September 6, 2016. http://forum.emule-project.net/index.php?showtopic=109705.

Enigmax. "RapidShare Slows Download Speeds to Drive Away Pirates." *TorrentFreak*, February 24, 2012. http://torrentfreak.com/rapidshare-slows-download-speeds-to -drive-away-pirates-120224/#disqus_thread.

Eriksson, Magnus. "Speech for Piratbyrån @ Bzoom Festival in Brno, Czech Rep." *Fade to Grey* (blog), October 14, 2006. http://fadetogrey.wordpress.com/2006/10/14/brno/.

Ernesto (Van der Sar). "BitTorrent's Future: DHT, PEX, and Magnet Links Explained." *Lifehacker*, November 24, 2009. http://lifehacker.com/5411311/bittorrents-future -dht-pex-and-magnet-links-explained.

Ernesto (Van der Sar). "Download a Copy of The Pirate Bay, It's Only 90 MB." *TorrentFreak*, February 9, 2012. http://torrentfreak.com/download-a-copy-of-the-pirate-bay-its -only-90-mb-120209/.

Ernesto (Van der Sar). "Pirate Bay Is the King of Torrents Once Again." *TorrentFreak*, August 14, 2016. https://torrentfreak.com/pirate-bay-king-torrents-160814/.

Ernesto (Van der Sar). "Rogers' BitTorrent Throttling Experiment Goes Horribly Wrong." *TorrentFreak*, December 13, 2010. https://torrentfreak.com/rogers-bittorrent -throttling-experiment-goes-horribly-wrong-101213/.

Ernesto (Van der Sar). "TalkTalk's P2P Throttling Kills OnLive Games." *TorrentFreak*, September 29, 2011. http://torrentfreak.com/talktalks-p2p-throttling-kills-onlive -games-110929/.

Ernesto (Van der Sar). "The Pirate Bay Appeal Verdict: Guilty Again." *TorrentFreak*, November 26, 2010. http://torrentfreak.com/the-pirate-bay-appeal-verdict-101126/.

Ernesto (Van der Sar). "The Pirate Bay Ships New Servers to Mountain Complex." *TorrentFreak*, May 16, 2011. http://torrentfreak.com/the-pirate-bay-ships-new -servers-to-mountain-complex-110516/.

Ernesto (Van der Sar). "Top 10 Most Popular Torrent Sites of 2016." *TorrentFreak*, June 2, 2016. https://torrentfreak.com/top-10-most-popular-torrent-sites-of-2016-160102/.

Ernesto (Van der Sar). "The Pirate Bay Turns 10 Years Old: The History." *TorrentFreak*,

August 10, 2013. https://torrentfreak.com/the-pirate-bay-turns-10-years-old-the
-history-130810/.

European Commission. "Telecoms: Commission Steps up UK Legal Action over Privacy
and Personal Data Protection." *European Commission Press Release Database*, October 29, 2009. http://europa.eu/rapid/press-release_IP-09-1626_en.htm?locale=en.

Ezrahi, Yaron. "Dewey's Critique of Democratic Visual Culture and Its Political Implications." In *Sites of Vision: The Discursive Construction of Sight in the History of Philosophy*, edited by David Kleinberg-Levin, 315–36. Cambridge, Mass.: MIT Press,
1999.

Farrand, Benjamin, and Helena Carrapico. "Networked Governance and the Regulation
of Expression on the Internet: The Blurring of the Role of Public and Private Actors as Content Regulators." *Journal of Information Technology & Politics* 10, no. 4
(October 2013): 357–68. DOI: 10.1080/19331681.2013.843920.

Fault. Comment on Shifthead, "Rogers ISP, WoW, and You!" *World of Warcraft Forums*,
December 19, 2010. http://us.battle.net/forums/en/wow/topic/1568009046?page
=2#post-27.

Feamster, Nick, Jennifer Rexford, and Ellen Zegura. "The Road to SDN: An Intellectual
History of Programmable Networks." *SIGCOMM Computer Communication Review* 44, no. 2 (April 2014): 87–98. DOI: 10.1145/2602204.2602219.

Federal Communications Commission (FCC). *Report and Order on Remand, Declaratory Ruling, and Order.* Washington, D.C.: Federal Communications Commission,
March 12, 2015. https://apps.fcc.gov/edocs_public/attachmatch/FCC-15-24A1.pdf.

Federal Trade Commission (FTC). *Protecting Consumer Privacy in an Era of Rapid
Change: Recommendations for Businesses and Policymakers.* Washington, D.C.:
Federal Trade Commission, March 2012. https://www.ftc.gov/sites/default/files
/documents/reports/federal-trade-commission-report-protecting-consumer
-privacy-era-rapid-change-recommendations/120326privacyreport.pdf.

Feenberg, Andrew. *Questioning Technology.* New York: Routledge, 1999. http://www.loc
.gov/catdir/enhancements/fy0649/98037421-d.html.

Feuz, Martin, Matthew Fuller, and Felix Stalder. "Personal Web Searching in the Age of
Semantic Capitalism: Diagnosing the Mechanisms of Personalisation." *First Monday* 16, no. 2 (2011). http://www.firstmonday.org/htbin/cgiwrap/bin/ojs/index.php
/fm/article/view/3344/2766.

Fevolden, Arne Martin. "The Best of Both Worlds? A History of Time-Shared Microcomputers, 1977–1983." *IEEE Annals of the History of Computing* 35, no. 1 (2013):
23–34.

Fichtner, Franco. "Bye Bye OpenDPI." *Lastsummer.de* (blog), August 6, 2012. http://
lastsummer.de/bye-bye-opendpi/.

Filip, Ondrej, Pavel Machek, Martin Mares, and Ondrej Zajicek. "The BIRD Internet
Routing Daemon Project." *cz.nic.* Accessed August 9, 2016. http://bird.network
.cz/?get_doc&f=bird-1.html#ss1.1.

Finnie, Graham, and Heavy Reading (organization). *ISP Traffic Management Technologies: The State of the Art.* Ottawa, Ont.: Canadian Radio Television and Telecommunications Commission, 2009.

Fleischer, Rasmus. "Pirate Politics: From Accelerationism to Escalationism?" *COPYRIOT* (blog), January 13, 2010. http://copyriot.se/2010/01/13/pirate-politics-from-accelerationism-to-escalationism/.

Fleischer, Rasmus. "Piratbyran's Speech at Reboot." *COPYRIOT* (blog), June 3, 2006. http://copyriot.blogspot.com/2006/06/piratbyrans-speech-at-reboot.html.

Flyverbom, Mikkel. "Transparency: Mediation and the Management of Visibilities." *International Journal of Communication* 10 (2016): 110–22.

Ford, L. R., and D. R. Fulkerson. "Maximal Flow through a Network." *Canadian Journal of Mathematics* 8 (1956): 399–404. DOI: 10.4153/CJM-1956-045-5.

Foucault, Michel. *Security, Territory, Population: Lectures at the College de France, 1977–1978.* Edited by Michel Senellart. Translated by Graham Burchell. New York: Palgrave Macmillan, 2007.

Foucault, Michel. "Truth and Power." In *Power,* edited by Paul Rabinow and James D. Faubion, 111–33. New York: New Press, 2000.

Frank, Howard. "Interview by Judy O'Neill." March 30, 1990. Oral History series. Charles Babbage Institute, Center for the History of Information Processing, University of Minnesota. https://conservancy.umn.edu/handle/11299/107294.

Frank, Howard (principal investigator and project manager) and the National Analysis Corporation (NAC). *First Annual Technical Report (15 October 1969 –15 June 1970) for the Project "Analysis and Optimization of Store-and-Forward Computer Networks."* October 15, 1970. Sponsored by Advanced Research Projects Agency, Department of Defense: ARPA Order No. 1523. http://www.dtic.mil/dtic/tr/fulltext/u2/707438.pdf.

Frank, Robert, Robert E. Kahn, and Leonard Kleinrock, "Computer Communication Network Design Experience with Theory and Practice." 1972. https://archive.org/details/ComputerCommunicationNetworkDesignExperienceWithTheoryAndPractice.

Frank, Sam. "Come with Us If You Want to Live." *Harper's Magazine,* January 2015. http://harpers.org/archive/2015/01/come-with-us-if-you-want-to-live/.

FunChords [Robb Topolski]. "Comcast Is Using Sandvine to Manage P2P Connections." *DSL Reports Forums.* Accessed September 6, 2016. https://www.dslreports.com/forum/r18323368-Comcast-is-using-Sandvine-to-manage-P2P-Connections.

Gabrys, Jennifer, Helen Pritchard, and Benjamin Barratt. "Just Good Enough Data: Figuring Data Citizenships through Air Pollution Sensing and Data Stories." *Big Data & Society* 3, no. 2 (July–December 2016): 1–14. DOI: 10.1177/2053951716679677.

Galison, Peter Louis. "The Ontology of the Enemy: Norbert Wiener and the Cybernetic Vision." *Critical Inquiry* 21, no. 1 (1994): 228–66.

Galison, Peter Louis. "War Against the Center." *Grey Room,* no. 4 (Summer 2001): 5–33.

Galloway, Alexander. *Protocol: How Control Exists After Decentralization.* Cambridge, Mass.: MIT Press, 2004.

Galloway, Alexander, and Eugene Thacker. "Protocol, Control, and Networks." *Grey Room,* no. 17 (Fall 2004): 6–29.

Galloway, Alexander, and Eugene Thacker. *The Exploit: A Theory of Networks.* Minneapolis: University of Minnesota Press, 2007.

Geere, Duncan. "Pirate Bay to Abandon .torrent Files for Magnet Links." *Ars Technica,* January 13, 2012. http://arstechnica.com/tech-policy/news/2012/01/pirate-bay -to-abandon-torrent-files-for-magnet-links.ars.

Gehl, R. W. "The Archive and the Processor: The Internal Logic of Web 2.0." *New Media & Society* 13, no. 8 (December 1, 2011): 1228–44. DOI: 10.1177/1461444811401735.

Gehl, Robert W. "Power/Freedom on the Dark Web: A Digital Ethnography of the Dark Web Social Network." *New Media & Society* 18, no. 7 (August 1, 2016): 1219–35. DOI: 10.1177/1461444814554900.

Geist, Michael. "All Your Internets Belong to US, Continued: The Bodog.Com Case." *Michael Geist* (blog), March 6, 2012. http://www.michaelgeist.ca/2012/03/bodog -case-column-post/.

Geist, Michael. "CRTC Issues Warning to Rogers: Address Throttling Concern or Face Public Hearing." *Michael Geist* (blog), July 14, 2011. http://www.michaelgeist.ca /2011/07/crtc-warning-on-throttling/.

Geist, Michael. "CRTC Sets Net Neutrality Framework but Leaves Guarantees More Complaints." *Michael Geist* (blog), October 21, 2009. http://www.michaelgeist.ca /content/view/4478/125/.

Geist, Michael. "Rogers Faces More Questions on World of Warcraft Throttling." *Michael Geist* (blog), March 30, 2011. http://www.michaelgeist.ca/2011/03/rogers-wow -throttling/.

Georgescu-Roegen, Nicholas. "Entropy." In *The New Palgrave Dictionary of Economics,* edited by Steven N. Durlauf and Lawrence E. Blume. 2nd ed. 8 vols. New York: Palgrave Macmillan, 2008. http://www.dictionaryofeconomics.com/article?id =pde1987_X000712.

Gerovitch, Slava. "InterNyet: Why the Soviet Union Did Not Build a Nationwide Computer Network." *History and Technology* 24, no. 4 (2008): 335–50.

Gillespie, Tarleton. "Algorithms, Clickworkers, and the Befuddled Fury around Facebook Trends." *Culture Digitally,* May 18, 2016. http://culturedigitally.org/2016/05 /facebook-trends/.

Gillespie, Tarleton. "Designed to 'Effectively Frustrate': Copyright, Technology and the Agency of Users." *New Media & Society* 8, no. 4 (August 1, 2006): 651–69.

Gillespie, Tarleton. "Engineering a Principle: 'End-to-End' in the Design of the Internet." *Social Studies of Science* 36, no. 3 (2006): 427–57.

Gillespie, Tarleton. "The Politics of 'Platforms.'" *New Media & Society* 12, no. 3 (May 1, 2010): 347–64.

Gillespie, Tarleton. "The Relevance of Algorithms." In *Media Technologies,* edited by Tarleton Gillespie, Pablo Boczkowski, and Kirsten Foot, 167–94. Cambridge, Mass.: MIT Press, 2014.

Gillespie, Tarleton. *Wired Shut: Copyright and the Shape of Digital Culture.* Cambridge, Mass.: MIT Press, 2007.

Goldmonger. "Canada ISP Latency Issues." *World of Warcraft Forums,* January 26, 2011. http://us.battle.net/forums/en/wow/topic/1965838937.

Goldsmith, Jack L., and Tim Wu. *Who Controls the Internet? Illusions of a Borderless World.* New York: Oxford University Press, 2006.

Goodin, Dan. "It Wasn't Easy, but Netflix Will Soon Use HTTPS to Secure Video Streams." *Ars Technica*, April 16, 2015. http://arstechnica.com/security/2015/04/it-wasnt-easy-but-netflix-will-soon-use-https-to-secure-video-streams/.

Google. "Load AMP Pages Quickly with Google AMP Cache." Google Developers. Accessed June 16, 2016. https://developers.google.com/amp/cache/.

Grand View Research. *Deep Packet Inspection (DPI) Market Analysis by Product (Standalone, Integrated), by Application (Government, Internet Service Provider, Enterprises, Education) and Segment Forecasts to 2020.* June 2014. http://www.grandviewresearch.com/industry-analysis/deep-packet-inspection-market.

Grand View Research. *Global Software Defined Networking (SDN) Market Analysis and Segment Forecasts to 2020: Software Defined Networking (SDN) Market Industry, Outlook, Size, Application, Product, Share, Growth Prospects, Key Opportunities, Dynamics, Trends, Analysis, Software Defined Networking (SDN) Report.* April 2014. http://www.grandviewresearch.com/industry-analysis/software-defined-networking-sdn-market-analysis.

Greenberg, Andy. "Meet Telecomix, the Hackers Bent on Exposing Those Who Censor and Surveil the Internet." *Forbes*, December 26, 2011. http://www.forbes.com/sites/andygreenberg/2011/12/26/meet-telecomix-the-hackers-bent-on-exposing-those-who-censor-and-surveil-the-internet/.

Greenberger, Martin, ed. *Computers and the World of the Future.* Cambridge, Mass.: MIT Press, 1964.

Greene, T., and L. Brown. "Route Control in AUTOVON Electronic Switching Centers." *IEEE Transactions on Communication Technology* 17, no. 4 (1969): 442–46.

Greenwald, Glenn. "How Covert Agents Infiltrate the Internet to Manipulate, Deceive, and Destroy Reputations." *The Intercept*, February 24, 2014. https://firstlook.org/theintercept/2014/02/24/jtrig-manipulation/.

Greenwald, Glenn, and Ewen MacAskill. "NSA Prism Program Taps in to User Data of Apple, Google and Others." *The Guardian*, June 7, 2013. http://www.theguardian.com/world/2013/jun/06/us-tech-giants-nsa-data.

Gregg, Melissa, and Gregory J. Seigworth, eds. *The Affect Theory Reader.* Durham, N.C.: Duke University Press, 2010.

Grier, David Alan, and Mary Campbell. "A Social History of Bitnet and Listserv, 1985–1991." *IEEE Annals of the History of Computing* 22, no. 2 (2000): 32–41.

Guenin, B., J. Könemann, and Levent Tuncel. *A Gentle Introduction to Optimization.* Cambridge: Cambridge University Press, 2014.

Guillory, John. "The Memo and Modernity." *Critical Inquiry* 31, no. 1 (2004): 108–32.

Guins, Raiford. *Edited Clean Version: Technology and the Culture of Control.* Minneapolis: University of Minnesota Press, 2009.

Haakonii. Comment on Shifthead, "Rogers ISP, WoW, and You!" *World of Warcraft Forums*, December 22, 2010. http://us.battle.net/forums/en/wow/topic/1568009046?page=4#post-76.

Hafner, Katie, and Matthew Lyon, *Where Wizards Stay Up Late: The Origins of the Internet.* New York: Simon and Schuster, 1996.

Halliday, Josh. "British ISPs Will Block The Pirate Bay within Weeks." Technology, *The*

Guardian, April 30, 2012. http://www.guardian.co.uk/technology/2012/apr/30
/british-isps-block-pirate-bay.

Hallinan, B., and T. Striphas. "Recommended for You: The Netflix Prize and the Production of Algorithmic Culture." *New Media & Society*, 18, no. 1 (January 1, 2016): 117–37. DOI: 10.1177/1461444814538646.

Halsall, Andy. "The Pirate Bay Proxy, an Open Internet and Censorship." *Pirate Party UK*, May 10, 2012. http://www.pirateparty.org.uk/blog/2012/may/10/pirate-bay
-proxy-open-internet-and-censorship/.

Hamzeh, Kory, Gurdeep Singh Pall, William Verthein, Jeff Taarud, W. Andrew Little, and Glen Zorn. "RFC 2637—Point-to-Point Tunneling Protocol (PPTP) (RFC2637)." *faqs.org*, July, 1999. http://www.faqs.org/rfcs/rfc2637.html.

Haralanova, Christina, and Evan Light. "Enmeshed Lives? Examining the Potentials and the Limits in the Provision of Wireless Networks: The Case of Réseau Libre." *Journal of Peer Production*, no. 9 (2016). http://peerproduction.net/issues/issue
-9-alternative-internets/peer-reviewed-papers/enmeshed-lives/.

Haraway, Donna J. "Manifesto for Cyborgs: Science, Technology, and Socialist Feminism in the Late Twentieth Century." In *Simians, Cyborgs, and Women: The Reinvention of Nature*, 149–82. New York: Routledge, 1991. Originally published in *Socialist Review*, no. 80 (1985): 65–108.

Harvey, David. "The Fetish of Technology: Causes and Consequences." *Macalester International* 13, no. 1 (July 1, 2003), article 7. http://digitalcommons.macalester.edu
/cgi/viewcontent.cgi?article=1411&context=macintl.

Hassan, Robert. *Empires of Speed: Time and the Acceleration of Politics and Society*. Leiden: Brill, 2009.

Hayles, N. Katherine. *How We Became Posthuman: Virtual Bodies in Cybernetics, Literature, and Informatics*. Chicago: University of Chicago Press, 1999.

Hayles, N. Katherine. "Print Is Flat, Code Is Deep: The Importance of Media-Specific Analysis." *Poetics Today* 25, no. 1 (2004): 67–89.

Hayles, N. Katherine. "Self-Reflexive Metaphors in Maxwell's Demon and Shannon's Choice: Finding the Passages." In *Literature and Science: Theory & Practice*, edited by Stuart Peterfreund, 209–38. Boston: Northeastern University Press, 1990.

Heart, Frank E., Robert E. Kahn, S. M. Ornstein, W. R. Crowther, and David C. Walden. "The Interface Message Processor for the ARPA Computer Network." In *Proceedings of the May 5–7, 1970, Spring Joint Computer Conference*, 551–67. New York: Association for Computing Machinery, 1970. http://dl.acm.org/citation.cfm?id=1477021.

Helmond, Anne. "Adding the Bling: The Role of Social Media Data Intermediaries." *Culture Digitally* (blog), May 7, 2014. http://culturedigitally.org/2014/05/adding-the-bling
-the-role-of-social-media-data-intermediaries/.

Hicks, Marie. *Programmed Inequality: How Britain Discarded Women Technologists and Lost Its Edge in Computing*. History of Computing. Cambridge, Mass.: MIT Press. 2017.

Higginbotham, Stacey. "More Bad News about Broadband Caps: Many Meters Are Inaccurate." *GigaOM*, February 7, 2013. http://gigaom.com/2013/02/07/more-bad
-news-about-broadband-caps-many-meters-are-inaccurate/.

Hildebrandt, Amber, Michael Pereira, and Dave Seglins. "CSE Tracks Millions of Downloads Daily: Snowden Documents." CBC News, January 27, 2015. http://www.cbc.ca/1.2930120.

Hogan, M. "Data Flows and Water Woes: The Utah Data Center." *Big Data & Society* 2, no. 2 (August 10, 2015): 1–12. DOI: 10.1177/2053951715592429.

Holt, Jennifer. "Regulating Connected Viewing: Media Pipelines and Cloud Policy." In *Connected Viewing: Selling, Streaming, and Sharing Media in the Digital Age*, edited by Jennifer Holt and Kevin Sanson, 19–39. New York: Routledge, 2014.

Hookway, Branden. *Pandemonium: The Rise of Predatory Locales in the Postwar World*. New York: Princeton Architectural Press, 1999.

Hörning, Karl H., Daniela Ahrens, and Anette Gerhard. "Do Technologies Have Time? New Practices of Time and the Transformation of Communication Technologies." *Time & Society* 8, no. 2–3 (September 1, 1999): 293–308. DOI: 10.1177/0961463X99008002005.

Hossfeld, Tobias, Sebastian Egger, Raimund Schatz, Markus Fiedler, Kathrin Masuch, and Charlott Lorentzen. "Initial Delay vs. Interruptions: Between the Devil and the Deep Blue Sea." In *Fourth International Workshop on Quality of Multimedia Experience (QoMEX), 2012*, 1–6. New York: IEEE, 2012. http://ieeexplore.ieee.org/xpls/abs_all.jsp?arnumber=6263849.

Howard, Philip N. *Pax Technica: How the Internet of Things May Set Us Free or Lock Us Up*. New Haven, Conn.: Yale University Press, 2015.

Hu, Tung-Hui. *A Prehistory of the Cloud*. Cambridge, Mass.: MIT Press. 2015.

Huston, Geoff. *ISP Survival Guide: Strategies for Running a Competitive ISP*. New York: Wiley, 1999. http://www.loc.gov/catdir/description/wiley033/98038660.html.

Ingham, Kenneth, and Stephanie Forrest. "Network Firewalls." In *Enhancing Computer Security with Smart Technology*, edited by V. Rao Vemuri, 9–40. Boca Raton, Fla.: Auerbach, 2005.

Innis, Harold Adams. *The Bias of Communication*. 2nd ed. Toronto: University of Toronto Press, 1951.

Internet Corporation for Assigned Names and Numbers (ICANN). "First IDN CcTLDs Available." *ICANN*, May 5, 2010. https://www.icann.org/news/announcement-2010-05-05-en.

Irix. Comment on Ressy, "Rogers Throttling/Deprioritizing World of Warcraft." *Rogers Community Forums*, January 28, 2011. http://communityforums.rogers.com/t5/forums/forumtopicpage/board-id/Getting_connected/message-id/705#M705.

ISC8 Inc. "ISC8 Acquires Key Assets of Bivio Networks to Expand into 'Big Data' Network Cybersecurity Market." *Marketwired*, September 4, 2012. http://www.marketwired.com/press-release/isc8-acquires-key-assets-bivio-networks-expand-into-big-data-network-cybersecurity-market-otcbb-isci-1696769.htm.

Isenberg, David S. "The Dawn of the 'Stupid Network.'" *NetWorker* 2, no. 1 (1998): 24–31.

Jacobs, John E. "SAGE Overview." *Annals of the History of Computing* 5, no. 4 (1983): 4.

Johns, Adrian. *Piracy: The Intellectual Property Wars from Gutenberg to Gates*. Chicago: University of Chicago Press, 2010.

Jones, Ben. "The Pirate Bay in the Hot Seat." *TorrentFreak*, January 24, 2007. http://torrentfreak.com/the-pirate-bay-in-the-hot-seat/.

Jowett, Garth, I. C. Jarvie, and Kathryn H. Fuller. *Children and the Movies: Media Influence and the Payne Fund Controversy.* Cambridge: Cambridge University Press, 1996.

Julkunen, H., and C. E. Chow. "Enhance Network Security with Dynamic Packet Filter." In *Proceedings of the 7th International Conference on Computer Communications and Networks, 1998,* 268–75. New York: IEEE, 1998. DOI: 10.1109/ICCCN.1998.998786.

Juniper Networks. "NorthStar Controller Web User Interface Guide." July 13, 2016. http://www.juniper.net/techpubs/en_US/northstar2.1.0/information-products/pathway-pages/2.1/northstar-web-user-interface.pdf.

Juniper Networks. "NorthStar WAN SDN Network Controller." Accessed July 21, 2016. https://www.juniper.net/us/en/products-services/sdn/northstar-network-controller/.

Kafka, Peter. "How One Company Figured Out How Many People Watch Netflix's New Shows—And How Netflix Stopped Them." *Recode,* August 8, 2014. http://www.recode.net/2014/8/8/11629692/how-one-company-figured-out-how-many-people-watch-netflixs-new-shows.

Kahn, Robert E. "Interview by Judy O'Neill." April 24, 1990. Oral History series. Charles Babbage Institute, Center for the History of Information Processing, University of Minnesota. https://conservancy.umn.edu/handle/11299/107387.

Kaiser, Christian. "HTML5 and Video Streaming." *The Netflix Tech Blog,* December 22, 2010. http://techblog.netflix.com/2010/12/html5-and-video-streaming.html.

Kakhki, Arash Molavi, Fangfan Li, David Choffnes, Ethan Katz-Bassett, and Alan Mislove. "BingeOn Under the Microscope: Understanding T-Mobiles Zero-Rating Implementation." David Choffnes website. http://david.choffnes.com/pubs/bingeon_sigcomm16.pdf. DOI: 10.1145/2940136.2940140.

Kaplan, Steven M. *Wiley Electrical and Electronics Engineering Dictionary.* Hoboken, N.J.: Wiley-Interscience, 2004.

Karas, D. "Network Measurement Program (NMP)." June 30, 1970. Kleinrock Internet History Center. http://digital2.library.ucla.edu/viewItem.do?ark=21198/zz002dj6tj.

Karpf, David. *The MoveOn Effect: The Unexpected Transformation of American Political Advocacy.* New York: Oxford University Press, 2012.

Kelty, Christopher. *Two Bits: The Cultural Significance of Free Software.* Durham, N.C.: Duke University Press, 2008.

Kimball, Danny. "Wonkish Populism in Media Advocacy and Net Neutrality Policy Making." *International Journal of Communication* 10 (2016): 5949–68.

KingNerd. Comment on Ressy, "Rogers Throttling/Deprioritizing World of Warcraft." *Rogers Community Forums,* January 25, 2011. http://communityforums.rogers.com/t5/forums/forumtopicpage/board-id/Getting_connected/message-id/633#M633.

Kiss, Jemima. "The Pirate Bay Trial: Guilty Verdict." *The Guardian,* April 17, 2009. http://www.guardian.co.uk/technology/2009/apr/17/the-pirate-bay-trial-guilty-verdict.

Kita, Chigusa Ishikawa. "J. C. R. Licklider's Vision for the IPTO." *IEEE Annals of the History of Computing* 25, no. 3 (July 2003): 62–77. DOI: 10.1109/MAHC.2003.1226656.

Kittler, Friedrich A. *Gramophone, Film, Typewriter*. Stanford, Calif.: Stanford University Press, 1999.

Kleinrock, Leonard. "An Early History of the ARPANET." *IEEE Communications Magazine* 48, no. 8 (August 2010): 26–36. http://ieeexplore.ieee.org/stamp/stamp.jsp?tp=&arnumber=5534584

Kleinrock, Leonard. "On Flow Control in Computer Networks." In *ConferenceRecord: 1978 International Conference on Communications, Toronto, Canada, June 4–7, 1978*, 2:27.2.1–5. New York: IEEE, 1978. https://www.lk.cs.ucla.edu/data/files/Kleinrock/On%20Flow%20Control%20in%20Computer%20Networks.pdf.

Kleinrock, Leonard. "Principles and Lessons in Packet Communications." *Proceedings of the IEEE* 66, no. 11 (1978): 1320–29.

Kleinrock, Leonard. *Communication Nets: Stochastic Message Flow and Delay*. New York: McGraw-Hill, 1964.

Kleinrock, Leonard. "Optimum Bribing for Queue Position." *Operations Research*, April 1, 1967, 304–17. DOI: 10.1287/opre.15.2.304.

Kline, Stephen, Nick Dyer-Witheford, and Greig de Peuter. *Digital Play: The Interaction of Technology, Culture, and Marketing*. Montreal: McGill-Queen's University Press, 2003.

Klose, Simon, dir. *TPB AFK: The Pirate Bay Away from Keyboard*. 2013. YouTube Video. 1:22:07. https://www.youtube.com/watch?v=eTOKXCEwo_8.

Krashinsky, Susan. "Rogers to Offer Promotional Ads by Text." *Globe and Mail*, October 2, 2013. http://www.theglobeandmail.com/report-on-business/industry-news/marketing/rogers-to-offer-promotional-ads-by-text/article14646004/.

Kreiss, Daniel. *Taking Our Country Back: The Crafting of Networked Politics from Howard Dean to Barack Obama*. New York: Oxford University Press, 2012.

Krishnan, S. Shunmuga, and Ramesh K. Sitaraman. "Video Stream Quality Impacts Viewer Behavior: Inferring Causality Using Quasi-Experimental Designs." In *Proceedings of the 2012 ACM Conference on Internet Measurement Conference*, 211–24. New York: Association for Computing Machines, 2012. http://people.cs.umass.edu/~ramesh/Site/PUBLICATIONS_files/imc208-krishnan.pdf.

Kuehn, Andreas, and Milton Mueller. *Profiling the Profilers: Deep Packet Inspection and Behavioral Advertising in Europe and the United States*. Rochester, N.Y.: Social Science Research Network, September 1, 2012. http://papers.ssrn.com/abstract=2014181.

Kuerbis, Brenden, and Milton Mueller. "Securing the Root." In DeNardis, *Opening Standards*, 45–62.

Kupferman, Steve. "How World of Warcraft Players Got Rogers to Admit It Was Wrong." *Torontoist*, April 5, 2011. http://torontoist.com/2011/04/how_world_of_warcraft_players_got_rogers_to_admit_it_was_wrong/.

Kurra, Babu. "Egypt Shut Down Its Net with a Series of Phone Calls." *Wired*, January 28, 2011. http://www.wired.com/2011/01/egypt-isp-shutdown/.

Kurs, Simon. "Yo Ho Ho: Buccanerds Give Studios a Broadside." *Sunday Times*, January 7, 2007. https://www.thetimes.co.uk/article/yo-ho-ho-buccanerds-give-studios-a-broadside-hshv9lcgw3x.

Kushner, Scott. "The Freelance Translation Machine: Algorithmic Culture and the Invisible Industry." *New Media & Society* 15, no. 8 (December 1, 2013): 1241–58. DOI: 10.1177/1461444812469597.

Lampland, Martha, and Susan Leigh Star, eds. *Standards and Their Stories: How Quantifying, Classifying, & Formalizing Shape Everyday Life.* Ithaca, N.Y.: Cornell University Press, 2009.

Land, Chris. "Flying the Black Flag: Revolt, Revolution and the Social Organization of Piracy in the 'Golden Age.'" *Management & Organizational History* 2, no. 2 (2007): 169–92.

Langlois, Ganaele. "Meaning, Semiotechnologies and Participatory Media." *Culture Machine* 12 (2011):1–27.

Langlois, Ganaele, and Greg Elmer. "Wikipedia Leeches? The Promotion of Traffic through a Collaborative Web Format." *New Media & Society* 11, no. 5 (August 1, 2009): 773–94.

Langlois, Ganaele, Greg Elmer, Fenwick McKelvey, and Zachary Devereaux. "Networked Publics: The Double Articulation of Code and Politics on Facebook." *Canadian Journal of Communication* 34, no. 3 (2009): 415–33.

Langlois, Ganaele, Fenwick McKelvey, Greg Elmer, and Kenneth Werbin. "Mapping Commercial Web 2.0 Worlds: Towards a New Critical Ontogenesis." *Fibreculture* 14 (2009). http://fourteen.fibreculturejournal.org/fcj-095-mapping-commercial-web-2-0-worlds-towards-a-new-critical-ontogenesis/.

Lash, Scott. *Critique of Information.* Thousand Oaks, Calif.: SAGE, 2002.

Lash, Scott. "Power after Hegemony: Cultural Studies in Mutation?" *Theory, Culture & Society* 24, no. 3 (2007): 55–78.

Latham, Robert. "Border Formations: Security and Subjectivity at the Border." *Citizenship Studies* 14, no. 2 (April 2010): 185–201. DOI: 10.1080/13621021003594858.

Latham, Robert. "Networks, Information, and the Rise of the Global Internet." In *Digital Formations: IT and New Architectures in the Global Realm,* edited by Robert Latham and Saskia Sassen, 146–77. Princeton, N.J.: Princeton University Press, 2005.

Lawson, Stephen. "Blue Coat to Acquire Packeteer for $268 Million." *COMPUTERWORLD,* April 22, 2008. https://www.computerworld.com/article/2536756/networking/blue-coat-to-acquire-packeteer-for--268m.html.

Lazar, Jonathan, Adam Jones, and Ben Shneiderman. "Workplace User Frustration with Computers: An Exploratory Investigation of the Causes and Severity." *Behaviour & Information Technology* 25, no. 3 (May 2006): 239–51. DOI: 10.1080/01449290500196963.

Le, Tung M., and Jason But. *Bittorrent Traffic Classification: Technical Report 91022A.* Melbourne, Australia: Centre for Advanced Internet Architectures, Swinburne University of Technology, October 2009. https://www.researchgate.net/publication/228786640_BitTorrent_Traffic_Classification.

Lee, J. A. N. "Claims to the Term 'Time-Sharing.'" *IEEE Annals of the History of Computing* 14, no. 1 (1992): 16–17.

Lee, J. A. N., John McCarthy, and Joseph Carl Robnett Licklider. "The Beginnings at MIT." *IEEE Annals of the History of Computing* 14, no. 1 (1992): 18–54. DOI: 10.1109/85.145317.

Lee, Terence. "Internet Control and Auto-Regulation in Singapore." *Surveillance & Society* 3, no. 1 (2005): 74–95.

Lee, Timothy B. "Report: NSA Can 'Reach Roughly 75% of All U.S. Internet Traffic.'" *Washington Post*, August 20, 2013. http://www.washingtonpost.com/blogs/the-switch/wp/2013/08/20/report-nsa-can-reach-roughly-75-of-all-u-s-internet-traffic/.

Leff, Harvey S., and Andrew F. Rex. *Maxwell's Demon: Entropy, Information, Computing.* Princeton, N.J.: Princeton University Press, 1990.

Legout, A., G. Urvoy-Keller, and P. Michiardi. "Understanding Bittorrent: An Experimental Perspective." Technical Report for Inria Sophia Antipolis - Méditerrané, Iria Grenoble-Rhône-Alpes, and Institut Eurecom, November 9, 2005. http://www.eurecom.fr/en/publication/1933/download/ce-urvogu-051109.pdf.

Leiner et al. "The Past and Future History of the Internet." *Communications of the ACM* 40, no. 2 (February 1997): 102–8.

Lessig, Lawrence. *Code: Version 2.0.* New York: Basic Books, 2006.

Levy, Steven. "(Some) Attention Must Be Paid!" *Newsweek*, March 26, 2006. http://www.newsweek.com/some-attention-must-be-paid-106439.

Lewis, Michael. "The Wolf Hunters of Wall Street: An Adaptation from 'Flash Boys: A Wall Street Revolt,' by Michael Lewis." *New York Times*, March 31, 2014. http://www.nytimes.com/2014/04/06/magazine/flash-boys-michael-lewis.html.

Lewis, Michael. *Flash Boys: A Wall Street Revolt.* New York: W. W. Norton, 2014.

Leyshon, Andrew. "Time–Space (and Digital) Compression: Software Formats, Musical Networks, and the Reorganisation of the Music Industry." *Environment and Planning A: Economy and Space* 33, no. 1 (2001): 49–77.

Li, Fangfan, Arash Molavi Kakhki, David Choffnes, Phillipa Gill, and Alan Mislove. "Classifiers Unclassified: An Efficient Approach to Revealing IP Traffic Classification Rules." Paper presented at the 16th Annual Association for Computing Machines Internet Measuring Conference, Los Angeles, Calif., October 31 through November 2, 2016. http://david.choffnes.com/pubs/ClassifiersUnclassified-IMC16.pdf.

Libbenga, Jan. "The Pirate Bay Plans to Buy Sealand." *The Register*, January 12, 2007. http://www.theregister.co.uk/2007/01/12/pirate_bay_buys_island/.

Licklider, Joseph Carl Robnett. "Man-Computer Symbiosis." *IRE Transactions on Human Factors in Electronics* HFE-1, no. 1 (1960): 4–11.

Licklider, Joseph Carl Robnett. "Memorandum for Members and Affiliates of the Intergalactic Computer Network," December 11, 2001. http://www.kurzweilai.net/memorandum-for-members-and-affiliates-of-the-intergalactic-computer-network.

Licklider, Joseph Carl Robnett, and Robert W. Taylor. "The Computer as a Communication Device." *Science and Technology for the Technical Men in Management*, April 1968. http://memex.org/licklider.pdf.

Light, Jennifer S. "When Computers Were Women." *Technology and Culture* 40, no. 3 (1999): 455–83.

Lindgren, Simon, and Jessica Linde. "The Subpolitics of Online Piracy: A Swedish Case

Study." *Convergence: The International Journal of Research into New Media Technologies* 18, no. 2 (March 1, 2012): 143–64. DOI: 10.1177/1354856511433681.

Lippmann, Walter. *Public Opinion.* New York: Macmillan, 1922. Reprint, New York: Free Press Paperbacks, 1997.

Löblich, Maria, and Francesca Musiani. "Network Neutrality and Communication Research: The Implications of Internet Infrastructure for the Public Sphere." In *Communication Yearbook 38,* edited by Elisia L. Cohen, 339–68. New York: Routledge, 2014.

Lohr, Steve. "Impatient Web Users Flee Slow-loading Sites." Technology, *New York Times,* February 29, 2012. http://www.nytimes.com/2012/03/01/technology/impatient -web-users-flee-slow-loading-sites.html.

Lukasik, Stephen J. "Why the ARPANET Was Built." *IEEE Annals of the History of Computing* 33, no. 3 (2011): 4–21.

Lungu, Dov, and Zbigniew Stachniak. "Following TRACE: The Computer Hobby Movement in Canada." *Scientia Canadensis: Canadian Journal of the History of Science, Technology and Medicine* 34, no. 1 (2011): 1. DOI: 10.7202/1006926ar.

MacAskill, Ewen, Julian Borger, Nick Hopkins, Nick Davies, and James Ball. "GCHQ Taps Fibre-Optic Cables for Secret Access to World's Communications." *The Guardian,* June 21, 2013. http://www.theguardian.com/uk/2013/jun/21/gchq-cables-secret -world-communications-nsa.

Mackay, Robin, and Armen Avanessian, eds. *#Accelerate: The Accelerationist Reader.* Falmouth, UK: Urbanomic, 2014.

Mackenzie, Adrian. "Java: The Practical Virtuality of Internet Programming." *New Media & Society* 8, no. 3 (June 1, 2006): 441–65.

Mackenzie, Adrian. *Wirelessness: Radical Empiricism in Network Cultures.* Cambridge, Mass.: MIT Press, 2010.

Mackenzie, Adrian. *Transductions: Bodies and Machines at Speed.* Technologies: Studies in Culture & Theory. New York: Continuum, 2002.

Mager, Astrid. "Algorithmic Ideology: How Capitalist Society Shapes Search Engines." *Information, Communication & Society* 15, no. 5 (June 2012): 769–87. DOI: 10.1080/ 1369118X.2012.676056.

Mailland, Julien, and Kevin Driscoll. *Minitel: Welcome to the Internet.* Platform Studies. Cambridge, Mass.: MIT Press, 2017.

Manjoo, Farhad. "Facebook's Bias Is Built-In, and Bears Watching." Technology, *New York Times,* May 11, 2016. http://www.nytimes.com/2016/05/12/technology/facebooks -bias-is-built-in-and-bears-watching.html.

Mansell, Robin. "From Digital Divides to Digital Entitlements in Knowledge Societies." *Current Sociology* 50, no. 3 (May 1, 2002): 407–26. DOI: 10.1177/ 0011392102050003007.

Mansell, Robin. *Imagining the Internet: Communication, Innovation, and Governance.* New York: Oxford University Press, 2012.

Margonis, Frank. "John Dewey's Racialized Visions of the Student and Classroom Community." *Educational Theory* 59, no. 1 (February 1, 2009): 17–39. DOI: 10.1111/ j.1741–5446.2009.00305.x.

Marill, Thomas, and Lawrence Roberts. "Toward a Cooperative Network of Time-Shared

Computers." In *Proceedings of the November 7–10, 1966, Fall Joint Computer Conference*, 425–31. New York: Association for Computing Machines, 1966

Marques, Eduardo, Lina de Bito, Paulo Sampaio, and Laura Rodriguez Peralta. "An Analysis of Quality of Service Architectures: Principles, Requirements, and Future Trends." In *Intelligent Quality of Service Technologies and Network Management: Models for Enhancing Communication,* edited by Pattarasinee Bhattarakosol, 15–35. Hershey, Pa.: IGI Global, 2010.

Marquis-Boire, Morgan, Jakub Dalek, Sarah McKune, Matthew Carrieri, Masashi Crete-Nishihata, Ron Deibert, Saad Omar Khan, Helmi Noman, John Scott-Railton, and Greg Wiseman. *Planet Blue Coat: Mapping Global Censorship and Surveillance Tools.* Toronto, Ontario: The Citizen Lab, January 15, 2013. https://citizenlab.org /2013/01/planet-blue-coat-mapping-global-censorship-and-surveillance-tools/.

Marres, Noortje. "Front-Staging Nonhumans: Publicity as a Constraint on the Political Activity of Things." In *Political Matter: Technoscience, Democracy, and Public Life,* edited by Bruce Braun and Sarah J. Whatmore, 177–210. Minneapolis: University of Minnesota Press, 2010.

Marsden, Christopher T. *Network Neutrality: From Policy to Law to Regulation.* Manchester, UK: Manchester University Press, 2017.

Massumi, Brian. "Potential Politics and the Primacy of Preemption." *Theory & Event* 10, no. 2 (2007). http://muse.jhu.edu/journals/theory_and_event/v010/10.2massumi .html. DOI: 10.1353/tae.2007.0066

Massumi, Brian. *The Power at the End of the Economy.* Durham, N.C.: Duke University Press, 2015.

Massumi, Brian. "Translator's Note." In Deleuze and Guattari, *A Thousand Plateaus,* xvii–xix.

Mathison, Stuart L., Lawrence G. Roberts, and Philip M. Walker. "The History of Telenet and the Commercialization of Packet Switching in the U.S." *IEEE Communications Magazine* 50, no. 5 (May 2012): 28–45. DOI: 10.1109/MCOM.2012.6194380.

Maxwell, James. *Theory of Heat.* New York: D. Appleton, 1872.

May, Jon, and Nigel Thrift, eds. *TimeSpace: Geographies of Temporality.* London: Routledge, 2001.

Mayer, Jonathan. "How Verizon's Advertising Header Works." *Web Policy,* October 24, 2014. http://webpolicy.org/2014/10/24/how-verizons-advertising-header-works/.

Mayr, Otto. *The Origins of Feedback Control.* Cambridge, Mass.: MIT Press, 1970.

McCormick, Rich. "4.6 Million Snapchat Phone Numbers and Usernames Leaked." *The Verge,* January 1, 2014. http://www.theverge.com/2014/1/1/5262740/4–6-million -snapchat-phone-numbers-and-usernames-leaked.

McKelvey, Fenwick. "A Programmable Platform? Drupal, Modularity, and the Future of the Web." *Fibreculture,* no. 18 (2011): 232–54.

McKelvey, Fenwick. "Ends and Ways: The Algorithmic Politics of Network Neutrality." *Global Media Journal—Canadian Edition* 3, no. 1 (2010): 51–73.

McKelvey, Fenwick. "Openness Compromised? Questioning the Role of Openness in Digital Methods and Contemporary Critical Praxis." In *Compromised Data: From*

Social Media to Big Data, edited by Greg Elmer, Ganaele Langlois, and Joanna Redden, 126–46. New York: Bloomsbury Academic, 2015.

McKelvey, Fenwick. "We Like Copies, Just Don't Let the Others Fool You: The Paradox of The Pirate Bay." *Television & New Media* 16, no. 8 (2015): 734–50. DOI: 10.1177/1527476414542880.

McKelvey, Fenwick. "Algorithmic Media Need Democratic Methods: Why Publics Matter." *Canadian Journal of Communication* 39, no. 4 (2014): 597–613. http://www.fenwickmckelvey.com/wp-content/uploads/2014/11/2746-9231-1-PB.pdf.

McKelvey, Fenwick, Matthew Tiessen, and Luke Simcoe. "A Consensual Hallucination No More? The Internet as Simulation Machine." *European Journal of Cultural Studies* 18, no. 4–5 (2015): 577–94.

McMahon, Rob, Michael Gurstein, Brian Beaton, Susan O'Donnell, and Tim Whiteduck. "Making Information Technologies Work at the End of the Road." *Journal of Information Policy* 4, no. 1 (May 27, 2014): 250–69. DOI: 10.5471/jip.v4i0.146.

McQuillan, John M. "The Birth of Link-State Routing." *IEEE Annals of the History of Computing* 31, no. 1 (2009): 68–71.

McQuillan, John M., William R. Crowther, Bernard P. Cosell, David C. Walden, and Frank E. Heart. "Improvements in the Design and Performance of the ARPA Network." In *Proceedings of the December 5–7, 1972, Fall Joint Computer Conference, Part II*, 741–54. New York: Association for Computing Machines, 1972. http://dl.acm.org/citation.cfm?id=1480096.

McStay, Andrew. "Profiling Phorm: An Autopoietic Approach to the Audience-as-Commodity." *Surveillance & Society* 8, no. 3 (2010): 310–22.

Menn, Joseph, and Dustin Volz. "Google, Facebook Quietly Move toward Automatic Blocking of Extremist Videos." Reuters, June 24, 2016. http://www.reuters.com/article/us-internet-extremism-video-exclusive-idUSKCN0ZB00M.

Menzies, Heather. *No Time: Stress and the Crisis of Modern Life*. Vancouver, British Columbia: Douglas & McIntyre, 2005.

Meyer, Robinson. "Everything We Know About Facebook's Secret Mood Manipulation Experiment." *The Atlantic*, June 28, 2014. http://www.theatlantic.com/technology/archive/2014/06/everything-we-know-about-facebooks-secret-mood-manipulation-experiment/373648/.

Miegel, Fredrik, and Tobias Olsson. "From Pirates to Politician: The Story of the Swedish File Sharers Who Became a Political Party." In *Democracy, Journalism and Technology: New Developments in an Enlarged Europe*, edited by Nico Carpentier, Pille Pruulmann-Vengerfeldt, Kaarle Nordenstreng, Maren Hartmann, Peeter Vihalemm, Bart Cammaerts, Hannu Nieminen, and Tobias Olsson, 203–17. Tartu, Estonia: Tartu University Press, 2008.

Miller, Robert B. "Response Time in Man-Computer Conversational Transactions." In *Proceedings of the December 9–11, 1968, Fall Joint Computer Conference, Part I*, 267–77. New York: Association for Computing Machines, 1968. DOI: 10.1145/1476589.1476628.

Mills, D. L. "The Fuzzball." In *SIGCOMM '88: Proceedings of the ACM Symposium on*

Communications Architectures and Protocols, 115–22. New York: Association for Computing Machines, 1988. DOI: 10.1145/52324.52337.

Mindell, David A. *Between Human and Machine: Feedback, Control, and Computing before Cybernetics.* Baltimore, Md.: Johns Hopkins University Press, 2002.

Mirowski, Philip. *Machine Dreams: Economics Becomes a Cyborg Science.* New York: Cambridge University Press, 2002.

Mirowski, Philip, and Edward Nik-Khah. *The Knowledge We Have Lost in Information: The History of Information in Modern Economics.* New York: Oxford University Press, 2017.

Mittelstadt, B. D., P. Allo, M. Taddeo, S. Wachter, and L. Floridi. "The Ethics of Algorithms: Mapping the Debate." *Big Data & Society* 3, no. 2 (December 1, 2016). DOI: 10.1177/2053951716679679.

Molyneux, Robert, and Robert Williams. "Measuring the Internet." In *Annual Review of Information Science and Technology* 34 (1999): 287–339.

Moschovitis, Christos J. P. *History of the Internet: A Chronology, 1843 to the Present.* Santa Barbara, Calif.: ABC-CLIO, 1999.

Mosco, Vincent. *The Digital Sublime: Myth, Power, and Cyberspace.* Cambridge, Mass.: MIT Press, 2004.

Mosco, Vincent. *The Political Economy of Communication: Rethinking and Renewal.* 2nd ed. Thousand Oaks, Calif.: SAGE, 2009.

Moya, Jared. "Swedish Prosecutor Won't Investigate Top Cop's MPAA Ties." *ZeroPaid,* July 9, 2008. http://www.zeropaid.com/news/9622/swedish_prosecutor_wont _investigate_top_cops_mpaa_ties/.

Mueller, Milton. *Ruling the Root: Internet Governance and the Taming of Cyberspace.* Cambridge, Mass.: MIT Press, 2002.

Mueller, Milton, and Hadi Asghari. "Deep Packet Inspection and Bandwidth Management: Battles over BitTorrent in Canada and the United States." Paper presented at the Telecommunications Policy Research Conference, 2011. https://papers.ssrn .com/sol3/papers.cfm?abstract_id=1989644##.

Mueller, Milton, and Hadi Asghari. "Deep Packet Inspection and Bandwidth Management: Battles over BitTorrent in Canada and the United States." *Telecommunications Policy* 36, no. 6 (July 2012): 462–75. DOI: 10.1016/j.telpol.2012.04.003.

Mueller, Milton, Andreas Kuehn, and Stephanie Michelle Santoso. "Policing the Network: Using DPI for Copyright Enforcement." *Surveillance & Society* 9, no. 4 (2012): 348–64.

Mumford, Lewis. *Technics and Civilization.* New York: Harcourt, Brace, 1934.

Murphy, Brian Martin. "A Critical History of the Internet." In Elmer, *Critical Perspectives on the Internet,* 27–45.

Muuss, Mike. "The Story of the PING Program." Accessed March 31, 2014. http://ftp.arl .army.mil/~mike/ping.html.

Nagy, P., and G. Neff. "Imagined Affordances: Reconstructing a Keyword for Communication Theory." *Social Media + Society* 1, no. 2 (2015): 1–9. DOI: 10.1177/ 2056305115603385.

Negri, Antonio. *The Savage Anomaly: The Power of Spinoza's Metaphysics and Politics.* Minneapolis: University of Minnesota Press, 1991.

Neilson, Brett, and Ned Rossiter. "Precarity as a Political Concept, or, Fordism as Exception." *Theory, Culture & Society* 25, no. 7–8 (December 1, 2008): 51–72. DOI: 10.1177/0263276408097796.

NetFlix. *2012 Annual Report.* Los Gatos, Calif.: Netflix, 2012. https://ir.netflix.com/static-files/96d37061-9312-4853-9a41-8c5df8efbca8.

Nhan, Johnny, Laura Huey, and Ryan Broll. "Digilantism: An Analysis of Crowdsourcing and the Boston Marathon Bombings." *British Journal of Criminology* 57, no. 2 (March 1, 2017): 341–61. DOI: 10.1093/bjc/azv118.

Noam, Eli M. *Interconnecting the Network of Networks.* Cambridge, Mass.: MIT Press, 2001.

Norberg, Arthur L., and Judy E. O'Neill. *Transforming Computer Technology: Information Processing for the Pentagon, 1962–1986.* Baltimore, Md.: Johns Hopkins University Press, 1996.

Norris, Pippa. *Digital Divide: Civic Engagement, Information Poverty, and the Internet Worldwide.* Cambridge: Cambridge University Press, 2001.

Norton, Quinn. "Secrets of the Pirate Bay." *Wired,* August 16, 2006. http://www.wired.com/science/discoveries/news/2006/08/71543.

Nowak, Peter. "CRTC Opens Net Neutrality Debate to Public," Technology & Science, CBC News, May 15, 2008. http://www.cbc.ca/news/technology/story/2008/05/15/tech-internet.html.

Noys, Benjamin. *Malign Velocities: Accelerationism and Capitalism.* London: Zero Books, 2014.

Obar, Jonathan A. "Closing the Technocratic Divide? Activist Intermediaries, Digital Form Letters, and Public Involvement in FCC Policy Making." *International Journal of Communication* 10 (November 8, 2016): 5865–88.

Office of the Privacy Commissioner of Canada, ed. *Deep Packet Inspection Essay Project,* March 28, 2013. https://www.priv.gc.ca/en/opc-actions-and-decisions/research/explore-privacy-research/?Page=9.

O'Neill, Judy. "The Role of ARPA in the Development of the ARPANET, 1961–1972." *IEEE Annals* 17, no. 4 (1995): 76–81.

O'Neill, Megan. "YouTube Responds to Reply Girls, Changes Related & Recommended Videos Algorithm." *SocialTimes,* March 13, 2012. http://www.adweek.com/socialtimes/youtube-reply-girls/92439.

Openwave Mobility. "Openwave Mobility First to Use Quality-Aware Optimization for Live Gaming Broadcasts." *Openwave Mobility Press Releases,* October 15, 2015. https://owmobility.com/press-releases/openwave-mobility-first-use-quality-aware-optimization-live-gaming-broadcasts/.

Oram, Andrew, ed. *Peer-to-Peer: Harnessing the Power of a Disruptive Technology.* Sebastopol, Calif.: O'Reilly, 2001. http://library.uniteddiversity.coop/REconomy_Resource_Pack/More_Inspirational_Videos_and_Useful_Info/Peer_to_Peer-Harnessing_the_Power_of_Disruptive_Technologies.pdf.

Orman, H. "The Morris Worm: A Fifteen-Year Perspective." *Security & Privacy, IEEE* 1, no. 5 (2003): 35–43.

Oxford English Dictionary. "Metastable, Adj." *OED Online*. Oxford University Press. Accessed September 22, 2016. http://www.oed.com.

Paasonen, Susanna, Ken Hillis, and Michael Petit. "Introduction: Networks of Transmission: Intensity, Sensation, Value." In *Networked Affect*, edited by Ken Hillis, Susanna Paasonen, and Michael Petit, 1–26. Cambridge: MIT Press, 2015.

Packeteer Inc. *Packeteer's PacketShaper/ISP.* 2001. http://archive.icann.org/en/tlds/org /applications/unity/appendices/pdfs/packeteer/PSISP_colorB1101.pdf.

Packeteer Inc. *Packetshaper Packetseeker Getting Started Guide.* 2002. https://bto .bluecoat.com/packetguide/5.3.0/documents/PacketShaper_Getting_Started_v53 .pdf.

Paine, Jeff. "50 Shades of Net Neutrality Is Here." *Saisei* (blog), November 10, 2014. http:// saisei.com/50-shades-net-neutrality/.

Papacharissi, Zizi. *Affective Publics: Sentiment, Technology, and Politics.* Oxford Studies in Digital Politics. New York: Oxford University Press, 2015.

Pargman, Daniel, and Jacob Palme. "ASCII Imperialism." In Lampland and Star, *Standards and Their Stories*, 177–99.

Pariser, Eli. *The Filter Bubble: What the Internet Is Hiding from You.* New York: Penguin Press, 2011.

Parks, Lisa. "Infrastructure." In *Keywords for Media Studies*, edited by Laurie Ouellette and Jonathan Gray, 106–7. New York: New York University Press, 2017.

Parks, Lisa, and Nicole Starosielski. "Introduction." In *Signal Traffic: Critical Studies of Media Infrastructures*, edited by Lisa Parks and Nicole Starosielski, 1–30. Champaign: University of Illinois Press, 2015.

Parnell, Brid-Aine. "Epic Net Outage in Africa as FOUR Undersea Cables Chopped." *The Registrar*, February 28, 2012. http://www.theregister.co.uk/2012/02/28/east _africa_undersea_cables_cut/.

Parsons, Christopher. *Deep Packet Inspection in Perspective: Tracing Its Lineage and Surveillance Potentials.* Kingston, Ont.: The New Transparency, Queens University Department of Sociology, January 10, 2008. https://qspace.library.queensu.ca /bitstream/1974/1939/1/WP_Deep_Packet_Inspection_Parsons_Jan_2008.pdf.

Parsons, Christopher. "Rogers, Network Failures, and Third-Party Oversight." *Technology, Thoughts & Trinkets* (blog), December 2, 2010. https://www.christopher-parsons .com/rogers-network-failures-and-third-party-oversight/.

Parsons, Christopher. "The Politics of Deep Packet Inspection: What Drives Surveillance by Internet Service Providers?" PhD diss., University of Victoria, 2013.

Pasquale, Frank. *The Black Box Society: The Secret Algorithms That Control Money and Information.* Cambridge, Mass.: Harvard University Press, 2015.

Paterson, Nancy. "Bandwidth Is Political: Reachability in the Public Internet." Rochester, N.Y.: Social Science Research Network, November 18, 2013. https://papers.ssrn.com /sol3/papers.cfm?abstract_id=2355762.

Paterson, Nancy. "End User Privacy and Policy-Based Networking." *Journal of Infor-*

mation Policy 4 (2014): 28–43. https://papers.ssrn.com/sol3/papers.cfm?abstract _id=2401834.

Patowary, Kaushik. "Security Flaw Makes PPTP VPN Useless for Hiding IP on BitTorrent." *Instant Fundas*, June 18, 2010. http://www.instantfundas.com/2010/06/security -flaw-makes-pptp-vpn-useless.html.

Paul, Ryan. "Canadian ISP Tests Injecting Content into Web Pages." *Ars Technica*, December 11, 2007. http://arstechnica.com/uncategorized/2007/12/canadian-isp-tests -injecting-content-into-web-pages/.

Paulsen, Gard. "When Switches Became Programs: Programming Languages and Telecommunications, 1965–1980." *IEEE Annals of the History of Computing* 36, no. 4 (2014): 38–50.

Pearce, Katy E., and Jessica Vitak. "Performing Honor Online: The Affordances of Social Media for Surveillance and Impression Management in an Honor Culture." *New Media & Society* 18, no. 11 (December 1, 2016): 2595–612. DOI: 10.1177/ 1461444815600279.

Peters, Benjamin. *How Not to Network a Nation: The Uneasy History of the Soviet Internet.* Cambridge, Mass.: MIT Press, 2016.

Peters, John Durham. *The Marvelous Clouds: Toward a Philosophy of Elemental Media.* Chicago: University of Chicago Press, 2015.

Peterson, Kim. "Speakeasy Founder Leaves for New Venture," Business & Technology, *Seattle Times*, April 4, 2006. http://community.seattletimes.nwsource.com/archive /?date=20060404&slug=webookla04.

Pfaffenberger, Bryan. "'If I Want It, It's OK': Usenet and the (Outer) Limits of Free Speech." *Information Society* 12, no. 4 (November 1, 1996): 365–86. DOI: 10.1080/ 019722496129350.

Pickering, Andrew. "Cyborg History and the World War II Regime." *Perspectives on Science* 3, no. 1 (1995): 1–48.

Pike, Rob. *Systems Software Research Is Irrelevant.* February 21, 2000. http://www.inf.ufes .br/~raulh/ufes/teaching/courses/sc/page/texts/utah200.pdf.

Pike, Rob, Dave Presotto, Sean Dorward, Bob Flandrenda, Ken Thompson, Howard Trickey, and Phil Winterbottom. "Plan 9 from Bell Labs." *Computer Systems* 8, no. 3 (1995): 221–54.

Pirate Bay, The. "POwr, xxxx, Broccoli and KOPIMI." February 25, 2009. http://cs .gettysburg.edu/~duncjo01/assets/writings/library/kopimi.html.

Plambeck, Joseph. "Court Rules That LimeWire Infringed on Copyrights." *New York Times,* May 12, 2010. http://www.nytimes.com/2010/05/13/technology/13lime.html.

Poon, Martha A. "From New Deal Institutions to Capital Markets: Commercial Consumer Risk Scores and the Making of Subprime Mortgage Finance." *Accounting, Organizations and Society* 34 (2009): 654–74. https://socfinance.files.wordpress .com/2010/01/poon_subprime_aos-2009.pdf.

Popper, Ben. "The Wireless and Cable Industries Just Sued to Kill Net Neutrality." *The Verge,* April 14, 2015. http://www.theverge.com/2015/4/14/8411033/ctia-wireless -cable-sue-lawsuit-fcc-net-neutrality.

Price, W. L. "Simulation of Packet-Switching Networks Controlled on Isarithmic Principles." In *DATACOMM 1973: Proceedings of the Third ACM Symposium on Data Communications and Data networks: Analysis and Design*, 44–49. New York: Association for Computing Machinery, 1973.

Procera Networks. *PacketLogic Policy & Charging Control: 3GPP-Based Service Innovation*. Accessed July 28, 2016. https://www.proceranetworks.com/hubfs /Datasheets/Procera_DS_3GPP_PCC.pdf.

Protalinski, Emil. "BitTorrent Performance Test Shows How Much Faster Sync Is Compared to Google Drive, OneDrive, and Dropbox." *Venture Beat*, October 22, 2014. http://venturebeat.com/2014/10/22/bittorrent-performance-test-shows-how -much-faster-sync-is-compared-to-google-drive-onedrive-and-dropbox/.

Protalinski, Emil. "The Pirate Bay Criticizes Anonymous for DDoS Attack." *ZDNet*, May 10, 2012. http://www.zdnet.com/blog/security/the-pirate-bay-criticizes-anonymous -for-ddos-attack/12072.

Quarterman, John S., and Josiah C. Hoskins. "Notable Computer Networks." *Communications of the ACM* 29, no. 10 (1986): 932–71.

Raboy, Marc, and Jeremy Shtern, eds. *Media Divides: Communication Rights and the Right to Communicate in Canada*. Vancouver: University of British Columbia Press, 2010.

Rainie, Lee, Sara Kiesler, Ruogu Kang, and Mary Madden. "Anonymity, Privacy, and Security Online." *Pew Research Center: Internet, Science & Tech*, September 5, 2013. http:// www.pewinternet.org/2013/09/05/anonymity-privacy-and-security-online/.

Rainie, Lee, and Mary Madden. "Americans' Privacy Strategies Post-Snowden." *Pew Research Center: Internet, Science & Tech*, March 16, 2015. http://www.pewinternet.org /2015/03/16/americans-privacy-strategies-post-snowden/.

Randell, Brian. "An Annotated Bibliography of the Origins of Digital Computers." *Annals of the History of Computing* 1, no. 2 (1979): 101–207.

Raymond, Eric S. *The New Hacker's Dictionary*. Cambridge, Mass.: MIT Press, 1996.

Reagle, Joseph Michael, Jr. *Good Faith Collaboration: The Culture of Wikipedia*. Cambridge, Mass.: MIT Press, 2010.

Reddit. "Reflections on the Recent Boston Crisis." *Upvoted* (blog), April 22, 2013. https:// redditblog.com/2013/04/22/reflections-on-the-recent-boston-crisis/.

Redmond, Kent C., and Thomas Malcolm Smith. *From Whirlwind to MITRE: The R&D Story of the SAGE Air Defense Computer*. Cambridge, Mass.: MIT Press, 2000.

Rens, Andrew. "Open Document Standards for Government: The South African Experience." In DeNardis, *Opening Standards*, 63–72.

Ressie. Comment on Goldmonger, "Canada ISP Latency Issues." *World of Warcraft Forums*, February 23, 2011. http://us.battle.net/forums/en/wow/topic/1965838937 ?page=43#post-848.

Ressy [Teresa Murphy]. "Rogers Throttling/Deprioritizing World of Warcraft." *Rogers Community Forums*, January 17, 2011. http://communityforums.rogers.com/t5 /forums/forumtopicpage/board-id/Getting_connected/message-id/557#M557.

Rheingold, Howard. *The Virtual Community: Homesteading on the Electronic Frontier*. Cambridge, Mass.: MIT Press, 2000.

Roberts, Lawrence. "The Evolution of Packet Switching." *Proceedings of the IEEE* 66, no. 11 (1978): 1307–13.

Roberts, Lawrence. "Multiple Computer Networks and Intercomputer Communication." In *SOSP 1967: Proceedings of the First ACM Symposium on Operating System Principles*, 3.1–6. New York: Association for Computing Machines, 1967.

Roberts, Sara T. "Behind the Screen: The Hidden Digital Labor of Commercial Content Moderation." PhD diss., University of Illinois at Urbana-Champaign, 2014. https://www.ideals.illinois.edu/handle/2142/50401.

Roderick, Ian. "(Out of) Control Demons: Software Agents, Complexity Theory and the Revolution in Military Affairs." *Theory & Event* 10, no. 2 (2007). DOI: 10.1353/tae.2007.0070.

Rogers Communications. "Hi-Speed Internet." http://www.rogers.com/web/link/hispeedBrowseFlowDefaultPlans.

Rogers Communications. *Comment on Public Notice 2008–19—Review of the Internet Traffic Management Practices of Internet Service Providers.* 2009. http://www.crtc.gc.ca/public/partvii/2008/8646/c12_200815400/1029665.zip.

Rogers Internet. "Rogers Network Management Policy." Accessed October 29, 2016. http://www.rogers.com/web/content/network_management.

Rogers Internet. "Rogers Commercial." YouTube video, 0:30. Posted by Hollerado. March 11, 2011.

RogersKeith. Comment on Vindari, "[Extreme Plus] Utorrent Settings and Rogers." *DSL Reports Forums,* October 2010. http://www.dslreports.com/forum/r24994463-.

Rosa, Hartmut. "Social Acceleration: Ethical and Political Consequences of a Desynchronized High–Speed Society." *Constellations* 10, no. 1 (March 1, 2003): 3–33. DOI: 10.1111/1467–8675.00309.

Rosa, Hartmut, and William E. Scheuerman, eds. *High-Speed Society: Social Acceleration, Power, and Modernity.* University Park, Pa.: Penn State University Press, 2008.

Rosen, E., A. Viswanathan, and R. Callon. *RFC 3031: Multiprotocol Label Switching Architecture.* January 2001. http://www.ietf.org/rfc/rfc3031.txt.

Rosenberg, Howard, and Charles S. Feldman. *No Time to Think: The Menace of Media Speed and the 24-hour News Cycle.* New York: Continuum, 2008.

Rosenzweig, Roy. "The Road to Xanadu: Public and Private Pathways on the History Web." *The Journal of American History* 88, no. 2 (September 2001): 548. DOI: 10.2307/2675105.

Roth, Daniel. "The Dark Lord of Broadband Tries to Fix Comcast's Image." *Wired,* January 19, 2009. http://www.wired.com/2009/01/mf-brianroberts/.

Russell, Andrew L. *Open Standards and the Digital Age: History, Ideology, and Networks.* Cambridge: Cambridge University Press, 2014. http://www.cambridge.org/ca/academic/subjects/history/twentieth-century-american-history/open-standards-and-digital-age-history-ideology-and-networks.

Russell, Andrew L., and Valérie Schafer. "In the Shadow of ARPANET and Internet: Louis Pouzin and the Cyclades Network in the 1970s." *Technology and Culture* 55, no. 4 (2014): 880–907. DOI: 10.1353/tech.2014.0096.

Ryan, Gerard, and Mireia Valverde. "Waiting Online: A Review and Research Agenda." *Internet Research* 13, no. 3 (2003): 195–205.

Rybczynski, Tony. "Commercialization of Packet Switching (1975–1985): A Canadian Perspective." *Communications Magazine, IEEE* 47, no. 12 (2009): 26–31.

Saisei Networks. "Products: Every Flow Tells a Story." Saisei. Accessed July 28, 2016. http://saisei.com/products/.

Saltzer, Jerome H., David P. Reed, and David D. Clark. "End-to-End Arguments in System Design." *ACM Transactions on Computer Systems* 2, no. 4 (1984): 277–88.

Salus, Peter H. *Casting the Net: From ARPANET to Internet and Beyond.* Boston: Addison-Wesley, 1995.

Sandvig, Christian. "Network Neutrality Is the New Common Carriage." *Info: The Journal of Policy, Regulation, and Strategy* 9, no. 2/3 (2007): 136–47.

Sandvig, Christian. "Shaping Infrastructure and Innovation on the Internet: The End-to-End Network That Isn't." In *Shaping Science and Technology Policy: The Next Generation of Research,* edited by David Guston and Daniel Sarewitz, 234–55. Madison: University of Wisconsin Press, 2006.

Sandvig, Christian. "The Internet as Infrastructure." In *The Oxford Handbook of Internet Studies,* edited by William H. Dutton, 86–108. Oxford: Oxford University Press, 2013.

Sandvig, Christian, K. Hamilton, K. Karahalios, and C. Langbort. "An Algorithm Audit." In *Data and Discrimination: Collected Essays,* edited by Seeta Peña Gangadharan, 6–10. Washington, D.C.: New America Foundation, 2014.

Sandvine Inc. *Meeting the Challenge of Today's Evasive P2P Traffic: Service Provider Strategies for Managing P2P Filesharing.* 2004. http://www.larryblakeley.com /Articles/p2p/Evasive_P2P_Traffic.pdf.

Sandvine Inc. *Sandvine Essentials Training (SET): Module 1: Overview and Platform Hardware.* 2014. https://www.scribd.com/doc/281100047/Sandvine-Overview.

Sandvine Inc. *Sandvine Policy Traffic Switch (PTS 8210): Characterize, Control and Secure Broadband Traffic.* September 27, 2004. https://web.archive.org/web /20060325102059/http://www.sandvine.com/general/getfile.asp?FILEID=18.

Sandvine Inc. *Session Management: BitTorrent Protocol: Managing the Impact on Subscriber Experience.* December 2014. https://web.archive.org/web/20060325102710 /http://www.sandvine.com/general/getfile.asp?FILEID=21.

Sauter, Molly. *The Coming Swarm: DDOS Actions, Hacktivism, and Civil Disobedience on the Internet.* New York: Bloomsbury Academic, 2014.

Schaffer, Simon. "Babagge's Intelligence: Calculating Engines and the Factory System." *Critical Inquiry* 21, no. 1 (1994): 203–27.

Scheuerman, William E. "Liberal Democracy and the Empire of Speed." *Polity* 34, no. 1 (2001): 41–67.

Scheuerman, William E. *Liberal Democracy and the Social Acceleration of Time.* Baltimore, Md.: Johns Hopkins University Press, 2004.

Schneider, Christopher J., and Dan Trottier. "The 2011 Vancouver Riot and the Role of Facebook in Crowd-Sourced Policing." *BC Studies: The British Columbian Quar-*

terly, no. 175 (July 26, 2012): 57–72. http://ojs.library.ubc.ca/index.php/bcstudies /article/view/182403.

Schoen, Seth. "Comcast and BitTorrent." *Electronic Frontier Foundation*, September 13, 2007. https://www.eff.org/deeplinks/2007/09/comcast-and-bittorrent.

Schoen, Seth. "Detecting Packet Injection: A Guide to Observing Packet Spoofing by ISPs." *Electronic Frontier Foundation*, November 28, 2007. https://www.eff.org/files/packet _injection_0.pdf.

Schoen, Seth. "EFF Tests Agree with AP: Comcast Is Forging Packets to Interfere with User Traffic." *Electronic Frontier Foundation*, October 19, 2007. https://www.eff .org/deeplinks/2007/10/eff-tests-agree-ap-comcast-forging-packets-to-interfere.

Schrock, Andrew Richard. "HTML5 and Openness in Mobile Platforms." *Continuum*, August 12, 2014, 1–15. DOI: 10.1080/10304312.2014.941333.

Schrock, Andrew, and Gwen Shaffer. "Data Ideologies of an Interested Public: A Study of Grassroots Open Government Data Intermediaries." *Big Data & Society* 4, no. 1 (January–June 2017): 1–10. DOI: 10.1177/2053951717690750.

Schwarz, Jonas Andersson. *Online File Sharing: Innovations in Media Consumption*. Comedia. New York: Routledge, 2014.

Schwarz, Jonas Andersson (as "Jonas Andersson"). "For the Good of the Net: The Pirate Bay as a Strategic Sovereign." *Culture Machine* 10 (2009): 64–108. http://www .culturemachine.net/index.php/cm/article/view/346/349.

Scott, Jason, dir. *BBS: The Documentary*. 2004. DVD and Creative Commons Attribute-ShareAlike 2.0 License. http://www.bbsdocumentary.com.

Selfridge, Oliver. "Pandemonium: A Paradigm for Learning." In *Mechanisation of Thought Processes: Proceedings of a Symposium Held at the National Physical Laboratory on 24th, 25th, 26th and 27th November 1958*, 511–29. London: Her Majesty's Stationery Office, 1959.

Selfridge, Oliver, and Ulric Neisser. "Pattern Recognition by Machine." *Scientific American*, August 1960, 60–68. DOI: 10.1038/scientificamerican0860-60. Reprinted in *Computer and Thought*, edited by Edward A. Feigenbaum and Julian Freedman, 237–50, Cambridge, Mass.: MIT Press, 1995.

Senft, Adam, Helmi Noman, Jakub Dalek, Masashi Crete-Nishihata, Matthew Carrieri, Ron Deibert, and Saad Omar Khan. *Internet Filtering in a Failed State: The Case of Netsweeper in Somalia*. Toronto: Citizen Lab, February 20, 2014. https://citizenlab .org/2014/02/internet-filtering-failed-state-case-netsweeper-somalia/.

Senft, Theresa M. "Bulletin-Board Systems." In *Encyclopedia of New Media: An Essential Reference to Communication and Technology*, edited by Steve Jones. Thousand Oaks, Calif.: Sage, 2003.

Shade, Leslie Regan. "Computer Networking in Canada: From CAnet to CANARIE." *Canadian Journal of Communication* 19, no. 1 (1994): 53–69.

Shade, Leslie Regan. "Public Interest Activism in Canadian ICT Policy: Blowing in the Policy Winds." *Global Media Journal—Canadian Edition* 1, no. 1 (2008): 107–21.

Shade, Leslie Regan. "Roughing It in the Electronic Bush: Community Networking in Canada." *Canadian Journal of Communication* 24, no. 2 (1999): 179–98.

Shah, Rajiv C., and Jay P. Kesan. "The Privatization of the Internet's Backbone Network." *Journal of Broadcasting & Electronic Media* 51, no. 1 (2007): 93–109.

Shahani, Aarti. "In Google Newsroom, Brazil Defeat Is Not a Headline." NPR, July 9, 2014. http://www.npr.org/blogs/alltechconsidered/2014/07/09/330003058/in-google -newsroom-brazil-defeat-is-not-a-headline.

Shannon, Claude E. "A Mathematical Theory of Communication." *Bell System Technical Journal* 27, no. 3 (July 1, 1948): 379–423. DOI: 10.1002/j.1538–7305.1948.tb01338.x.

Shannon, Claude E. "Programming a Computer for Playing Chess." *Philosophical Magazine* 41, ser. 7, no. 314 (1950): 256–74. http://vision.unipv.it/IA1/aa2009-2010 /ProgrammingaComputerforPlayingChess.pdf.

Sharma, Sarah. *In the Meantime: Temporality and Cultural Politics*. Durham, N.C.: Duke University Press, 2014.

Sharma, Sarah. "It Changes Space and Time: Introducing Power-Chronography." In *Communication Matters: Materialist Approaches to Media, Mobility, and Networks*, edited by Jeremy Packer and Steve Wiley, 66–77. New York: Routledge, 2011.

Sharma, Sarah. "The Biopolitical Economy of Time." *Journal of Communication Inquiry* 35, no. 4 (October 1, 2011): 439–44. DOI: 10.1177/0196859911417999.

Shifman, Limor. "An Anatomy of a YouTube Meme." *New Media & Society* 14, no. 2 (March 1, 2012): 187–203. DOI: 10.1177/1461444811412160.

Shifthead. "Rogers ISP, WoW, and You!" *World of Warcraft Forums*, December 18, 2010. http://us.battle.net/forums/en/wow/topic/1568009046#post-1.

Shneiderman, Ben, and Catherine Plaisant. *Designing the User Interface: Strategies for Effective Human-Computer Interaction*. 5th ed. Boston: Addison-Wesley, 2010.

Simon, Herbert. "Reflections on Time Sharing from a User's Point of View." In *Computer Science Research Review*, edited by Joyce Nissenson, 43–52. Pittsburgh, Pa.: Carnegie Institute of Technology, 1966. http://www.dtic.mil/dtic/tr/fulltext/u2/645294.pdf.

Sinnreich, Aram. "Sharing in Spirit: Kopimism and the Digital Eucharist." *Information, Communication & Society* 19, no. 4 (April 2, 2016): 504–17. DOI: 10.1080/ 1369118X.2015.1036766.

Smythe, Dallas Walker. *Dependency Road: Communications, Capitalism, Consciousness and Canada*. Norwood, N.J.: Ablex, 1981.

Snader, Jon C. *VPNs Illustrated: Tunnels, VPNs, and IPsec*. Boston: Addison-Wesley Professional, 2005.

Söderberg, Johan. "Misuser Inventions and the Invention of the Misuser: Hackers, Crackers and Filesharers." *Science as Culture* 19, no. 2 (June 2010): 151–79. DOI: 10.1080/ 09505430903168177.

Spilker, Hendrik Storstein, and Svein Hoier. "Technologies of Piracy? Exploring the Interplay between Commercialism and Idealism in the Development of MP3 and DivX." *International Journal of Communication* 7 (2013): 2067–86.

Sprenger, Florian. *The Politics of Micro-Decisions: Edward Snowden, Net Neutrality, and the Architectures of the Internet*. Translated by Valentine A. Pakis. Lüneburg, Germany: Meson Press, 2015.

Srnicek, Nick, and Alex Williams. *Inventing the Future: Postcapitalism and a World Without Work*. New York: Verso, 2015.

Star, Susan Leigh. "The Ethnography of Infrastructure." *American Behavioral Scientist* 43, no. 3 (November 1, 1999): 377–91. DOI: 10.1177/00027649921955326.

Starosielski, Nicole. "Fixed Flow: Undersea Network as Media Infrastructure." In Parks and Starosielski, *Signal Traffic*, 53–70.

Starosielski, Nicole. *The Undersea Network*. Sign, Storage, Transmission, edited by Jonathan Sterne and Lisa Gitelman. Durham, N.C.: Duke University Press, 2015.

Stastna, Kazi. "Bell's Discounting of Mobile TV against the Rules, Complaint Claims." CBC News, December 16, 2013. http://www.cbc.ca/1.2445059.

Sterling, Bruce. *The Hacker Crackdown: Law and Disorder on the Electronic Frontier.* New York: Bantam Books, 1992.

Sterne, Jonathan. *MP3: The Meaning of a Format*. Sign, Storage, Transmission, edited by Jonathan Sterne and Lisa Gitelman. Durham, N.C.: Duke University Press, 2012.

Stevenson, John Harris. *The Master Switch and the Hyper Giant: Google's Infrastructure and Network Neutrality Strategy in the 2000s*. Rochester, N.Y.: Social Science Research Network, August 14, 2014. https://papers.ssrn.com/abstract=2418784.

Striphas, Ted. *The Late Age of Print: Everyday Book Culture from Consumerism to Control*. New York: Columbia University Press, 2009.

Stuart, Tessa. "Megan Lee Heart and Reply Girls Game the System." *LA Weekly*, June 27, 2012. http://www.laweekly.com/arts/megan-lee-heart-and-reply-girls-game-the -system-2371955.

Suarez, Daniel. *DAEMON*. New York: Signet Books, 2009.

Sunde, Peter. "The Pirate Bay Interview (Chaosradio International: CRI009)." Mp3 audio podcast, 43:16. Hosted by Tim Pritlove. February 6, 2006. Chaosradio. Accessed November 28, 2012. http://chaosradio.ccc.de/cri009.html.

Svensson, Peter. "Comcast Blocks Some Internet Traffic." Associated Press, October 19, 2007. Archived at Wayback Machine, https://web.archive.org/web /20071101114042/http://news.yahoo.com/s/ap/20071019/ap_on_hi_te/comcast _data_discrimination.

Synergy Research Group. *Cisco's Dominant Share of Switching & Routers Holds Steady.* February 24, 2016. https://www.srgresearch.com/articles/ciscos-dominant-share -switching-routers-holds-steady?ref=il.

Take Our Word for It. "Sez You . . . [email chain on 'daemon']." *Take Our Word for It* (blog), no. 146, 4. Accessed June 3, 2016. http://www.takeourword.com/TOW146/page4 .html.

Tanenbaum, Andrew S. *Computer Networks*. 4th ed. Englewood Cliffs, N.J.: Prentice Hall, 2002.

Tay, Liz. "Pirate Bay's IPREDator Not a Place to Hide." *ITnews*, August 4, 2009. http://www .itnews.com.au/News/151988,pirate-bays-ipredator-not-a-place-to-hide.aspx.

Taylor, Astra. *The People's Platform: Taking Back Power and Culture in the Digital Age.* Toronto: Random House Canada, 2014.

Tencer, David. "Gamers' Group on Traffic Throttling: CRTC Ignoring Consumer Protection Laws." Business, *The Huffington Post*, September 22, 2011. http://www .huffingtonpost.ca/2011/08/22/crtc-rogers-traffic-shaping_n_933370.html.

Terranova, Tiziana. *Network Culture: Politics for the Information Age.* Ann Arbor, Mich.: Pluto Press, 2004.

Tetzlaff, David. "Yo-Ho-Ho and a Server of Warez: Internet Software Piracy and the New Global Information Economy." In *The World Wide Web and Contemporary Cultural Theory: Magic, Metaphor, Power,* edited by Andrew Herman and Thomas Swiss, 99–126. New York: Routledge, 2000.

Thaler, Richard H., and Cass R. Sunstein. *Nudge: Improving Decisions About Health, Wealth, and Happiness.* New York: Penguin Books, 2009.

Third Generation Partnership Project (3GPP). "Partners." 3GPP: A Global Initiative. http://www.3gpp.org/about-3gpp/partners.

Tiessen, Matthew. "High-Frequency Trading and the Centering of the (Financial) Periphery." *The Trading Mesh* (blog), 2013. http://www.thetradingmesh.com/pg/blog/mtiessen/read/70969.

Timberg, Craig. "NSA Slide Shows Surveillance of Undersea Cables." *Washington Post,* July 10, 2013. http://www.washingtonpost.com/business/economy/the-nsa-slide -you-havent-seen/2013/07/10/32801426-e8e6-11e2-aa9f-c03a72e2d342_story .html.

Tkacz, Nathaniel. *Wikipedia and the Politics of Openness.* Chicago: University of Chicago Press, 2014.

Touloumis, Tara. "Buccaneers and Bucks from the Internet: Pirate Bay and the Entertainment Industry." *Seton Hall Journal of Sports and Entertainment Law* 19 (2009): 253.

Turing, Alan M. "Computing Machinery and Intelligence." *Mind: A Quarterly Review of Psychology and Philosophy* 59, no. 236 (1950): 433–60. DOI: 10.1093/mind/LIX.236.433.

Turkle, Sherry. *Life on the Screen: Identity in the Age of the Internet.* New York: Touchstone, 1997.

Turner, Fred. *From Counterculture to Cyberculture: Stewart Brand, the Whole Earth Network, and the Rise of Digital Utopianism.* Chicago: University of Chicago Press, 2006.

Tutt, Andrew. "An FDA for Algorithms." *Administrative Law Review* 69, no. 1 (Winter 2017): 83–124.. https://papers.ssrn.com/abstract=2747994.

Umeaenergi. "Living with Lag—an Oculus Rift Experiment." YouTube video, 2:58. April 27, 2014. https://www.youtube.com/watch?v=_fNp37zFn9Q.

Umeaenergi. "Living with Lag—Lag View." YouTube video, 2:58. April 27, 2014. https://www.youtube.com/watch?v=P2VMHzN-bq8.

United States Army, Department of the. "Request for Quotations—DAHC15 69 Q 0002," Defense Supply Services, June 29, 1968.

Valentino-DeVries, Jennifer. "More Predictions on the Huge Growth of 'Cloud Computing.'" *Digits* (*Wall Street Journal* blog), April 21, 2011. http://blogs.wsj.com/digits /2011/04/21/more-predictions-on-the-huge-growth-of-cloud-computing/.

Valley, George E., Jr. "How the SAGE Development Began." *Annals of the History of Computing* 7, no. 3 (1985): 196–226.

Van Beijnum, Iljitsch. "Meet DOCSIS, Part 1: The Unsung Hero of High-Speed Cable Internet Access." *Ars Technica*, May 5, 2011. http://arstechnica.com/business/news/2011/05/docsis-the-unsung-hero-of-high-speed-cable-internet-access.ars.

Van Dijck, Jose. "Datafication, Dataism and Dataveillance: Big Data between Scientific Paradigm and Ideology." *Surveillance & Society* 12, no. 2 (May 9, 2014): 197–208.

Van Dijck, Jose. *The Culture of Connectivity: A Critical History of Social Media.* Oxford: Oxford University Press, 2013.

Van Eeten, Michel J. G., and Milton Mueller. "Where Is the Governance in Internet Governance?" *New Media & Society* 15, no. 5 (August 1, 2013): 720–36. DOI: 10.1177/1461444812462850.

Van Schewick, Barbara. *Internet Architecture and Innovation.* Cambridge, Mass.: MIT Press, 2010.

Van Schewick, Barbara. *Network Neutrality and Quality of Service: What a Non-Discrimination Rule Should Look Like.* Stanford, Calif.: Center for Internet & Society, June 11, 2012. http://cyberlaw.stanford.edu/downloads/20120611-NetworkNeutrality.pdf.

Varadhan, K. *Request for Comments 1403: BGP OSPF Interaction.* January 1993. https://www.rfc-editor.org/rfc/rfc1403.txt.

Vincent, James. "Google Received More than 345 Million Link Takedown Requests Last Year." *The Verge*, January 6, 2015. http://www.theverge.com/2015/1/6/7500431/google-piracy-takedown-requests-345-million-2014.

Virilio, Paul. *Speed & Politics.* Translated by Mark Polizzotti. New York: Semiotext(e), 2006. Originally published 1997.

Virilio, Paul. *The Art of the Motor.* Translated by Julie Rose. Minneapolis: University of Minnesota Press, 1995.

Vuze. "Bad ISPs." Accessed September 6, 2016. http://wiki.vuze.com/mediawiki/index.php?title=Bad_ISPs&oldid=5484.

Wajcman, J. "Life in the Fast Lane? Towards a Sociology of Technology and Time." *British Journal of Sociology* 59, no. 1 (2008): 59–77.

Wakefield, Jane. "Rage against the Machine—Survey." *ZDNet*, May 27, 1999. http://www.zdnet.com/article/rage-against-the-machine-survey/.

Walden, David. "The Arpanet IMP Program: Retrospective and Resurrection." *Annals of the History of Computing, IEEE* 36, no. 2 (2014): 28–39.

Waldrop, M. Mitchell. *The Dream Machine: J.C.R. Licklider and the Revolution That Made Computing Personal.* New York: Penguin Books, 2002.

Warner, Michael. "Publics and Counterpublics." *Public Culture* 14, no. 1 (2002): 49–90.

Webb, Adam. "Gamers vs. Rogers: One Month at a Time." *Open Media*, May 24, 2011.

Wiener, Norbert. *Cybernetics or, Control and Communication in the Animal and the Machine.* New York: J. Wiley, 1948.

Wiener, Norbert. *The Human Use of Human Beings.* Cambridge, Mass.: Houghton Mifflin, 1950.

Wilkinson, Roger I. "Theories for Toll Traffic Engineering in the U.S.A." *Bell Systems Technical Journal* [online] 35, no. 2 (July 2013) [originally 1956]. DOI: 10.1002/j.1538-7305.1956.tb02388.

Williams, James. *Gilles Deleuze's Philosophy of Time: A Critical Introduction and Guide.* Edinburgh: Edinburgh University Press, 2011.

Williams, Raymond. *Keywords: A Vocabulary of Culture and Society.* Revised edition. London: Fontana Paperbacks, 1983. Originally published 1976.

Williams, Raymond. *Marxism and Literature.* Marxist Introductions. Oxford: Oxford University Press, 1977.

Williamson, Wade. "A Revolutionary New Approach to Detecting Malicious Covert Communications." *Vectra* (blog), October 28, 2015. http://blog.vectranetworks.com/blog/a-revolutionary-new-approach-to-detecting-malicious-covert-communications.

Winderans. Comment on Shifthead, "Rogers ISP, WoW, and You!" *World of Warcraft Forums,* December 19, 2010. http://us.battle.net/forums/en/wow/topic/1568009046#post-18.

Winner, Langdon. *The Whale and the Reactor: A Search for Limits in an Age of High Technology.* Chicago: University of Chicago Press, 1986.

Winseck, Dwayne. "Netscapes of Power: Convergence, Consolidation and Power in the Canadian Mediascape." *Media, Culture & Society* 24, no. 6 (2002): 795–819.

Wise, John MacGregor. "Attention and Assemblage in a Clickable World." In *Communication Matters: Materialist Approaches to Media, Mobility and Networks,* edited by Jeremy Packer and Steve Wiley, 159–72. New York: Routledge, 2011.

Wolin, Sheldon. "What Time Is It?" *Theory & Event* 1, no. 1 (1997). http://muse.jhu.edu/journals/theory_and_event/v001/1.1wolin.html.

Wood, D., V. Stoss, L. Chan-Lizardo, G. S. Papacostas, and M. E. Stinson. "Virtual Private Networks." In *International Conference on Private Switching Systems and Networks, 1988,* 132–36. New York: IEEE, 1988.

Wood, Gaby. *Edison's Eve: A Magical History of the Quest for Mechanical Life.* New York: Alfred A. Knopf, 2002.

Woolley, Samuel C. "Automating Power: Social Bot Interference in Global Politics." *First Monday* 21, no. 4 (March 10, 2016). http://journals.uic.edu/ojs/index.php/fm/article/view/6161.

Woolley, Samuel C., and Philip N. Howard. "Political Communication, Computational Propaganda, and Autonomous Agents—Introduction." *International Journal of Communication* 10 (October 12, 2016): 4882–90.

Wortham, Jenna. "Snapchat, a Growing App, Lets You See It, Then You Don't." Technology, *New York Times,* February 8, 2013. http://www.nytimes.com/2013/02/09/technology/snapchat-a-growing-app-lets-you-see-it-then-you-dont.html.

Wray, Stefan. "Electronic Civil Disobedience and the World Wide Web of Hacktivism: A Mapping of Extraparliamentarian Direct Action Net Politics." *Switch* 4, no. 2 (1998). http://switch.sjsu.edu/web/v4n2/stefan/.

Wu, Tim. "Network Neutrality, Broadband Discrimination." *Journal on Telecommunication & High Technology Law* 2 (2003): 141–79.

Wu, Tim. "When Code Isn't Law." *Virginia Law Review* 89, no. 4 (June 2003): 679–751. DOI: 10.2307/3202374.

Yates, JoAnne. *Control through Communication: The Rise of System in American Management.* Baltimore, Md.: Johns Hopkins University Press, 1989.

Yeung, Karen. "'Hypernudge': Big Data as a Mode of Regulation by Design." *Information, Communication & Society* 20, no. 1 (2017): 1–19. DOI: 10.1080/1369118X.2016.1186713.

YouTube Help. "How Content ID Works." YouTube video, 2:05. N.D. https://support.google.com/youtube/answer/2797370?hl=en.

Zittrain, Jonathan. *The Future of the Internet and How to Stop It.* New Haven, Conn.: Yale University Press, 2008.

INDEX

accelerationism, 165, 166, 180; academic interest in, 165–66; as encouraging flow control, 180–81; vs. escalationism, 178–79; Land's interpretation of, 166; and optimization, 181–82; and piracy, 166, 181; and The Pirate Bay, 166–71

accountability gaps, 202–3

Active Threat Level Analysis System (ATLAS), 98, 175, 226

adaptive routing, 56, 65

Advanced Research Projects Agency (ARPA), 4, 47. *See also* ARPANET

advertisements: and affects, 139; "Dancing Alone" (AT&T), 147–50; and internet affects, 136–37, 139–40; "Living with Lag" (ume.net), 156–58; "Not Fair" (Rogers), 150–53; RoadRunner ISP, 153–56; "SpeedBoost" (Rogers), 142–47; and structures of feeling, 139; television, 146; "We Own Faster" (Comcast), 134, 140–42

affects, 137; and bandwidth caps, 149; and buffering, 135–36, 139; of delay, 143–47; of DRM, 145; flow control's influence on, 138–39, 142, 149–50, 152, 157; and media infrastructures, 136; networked, 137–38; and optimization, 155–56; priming, 138–39; of social acceleration, 150–51; and

social temporalities, 147–49, 153; and structures of feeling, 19, 139–40, 149, 190. *See also* advertisements

algorithms, 12; and bias, 131; and ethics, 202–3; and online content, 222; and regulation, 131–32; as social control, 21

Allot Communications, 99, 109, 164, 210–11

Amoore, Louise, 131–32

Anonymous, 166–67, 172

AppNav Controllers (ANC), 111

Ares Galaxy, 117–18, 124–25

Aria Networks, 130

ARPANET, 43; communication subnet, 76; email, 66; FTP, 66; measuring, 233–34; Network Control Program, 72–73, 78–80; optimization of, 61–67; origins of, 32; packet-switching networks attached to, 81; preventing delays in, 61; proposal for, 51–53; proposed diagrams of, 73, 76; queuing in, 58–59, 61; RFC discussions, 66; RFQ (1968), 57–61; routing in, 60–61, 103–5; simulations of, 62; as social, 66; and TCP/IP, 80, 90; topology of, 63–64; user subnet, 76, 78–79; voice communication, 66. *See also* Interface Message Processors

delay: affects of, 143–47; buffering, 58, 135–36, 139; and control, 154; and flow control, 146–47; and social acceleration, 150–51

Deleuze, Gilles: accelerationism, 166; communication, 171; control, 40; control societies, 15, 41–42, 171, 240n53; diagrams, 13, 74–75; dividuality, 192–93; mediators, 196; metastability concept, 42; modulation, 41; rhizomes, 164; on the war machine, 164, 180

DeNardis, Laura, 96–97

Dewey, John, 20, 189, 194–95, 206–7

diagrams, 13; Comcast's infrastructure, 118, 127; and daemons, 14, 75–76; Deleuze and Guattari on, 74–75; and flow control, 13; Foucault on, 74; of the internet, 82–85; and internet history, 75; and protocols, 75

Differentiated Services (DiffServ) protocol, 110

digest networks, 87

Digital Rights Management (DRM), 145, 224, 263n32

digital sublime, the, 141

discrimination, 21, 29, 50, 116, 126, 131

distance-vector routing, 103–4

Distributed Denial of Service (DDoS) attacks, 167

distributive agency: and accountability, 202–3; and flow control, 41, 112, 209; novelty of, 57; in "Pandemonium," 13–14

dividuality, 192–93

domain name seizures, 217

Domain Name System (DNS), 218, 224

dromology, 141

duration concept, 31, 54

Dynamic Adaptive Streaming over HTTP (DASH), 100

Electronic Frontier Foundation (EFF), 88, 117, 125–26

email, 42, 66, 84, 87, 148, 176, 236

eMule, 1, 3, 100, 116, 120

enchantment, 131–32

encryption, 97, 101, 173

End-to-End principle (E2E), 80, 94, 113–15, 125, 253n80

entropy, 3, 24–26, 28, 210

escalationism, 165, 171, 180; vs. accelerationism, 178–79; and confrontation, 166, 181; and flow control, 180–81; IPREDator as, 179; and obfuscation, 99, 120–21, 174, 179, 181; and optimization, 182; and piracy, 179, 181–82; tactics of, 179–80; TOR, 90, 172, 179. *See also* virtual private networks

ethics, 131, 203–4

exploits, 41, 88–89, 217

Facebook: as algorithmic media, 21, 190; as human content moderation, 226; Instant Articles, 223; Local Awareness, 222; news feed, 131, 221; as platform, 220–21; sentiment analysis, 221; TPB's use of, 167, 183; use of HTTP, 99

Federal Communications Commission (FCC): Comcast investigation, 2–3, 116, 121, 212; and net neutrality, 17, 141; on right to regulate internet, 3; Verizon investigation, 146

FIDONET, 89

File Transfer Protocol (FTP), 66, 84, 99, 175–76

firewalls, 77–78, 97–98

Five Eyes, 225, 265n78

Fleischer, Rasmus, 164–68, 171, 181

FlowCommand (Saisei Networks), 129–30, 132, 181

flow control, 4–5, 14, 42, 67; as affective influence, 138–39, 142, 149–50, 152, 157; daemons enabling, 4–6, 41–42; and delay, 145; and diagrams, 13; as discrimination, 126; as distributive agency, 41; gateways, 73, 80–82, 105; as inter-network relation, 68–69;

Kleinrock on, 16, 59, 247n53; and metastability, 42; and net neutrality, 20–21; and network diversity, 211; and nudge theory, 145–46; and optimalities, 42; Packeteer PacketShaper 8500, 175–79; via packet inspection, 102; in Pandaemonium, 132 33; policy management, 110–12; and queuing, 59; routing as, 60; and social acceleration, 150–51; and social temporalities, 148–49; Software-Defined Networking, 93, 111–12; stakes of, 210–11; and tiers, 210; traffic accelerators, 109; traffic shaping, 108–9, 176–77. *See also* Deep Packet Inspection; Interface Message Processors; optimization; packet inspection; packet switching; Peer-to-Peer networking; queuing; routing

flows, 35

Ford–Fulkerson algorithm, 12

Foucault, Michel, 13, 39, 74, 223, 225

Frank, Howard, 62–63, 247n65–66

Fuzzballs (gateways), 82, 85

Galloway, Alexander, 13–15, 41, 75, 219

gamer publics, 195–96, 199, 202. *See also* Rogers Internet connection issues

gateways, 73, 80–82, 105

Gatlinburg ACM symposium (1967), 46, 51, 53, 55, 75

Geist, Michael, 188, 200

Gillespie, Tarleton, 21, 117, 138, 145, 224

Glasnost, 196, 201, 237

Gnutella, 117–18

"good enough" data, 206–7

Google: Accelerated Mobile Page (AMP), 223; as algorithmic media, 21; Brillo, 220; content moderation, 226; and HTTP, 99; and IP enforcement, 224; and ISPs, 217; and machine learning, 219; News, 221; and SDN, 111; search algorithms, 21

Gore, Al, 90–91

Guattari, Félix, 74, 164, 166, 180, 256n28

Haraway, Donna, 15–17, 23, 27

Hayles, Katherine, 23, 25–27, 210

heterarchy, 72, 91, 112–13

High Performance Computing Act, 90–91

hot-potato routing, 56, 60

hubs, 67, 77

human–computer interaction, 30, 143–45. *See also* man–computer symbiosis

Hypertext Transfer Protocol (HTTP): and DASH, 100; in internet measurement, 237–38, 238; and packet injection, 103; and packet inspection, 96, 99–100; and ports misuse, 99–100, 175; traffic shaping of, 175–76

Inferno operating system, 213–14

Information Processing Techniques Office (IPTO), 46–47, 52; IMP proposal paper (1967), 51–53; and Licklider, 47–49; and modern packet switching, 67; and NAC, 62; networking memo (1963), 48–49; researchers at, 48

information theory, 17, 26–28, 43

infrastructure: centralization of, 217; coaxial cable, 117, 119, 126; Comcast's, 117–19, 126–28; computers as, 24, 34, 50; and control, 39, 215–16; for early networking, 50, 79; failures in, 185–86; internet fiber, 215; managed vs. unmanaged, 210; and media policy, 204; for mobile devices, 134

intellectual property, 161, 164, 172, 224, 226

Intellectual Property Rights Enforcement Directive (IPRED), 172, 174

Interface Message Processors (IMPs): as abstract components, 76–77; and ARPANET, 46, 57–61, 75; BBN on, 95; daemons replacing, 95; deprecation of, 80; diagram for, 73; functions of, 58–59, 95; as infrastructure, 79; IPTO proposal paper (1967), 51–53; Kleinrock on, 52; in modern network devices, 67, 77; monitoring of, 62; NAC's reports on, 62–64; name origin, 52; and OLIVERs, 74; as optimistic, 104; as optimizers, 56, 62, 64; origins of, 14, 46, 56–57, 61–67; as protocological, 75; and queuing, 58, 107; routing functions, 58–60, 103–5; trace bits, 233; types of, 75, 77

internet, the: as competing operating systems, 214–15; diagram of, 82–85; fragmentation of, 219–20; as heterarchy, 91; layers of, 83–84; metastability of, 68, 91–92, 112–14; as multiple networks, 36, 85; optimization of, 113, 131–32; origins of, 72, 80, 90–91; as pandaemonium, 7, 94; reliance on daemons, 4–5, 7, 11, 46, 95, 209; and temporalities, 37; and vibrant materialism, 8. *See also* ARPANET

Internet Assigned Numbers Authority (IANA), 84

Internet Detailed Record Collector servers, 128

Internet Explorer, 135

internet measurement, 233; active, 235; ARPANET, 233–34; CAIDA, 234; Cerf on, 234; crowdsourced, 235–36, 238; frankenflows, 236–37; Glasnost, 196, 201, 237; Measurement Lab, 144, 196, 236; and mediators, 196–97, 205; need for, 187; Ookla's Speedtest, 235; passive, 235; ping tool, 234; public participation in, 206; and regulation, 206, 236–37; reliance on HTTP, 238; as research, 234–35; SamKnows, 236; traceroutes, 234, 237; WeHe, 237

Internet of Things (IoT), 219, 227

Internet Protocol (IP) addressing, 84, 97

Internet Relay Chat (IRC), 90

internet service providers (ISPs): bandwidth caps, 123, 149; Bell Canada, 169–70; BitTorrent throttling, 2–3, 6, 20, 124–25, 169–70; Verizon, 103, 146, 216; zero-rating programs, 149, 208,

218, 236. *See also* Comcast; Rogers Communications

iPoque, 100

IPREDator VPN, 172–74, 176–80

isarithmic networks, 64–65

ISC8 Inc., 98–99

Java, 213–14

Jennings, Tom, 89

Juniper Networks, 93, 108, 110–11

Kahn, Robert, 60–61, 67, 80–82, 84

Kelty, Chris, 186, 195

Kleinrock, Leonard: on flow control, 16, 59, 247n53; and Frank, 63; on IMPs, 52; on Licklider, 49; at NMC, 233; queuing theory dissertation, 58–59

Kopimism, 163–64

lag. *See* delay

Lash, Scott, 15, 213

latency, 187

layering, 82–83

Licklider, J. C. R.: and ARPA, 47; career of, 29–30; "The Computer as a Communication Device," 71–74, 85–86; at IPTO, 47–49; on man–computer symbiosis, 23, 29–32, 48–49; networking memo, 48–49; as optimist, 32, 48, 71

Lincoln Laboratory, 29–30, 32, 49–51

loading indicators, 155

MacKenzie, Adrian, 68, 138, 213

man–computer symbiosis, 23, 29–32, 48

Marill, Thomas, 49–51, 96

Massachusetts Institute of Technology (MIT): Air Force funding of, 32; computing culture of, 47; "daemon" term origination, 18, 24; MULTICS, 38; Project MAC, 34, 38, 43, 45, 53–54, 59; SAGE, 32; time-sharing experiments, 32, 34–35

materialism, 17

Maxwell's demon, 24–25; and cyborg

P2P file sharing, 92. *See also* Pirate
 Bay, The
Piratbyrån ("Piracy Bureau"), 163; and
 accelerationism, 165–66, 168; and
 escalationism, 165–66, 181; Rasmus
 Fleischer on, 164–68, 171, 181; and
 the intellectual property regime, 164;
 Kopimism, 163–64; and The Pirate
 Bay launch, 163, 165, 167–68; and
 resisting daemons, 164
Pirate Bay, The (TPB), 161; as accelerating piracy, 168; and accelerationism,
 166–71; administrator trial and
 arrest, 161–62, 182–83; British ban
 on, 166–67, 217; copyright politics
 of, 161–62; as eluding flow control,
 162–63; and escalationism, 172–74,
 179; hosting of, 170–71; IPREDator
 VPN, 172–74, 176–80; launch of,
 163, 165, 167–68, 183; police raid
 on, 161–62, 182; policies of, 162; as
 political act, 167; relaunch of, 162;
 resilience of, 168, 170–71; size of, 170
pirate political parties, 165, 174, 182–83
Plan 9, 213, 220
platforms, 213, 220–24
Policy and Charging Control (PCC), 134
policy management, 110–12
Policy Traffic Switch (PTS) 8210, 121–25
political bots, 222
Pouzin, Louis, 67, 81
power: algorithmic, 21; constituent vs.
 constituted, 39, 41; and control, 39;
 control societies, 15, 41–42, 171,
 240n53; diagrams describing, 13, 18,
 74; and materiality, 11; "netscapes" of,
 115, 130; and time, 68, 152. *See also*
 control, networked techniques of;
 flow control
priming (affect theory), 138–39
privacy, 90, 121–22, 172, 179. *See also*
 escalationism; Virtual Private
 Networks
Procera Networks, 93, 100, 134

progress bars, 155
Project MAC, 34, 38, 43, 45, 53–54, 59
protocols, 51, 96; administration of, 218;
 consequences of, 219; Galloway's
 theory of, 75; Open Shortest Path
 First, 105–6; as political, 96–97; and
 routing, 103–4; VPN, 173
proxy servers, 167, 172, 217
publics, 186; and daemons, 186, 192–93,
 195; forming of, 191, 194–95; gamer,
 195–96, 199, 202; and information,
 194; and institutions, 205; as intelligences, 194; and the internet, 186; and
 mediators, 196–97; and nonhumans,
 195; problematic, 206; recursive, 195;
 reflexive apparatuses in, 191–92, 197;
 research by, 194–95; scope issues, 207;
 and self-awareness, 207–8; and systematic care, 207–8. *See also* Rogers
 Internet connection issues

queuing, 106; "class-based weighted fair,"
 108–9; IMPs, 107; "leaky bucket" algorithm, 107–8; measuring, 237; and
 prioritization, 109–10; round-robin
 technique, 106–7; theories of, 58–59;
 in time-sharing computing, 59, 106–7;
 "token bucket" algorithm, 108; traffic
 shaping, 108–9

real-time computing, early, 32–33, 43,
 243n51. *See also* Semi-Automatic
 Ground Environment
Reddit, 90, 206
Reed, David, 113–14, 253n80
reflexive apparatuses, 191–92, 197
reification, 11–12
"reply girls," 222
reset packets, 125–26
resisting. *See* accelerationism;
 escalationism
Resource reSerVation Protocol (RSVP),
 110
rhizomes, 164

(continued from page ii)